NORTHERN AFRICA

Reference Sources in the Social Sciences Series

Robert H. Burger, Series Editor

Psychology: A Guide to Reference and Information Sources. By Pam M. Baxter

American Military History: A Guide to Reference and Information Sources. By Daniel K. Blewett

Sociology: A Guide to Reference and Information Sources. Second edition. By Stephen H. Aby

Education: A Guide to Reference and Information Sources. Second edition. By Nancy P. O'Brien

Northern Africa: A Guide to Reference and Information Sources. By Paula Youngman Skreslet

NORTHERN AFRICA
AFRICA

A Guide to Reference and Information Sources

PAULA YOUNGMAN SKRESLET

William Smith Morton Library
Union Theological Seminary and
Presbyterian School of Christian Education
Richmond, Virginia

2000
Libraries Unlimited, Inc.
Englewood, Colorado

Libraries Unlimited, Inc.
P.O. Box 6633
Englewood, CO 80155-6633
1-800-237-6124
www.lu.com

Library of Congress Cataloging-in-Publication Data

Skreslet, Paula Youngman.
    Northern Africa : a guide to reference and information sources / Paula Youngman Skreslet.
        p. cm.
    Includes bibliographical references and indexes.
    ISBN 1-56308-684-0 (cloth)
    1. Africa, North--Reference books--Bibliography. 2. Africa, North--Electronic information resources. 3. Africa, Northwest--Reference books--Bibliography. 4. Africa, Northwest--Electronic information resources. 5. Sahel--Reference books--Bibliography. 6. Sahel--Electronic information resources. I. Title.

Z3515 .S57 2000
[[DT185]]
016.961--dc21

00-040543

CONTENTS

V

PART THREE
REFERENCE SOURCES
BY COUNTRY AND REGION

PREFACE

Research in area studies is rewarding precisely because the field challenges the writer to become informed about every aspect of life in a certain part of the world. Not many of us are equally expert in subject areas ranging from economics to astronomy, fine arts to physical geography, education to theology to law. Preparing an annotated bibliography of reference works in area studies reveals one's limitations and motivates learning in a serious way.

The purpose of preparing such a bibliography is to assist the student, research scholar, librarian, or information professional gaining a foothold in this field. Collecting current and important materials from a range of sources and subject areas; categorizing them for easy access; and providing concise, informative notices of their contents and applicability should help those selecting reference works and move them a few steps forward in the process.

This volume provides an annotated bibliography of reference materials pertaining to the northern portion of the African continent: the predominantly Arabic-speaking Maghreb and Egypt, the Sahel or Sahara region and the Horn of Africa. It includes reference materials in English, French, German and transliterated Arabic. A full spectrum of area studies topics is considered. Formal reference works (encyclopedias, dictionaries, atlases, collective biographies, and so forth) form the basis of the bibliography, but nontraditional sources are also included if they represent important sources of information on neglected countries, regions or topics.

Annotations indicate the nature of each work and its relevance to the field. The basic premise or approach of each work, the degree to which it is regarded as authoritative and accurate, extra features that increase its reference value (maps, tables of data, appendices, illustrations, etc.), effectiveness of organization and access and any special biases or agendas are reported insofar as possible. If a work seems particularly suited to classroom teaching, to an undergraduate library or to the more advanced scholar, this observation is noted. Flaws or shortcomings in the work are commented upon, in what is meant to be a constructive way. Several years of teaching, research and collection development experience have shaped these priorities.

Scope

The coverage of an area studies bibliography is not always self-evident. Where the continent of Africa is concerned, geographic divisions are especially difficult.

What Is "North Africa?"

The first thing a researcher discovers is that reference works and mono-graphs frequently use the term "North Africa," and just as frequently disagree about what this term means. For French scholars, *l'Afrique du Nord* may mean only Morocco, Algeria and Tunisia; sometimes, Libya is included. The term "Maghreb" or "West" usually encompasses Libya, but not always. Egypt and Sudan may be part of North Africa, or part of the "Middle East" (another dis-puted term). The inland countries of the Sahel are often considered "sub-Saharan" Africa, mainly because their capitals and population centers generally lie in the south, below their desert territory. One may choose an arbitrary geo-graphical delimiter, like the Tropic of Cancer, or the 20° N latitude line; one of these clearly includes the Sahel, but the other does not. Perhaps only those states with a Mediterranean coastline should be eligible.

In terms of culture, history and politics, the picture is even more complex. Is Mauritania in West Africa or North Africa? Is it Maghreb or Sahel? Does the dispute with Morocco over the Western Sahara enter into this issue? What about Chad's long-term territorial problems with Libya? Or Ethiopia's ancient ties with Egypt? Or the complex history of the Nile Basin peoples of Egypt, Nubia, and Sudan, which both unites and divides them? Or the close proximity, both physical and spiritual, of Somalia and the Saudi peninsula? Do the oil-based economies of the area belong in a special category? What role should language, colonial experience, religion or race play in these decisions?

For this bibliography, the term "northern Africa" has been chosen to desig-nate the region touching on the Mediterranean and the North Atlantic, rimming the great Sahara, and forming the eastern spur known as the Horn. The volume's table of contents defines the area. (Since Eritrea's independence in 1993, there may be fourteen nations or fifteen, depending upon the status of the Western Sa-hara.) These states are clustered into three groups: Egypt and Libya are bundled into the Maghreb, Mauritania rests uneasily between the Maghreb and Sahel, and Sudan behaves as a special case throughout. Generally speaking, these are states that seem to consider themselves to be regionally related, as suggested by their various affiliations through the Arab League, Organization of African Unity, Organization of the Islamic Conference and Islamic Development Bank, and other political, historical, economic and cultural ties.

What About Dates?

Any area studies bibliography must limit itself chronologically in two ways: the historical coverage of the region and the publication dates of the mate-rials included.

The history of northern Africa might be thought of as beginning with the bones of our near-human ancestors discovered in the earth at Hadar: indeed, comprehensive works like *The Cambridge History of Africa* open with palaeo-archaeology. Recorded history reaches back to Egypt's Old Kingdom, whose people were already highly literate, creative and accomplished five thousand years ago; it was both an ancient and an advanced civilization. This bibliography includes representative materials dealing with all of the region's ages, although a comprehensive account of Pharaonic materials would require a volume of its own.

Because of the existence of a number of very helpful bibliographies published in the 1970s (Atiyeh, Howard, Drabek and Knapp, Marcus, Simon, Schultz and Littlefield, among others), this volume emphasizes works published after that, in the 1980s and 1990s. Earlier works are included if they are unique and have not been superceded, or if they are still cited by scholars. More than one edition of a work may be included if they are still widely used, or if the editions differ substantially. In some cases, several issues of an annual publication may be described to indicate the work's typical coverage and content; sometimes, a representative issue or a general description of the serial will suffice.

Reprints and classic works found in research libraries may be included: In some subject areas (language, religion, art, history) they remain the standard and authoritative works in the field. If a work is obsolete in some ways but still valuable in others (often the case with atlases), an effort is made to call attention to this fact in the annotation.

Types of Material Included

Fundamental reference materials form the core of this bibliography: dictionaries and encyclopedias, collective biographies and who's who's, atlases, directories and almanacs, guides, handbooks and yearbooks and of course, bibliographies. Other introductory and comprehensive works are also of substantial reference value for area studies (especially comprehensive histories), and some monographs, articles and essay collections appear if they provide unusual and hard-to-find information in a form that lends itself to reference work. Out of the large number of commercial tourist guidebooks available, a representative selection is included. Periodicals and indexes appear here if they pertain to northern Africa or are likely to contain relevant materials. Works that are distributed in electronic formats or microform are noted. Considerable care has been taken to sort through the vast number of statistical publications available, to describe those that are often consulted in area studies research, and to indicate their typical coverage of northern Africa. More than a thousand works in print are cited, with annotations.

Every researcher has experienced the disappointment of going to great lengths to obtain a work with a promising title or catalog record, only to find that the work is not at all helpful. To save the researcher's time, a number of inadequate sources are mentioned here, with annotations noting their drawbacks. Likewise, valuable reference assets can be found in unexpected places. For this reason, some select pamphlets, post reports and similar sources are included.

Electronic reference resources tend to fall into two categories: proprietary databases or services (requiring a purchase, subscription or site license) and public Internet websites. About 400 of these have been cited here, out of the countless materials available; they have been selected on the basis of authority, currency, scope and uniqueness. Well-maintained institutional or corporate sites that are likely to be operating in the future took priority, but a few individual or informal sites were included if they offered especially interesting information not easy to find elsewhere. Website entries are annotated as needed, to explain their purpose or to call attention to unusual features.

As always, the Internet is a volatile environment: If a given URL proves inoperative, one can usually trace a website by entering its title as a term in any large search engine (such as Metacrawler). Current usenet groups, listservs, electronic bulletin boards and e-mail groups are listed at the websites of academic and professional organizations pertinent to the Middle East or African Studies—for instance, the Middle East Network Information Center, provided by the Center for Middle East Studies at the University of Texas at Austin. Associations based upon particular subject areas within area studies—archaeology, for example—can also be a valuable source of news and information.

Arrangement and Organization

This volume relies on a traditional area studies structure. Materials concerning the region as a whole, or each of the countries of northern Africa, are grouped in the first large section. The citations are organized topically, covering as many of the various aspects of area studies as time and space and the author's own limitations permit. Thereafter, materials pertaining to one of the regional subdivisions of northern Africa (the Maghreb, Sahel and Horn), or to one specific country, are organized geographically.

Each citation includes all of the bibliographic data available, except prices (these are valid only when a publication is actually ordered, so they must be obtained at the time of purchase in any case). A table of contents, a names index, a titles index and a subject index are provided to help guide the reader. Entries for materials relevant to more than one subject area may be repeated, allowing the reader to browse by topic without constantly searching around for citations.

ACKNOWLEDGMENTS

The author is very much indebted to Dr. Robert H. Burger, Director of the Slavic and East European Library at the University of Illinois at Urbana-Champaign, who serves ably as the editor of this social science reference series. Also, a word of thanks is due to Professor Donald Krummel at the Graduate School of Library and Information Science at UIUC, who teaches that, in reference work, only the best is good enough. Nevertheless, all typographical errors, technical faults, and mental lapses are the author's alone.

The welcome of local academic libraries, especially the University of Richmond and Virginia Commonwealth University, is much appreciated. Reference assistance and interlibrary loan services were also provided by the William Smith Morton Library in Richmond. The author is lucky enough to live within travelling distance of Georgetown University and its Center for Contemporary Arab Studies, designated a National Resource Center on the Middle East; the College of William and Mary, home of the Reves Center for International Studies; the Alderman Library at the University of Virginia; and of course, the Africa and Middle East collections at the Library of Congress. I would also like to mention the warmth and kindness of Janet Wilgus, former Cultural Attaché at the American Embassy in Cairo, where I lived and worked for ten years as a teacher and academic librarian.

Nothing can compare to the patient encouragement of my husband Stan and our children, Tabor, Nathan and Rebecca. With loving thanks, this work is dedicated to them.

PART ONE

General Reference Works

General Works

Chapter **1**

Print and electronic sources basic to library reference collections and services are the backbone of this section. Materials relevant to area studies in general are included, but the emphasis is on sources featuring the Middle East or Africa. Many of these sources pertain only to certain parts of northern Africa; annotations indicate the scope and coverage of these sources.

Handbooks

1. **Africa.** Revised and updated edition. Edited by Sean Moroney New York: Facts on File, 1989. 2 v., continuously paginated. *Handbooks to the Modern World.* ISBN 0-8160-1623-2 (set).
  A clear two-volume format establishes the goals of this reference. Vol. 1 is composed of alphabetically-arranged encyclopedia-style entries (5-15 pages) on each country, with a map, basic data, and description organized under topical headings. Forty pages of World Bank statistics are provided at the end. Vol. 2 consists of substantial signed essays on important themes in political, economic and social affairs: Africa's problems are studied with a serious, mainly pessimistic view. Each of these essays includes footnotes and a brief bibliography. A carefully-prepared and competent index appears at the end of the second volume.

2. **Africa Today.** Second edition. Editor in Chief Raph Uwechue. London: Africa Books, 1991. xvi, 2056 p. *Know Africa.* ISBN 0-903274-16-7; 0-903274-19-1 (3-v. series).
  One of the three-volume *Know Africa* series, which "aims at terminating the era of publications on Africa which reflect the colonial perception of the continent" (Preface). This volume provides reference information on Africa as a unit, including regional and continental organizations, then presents the history of the political, economic and social development of each country. (Western Sahara is identified as a separate state known as the "Sahrawi Arab Democratic Republic.")

Photo portraits of African leaders, color images of national and organizational flags, monochrome maps of each country, tables of economic data, and an appendix containing 23 colorful thematic maps are included. In addition, there is a collection of topical essays (some of them polemical in tone) on apartheid, health, education, banking, sports, women's roles, African international relations, and other subjects, including one on the racial characteristics of ancient Egyptians. A new edition of this work is expected.

3. **The Middle East.** Eighth edition (expanded reference edition). Washington: Congressional Quarterly, 1995. 512 p. ISBN 1-56802-038-4.

A sort of briefing book comprised of informative articles and important themes in Middle East current events: the Arab-Israeli conflict, U.S. policy in the region, the Persian Gulf, the oil industry, and Islam. Individual country profiles make up Part 2 of this volume. Of the northern Africa states, only Egypt and Libya are included.

The work contains many helpful ready reference features: brief sketches of current and recent Middle East political leaders; two chronologies of events, 1900-44 and 1945-94; the verbatim text of several significant historical documents, including UN Security Council Resolution 242, the Camp David agreement, etc.; a short but interesting bibliography; a well-organized index; helpful "boxes" of key information set apart from the text; 19 simple maps; seven important tables of statistics on petroleum production and consumption. These features combined in one convenient and attractive volume make this a desirable classroom or reference-desk tool.

4. **The World: a Third World Guide 1995/96.** Montevideo: Institutio del Tercer Mundo, 1996. 623 p. ISBN 0-85598-291-8.

Distributed by Oxfam, this reference is intended to give "Northern readers access to Southern voices" (p. 3). The guide is published sporadically, and this appears to be the eighth edition. Information is organized by topic and geography, with country-by-country profiles covering all of the nations of northern Africa. Relevant tables of data are also found in topical sections on demography, health, education, labor, housing, etc. Many small maps, charts and graphics illustrate the articles, and there is a large color fold-out map. A bibliography and a general index are provided. This reference unapologetically presents a political point of view.

5. **Understanding Contemporary Africa.** Edited by April A. Gordon and Donald L. Gordon. Boulder; London: Lynne Rienner, 1992. xvi, 342 p. ISBN 1-55587- 256-5.

This introduction to the study of sub-Saharan Africa is organized around themes (politics, economics, population, religion, the environment, etc.) and does not lend itself readily to reference work, despite an adequate index. It does contain several good monochrome maps and some black-and-white photos, and each chapter provides a useful bibliography.

6. Arnold, Guy. **The Third World Handbook.** Second edition. London; Chicago: Cassell; Fitzroy Dearborn, 1996. xii, 213 p. ISBN 0-304-32837-5.

A small volume intended to do a big job: identifying the countries of the "Third World" or "the South," chronicling their independence struggles and the process of decolonization, explaining their regional and international alliances and organizations, and describing their current problems. This edition emphasizes the geopolitical changes brought about by the breakup of the USSR in 1989.

The Middle East and Africa are considered here, as are OPEC, the Non-Aligned Movement, the OAU, ECA, ADB, OIC, the Arab League, and the Muslim world in general. The monochrome maps used throughout are clear and pertinent. There is a section of brief biographical entries, a "country gazetteer" (ready reference data), and a helpful index.

7. Bacharach, Jere L. **A Middle East Studies Handbook.** Seattle: University of Washington Press, 1984. x, 160 p. ISBN 0-295-96138-4.

A loose collection of charts, maps, lists and other tidbits of information relating to the history and social geography of the Middle East. Coverage of the topic is very wide and very shallow. Of the northern Africa states, Egypt is included from the medieval period; some material touching on Sudan and Libya may be found here as well.

8. Bever, Edward. **Africa.** Phoenix, AZ: Oryx Press, 1996. vii, 302 p. *International Government and Politics Series.* ISBN 0-89774-954-5.

A convenient one-volume handbook introducing the reader to Africa's political life and its historical background. Early chapters (Part 1) describe the kingdoms and tribal states up through the Islamic conquest, European exploration and imperialism, then the rise of African nationalism and decolonization. A closing section (Part 3) presents "continental perspectives" on current issues of key importance in African politics: regional and intergovernmental alliances, the aftermath of the Cold War, IMF and World Bank policies, refugees, population and health issues, and so on.

In between (Part 2) is a section of brief country-by-country political profiles, three or four pages in length, summing up the current political pressures or forces active in each society. (This material is necessarily concise, even condensed, and some generalizations, assertions or conclusions could be challenged.) Regional maps and a little text on each area are provided; one might wish for bibliographical references pertaining to each country, instead of one very general bibliography at the end of the book.

All of the nations of northern Africa are represented here, even those that are sometimes overlooked. In addition, there is a detailed and helpful index.

9. Gresh, Alain and Dominique Vidal. **A to Z of the Middle East.** London: Zed Books, 1990. xxi, 261 p. ISBN 0-86232-880-2

Originally published in French as *Les Cent Portes du Proche-Orient.*

The title seems to suggest a comprehensive reference, but all it really means is that the very basic information in this introductory guide is arranged in alphabetized entries. Coverage of the Middle East is limited to Israel-Palestine, with forays into Lebanon, Egypt, Iran, etc. as they relate to this central concern. There is a useful appendix containing the text of 13 major international documents on Palestine, starting with the Balfour Declaration. A simple bibliography and index are included.

10. Griffiths, Ieuan Ll. **The Atlas of African Affairs.** Second edition. London and New York: Routledge (Witwatersrand University Press), 1994. x, 233 p. ISBN 0-415-05487-7.

The word "atlas" may be a misleading one for this small and useful volume. While it provides many clear and informative maps, these function as illustrations for the text, which is composed of 65 tightly-focused articles on the environment/geography, history, politics and economics of the African continent. The format of brief articles (2-4 pages) on distinct topics lends itself easily to reference work; however, choosing a topic from the table of contents is likely to be more efficient than trying to use the rather clumsy index. Several appendices offer a chronology, bibliography and basic statistical information. The book would be well-suited to classroom use, or to the high school and undergraduate library.

11. Knapp, Wilfrid. **North West Africa: a Political and Economic Survey.** Third edition. Oxford: Oxford University Press, 1977. vii, 453 p. ISBN 0-19-215635-7.

A very convenient handbook to the Maghreb states, with introductory and thematic material on the area as a whole (including an article on "Literature in North West Africa") , and individual chapters on Algeria, Libya, Mauritania and the Southern Sahara, Morocco and Tunisia. This structure, plus a careful index, help make the volume useful for reference work. It also provides a glossary of romanized Arabic terms, an appendix with 15 tables of statistical data, a topical bibliography and four maps. Each country chapter does the work of a good encyclopedia article, with sections on geography and population, history and politics, the economy, foreign relations, the armed forces and security, education and society. A useful resource for information up to 1977.

12. Munro, David and Alan J. Day. **A World Record of Major Conflict Areas.** Chicago; London: St. James Press, 1990. 373 p. ISBN 1-55862-066-4.

This interesting volume is meant to summarize the events in 28 major conflicts current at the time of publication (Iraq had just invaded Kuwait). Each article provides a simple fact-box profile, a descriptive summary of the conflict, a chronology of events, a "who's who" identifying major figures on all sides, a similar listing of place names, and a glossary covering other unique terms.

Each article also has its own select bibliography and simple but clearly-printed monochrome map. In Africa, this volume covers the Sudan, Ethiopia and Western Sahara (but not Algeria or Somalia). There is no index.

13. Prpic, George J. **The Modern Middle East: a Reference Guide.** Second revised and enlarged edition. Cleveland: John Carroll University, 1987. iii, 178 p.

Published by the author in cooperation with the Institute for Soviet and East European Studies [sic], this work was prepared "for use by our graduate students in courses dealing with the Middle East" (verso). The Mediterranean coast of Africa and the Sudan are included in its scope.

The materials collected here are meant to be used by high school history teachers to enrich their classroom teaching. A basic unannotated bibliography of monographs and reference works is subdivided by topic. A chronology of events 1945-1987 and profiles of seven contemporary leaders in the region (including Qaddafi of Libya, but not Hosni Mubarak) are provided. There are no indexes.

14. Sluglett, Peter and Marion Farouk-Sluglett. **The Times Guide to the Middle East: the Arab World and Its Neighbours.** Third edition. London: Times Books, 1996. 349 p. ISBN 0-7230-0868-X.

A handbook composed of short chapters (10-20 pages) offering an overview of the 19th-20th century history, political events, social and cultural character of 16 states or groups of states (or stateless peoples, such as the Palestinians and the Kurds) in this wide region. Egypt, Libya and Sudan each command a chapter, while Algeria, Morocco and Tunisia are dealt with together in Chapter 10, "The Maghrib." Two topics, "Oil in the Middle East" and "Islam" are singled out for special (though brief) chapters. There is a limited bibliography, divided by topic, citing works that are likely to be available in any college library. Simple but useful maps are provided for each country or people. This reference could be handy for undergraduates or for high-school teachers of current events.

15. Sluglett, Peter and Marion Farouk-Sluglett. **Tuttle Guide to the Middle East.** Boston: Charles E. Tuttle, 1992. 320 p. ISBN 0-8048-1814-2.

This American edition of Slugletts' *Times Guide to the Middle East* (third edition, 1996) differs superficially from that published in the UK. The content and organization are similar, though the Tuttle guide contains some statistical and documentary appendices the *Times Guide* lacks. There is, however, little reason to buy both.

Dictionaries

16. **The World Bank Glossary.** Prepared by the Terminology Unit of the Language Services Division. Washington: World Bank, 1986. 2 v. ISBN 0-8213-1733-4 (v.1) and 0-8213-1734-2 (v.2)

Also titled: *Glossaire de la Banque Mondiale*; *Glosario del Banco Mundial*.

This reference is simple in concept and extremely effective in practical terms: it offers a direct equivalent in three languages for "financial and economic terminology and terms relating to the Bank's procedures and practices ... [and] terms that frequently occur in Bank documents ... relating to such fields as agriculture, education, energy, housing, law, technology and transportation" (Foreword). Each volume also contains a list of acronyms defined in the Glossary, and of the scores of national and intergovernmental banks and agencies and NGOs involved in development work worldwide. The 2-volume format (Vol. 1 for French, Vol. 2 for Spanish) is convenient as well.

17. Arnold, Guy. **Political and Economic Encyclopedia of Africa.** Essex: Longman Current Affairs, 1993. x, 342 p. ISBN 0-582-209951.

An alphabetized dictionary-style ready reference providing concise, informative articles on African affairs, falling into four categories: country entries, covering essential data on every nation or area, including Western Sahara (Eritrea is still represented as a region of Ethiopia); organization entries, for institutions such as the OAU or ECOWAS; individual entries for persons or political parties; general entries, for "problems or topics common to a number of countries or the region as a whole"—for example, REFUGEES. One topical/political map is included. The index is useful, but could be greatly improved by topical subdivisions.

18. Beti, Mongo and Odile Tobner. **Dictionnaire de la Négritude.** Paris: Éditions L'Harmattan, 1989. 246 p. ISBN 2-7384-0494-4.

A ready reference composed of brief entries (1-10 paragraphs) identifying persons, places, organizations and concepts pertaining to Africa or people of African descent. The idea of *négritude*, as represented particularly in the writings of Léopold Senghor of Senegal, posited a kind of spiritual unity among people of color. African-Americans are included (e.g., Martin Luther King Jr., Billie Holiday), from all walks of life: politics, sports, the arts, etc. The approach of the work is not geographical, so finding information about northern Africa depends upon the topic or person used as the search term: for example, Hailé Sélassié of Ethiopia.

19. Hadjor, Kofi Buenor. **Dictionary of Third World Terms.** London; New York: I.B. Tauris and Co., 1992. 303 p. ISBN 1-85043-346-1.

This wide-ranging reference seeks to define key terms pertaining to the life and history of developing countries worldwide, from African Socialism to Zionism. There are some odd omissions: no entry for the Non-Aligned Movement, and no mention of it even in the entries for "Cold War" and "Nasser, Gamal Abdel."

Some entries offer bibliographical references, but many do not. Cross-references to terms within entries are provided, but there are no references from terms not used, meaning that Libya's head of state may be found under G but not under K or Q. There is no index to help find terms not used as headings.

The tone of some of the entries is partisan and tendentious (e.g., "Religion"). There is a useful table of dates of foreign control under "Colonization," a table that could be improved with further detail.

20. Hall, David E. **African Acronyms and Abbreviations: a Handbook.** London: Mansell, 1996. xi, 364 p. ISBN 0-7201-2275-9.

At first glance it seems surprising that more than 360 pages of two-column text are required for this reference, but clearly there is a vast amount of detail to cover here. Indeed, the unsystematic way such information has been handled in the past is part of the problem addressed by this work. An informative introduction explains why this reference is needed and how it contributes to African studies.

Governmental entities, educational and cultural institutions, business associations, political parties, NGOs and development agencies—both active and inactive—are listed, located and defined. Changes of name or initials are traced over time by means of cross-references. The whole of Africa is included, except Egypt.

21. Heravi, Mehdi. **Concise Encyclopedia of the Middle East.** Washington: Public Affairs Press, 1973. 336 p. LCCN 73-82012.

An alphabetized ready reference composed of one-paragraph entries on persons, historical events and cultural features of the region, through 1973. The author does not define the geographical or chronological scopes; material is included pertaining to at least some states of northern Africa, as far west as Mauritania and as far south as Sudan. Names are given in an idiosyncratic transliteration, with a few cross-references (not enough) and no index.

22. Hiro, Dilip. **Dictionary of the Middle East.** New York: St. Martin's, 1996. ix, 367 p. ISBN 0-312-12554-2.

A convenient one-volume ready reference. Ten clear monochrome maps are gathered together in the front. Entries include a phrase of identification and dates or alternate spellings if relevant, then an article of 1-5 paragraphs. Of the northern Africa nations, only Egypt is included; this definition of scope is unfortunate. Does it make sense in a dictionary of the Middle East to include Sultan Qaboos of Oman but not Muammar Qaddhafi of Libya? Articles on individual states provide a very concise country profile, but sometimes with dated information (statistics from 1992, for instance).

23. Korbani, Agnes. **The Political Dictionary of Modern Middle East.** Lanham, MD: University Press of America, 1995. 258 p. ISBN 0-8191-9579-0.

A compilation of 900 very brief identifications of persons, places and things pertaining to the Middle East, broadly construed; the geographical and chronological scopes are not defined, but seem to include at least some entries for Morocco, Algeria, Tunisia, Libya, Sudan and Egypt. The transliteration style is not specified, and there are no cross-references from other common forms of names or vocabulary terms.

24. Ziring, Lawrence. **The Middle East: a Political Dictionary.** Second edition. Santa Barbara, CA: ABC-Clio, 1992. x, 401 p. ISBN 0-87436-612-7.

Taking an unusual approach in a dictionary-style reference, the author has divided the entries into seven thematic sections: political geography and geopolitics, Islam, ethnicity and political culture, political parties and movements,

Israelis and Palestinians, diplomacy (detailing specific UN resolutions, treaties and doctrines) and conflict (itemizing outbreaks of war and violent incidents). This arrangement makes it possible to browse sections of closely-related material. The concise entries are alphabetized within their sections, and a carefully-subdivided and informative index overcomes any problems in locating material.

The writer has used another unusual and effective technique in preparing this volume. Each entry consists of a brief definition in as objective a manner as possible, then includes an interpretive paragraph headed "Significance" that explains the entity or event in its context.

For this volume, the Middle East includes all states from Morocco to Pakistan, including Sudan. It does not include Mauritania or the rest of the Sahel and Horn.

Encyclopedias

25. **Cambridge Encyclopedia of Africa.** Edited by Roland Oliver and Michael Crowder. Cambridge: Cambridge University Press, 1981. 492 p. ISBN 0-521-23096-9.

A convenient one-volume reference, organized by geography, chronology and topic. The volume is well illustrated with maps (several in color), tables of data, drawings and photographs. A detailed index (at the front of the book, for some reason) helps to locate specific material. Individual entries are quite brief, from a few paragraphs to 2-3 pages, and they do not provide bibliographies or cross-references. A list of materials for further reading appears at the back of the book. A traditional Eurocentric Orientalist viewpoint is rather obvious in some entries; for example, "The Muslim World" (p. 469-471). A new edition of this reference is perhaps overdue.

26. **Cambridge Encyclopedia of the Middle East and North Africa.** Edited by Trevor Mostyn and Albert Hourani. Cambridge: Cambridge University Press, 1988. 504 p. ISBN 0-521-32190-5.

A useful and attractive one-volume reference on the lands and peoples, history, societies and economies, culture and international relations of the region. The Mediterranean states of Africa, the Western Sahara and Sudan are covered; Somalia and Djibouti are included, but Ethiopia and Eritrea are not. Amply illustrated with black-and-white and color photos and maps. The information is conveyed in lengthy narrative articles on countries or themes, not in the alphabetized-entry structure generally expected of an encyclopedia. Each article provides a very simple and brief bibliography of "further reading." There is a detailed index.

27. **Current History Encyclopedia of Developing Nations.** New York: McGraw-Hill, 1982. ix, 394 p. ISBN 0-07-064387-3.

A traditional one-volume encyclopedia (dated now), offering country profiles with fact boxes, a 4-6 page article without subheadings, some black-and-white photos, and regional maps. Articles are signed, but there are no bibliographical references. The articles are grouped into regional sections: Mauritania, Sudan, the Sahel states and the Horn (except Djibouti) are all considered "Africa South of the Sahara," while the five Mediterranean states are part of "North Africa and the Middle East." A names and a subject index are provided.

28. **Encyclopedia of Africa South of the Sahara.** Editor in chief, John Middleton. New York: Charles Scribner's Sons (Macmillan Library Reference), 1997. 4 v. ISBN 0-684-80466-2 (set).

A substantial and attractive new multivolume reference on Africa, excluding the northern coast (from Western Sahara to Egypt), but including Mauritania, Sudan, the Sahel and the Horn. Some material is included on the Nile Valley, and on Egypt and the Arab states' historical and current relationships with sub-Saharan populations and cultures.

Very sharp monochrome maps and drawings, and somewhat less successful black-and-white photos, illustrate each volume. Valuable appendices are found in Vol. 4: material on African Studies as an academic discipline outside Africa itself; a comparative chronology of five different regions of the continent; a huge table of basic data on scores of ethnic and identity groups, suitable for ready reference (p. 480-563). A strong group of editors, consultants and contributors is identified in a directory. Vol. 4 also contains an extensive and detailed index.

29. **Encyclopedia of the Modern Middle East.** Edited by Reeva S. Simon, Philip Mattar, and Richard W. Bulliet. New York: Macmillan Reference USA, 1996. 4 v. ISBN 0-02-896011-4.

This new four-volume work seeks to present "scholarly, balanced and proportionate coverage" of the highly divisive issues and diverse peoples of the region. It includes 24 countries from Mauritania to Afghanistan (with Sudan, but not the Horn of Africa, Mali, Niger or Chad). The editors have tried to devote attention to minority ethnic and religious groups. Most of the information concerns events since 1800 (with some background on, for example, the Ottoman Empire). Each country is assigned to one of four levels of coverage; Egypt, Algeria and Tunisia are among those given priority.

Designed for ready reference, each entry provides a very concise definition or identification, a signed article with cross-references and a bibliography citing 1-12 sources, some of them of a popular nature. Articles may be illustrated with photos or simple maps (however, there is no map of the Western Sahara, despite territorial conflict over it). The historical articles tend to be the most detailed and informative. Biographical entries include many journalists, artists, scientists, business leaders and entertainers. Information on human rights groups and political dissidents is easy to find.

Two very useful appendices provide schematic genealogies of the major royal families (including Morocco and Egypt) and a classified list of the biographical entries, from "Archaeologists" to "Theatre, Film and Dance Artists." In the fourth volume is a detailed and well-organized index.

30. **Encyclopedia of World Cultures.** Vol. 9. Edited by David Levinson. Boston: G.K. Hall & Co., 1995. 10 v. ISBN 0-8161-1840-X (set).

This multivolume reference was "prepared under the auspices and with the support of the Human Resources Area Files at Yale University ... the foremost international research organization in the field of cultural anthropology" (verso). Volume 9 is devoted to Africa and the Middle East. Introductory articles on these two regions—with maps and bibliographies—open the volume; detailed articles on individual ethnic groups are ordered alphabetically.

The articles describe each group's history, "orientation" (name and basic affiliation or origin of the group), location, demography and language, type of settlements, economy, labor and land use, kinship and family ties, marriage and childbearing customs, social organization (clan, tribe, etc.), religion and art forms. Each article includes a small bibliography. Appendices provide a list of additional African cultures not covered by articles, an ethnonym index, glossary and filmography. Volume 10 supplies an index to the whole work.

31. **World Encyclopedia of Black Peoples.** Vol. 1: Conspectus. St. Clair Shores, MI: Scholarly Press, 1975. 317 p. ISBN 0-403-01796-3.

The scope of this multi-volume work is very broad, incorporating "people who consider themselves to be black, as well as persons who, being to some extent of black descent, are associated with the black tradition" (Foreword). Presumably, this would include much of northern Africa. Vol. 1, which is composed of lengthy articles on major theses and serves as an introductory volume, includes an essay by Ibrahim Abu-Lughod on "Islam in Africa" (pp. 283-289). Evidently, no other volumes in this projected work were published.

32. **Worldmark Encyclopedia of the Nations.** Eighth edition. New York: Gale Research, 1995. 5 v. ISBN 0-8103-9878-8 (set).

Adequately suited to area studies, this five-volume encyclopedia provides sizable articles on each country, with a fact box showing the flag, seal and basic data, a very clear monochrome map, and 5-25 pages of text. The text is subdivided under bold headings: topography, climate, languages, history, judicial system, political parties, industry, trade, health, education, libraries and museums, etc., using a standard format for all of the articles; locating and comparing data is made easier by this approach. Each article includes a select and fairly current bibliography. Vol. 2 is devoted entirely to Africa.

33. Gurney, Gene. **Kingdoms of Asia, the Middle East and Africa: an Illustrated Encyclopedia of Ruling Monarchs From Ancient Times to the Present.** New York: Crown, 1986. viii, 438 p. ISBN 0-517-55256-6.

The very broad scope of this work allows one chapter for all of Egyptian history from Neolithic times to the Revolution of 1952. Another chapter is devoted to Ethiopia, and one-page appendices are found pertaining to Libya and Morocco. Still, the text manages to hit the high points, and the simple, direct prose style would be accessible to high school or college students. Maps, drawings, paintings and black-and-white photos with helpful captions illustrate every page. Each chapter includes a dynastic table with dates. The volume includes a names index.

34. Kurian, George Thomas. **Encyclopedia of the Third World.** Fourth edition. New York: Facts on File, 1992. 3 v. ISBN 0-8160-2261-5 (set).

A handbook to 122 of the "politically nonaligned and economically developing and less industrialized nations of the world" (Preface). An initial section offers basic data on intergovernmental organizations important to development: OPEC, the ADB, the Arab League, etc. Country-by-country profiles follow. These employ a standard encyclopedia structure, with a basic fact box, descriptive section on the country's geography, climate, population (including language, religion and ethnicity), history, politics and government, the economy, education and defense. Statistical data is presented in convenient boxes; a map is provided, but no illustrations. A glossary, chronology and bibliography (sometimes quite dated) accompany each article.

Yearbooks and Annuals

Citations and annotations reflect the issue examined; some changes can be expected in later editions or issues of the same work.

35. **Africa 1994.** 29th edition. Edited by Pierre Etienne Dostert. Annual; 1966- . Harpers Ferry, WV: Stryker-Post, 1994. 234 p. ISBN 1-943448-82-4; ISSN 0084-2281.

An encyclopedia-style annual composed of articles (3-5 pages long) on Africa generally and each region or nation in particular. Background sections cover African history from prehistoric through colonial times; country articles offer basic data, a descriptive/historical text (including up-to-date material), small maps and quite a few large and interesting black-and-white photos. All of the countries of the continent are represented. There is a subdivided bibliography with at least some current sources. This reference would be suitable for a high school or college library, and would serve as a convenient means of updating the material in standard encyclopedic references.

36. **Africa Contemporary Record: Annual Survey and Documents.** Annual; 1969-1992. New York; London: Africana Publishing. Edited by Marion E. Doro and Colin Legum. ISBN 0-8419-0560-6; ISSN 0065-3845.

This informative work records and comments upon recent developments in Africa in several ways. Part I contains fairly lengthy signed articles with bibliographical references describing and analyzing current issues on the continent: refugees and displaced persons, trade unions, democratization, press freedom, activities of various Western powers in Africa, etc. Part II offers signed articles on recent events in individual countries; all of the northern states are covered. Part III presents the text of important documents, including constitutional

changes, official policy announcements, resolutions adopted by intergovernmental organizations, etc. In addition, tables of current demographic and economic data are provided (mostly from World Bank or IMF sources). There are
both a subject and a names index. Unfortunately, publication of this work has
been discontinued, and it is not clear whether it will resume.

37. **Countries of the World and Their Leaders Yearbook 1988.** Updated by
supplements. Detroit: Gale Research, 1988. 2 v. ISBN 0-7876-0054-7 (set);
ISSN 0196-2809.
　　This two-volume compilation of State Department information is packaged
like an almanac and encyclopedia together, with clearly-defined slots into which
current data will fit. The names of heads of state, cabinet ministers and ambassa-
dors occupy only a small amount of the space. The bulk of both volumes is the
country reports, with current statistics, good maps, a brief narrative history, description of the population, the government and political conditions, the economy, foreign relations and defense.
　　There is an emphasis on US relations with each government, and on travel
advisories and visa requirements for Americans, conditions of travel, and the US
embassies, consulates and foreign service posts in each location. All of the nations of northern Africa are covered (for Western Sahara, see Morocco).

38. **Europa World Year Book 1999.** London: Europa Publications. Annual;
1989- . 2 v. ISBN 1-85743-033-6 (set); ISSN 0956-2273.
　　The comprehensive companion to Europa's seven regional references
(among them *Africa South of the Sahara* and *The Middle East and North Africa*).
This two-volume set includes a 300-page section on international organizations,
many of which are active in northern Africa. The country-by-country coverage is
similar to that in the regional volumes.

39. **The Middle East and North Africa 1997.** 43rd edition. London: Europa
Publications, 1997. 1104 p. ISBN 1-85743-030-1; ISSN 0076-850.
　　This very useful annual by Europa provides a wide variety of information
for study and ready reference. Lengthy signed feature articles on broad topics
(the Islamist movement, the oil industry, water resources, banking, etc.) are followed by a section detailing the members, leadership, publications and activities
of regional organizations, those connected with the UN and independent ones
(OIC, the Arab League, OPEC and others). A third major section provides survey articles on the geography, history, economy and current events of 21 countries, including Egypt, Libya, Tunisia, Morocco and the Spanish North African
possessions. (Information pertinent to other nations may be found under regional
organizations: for example, Mauritania, Mali, Niger, Chad, Sudan, Somalia and
Djibouti are all subscribers to the Islamic Development Bank).
　　Especially convenient is the current directory information provided for
each country: government ministries, political parties, embassies, the judicial
system, news media and publishers, religious bodies, finance, trade, transport
and tourism offices are all listed, with some almanac-style entries (the text of a

nation's constitution, for instance) and several tables of statistical information derived from sources like UNESCO, the ILO, FAO and IMF. Maps are provided of particular areas that are politically sensitive. In addition, there is a chronology of events in the area during the previous year, and a page for late changes just before publication.

Note: For Sahel and Horn countries and regional organizations, see: *Africa South of the Sahara 1997*. 26th edition. London: Europa Publications, 1997. 1111 p. ISBN 1-85743-029-8; ISSN 0065-3896.

40. **Middle East Contemporary Survey.** Edited by Ami Ayalon and Bruce Maddy-Weitzman. Boulder, CO: Westview Press. Annual, 1977- . ISBN 0-8133-2776-8; ISSN 0163-5476.

Published for the Moshe Dayan Center for Middle Eastern and African Studies, The Shiloah Institute, Tel Aviv University.

This annual provides material for study and ready reference, including the complete text of some important documents, relevant maps and statistical tables, but most of the information is conveyed through lengthy and detailed signed articles. What distinguishes these articles is the set of source notes with each one: these draw heavily on newspapers, journals and other current-events sources, including national news agencies and radio and television monitoring services, offering access to material that might otherwise be difficult to obtain; for example, Radiodiffusion Télévision Marocaine in Rabat, or the Libyan daily *Al-Shams*. The topical essays in Part One concentrate on issues involving Israel, Palestine and the Arabian peninsula, but Part Two includes country surveys of Algeria, Egypt, Libya, Morocco, Sudan and Tunisia. Vol. 18, appearing in 1996, covers events in the region from January to December 1994.

41. **New African Yearbook, 1997-98.** 11th edition. Edited by Alan Rake. Annual; 1978- . London: IC Publications, 1998. 540 p. ISBN 0-905268-62-8; ISSN 0140-1378.

With this new edition, all of the countries of Africa are covered, including the Mediterranean states (though, oddly, a map of the whole continent is still titled "Sub-Saharan Africa"). This reference provides directory data, basic facts and descriptions for African regional organizations. Then, encyclopedia-style signed articles appear in a country-by-country format. A map is provided for each article, but no illustrations.

42. **Statesman's Yearbook: a Statistical, Political and Economic Account of the States of the World for the Year 1997-1998.** 134th edition. Edited by Brian Hunter. New York: St. Martin's Press, 1997. Annual; 1864- . 1700 p. ISSN 0081-4601.

Published regularly since 1864, this handy almanac complies a great deal of detailed, current information on international organizations (both UN-related and not), then country-by-country summaries of basic current and background data. Statistical information, names, dates and facts are stressed: there is almost no descriptive or interpretive material.

The names of current diplomatic representatives, heads of state and government ministers can be quickly found here. A few bibliographical references are added to each country article, and they are kept up-to-date. All of the nations of northern Africa except Western Sahara appear as entries (it is mentioned under Morocco).

43. **World Factbook.** Washington: Central Intelligence Agency, Office of Public and Agency Information. Annual, 1982- . SuDocs PrEx 3.15:994, etc.
   Also available on microfiche, diskette or CD-ROM.
   This annual is produced "by the CIA for the use of US Government officials, and the style, format, coverage and content are designed to meet their specific requirements" (title page). Evidently, what these readers require is two pages of statistical snippets on each country, with a tiny map, geographical data, population figures, basic political facts (e.g., the names of Algeria's 48 provinces), and bits of information on the economy, agriculture and industry, transport and communications, and defense; also appearing are the names of some current office-holders and opposition leaders. Several appendices present information on international organizations, including a helpful chart showing the relational scheme of all those UN agencies. A collection of 16 colorful but not-very-detailed maps is included.

44. **World Statistics Pocketbook.** Annual; prepared by the Department for Economic and Social Information and Policy Analysis, Statistical Division. *World Statistics in Brief;* Series V, no. 16 (1995). New York: United Nations, 1995. ISBN 92-1-161376-0; UN Doc. ST/ESA/STAT/SER.V/16; Sales no. E.95.XVII.7.
   An attempt to provide one-page summary tables for each country showing basic geographic, economic, social and environmental data. Current figures and those from 10 years earlier are given for comparison. Some tables appear for every part of northern Africa, even Western Sahara.

Comprehensive Histories and Chronologies

Guides to historical literature and historical dictionaries are also found here. For more specific topics in the history of the region, see Part Two, "History and Antiquities."

45. **Cambridge History of Africa.** Cambridge: Cambridge University Press, 1982-1984. 8 v. ISBN 0521-22215-X.
   In conformity with other Cambridge histories, this multi-volume work seeks to provide an "enduring historical survey" and an interpretive summation of Western scholarly research in its field. The eight volumes cover a comprehensive period from "the earliest times" or "palaeo-ecology" of the African continent up to about 1975. Very clear tables of contents in each volume offer access

to each geographical region during a particular era: for example, articles on Egypt and Sudan, the Maghreb, Ethiopia and the Horn. In each volume are found extensive bibliographical essays and bibliographies, and a detailed index. Some maps and tables are included.

46. **General History of Africa.** Prepared by the UNESCO International Scientific Committee for the Drafting of a General History of Africa. Berkeley: Heinemann, 1981. 8 v. ISBN 0-435-94807-5.

An extensive collection of essays, rich in detail, chronicling the course of many African civilizations from prehistoric times to about 1980. The methodology of history itself receives a great deal of attention; reliance on European sources is avoided, and the work intentionally rests upon the two bases of archaeology and oral tradition. The political agenda of the effort is spelled out in the Preface by Senegal's Amadou-Mahtar M'Bow, then Director-General of UNESCO: "... [formerly, in the scholarly community] there was a refusal to see Africans as the creators of original cultures which flowered and survived over the centuries in patterns of their own making and which historians are unable to grasp unless they forgo their prejudices and rethink their approach" (Vol. 1, p. xvii).

Vol. 2 concentrates on the ancient civilizations of Pharaonic Egypt, Nubia and Axum; finding other material on the peoples of the Maghreb, Sahel and Horn is not so easy, but is helped by detailed indexes in which one may search for place names or tribal ethnonyms (the Tuareg, Songhay, Fulani, etc.). Each volume contains illustrations and maps. An abridged edition published in 1990 is also available.

47. Bidwell, Robin. **Dictionary of Modern Arab History: an A to Z of Over 2000 Entries From 1798 to the Present Day.** London; New York: Kegan Paul International, 1998. ix, 456 p. ISBN 0-7103-0505-2.

A substantial tool for ready reference and research on the Arab world, including the Maghreb and Egypt. Lengthy and carefully-written entries distinguish this information-rich work. Unfortunately, the author's death left the work somewhat incomplete, in that there are no cross-references (not even from variant spellings of names) and no indexes, nor are there maps or other reference helps; but the quality of the writing may compensate. The work also exhibits a distinctive and personal point of view.

48. Fage, J. D. **A History of Africa.** Third edition. London; New York: Routledge, 1995. x, 595 p. ISBN 0-415-12721-1.

A new edition of a standard scholarly one-volume history of the continent. Part 2, "The Impact of Islam," concentrates upon medieval North Africa, and other relevant information can be found in the index (though the index is not as carefully classified as one might wish). The subdivided bibliography leads to sources pertaining to each of the historical eras and regions covered. Helpful historical maps are provided, and there are some illustrations and tables of data; however, the black-and-white photos are often dark and murky. On many pages, even the text is faint and poorly printed.

49. Freeman-Grenville, G. S. P. (Greville Stewart Parker). **Chronology of African History.** London: Oxford University Press, 1973. xxii, 312 p. ISBN 0-19-913174-0.

The fact that this reference dates from 1971 does not decrease its value, as the chronology begins in 1300 BC and covers the intervening centuries. The reader must take a few minutes to grasp the organization of the four major historical sections. Each one divides the page into columns and shows the events taking place simultaneously in 4-6 different geographical areas. Therefore, events in northern Africa in 1727, for example, may be compared at a glance to events in 1727 in Egypt and the Sudan, West Africa, East Africa, Central & Southern Africa, and "other countries" (usually Europe). The result is a fascinating volume one wishes to browse at leisure. A names and subject index makes it possible to locate specific information spread throughout the chronology.

50. Fritze, Ronald H. and et al. **Reference Sources in History: an Introductory Guide.** Santa Barbara, CA: ABC-Clio, 1990. xvii, 319 p. ISBN 0-87436-164-8.

A carefully-written handbook to major sources for historical research and study. Coverage of Africa and the Middle East is limited, but the annotations are so valuable that this work may still be worth consulting. Also, many of the sources described here contain material relevant to northern Africa, even if that is not their primary concern. A general index is provided.

51. Haarman, Ulrich. **Geschichte des Arabischen Welt.** Third enlarged edition. Munich: C.H. Beck Verlag, 1994. 756 p. *Becks Historische Bibliothek.* ISBN 3-406-38113-8.

A comprehensive but concise one-volume history in an updated and improved edition. The clarity of organization makes it easy to find material on North Africa before the Middle Ages (Chapter VI) and from 1300 to the present (Chapter X).

An important part of the volume is the substantial bibliographical essay (pp. 659-706), a detailed guide to primary sources and Western scholarship in each of the historical and topical areas covered. The volume includes 14 maps and a useful index.

52. Hourani, Albert. **A History of the Arab Peoples.** Cambridge, MA: Belknap (Harvard University Press), 1991. xx, 551 p. ISBN 0-674-39565-4.

A landmark work by one of the 20th century's great authorities on the Arab world. Its organization is both chonological and conceptual. The work devotes due attention to the "Maghrib" as well as the "Mashriq" or Middle East, and includes material on the Sudan. A very precise index leads the reader directly to these topics. Of great reference value are the 16 very clear original maps by John Flower, and the beautifully-organized select bibliography (pp. 500-529).

53. Isichei, Elizabeth. **A History of African Societies to 1870.** Cambridge: Cambridge University Press, 1997. viii, 578 p. ISBN 0-521-45444-1.

Written with perfect clarity by one of the leading authorities in the field, this is a well-organized comprehensive history of the African continent from prehistoric times, in one concise and convenient volume. It uses a deceptively simple plan: first, the ages of Africa's distant past, then more closely-focused regional histories.

Northern Africa, the northeast and Horn, the western Sahel, etc., are fully covered within their contemporary regional and tribal groupings. The author takes into account important interpretive factors, including gender concerns, ecology and the lives of ordinary people, not only the history of rulers or empires.

Five diagrams or charts and sixteen small but helpful historical maps illustrate the text. Meticulous footnotes and a current, annotated and subdivided bibliography lead the reader to valuable source material. In addition, there is an effective index.

54. Jenkins, Everett Jr. **Pan-African Chronology: a Comprehensive Reference to the Black Quest for Freedom in Africa, the Americas, Europe and Asia, 1400-1865.** Jefferson, NC: McFarland & Co., 1996. viii, 440 p. ISBN 0-7864-0139-7.

The geographical scope of this work is extremely broad, but careful discipline of the chronology helps keep order in this information-rich work. The writer's aim is to chronicle the complex interaction of Africans with the rest of the world during these very eventful years, with special attention to the displacement and enslavement of Africans and their efforts to recover their freedom. A not-very-successful names and subject index (subdivided by year) and a brief bibliography are included. The reader longs for source notes to document these events, but perhaps printing them would have swallowed the chronology in bibliographic detail. The work is nevertheless a valuable contribution to an underdocumented field.

55. Le Gall, Michel and Kenneth Perkins. **The Maghrib in Question: Essays in History and Historiography.** Austin: University of Texas Press, 1997. xxv, 258 p. ISBN 0-292-76576-2.

Not a reference book, this collection of specialized scholarly essays is mentioned here because it is, apparently, the only source providing "a serious assessment of the state of our field" (Preface). Each essay has bibliographical references, but unfortunately there is no general bibliography or index.

56. Mansfield, Peter. **A History of the Middle East.** New York: Viking, 1991. 373 p. ISBN 0-670-81515-2.

A new narrative history by well-known author Peter Mansfield, whose *Middle East: a Political and Economic Survey* (5th edition, 1980) is still consulted. This volume covers Egypt, and Sudan to a lesser extent; material on other parts of Arab North Africa may be found in the well-organized index.

57. Mantran, Robert. **Les Grandes Dates de l'Islam.** Paris: Larousse, 1990. 288 p. ISBN 2-03-740006-3.

A reference volume composed of chronologies and maps, with a handy glossary and dynastic tables. Brief introductions and boxes with significant quotes are also provided. The Abbasids, Fatimids, Almoravids, Almohads and Mamelouks are covered here, with specific attention to North African medieval events, even beyond the boundaries of the Ottoman Empire. The era of European imperialism in Africa is detailed in several chronologies, organized regionally, with material on Afrique Noire, the Maghreb and individual states or peoples. The emergence of independent modern states and of contemporary political Islam ("L'affirmation musulmane 1963-1989") are represented as well. The general index helps to locate more specific terms (e.g., "Berbères") but some significant terms mentioned in the work are not included (Songhay, Nubie, etc).

58. McEwan, Peter J. M. **Readings in African History.** London: Oxford University Press, 1968. 3 v.

This 3-volume collection of previously-published articles and essays, though dated, conveniently brings together important historical material from a variety of sources. The work deals briefly with ancient, medieval and early colonial Africa, then concentrates on the political issues of the 19th and 20th centuries. The same geographical pattern is followed throughout: West Africa, North Africa, Egypt, Ethiopia, East Africa, Southern Africa. This pattern places emphasis on the northern portion of the continent and "singles out" Egypt and Ethiopia for special attention. Some maps are provided; also a fairly simple bibliography and index.

59. Norton, Mary Beth. **The American Historical Association's Guide to Historical Literature.** Third edition. New York; Oxford: Oxford University Press, 1995. 2 v. ISBN 0-19-505727-9.

An important annotated guide that belongs at the reference desk of every university library. Many of the chapters relate to northern Africa, even if the chapter title does not reveal this: for example, Section 2, "Prehistory." Chapters specifically occupied with topics relevant to the region include "Pre-Roman North Africa" (within Section 7), "Islamic World to 1500," "Middle East and North Africa" and "Sub-Saharan Africa," all prepared by established scholars. Introductory material in each section is also quite valuable. If the clear arrangement of material in each section is not detailed enough, there is an immense subject index in Vol. 2 that should direct the reader to useful sources.

60. Robinson, Francis. **Atlas of the Islamic World Since 1500.** New York: Facts on File, 1982. 238 p. ISBN 0-87196-629-8.

A big, impressive "coffee table" book with an immense scope, covering 500 years of history in a very wide area, including all of Africa and Asia. The work is organized by chronology and theme. As such, it is more successful than the *Cambridge Illustrated History of the Islamic World*, also edited by Robinson.

The emphasis in this work is upon the cultural sophistication of various Muslim peoples and their contributions to world civilization, particularly in design: fine art, crafts and architecture. Fifty well-conceived and executed maps accompany the text; extraordinary full-color photos illustrate almost every page.

Part Two, "To Be a Muslim," provides a sympathetic view of religious and social life. The work is very frank about the troubled relations between Europe and Islam during this era, and the introductory essay, "Western Attitudes to Islam," could be assigned on its own as profitable reading for undergraduates.

The volume provides other useful reference helps: an unusually attractive chronological table, a list of rulers of Islamic states and regions since 1500, a simple glossary, a very precise gazetteer giving exact latitude and longitude (plus the page numbers of the relevant maps) for scores of locations, a carefully-subdivided index, a set of captions identifying the subject and source of all those excellent photos, and remarkably, a very competent bibliographical essay directing the reader to sources for further study.

61. Robinson, Francis. **Cambridge Illustrated History of the Islamic World.** Cambridge: Cambridge University Press, 1996. xxiii, 328 p. ISBN 0-521-43510-2.

An attractive, one-volume comprehensive history of the Islamic world in its broad geographic sense, encompassing the billion inhabitants of the globe who consider themselves Muslims. It is necessarily somewhat general in approach, and gives a superficial impression of dealing with something monolithic or homogeneous; it requires the reader to regard states and societies from Mauritania to Indonesia as a single entity or region. The text does attempt to deal with this problem, but it is inherent in the thematic—as opposed to chronological or geographical—organization of the whole volume. The work reflects very capably the ways in which these societies share historical and cultural characteristics.

Excellent maps and carefully-captioned black-and-white and color photos tastefully illustrate the volume. Feature pages call attention to outstanding historical figures, places or traditions, such as characteristically Islamic medieval house design. Several helpful reference features are included: a table of rulers of the Islamic world by country or dynasty (with names and dates), a small glossary, a dense but interesting bibliographical essay, and an index.

The most disappointing thing about this volume is its minimal coverage of Africa: Egypt is the only part of the continent that is well represented. Other areas are mentioned only in passing.

62. Shavit, David. **The United States in Africa: a Historical Dictionary.** New York: Greenwood Press, 1989. xxii, 298 p. ISBN 0-313-25887-2.

Not confining itself to official US government activities in Africa, this work has a far broader and more interesting function: to identify the "slavers ... colonists, ships and officers ... sea captains and traders, missionaries, diplomats, explorers, travellers and adventurers, soldiers, educators, authors and artists, scientists, mining engineers, hunters and other Americans and American institutions, organizations and business firms, which established a whole gamut of relation-ships between the United States and Africa" (Preface). This volume excludes the northernmost states of Africa, covering the Sahel east from Mauritania, and the Horn; see also Shavit's *The United States in the Middle East.*

An interesting bibliographical essay is provided, plus a general index, a list of all chiefs of American diplomatic missions in Africa 1863-1988, and a helpful ordering of biographical entries by profession or occupation.

63. Shavit, David. **The United States in the Middle East: a Historical Dictionary.** New York: Greenwood Press, 1988. xxiv, 441 p. ISBN 0-313-25341-2.

Another of Shavit's valuable references (see *The United States in Africa*), this volume documents contact between Americans and the people of the Middle East, including the Maghreb, Egypt and Sudan. "Missionaries, diplomats, ar-chaeologists, travelers and tourists, army officers, educators, authors and artists, scientists, engineers, petroleum geologists and other Americans and American institutions, organizations and business firms" (p. vii) fall within the scope of this work.

Concise (usually one paragraph) entries convey important biographical data about each person, with bibliographical references. Entries identifying sig-nificant places and organizations appear here as well. A chronology and brief in-troduction, bibliographical essay, list of US diplomats and an index categorizing persons by profession are provided, along with a general index. This volume be-longs on the desk within reach of anyone needing convenient ready-reference materials on the history of this region.

64. Stewart, John. **African States and Rulers: an Encyclopedia of Native, Colonial and Independent States and Rulers Past and Present.** Jefferson, NC: McFarland & Co., 1989. xx, 395 p. ISBN 0-89950-390-X.

Each entry in this reference provides a list of all known rulers or administra-tors of a given political unit and the dates of their tenure in office. There is no other biographical information on any of these individuals. The heading of each entry is the name of the political unit at that time. Therefore, the rulers of Algeria during the period from 1516 to 1520 will be found under "Algiers Pashalik [i]"; from 1671-1830 under "Algiers Regency," etc. An entry under the modern name of the state provides cross-references to all of the related entries. Ancient or me-dieval names may have separate entries and also be linked to a modern state (for example, Tagant Emirate, now part of Mauritania). A table of contents actually functions as a subject index, and there is a lengthy names index as well.

Statistical Sources and Guides

For demographic and economic figures pertaining to trade and development in the region, see Part Two, "Economics: Commerce, Industry and Aid."

65. Gale Country & World Rankings Reporter. Edited by Charity A. Dorgan. New York: Gale Research, 1995. lxix, 1091 p. ISBN 0-8103-9876-1; ISSN 1079-929X.

Tables of comparative data on every kind of human activity, from basic demographic statistics to the percentage of faculty members polled in 14 countries who believe that respect for academics is declining, or the percentage of people who feel comfortable using a VCR, or the price of golf balls in Asia. Serious information is communicated as well: e.g., the HIV prevalence in adults in 13 regions of the world (including North and sub-Saharan Africa), and the incidence of reported political detention or imprisonment. Source notes are provided for every table; a location index makes it possible to see what kind of information is available for each place: Chad, for instance, is represented on tables in 59 categories. A keyword index is also included.

66. Index to International Statistics: a Guide to the Statistical Publications of International Intergovernmental Organizations. Monthly, with quarterly and annual cumulations; 1983- . Bethesda, MD: Congressional Information Service. ISSN 0737-4461; ISBN 0-88692-418-9.

Also available monthly from CIS on microfiche; also available quarterly from CIS on CD-ROM as "Statistical Masterfile" and online as "Statistical Universe": see **www.cispubs.com/statuniv/**

Detailed abstracts of IO statistical publications in paper and electronic formats comprise Vol. 1 of the paper reference, while Vol. 2 provides a huge index by country or geographic area, names and subjects. Entries are abbreviated, but intelligible.

67. Statistical Abstract of the World. Edited by Marlita A. Reddy. New York: Gale Research, 1994. xx, 1111 p. ISBN 0-8103-9199-6; ISSN 1077-1360.

An attempt to organize data in a standard country-by-country format, with blocks of space provided for each topic. For information-poor countries like Djibouti, the result is a sprinkling of numbers on a largely empty page. The approach works better than expected for Mali, Sudan, etc.; however, the same information is readily available elsewhere.

68. Statistics Sources: a Subject Guide to Data on Industrial, Business, Social, Educational, Financial and Other Topics for the United States and Internationally. 22nd edition. Irregular; 1962- . Edited by Jacqueline Wasserman O'Brien and Steven R. Wasserman. Detroit: Gale Research, 1999. 2 v. ISBN 0-7876-2459-4 (set); ISSN 0585-198X.

An annotated guide to published sources (print and electronic) of statistical information. The subject orientation indicates places to find data on, for example, Algeria—Health or Algeria—Literacy, as well as much more specific keywords such as Algeria—Flour Production or Algeria—Goats. Descriptions of the huge array of World Bank and OECD sources are helpful, as well as lists of US government agency statistical databases. All of the nations of northern Africa are listed, even Western Sahara.

69. Bleaney, C. H. **Official Publications on the Middle East: a Selective Guide to the Statistical Sources.** Durham: Centre for Middle Eastern and Islamic Studies, 1985. 31 p. *Middle East Libraries Committee Research Guides;* 1.

This small package contains a very useful introduction to official publications originating in the Middle East, Mediterranean Africa and Sudan. More than a list of sources, this guide describes each type of publication (budgets, development plans, census data, central bank and Ministry reports, etc.) and offers a country-by-country summary of the available materials. In addition, Bleaney describes the international/intergovernmental organizations active in the region and notes what their publications have to offer. A bibliography of reference sources and a guide to institutions with relevant holdings in the UK are also included. One would like to see this valuable work renewed on a regular basis.

70. Kurian, George Thomas. **Global Data Locator.** Lanham, MD: Bernan Press, 1997. xvii, 375 p. ISBN 0-89059-039-7.

A successor to Kurian's *Sourcebook of Global Statistics* (1985), this reference is topically organized, with indexes of titles and publishers. A table of contents guides the reader to statistical reference works, from general global compendia to highly specialized sources. Materials in print, electronic databases in various formats and online services are included. Each entry provides a capsule profile of the reference source: its basic purpose and scope, its organization of data and methodology. Then, the contents of the work are reproduced, often in very great detail, with headings for all tables of data included.

71. Kurian, George Thomas. **The New Book of World Rankings.** Third edition. New York: Facts on File, 1991. xxi, 324 p. ISBN 0-8160-1931-2.

Tables of country rankings by topic, including geography, vital statistics, economic data, and some more unusual information: a "civil rights index," crime data, registered borrowers in public libraries, etc. One can determine, for instance, that Chad has the lowest percentage of paved roads in the world. Very brief country profiles and a topical index are provided.

72. Showers, Victor. **World Facts and Figures.** Third edition. New York: John Wiley & Sons (Interscience), 1989. xii, 721 p. ISBN 0-471-85775-0.

A one-volume reference specializing in rankings and comparison tables of the nations of the world on the basis of demographic indicators (birth rates, life expectancies, population density, etc.), economic data (GDP, energy use, volume of exports, transport and communications, etc.), and other factors. These other factors include geographic and man-made features of all kinds: coolest cities, oldest cities, longest bridges, highest dams, largest islands, lakes, rivers, mountains, waterfalls, and so on. The index is most helpful if one uses very specific search terms: not North Africa, or Morocco, but Rabat or Marrakesh.

73. Westfall, Gloria D. **Bibliography of Official Statistical Yearbooks and Bulletins.** Alexandria, VA: Chadwyck-Healey, 1986. 247 p. *Government Documents Bibliographies.* ISBN 0-85964-124-4.

A straightforward, helpful country-by-country guide to the publications of national statistics offices, covering physical environment, demography and economic, political, social and cultural affairs. This simple arrangement makes it possible to browse quickly through each section. Entries for each publication are quite detailed; in addition to basic bibliographic information, there is some publishing history, a description of each publication's coverage and some sales or availability information, including microform. All of the nations of northern Africa are included; many of these states publish their official statistical documents in French.

Collective Biographies

74. **Africa Who's Who.** Second edition. Editor in Chief Raph Uwechue. London: Africa Books, 1991. viii, 1863 p. *Know Africa.* ISBN 0-903274-17-5; 0-903274-19-1 (3-v. series).

One of the three-volume *Know Africa* series, which "aims at terminating the era of publications on Africa which reflect the colonial perception of the continent" (Preface). Composed of concise alphabetized entries, this volume provides current biographical data on about 12,000 prominent Africans. The entries list only birthdate and birthplace, family, education, professional titles and accomplishments, hobbies and a postal address. Persons listed represent all walks of life: academics, civil servants, professionals (lawyers, pharmacists, etc.), politicians, military officers, religious leaders, and so on. Unfortunately, there is no index by profession or nationality. A new edition of this work is expected.

75. **African Biographical Archive.** Edited by Victor Herrero Mediavilla; with Ulrike Kramme and ðelmíra Urra Muena. Munich: K.G. Saur, 1994-1997. Microfiche in 12 installments. ISBN 3-598-33101-0 and 3-598-33100-2

Also titled: *Archives Biographiques Africaines.*

A massive compilation of biographical data on about 75,000 persons significant in the history, politics and culture of the whole African continent, including the northern states. The information was compiled from some 214 reference sources (encyclopedias, collective biographies, etc.), published between 1840 and 1993, mainly in German, English, French and Italian. The work cannot be evaluated until the planned index appears.

76. **Burke's Royal Families of the World.** Vol. II: Africa and the Middle East. London: Burke's Peerage, 1980. xv, 320 p. ISBN 0-85011-029-7.

This important genealogical resource provides data on the former royal houses of Egypt, Ethiopia, Libya, Morocco, Tunisia and many Saharan families of Arab, Fulani and other tribal origins, from earliest recorded times to the most recent heirs. An appendix offers more general descriptions of pre-colonial African states and their dynasties (including Chad, Niger and Sudan). Some dynastic charts, a glossary of culture-specific terms, a bibliography and an index are provided. There is also a helpful map.

77. **Dictionary of African Biography.** Vol. 1. Edited by L. H. Ofosu-Appiah. Algonac, MI; New York: Reference Publications, 1977. *Encyclopaedia Africana.* ISBN 0-917256-01-8 (Vol. 1).

This reference is mainly concerned with sub-Saharan Africa; apparently, only three of a projected 20 volumes have been published, so only a few countries have been covered up to this point. About half of Vol. 1, however, is devoted to Ethiopia, and it is a most interesting information source. It includes an historical introduction by Richard Pankhurst, a glossary of Ethiopian titles and vocabulary terms, and three large, clear monochrome maps. The alphabetized, signed articles (1-12 columns of print) provide biographical material on some 150 individuals, both Ethiopian and foreign, who played key roles in the nation's history. A bibliography of 3-10 sources appears with each article, and many are accompanied by fascinating black-and-white portraits, nicely reproduced, in the form of photographs or contemporary drawings or paintings of the individual. In addition to political leaders, figures from the history of the Ethiopian church are well represented.

78. **Historic World Leaders.** Vol. 1: Africa, Middle East, Asia, Pacific. Edited by Anne Commire. Detroit: Gale Research, 1994. lix, 850 p. ISBN 0-8103-8409-4 (vol. 1).

A collection of alphabetized, signed encyclopedia-style articles on notable figures from antiquity to the recent past. The individuals are not classified by place of origin, but the general index is of some help in locating persons connected to the Sudan, for example, or Algeria. Each 3-5 page article provides a capsule identification, a picture of some kind (often a drawing or painting), quite a bit of historical detail, and a small bibliography. An appendix of chronologies and dynastic lists, and 30 pages of interesting historical maps (some rather murky, and all sorely in need of captions) are included.

79. **Makers of Modern Africa.** Second edition. Editor in Chief Raph Uwechue. London: Africa Books, 1991. 797 p. *Know Africa.* ISBN 0-903274-18-3; 0-903274-19-1 (3-v. series).

One of the three-volume *Know Africa* series, which "aims at terminating the era of publications on Africa which reflect the colonial perception of the continent" (Preface). Biographical articles, relating the life stories and explaining the significance of 680 persons important in African history, make up this volume.

Portraits accompany most of the articles; some prominent women are included. Most of those featured are political leaders, but there are also some educators, physicians, artists, etc. Indexes by profession and nationality would increase the usefulness of this reference. A new edition of this work is expected.

80. **Penseurs Maghrébins Contemporains.** Tunis: Cèrés Productions (Édition Tunisienne), 1993. 279 p. ISBN 9973-19-027-0

Déjà paru dans la collection *Horizon Maghrébin.*

A collection of nine essays examining the work of leading intellectuals in the arts, political science or philosophy. A one-page biographical sketch opens each article, followed by a detailed study (about 30 pages) of the individual's thought and work. All of the persons covered are from Algeria, Tunisia and Morocco, though some are connected with more than one of these, and others are active mainly in Europe. The volume has a substantial bibliography, but no index.

81. **Who's Who in the Arab World.** Munich: K.G. Saur and Publitec Publications. Biennial, 1966- . ISBN 3-598-07646-0; ISSN 0083-9752.

The thirteenth edition of this reference, dated 1997-98, consists of three major parts. About two-thirds of the volume presents a compendium of brief entries containing biographical data on "outstanding personalities and leading national figures" (p. 7). In typical Who's Who style, these entries provide just a chronology of an individual's career, with dates, birthplace, offices held or accomplishments, family data, education and mailing address if available; there is no narrative biography or assessment of the individual's significance.

Part 2 of the volume provides profile data on 19 Arab countries, including Algeria, Djibouti, Egypt, Libya, Mauritania, Morocco, Somalia, Sudan and Tunisia. Part 3 offers a thematic outline of history and modern issues in the region, activities of the Arab League, the Arab/Israeli peace process, banking, development and the petroleum industry, and one page devoted to "The Maghreb."

Unfortunately, the whole work has apparently suffered in translation: the English prose is sometimes very awkward and inaccurate, with prominent spelling and grammatical mistakes.

82. Auchterlonie, Paul. **Arabic Biographical Dictionaries: a Summary Guide and Bibliography.** Durham: Middle East Libraries Committee, 1987. iv, 60 p. *MELC Research Guides;* 2. ISBN 0-948889-01-2; ISSN 0269-0233.

A helpful introductory essay and annotations (from one sentence to a paragraph in length) add to the value of this collection of sources. Auchterlonie takes the wise step of separating classical Arabic sources—medieval in origin—from modern works, in both Arabic and Western languages. In addition, Chapter 4 lists scholarly studies and uses of biographical dictionaries. Sources from and about northern Africa are included. A names and titles index completes the work.

83. Brockman, Norbert C. **An African Biographical Dictionary.** Santa Barbara, CA: ABC-Clio, 1994. viii, 440 p. ISBN 0-87436-748-4.

Concise, readable entries (from 1 paragraph to 3 pages) identify and summarize the significant achievements of hundreds of political and cultural figures, scientists and religious leaders from Africa south of the Mediterranean coast, including the Sahel and Horn. Some entries include portraits, and most direct the reader to information available in other standard reference works (like *Contemporary Authors*).

Handy appendices include a table of colonial names for modern independent states, some historical maps, a list of names and dates by country for all African leaders since independence, a list of the biographical entries by nationality, and another listing the entries by field of activity, from heads of state to sports stars and poets. In addition, a very detailed and well-organized index is provided.

Brockman has dealt with the problem of principal or family names in different traditions by capitalizing the name under which the entry is found. When a person is significant in more than one country—for example, the Songhay Empire ruler Dawud—the person is listed more than once (e.g., under Mail and Niger). Emphasis is placed on the postcolonial and contemporary periods, but important figures from earlier eras are sometimes included.

84. Burke, Edmund III. **Struggle and Survival in the Modern Middle East.** Berkeley: University of California Press, 1993. xi, 400 p. ISBN 0-520-07566-8.

Not a typical collective biography, this volume aims to present life stories of "ordinary men and women" and shed light on "Middle Eastern history as it might appear when viewed from the bottom up" (Preface). The scope of the work includes the North coast of Africa, but not the Sahel or Horn. The stories are gathered into three sections, covering precolonial, colonial and contemporary lives. Each feature is more than a simple anecdote: these are detailed and well-researched narratives, each with its descriptive bibliography. A glossary of terms (mostly from Arabic) is provided, but there are no indexes; this is a work for study rather than ready reference.

85. Glickman, Harvey. **Political Leaders of Contemporary Africa South of the Sahara.** Westport, CT: Greenwood, 1992. xxii, 361 p. ISBN 0-313-26781-2.

"Contemporary," for purposes of this volume, means "since 1945," and thus a figure like Haile Selassie (who died in 1975) is included, along with 53 other important figures in the history of the continent. The predominantly Arab states of northern Africa and Sudan are excluded. Each biographical essay provides 5-6 pages of information, plus a brief bibliography. There is a names and subject index.

86. Lipschutz, Mark R. and R. Kent Rasmussen. **Dictionary of African Historical Biography.** Chicago: Aldine, 1978. xi, 292 p. ISBN 0-202-24144-0.

A ready reference intended for the student, and for the trained scholar in need of quick access to information outside his or her subject area. It includes the Sahel and Horn, and occasional references to persons active in the Mediterranean region of Africa. Each of the 800 entries (1-3 paragraphs in length) provides dates, a simple identification (e.g., "Reputed first Muslim ruler of the Mali empire") , a biographical sketch and very simple—somewhat dated—bibliographical references. Includes a subject index and a names index.

87. Rake, Alan. **100 Great Africans.** Metuchen, NJ: Scarecrow, 1994. ix, 431 p. ISBN 0-8108-2929-0.

Taking the long view of the continent's history, Rake has selected figures significant in the cultural and political fabric of Africa, from Queen Hatshepsut of Pharaonic Egypt to Flight Lieutenant Jerry Rawlings of Ghana. Lively descriptive entries, often with maps (but no portraits), are organized roughly by chronology and theme. An index lists the names alphabetically. Oddly, there are no bibliographical references or source notes to document Rake's assertions, which are often highly flavored with opinion, speculation and value judgments.

88. Rake, Alan. **Who's Who in Africa: Leaders for the 1990s.** Metuchen, NJ: Scarecrow, 1992. vii, 448 p. ISBN 0-8108-2557-0.

Concentrating on sub-Saharan Africa, this work includes entries for Chad, Djibouti, Ethiopia, Mali, Mauritania, Niger, Somalia and Sudan. It is not a "Who's Who" in the usual sense of containing very brief directory-style items; for each individual in this volume, a descriptive entry of 3-4 paragraphs to 3-4 pages is provided. An emphasis on political activity is maintained throughout, and purely cultural, artistic, religious or business leaders are not included. Entries are organized by country, with a names index to give alphabetical access.

89. Reich, Bernard. **Political Leaders of the Contemporary Middle East and North Africa: a Biographical Dictionary.** New York: Greenwood Press, 1990. 557 p. ISBN 0-313-26213-6.

This work is really a collection of biographical essays on 70 of the most significant political figures of the region in the latter half of the 20th century. The articles range from 4-10 pages in length and each offers a bibliography of 6-8 sources, including any major works written by the subject. Golda Meir is the only woman included, and some of the entries are not contemporary (Abdullah Ibn Hussein, for example, died in 1951) but are historically important for current events. The difficult problem of transliteration and alphabetizing of Arabic, Turkish, Persian and Hebrew names makes searching the table of contents rather slow, and the list of entries by country provides no page numbers. The index is very limited; a chunk of 59 page numbers under "Soviet Union" is not subdivided in any way. The tone of the essays is sometimes judgmental. Nevertheless, the articles provide a great deal of information in narrative form.

90. Shimoni, Yaacov. **Biographical Dictionary of the Middle East.** New York: Facts on File, 1991. 255 p. ISBN 0-8160-2458-8.

This ready reference concentrates on the Middle East but includes some public figures of Libya, Tunisia, Algeria and Morocco. Intellectuals and religious leaders are mentioned "from the point of view of their influence on the [current] political scene." Entries range from one concise paragraph to 2-3 pages; no bibliographies are given. Some black-and-white photos appear, several of them curiously out-of-date. There is a collection of maps at the end, many rather poorly reproduced and too small to be useful. No index is included, but cross-references are given from well-known forms of certain names: NASSER see Abd-ul-Nasser, Gamal. Some of the articles are tendentious in tone (e.g., 'Arafat, Yasser); no Arab or African contributors, editors or researchers were involved in preparing this volume.

91. Wiseman, John A. **Political Leaders in Black Africa: a Biographical Dictionary of the Major Politicians Since Independence.** Brookfield, VT: Edward Elgar, 1991. xxiii, 248 p. ISBN 1-85278-047-9.

This convenient reference covers African history since about 1960, and provides one-column sketches not only of African office-holders, but also of opposition politicians and leaders of militant or insurgent groups, both living and deceased. Entries are organized alphabetically, with a list showing the country of origin and the part of the name used for the entry heading (a difficult problem in many collective biographies).

A brief country-by-country chronology helps to place leaders readily in their proper sequence, and would be helpful to a reader who knows the country concerned but not the individual's exact name. A geographical index is provided, but it shows only entry numbers and not names; a reader might have to look up dozens of entries to find the one wanted.

The states of the northern coast are not included in this volume, but Mauritania, Sudan, the Sahel and Horn are covered.

Travel Information

Well-written travel guides contain a great deal of general information about the history, archaeology, geography, culture and people of a given area. For many more travel guidebooks, see chapters for specific countries in Part Three.

92. **North African Handbook: With Andalucia—Moorish Southern Spain.** Second edition. By Anne and Keith McLachlan. Chicago: Passport Books, 1995. 928 p. ISBN 0-8442-8978-7.

A travel guide covering the region in general, then Morocco, Mauritania, Algeria, Tunisia, Libya, Egypt and Sudan. Each section provides some maps and city plans, distance and climate charts, a basic country profile, information about hotels, food, shopping and transport, and sometimes a special feature box—for example, a diagram explaining the way a mirage is formed in the desert. There is a simple glossary and three indexes.

93. Laffin, John. **Know the Middle East.** Gloucester: Alan Sutton, 1985. 188 p. ISBN 0-86299-215-X.

A pocket paperback reference intended for "the foreign businessman, traveller, writer and politician and the ordinary tourist" (Author's Note). It is meant to help one avoid misunderstandings and mishaps that may befall a Western visitor who is unaware of the basic social customs and realities he or she will encounter. The scope is said to be "the entire Arab world"—including the Mediterranean states of Africa and the Sudan. The book is not organized geographically: it is composed of short alphabetized topical entries, from Alawites to Zionism. Small maps are included. A disturbing characteristic of this brief format is its reliance upon simplistic judgments and generalizations that are very frequently negative: religious fanaticism, dictatorship and backwardness appear often, and the tone is patronizing.

Websites

94. Focus Multimedia Online Magazine. **www.focusmm.com.au/welcome.htm**
Travel, entertainment and cultural features on the Mediterranean countries, including Egypt, Tunisia and Morocco.

95. Fodor's Resource Center. Smart Travel Tips. **www.fodors.com/resource/**
General travel information.

96. Lonely Planet. Destinations: Africa. **www.lonelyplanet.com/dest/afr/des-afr.htm**
Travel information. So far, weak on northern Africa.

97. The Middle East and North Africa Travel Network. **www.mideasttravelnet.com/**
Descriptions of each country, plus more specific travel information: airlines serving certain locations, flight times, accommodations, local transport, entertainment, attractions, business contacts, etc. Covers Morocco, Algeria, Tunisia, Libya and Egypt.

98. Virtual Tourist. Africa. **www.vtourist.com/Africa/**
For Egypt, see the Middle East page.

99. World Tourism Organization. Africa. **www.world-tourism.org/ows-doc/africa.htm**
Directory data for official ministries and national tourism offices in all of the countries of northern Africa. Names, mailing addresses and phone numbers, but few websites.

100. World Travel Guide Online. Africa Page. **www.wtgonline.com/navigate/default.asp**
A good deal of useful background information for the visitor; pages on each country.

Bibliographies

More specific topical bibliographies will be found in later chapters pertaining to particular subjects and countries (Part Two and Part Three).

General and Topical Bibliographies

101. **Bibliographie de la Culture Arabe Contemporaine.** Under the direction of Jacque Berque. Paris: Sindbad (UNESCO), 1981. 476 p. ISBN 92-3-201758-X and 2-7274-0059-4.

An introductory essay on Arab culture accompanies an extensive compilation of over 1600 works in European languages and Arabic, topically arranged. Critical and scholarly studies of the Arab world cover not only "culture" in the sense of fine art and literature, but also law, urban studies and the environment, political crises (including the Arab-Israeli conflict), Arab nationalism and other ideologies, economics, women's status, technology and industry and their effects on society, etc. The materials included were published from the end of the 1940s up to the beginning of the 1970s.

Many of the entries include abstracts or annotations, often lengthy, in either French or English. A names index in the Roman alphabet, an author index in Arabic script and an index of Arabic titles are provided.

102. **Bibliographie der Deutschsprachigen Arabistik und Islamkunde: von den Anfängen bis 1986 nebst Literatur über die Arabischen Länder der Gegenwart.** Produced by Fuat Sezgin. Frankfurt am Main: Institut für Geschichte der Arabisch-Islamischen Wissenschaften, 1990. 21 v. *Reihe A: Texte und Studien.*

A monumental work of scholarship comprising 21 large volumes (the last is a huge index), covering: general works and research helps; the religion of Islam (theology, law and custom); the Arabic language and philology; poetry and prose literature; science, philosophy, medicine and historiography; handcrafts, arts and folklore; history and economics, geography, sociology and ethnology. Eight large topical divisions involve at least one volume each. Scholarly articles as well as books are included; entries are not annotated.

103. **Books in Print in the United Nations System.** First edition. Compiled by the Advisory Committee for the Co-Ordination of Information Systems (ACCIS). New York: United Nations, 1992. xviii, 721 p. ISBN 92-1-100379-2; UN Sales No. GV.E.92.0.18.

United Nations official materials now amount to over 14,000 "system publications," many of which are relevant to area studies. Indeed, "collectively the UN system is one of the world's most prolific publishers, with a vast range of printed materials in almost every area of learning, research and development" (p. vii).

This topically-organized guide can help the scholar or acquisitions librarian identify these materials and determine how to obtain them. Four indexes are provided to speed access, and directory/contact data for sales agents and publishers is included.

104. **Contemporary African Politics and Development: a Comprehensive Bibliography, 1981-1990.** Compiled by Vijitha Mahadevan. Boulder and London: Lynne Rienner, 1994. xxi, 1314 p. ISBN 1-55587-334-0.

A compilation of almost 17,000 citations of materials in English and French published during a very active decade of scholarship on Africa. Books and monographs, articles and essays in journals and edited volumes, reference works and government documents are included. Many entries offer a brief synopsis or abstract, and all provide at least a note indicating subject headings and keywords that correspond to the work's contents. An opening section on Africa generally (organized by topic) is followed by materials on each country; the "expanded contents" at the beginning of the book facilitates a quick browse through the whole work. Appendices and indexes offer a few more helps in locating and identifying material (though the keyword index is not entirely successful).

105. **Guide to Country Information in International Governmental Organization Publications.** Edited by Marian Shaaban. American Library Association Government Documents Round Table, 1996. xviii, 343 p.

An annotated bibliography of documents, organized by region. Materials of a world scope are arranged by topic, covering a wide range of political, economic and social issues. Section 2, "Africa" and Section 6, "Middle East" contain many relevant publications. The volume is indexed by the documents' "issuing source" and by title, with a handy membership list and directory data for each organization in appendices.

106. **Guide to Official Publications of Foreign Countries.** American Library Association: Government Documents Round Table, 1990. xxi, 359 p.

Every research library should be aware of the materials collected in this useful guide, which covers directories, economic data and statistics, banking and development, population and census reports, law, health, education, and some cultural activities (publishing and bibliography, for instance). Each entry is briefly annotated, and acquisitions information is given if possible. Entries are organized by country, and all of the nations of northern Africa are represented.

107. **Guide to Reference Sources on Africa, Asia, Latin America and the Caribbean, Middle East and North Africa, Russia and East Europe: Selected and Annotated.** Edited by James R. Kennedy et al. Williamsport, PA: Bro-Dart, 1972. xiv, 73 p. *Foreign Area Materials Center, Occasional Publications;* no. 17. ISBN 87272-023-3.

A simple guide to reference materials "on non-Western European areas," meant to be useful to the undergraduate doing research in a college library. Materials on northern Africa can be found subsumed under Africa generally or the Middle East. Ample annotations may be helpful in the evaluation of collections.

108. **The Middle East in Conflict: a Historical Bibliography.** Santa Barbara, CA: ABC-Clio, 1985. ix, 302 p. *Clio Bibliography Series;* no. 19. ISBN 0-87436-381-0.

An index of journal literature studying developments in the Middle East, the Maghreb, Sudan and, to a lesser extent, Ethiopia and Somalia in the 20th century (up to 1982). Entries pertaining to history and related social sciences and humanities are organized topically and geographically; topics include the Western Sahara conflict of 1973-83. More than 2000 journals in 40 languages (both European and some Middle Eastern and African publications) are covered. Abstracts are provided for every entry. A detailed subject index built upon strings of descriptors offers efficient access to this useful compendium of material.

109. Aman, Mohammed M. **Arab Periodicals and Serials: a Subject Bibliography.** New York: Garland, 1979. x, 252 p. *Garland Reference Library of Social Science;* 57. ISBN 0-8240-9816-1.

Though dated, this guide to "periodicals in Arabic, English, French and other European languages published in the Arab countries or in the Western hemisphere" (p. ix) is a place to start. The work is organized by topic or theme; unfortunately, there is no title index, nor an index by place of publication. Annotations describing the typical coverage or readership of these publications would enormously increase this work's usefulness.

110. Atiyeh, George N. **The Contemporary Middle East, 1948-1973: a Selective and Annotated Bibliography.** Boston: G.K. Hall, 1975. xxvi, 664 p. ISBN 0-8161-1085-9.

Atiyeh's major work cites more than 6000 monographs and journal articles, chiefly in the social sciences. Materials listed are mainly in English, French, German, Italian and Spanish, but also include some in Arabic, Turkish and Persian.

The compilation is organized geographically, with large sections on the Middle East and Arab countries generally; one section covers the Nile Valley (Egypt and Sudan), and another North Africa (the Maghreb as a region, then Libya, Tunisia, Algeria and Morocco). Within each section, works are organized topically. Atiyeh's annotations would be very valuable to the researcher, identifying the theme and conclusion of each work. An author index and helpful subject index are provided.

111. Auchterlonie, Paul. **Introductory Guide to Middle Eastern and Islamic Bibliography.** Oxford: Middle East Libraries Committee, 1990. v, 84 p. *MELC Research Guides;* 5. ISSN 0269-0233.

A "basic bibliography ... intended to provide concise and straightforward guidance to the range of reference works available in Middle Eastern studies" (Introduction). One finds here at least a few representative works from a wide range of subject areas, including Persian and Turkish studies; northern Africa is covered only insofar as materials pertaining generally to Islam or the Middle East are relevant to the area. Annotations range from one sentence to one paragraph in length. An author and title index is provided.

112. Auchterlonie, Paul. **Middle East and Islam: a Bibliographical Introduction.** Supplement, 1977-1983. Middle East Libraries Committee. Zug: Inter-Documentation, 1986. vi, 244 p. *Bibliotheca Asiatica;* 20. ISBN 3-300-00001-7.

A helpful supplement to the version produced in 1979 by Diana Grimwood-Jones.

113. Besterman, Theodore. **A World Bibliography of African Bibliographies.** Revised edition by J.D. Pearson. Oxford: Basil Blackwell, 1975. 241 columns of print (not paginated). ISBN 0-631-16900-8.

A companion volume to Besterman and Pearson's *A World Bibliography of Oriental Bibliographies*, this work reproduces the citations of the general materials on "the Tropics," colonization and economic development in Asia and Africa, then presents materials on Africa per se. North Africa as a region is covered, then each of the countries of the continent as they existed at the publication of the fourth edition of this work. There is a names and titles index.

114. Besterman, Theodore. **A World Bibliography of Oriental Bibliographies.** Revised edition by J.D. Pearson. Totowa, NJ: Rowman and Littlefield, 1975. 727 columns of print (not paginated). ISBN 0-87471-750-7.

An important reference still consulted by historians, this work encompasses topical bibliographies, map catalogs, library and archive holdings lists and other collections of material in a huge spectrum of languages, including Latin, Greek, Hebrew, Syriac, Russian and countless other European and Asian tongues and scripts. Coverage of the Middle East is limited to a section on the "Modern Near East (West Asia)" and Egypt (under "Arab Countries") . There is also a significant section on Arabic language and literature. A names and titles index is provided.

115. Blackhurst, Hector. **East and Northeast Africa Bibliography.** Lanham, MD: Scarecrow, 1996. xiv, 299 p. *Scarecrow Area Bibliographies;* no. 7. ISBN 0-8108-3090-6.

A careful compilation of books published from 1960-1995 (periodical articles, items in collective works and pamphlet publications under 40 pages are excluded). The humanities and social sciences form the core of this bibliography. Works in English, French, Italian and German are found here (but none in non-Roman script languages).

The citations are organized alphabetically by subject heading, using combined descriptors to subdivide large sections. For example, materials on Ethiopia are grouped together by the first term, then ordered into logical sequence by the second (from ETHIOPIA—AGRICULTURE to ETHIOPIA—WOMEN). Topical headings covering the region are also provided: e.g., REFUGEES—NORTHEAST AFRICA. This arrangement works well, though one might wish for a table of contents to browse. There is an author index.

The Horn of Africa is well covered here—Ethiopia, Eritrea, Somalia and Djibouti—along with states of the East African region.

116. Blake, David and Carole Travis. **Periodicals From Africa: a Bibliography and Union List of Periodicals Published in Africa.** First supplement. Boston: G.K. Hall, 1984. xvii, 217 p. *A Reference Publication in African Studies.* ISBN 0-8161-8525-5.

Prepared on behalf on the Standing Conference on Library Materials on Africa (SCOLMA), this reference provides a much-needed vantage point for identifying and locating important journals that are often hard to find. The journals and newsletters cited are organized geographically, with the countries of northern Africa properly covered. The periodicals title index makes it possible to go the other way, if one knows the title of a journal but not its country of origin. Location data is given for these periodicals for about 60 library collections in the United Kingdom. One might only wish for annotations explaining the typical approach and subject matter of these periodicals, as sometimes the titles are rather broad.

117. Fenton, Thomas P. and Mary J. Heffron. **Africa: a Directory of Resources.** Maryknoll: Orbis Books, 1987. xiv, 144 p. ISBN 0-88-344-532-8.

A fully-annotated compilation of resources—books, periodicals, pamphlets, articles and audiovisual materials—prepared expressly for "organizations that oppose the injustices in foreign military and economic intervention in the Third World" (Preface). It contains directory information about many such organizations of religious and political activists in human rights, relief and development, refugee services, women's status and justice issues. The entries are grouped by type of material, and there are five helpful indexes of names (individuals and organizations), titles, geographical areas and subjects. The majority of the works cited have to do with southern Africa (especially apartheid), but there are materials pertaining to famine and displacement of people in Ethiopia, Eritrea and Somalia.

118. Fenton, Thomas P. and Mary J. Heffron. **Third World Struggles for Peace With Justice: a Directory of Resources.** Maryknoll: Orbis, 1990. xviii, 188 p. ISBN 0-88344-660-X.

A helpful guide to a variety of books, periodicals, pamphlets and articles, audiovisual materials and organizations active in development. The work is part of the Third World Resources project undertaken to help combat social, political and economic injustice in the developing world, by informing activist groups about each other and increasing access to educational and motivational materials. The work is organized by type of material, but indexes provide access by individual and corporate names, titles, geographical areas and subjects. Africa and the Middle East are fairly well represented.

119. Gorman, G. E. and J. J. Mills. **Guide to Current National Bibliographies in the Third World.** Second revised edition. London: Hans Zell, 1987. xx, 372 p. ISBN 0-905450-34-5.

An important contribution to the ongoing work of bibliographic control of materials published in developing counries. This work provides full descriptions of each national bibliography or similar publication, plus a careful analysis of the currency, coverage, accuracy and reference value of each one.

Regional bibliographies or accessions lists exist for Africa and the Arab states, and individual entries for Algeria, Egypt, Libya, Morocco, Tunisia and Ethiopia are provided. The volume also offers a titles index. The publisher is apparently making an effort to keep this work current: a third edition is planned.

120. Grimwood-Jones, Diana. **Middle East and Islam: a Bibliographical Introduction.** Revised and enlarged edition. Middle East Libraries Committee. Zug: Inter-Documentation, 1979. ix, 429 p. *Bibliotheca Asiatica;* 15. ISBN 3-85750-032-8.

A well-organized topical compendium of materials (mostly scholarly monographs, but also some reference works and periodicals), prepared by noted authorities. A chapter on the history of the Maghreb, one on the oil industry, several on specific places (North Africa as a region, Egypt, Sudan), and one on Berber studies are all relevant. Some of the entries are briefly annotated. An index of authors is provided.

121. Howard, Harry et al. **Middle East and North Africa: a Bibliography for Undergraduate Libraries.** Williamsport, PA: Bro-Dart, 1971. xviii, 80 p. *Foreign Area Materials Center, Occasional Publication;* no. 14. ISBN 0-8727-2018-7.

A clearly-organized bibliography meant to assist libraries in collection development. The work emerges from the Center's "active concern with encouraging international studies in American colleges and universities" (Foreword). The materials are grouped into three categories: books on the topic that should be in all undergraduate libraries, books needed to support a few courses in the subject area, and books required for an area studies major or advanced program. The entries are not annotated, but reviews available in major journals are indicated. North Africa in general, Egypt, Tunisia, Algeria, Libya and Morocco are included, but not Sudan, the Sahel or Horn.

122. Khalil, Mufid. **Grundbestände Moderner Orientalia der Universitätsbibliothek Bielefeld: eine Auswahlbibliographie.** Bielefeld: Forschungsschwerpunkt Entwicklungssoziologie, 1988. v, 358 p. *Reihe Dokumentation;* no. 22.

Covering the Middle East and North Africa, this bibliography compiles and classifies the holdings of a major European library on the sociology/anthropology, religion, economic and political development of the region. This social-science approach distinguishes it from traditional literary and philological/linguistic Orientalism, particularly in German sources.

A carefully-organized table of contents sets forth the classification scheme. Unfortunately, the volume consists mainly of catalog-card records or printouts, often hard to read and certainly hard to search. There is a geographical index, but it is not subdivided in any way and thus contributes very little. The subject index is a bit more helpful. Of the states of northern Africa, Egypt, Libya, Algeria, Tunisia, Morocco and Sudan are included, as well as "Nordafrika" as a region.

123. Khoury, Fawzi W. and Michele S. Bates. **The Middle East in Micro-form: a Union List of Middle Eastern Microforms in North American Libraries.** Seattle: University of Washington Libraries, 1991. xv, 377 p.

Entries in this compilation are alphabetized by title, including those in romanized Arabic. Some states in northern Africa are included (apparently Egypt, Libya, Morocco, Algeria, Sudan, Somalia, Mauritania and Tunisia), but there is no index by country, since according to the editors it was difficult to determine the place of publication of many of these sources. There is an index by language, which is helpful. Entries identify the periodical, list issues extant, and supply location codes for library collections.

124. Littlefield, David W. **The Islamic Near East and North Africa: an Annotated Guide to Books in English for Non-Specialists.** Littleton, CO: Libraries Unlimited, 1977. 375 p. ISBN 0-87287-159-2.

Very helpful annotations describe a wide variety of works on Arab civilization, noting the appropriateness of each work for general, undergraduate or advanced research collections. The scope of material covered is extremely broad, both geographically and topically. It includes the Mediterranean coast of Africa and Sudan, but not the rest of the Sahel or Horn. This well-organized volume includes separate author, title and subject indexes.

125. McIlwaine, John. **Africa: a Guide to Reference Material.** London: Hans Zell, 1993. xxxv, 507 p. *Regional Reference Guides;* 1. ISBN 0-905450-43-4.

An important compilation of general references, handbooks, yearbooks, directories, statistical publications, collective biographies, atlases and gazetteers. The large section devoted to Africa as a whole is divided according to type of publication. Regional sections follow, with subdivisions for each country.

This bibliography is largely retrospective, including many very obscure sources published as long ago as the 1860s. Coverage of current titles is "more selective" (p. xx).

The emphasis in this volume is on sub-Saharan Africa, excluding the Mediterranean states. Some material is included on Sudan, the Horn and the Sahel. Entries are sometimes briefly annotated, or reference is made to a recent review. A substantial appendix identifies British colonial documents on Africa (including Somalia and Sudan). There is a general index.

126. Miller, E. Willard and Ruby M. Miller. **Northern and Western Africa: a Bibliography on the Third World.** Monticello, IL: Vance Bibliographies, 1981. 96 p. *Public Administration Series;* no. 818.

The Vance bibliographies on public administration are composed of topically arranged citations—up to about 1000 in each issue—of books and articles, government bulletins and other publications. The entries are sometimes briefly annotated. This issue covers (among other nations) Algeria, Egypt, Libya, Sudan, Tunisia, Chad, Mali, Mauritania and Niger during the 1970s.

127. Miller, E. Willard and Ruby M. Miller. **The Third World—Africa: Northern Desert Lands: a Bibliography.** Monticello, IL: Vance Bibliographies, 1990. 38 p. *Public Administration Series;* P-2973. ISBN 0-7920-0683-6.

The "northern desert lands" in this issue include the Sahel region in general, then Western Sahara, Mauritania, Mali, Niger, Chad, Sudan; the Horn of Africa in general, then Ethiopia, Somalia and Djibouti.

128. Miller, E. Willard and Ruby M. Miller. **The Third World: Islam, Muslims, Arab States: a Bibliography.** Monticello, IL: Vance Bibliographies, 1989. 37 p. *Public Administration Series;* P-2735. ISBN 0-7920-1295-4; ISSN 0193-970X.

This issue suffers from an overly broad scope: the sections on Islam include materials on Iran, Pakistan, India, Turkey and Indonesia, while the section on the Arab states is neither defined nor subdivided geographically.

129. Pfister, Roger. **Internet for Africanists and Others Interested in Africa.** Basel: Swiss Society of African Studies, 1996. 140 p. *Basler Afrika Bibliographien.* ISBN 3-905141-67-1.

A very helpful introduction and guide to the process of collecting Africa-related information electronically through the Internet. Most of the explanations and advice Pfister offers retain their validity, even if certain details have changed since the time of publication. The volume has a keyword index.

130. Scheven, Yvette. **Bibliographies for African Studies, 1980-1983.** Munich: Hans Zell (K.G. Saur), 1984. xiii, 300 p. ISBN 0-905450-13-2 and 3-598-10487-1.

One of the essential reference tools compiled by Scheven to help scholars locate bibliographies pertaining to African studies. Entries are topically organized and annotated, often with very useful descriptions. The Mediterranean states of Africa are not covered, but the countries of the Sahel and Horn (including Mauritania and Sudan, but not Niger or Mali) are within the scope of this volume. A unified index (names, titles, subjects) is provided.

131. Scheven, Yvette. **Bibliographies for African Studies, 1987-1993.** With Phyllis Bischof, Joseph J. Lauer, and Mette Shayne. London: Hans Zell, 1994. xiii, 176 p. ISBN 1-873836-51-1.

Scheven has added this compilation to update her very valuable series of bibliographies for African studies. This volume is compiled mainly from notices for Africana reference works appearing in the *African Book Publishing Record* during the years covered. The entries are carefully organized by topic, using somewhat modified Library of Congress subject headings; they are reorganized by author and subject in indexes, but not by title. Each entry is very briefly annotated. Unlike earlier editions, in this volume all the states of northern Africa are included.

132. Silverburg, Sanford R. **Middle East Bibliography.** Metuchen, NJ: Scarecrow, 1992. xxxi, 564 p. *Scarecrow Area Bibliographies;* no. 1. ISBN 0-8108-2469-8.

A listing of books dealing with the Middle East, published for the most part in the 1980s. The work is organized by alphabetically-arranged keyword strings, like Silverburg and Reich's *Asian States' Relations with the Middle East and North Africa: a Bibliography, 1950-1993.* A large section of listings pertains to the Arab world in general; of the states of northern Africa, only Egypt is specifically covered. The entries are not annotated. There is an author index; the volume also includes an introductory bibliographical essay.

133. Simon, Reeva S. **The Modern Middle East: a Guide to Research Tools in the Social Sciences.** Boulder, CO: Westview Press, 1978. xv, 283 p. *Westview Special Studies on the Middle East.* ISBN 0-89158-059-X.

This unusually comprehensive bibliography of reference works covers the past two centuries of writing on Middle East issues. Materials published in Arabic, Hebrew, Persian, and Turkish as well as Western languages are included; Egypt, Sudan and the Maghreb states are within the scope of this volume.

Not all titles pertain directly to the subject area: basic research tools, library catalogs and bibliographies of social science generally are also cited. Some works listed are monographs containing noteworthy bibliographies. The entries are organized by type of work cited: i.e., periodicals, bibliographies, catalogs, encyclopedias, etc.; entries are briefly annotated. A single – rather awkward – index of names, titles and subjects is provided.

134. Vidergar, John J. **Bibliography on Afghanistan, the Sudan and Tunisia.** Monticello, IL: Vance Bibliographies, 1978. 7 p. *Public Administration Series;* no. 141.

The Vance bibliographies on public administration are composed of topically arranged citations—up to about 1000 in each issue—of books and articles, government bulletins and other publications. The entries are sometimes briefly annotated. This issue is no more than a little leaflet offering a few sources, but the books and journals cited are scholarly ones (in English and French).

135. Williams, Michael W. **Pan-Africanism: an Annotated Bibliography.** Pasadena, CA: Salem Press, 1992. ix, 142 p. *Magill Bibliographies.* ISBN 0-89356-674-8.

The relevance of Pan-Africanism as an ideology to the people of northern Africa is problematic, and this book does very little to clarify the issue. The materials cited here (with excellent annotations) are important and interesting, but reflect the concerns of African-Americans for the most part.

136. Zell, Hans M. and Cécile Lomer. **The African Studies Companion: a Resource Guide and Directory.** Second revised and expanded edition. London: Hans Zell, 1997. xvi, 276 p. ISBN 1-873836-41-4.

A welcome update to the original 1989 edition, this annotated guide provides access to a variety of information sources for African studies. A directory of major Western libraries and documentation centers with substantial holdings in this subject area provides contact data, access conditions and a brief indication of the extent of each collection. Entries are organized by location, then listed by name in the index.

This volume also features important journals and news magazines devoted to Africa, serial bibliographies, and general reference sources. In addition, publishers, book dealers and distributors with considerable African studies materials are listed, with contact information. Organizations and associations, foundations and donor agencies with an interest in Africa are also mentioned, often with extensive descriptions.

Indexes and Guides

137. **Africa Bibliography.** Edited by Christopher H. Allen. Edinburgh: Edinburgh University Press, for the International African Institute in London. Annual; 1985- . ISBN 0-7486-0878-8; ISSN 0266-6731.

An authoritative guide to publications in European languages on Africa "principally in the social and environmental sciences, humanities and arts," covering the entire continent. Each issue includes material published in that calendar year, plus any earlier citations not yet listed. Books or monographs and journal articles are included. The work is organized geographically, with an opening section for materials dealing with Africa in general. Author and subject indexes are provided. In addition, some articles of interest to librarians, bibliographers and information professions appear in each issue: in 1995, for example, an article by Olivier Coeur de Roy on "The Internet in Africa" and two others on building up library systems and collections were published. Entries are not annotated, and there are no abstracts.

138. **International Bibliography of Political Science/Bibliographie Internationale de Science Politique.** Vol. XLV. Annual; 1961- . London: Routledge (for the British Library of Political and Economic Science), 1996. xciii, 493 p. *International Bibliography of the Social Sciences.* ISBN 0-415-16081-2; ISSN 0085-2058

Also available on CD-ROM through SilverPlatter, and online to subscribers in the UK, Australia and New Zealand.

One segment of the four-part *International Bibliography of the Social Sciences*, this compilation of journal articles, monographs and collective works is topically organized, with a hierarchical structure. Under "Political Systems," one may choose "Political Change," then "Africa"; or "Political Life," then "Religious Forces," then "Islam." The subject index and place name index are of some help here (there is also an index in French). The other portions of this work concentrate on economics, sociology and anthropology.

139. **International Political Science Abstracts/Documentation Politique Internationale.** Bimonthly; 1951- . Paris: International Political Science Association. ISSN 0020-8345.

Also available on CD-ROM and online through SilverPlatter to subscribers only; see also **www.ucd.ie/~ipsa/index.html**

Using the same basic classification scheme as the *International Bibliography of Political Science*, this publication presents the full abstracts of scholarly articles in the field. Each issue is indexed, and the last issue of each volume contains a cumulated subject index. Abstracts appear in English or French.

140. **Middle East Abstracts and Index.** 21st edition. Annual; 1978- . Edited by James Joseph Sanchez. Seattle: Reference Corporation (Aristarchus Knowledge Industries), 1998. 5 v.

The first four volumes of this substantial index to journal literature on the Middle East are geographical in approach, with Volume D focused upon the Maghreb, Sahel and Horn. Fifteen countries of northern Africa are individually covered (Egypt is included in Volume A, "Near East") . Since 1997, a fifth volume of each edition will concentrate upon a different special topic in Middle East studies. In 1997, the focus was "Women in the Middle East"; in 1998, it was "Oil, Natural Gas and Petrochemical Industries."

Entries may include citations and abstracts only, or the full text of scanned articles, editorials, government and United Nations documents, research reports, press releases, interviews and other materials. News sources as well as scholarly journals are included. Each volume is supplied with indexes for authors, corporate and personal names, and subjects (keywords).

141. **PAIS International in Print.** Annual cumulation; 1991- . New York: Public Affairs Information Service. 2 v.; Vol. 2 is author index. ISSN 1076-2094.

Also available on CD-ROM or tape; available online through DIALOG, OCLC and other vendors to subscribers only. See also **www.pais.org**

A massive compilation of social science literature, with abstracts. Books, articles, government documents, statistical publications, research and conference reports are all included. Languages covered are English, German, Spanish, French, Italian and Portuguese. The entries are topically arranged, with specific countries as separate headings, making it possible quickly to browse the current literature on Chad, for example. A basic information source.

142. Gorman, G. E. and J. J. Mills. **Guide to Current Indexing and Abstracting Services in the Third World.** London: Hans Zell, 1992. xvii, 260 p. ISBN 0-905450-85-X.

An informative and useful guide to indexes giving access to the contents of serials, conference proceedings, workshop papers and other current publications of multiple authorship originating in the "Third World." Not only are these materials themselves often hard to find, but even the indexes and indexing services are unknown outside their immediate area. This reference brings more than 120 of these important information sources to the surface.

Each entry gives publication data or online database location, a statement of scope, a description of the organization and content of the index, and an assessment of its quality. The entries are simply alphabetized, but a subject index allows the reader to search for specific topics or countries covered.

Indexes covering literature pertaining to Africa and the Arab world, plus Egypt, Libya, Mali, Morocco, Ethiopia and Sudan, may be found in this volume. An appendix lists services not examined by the writers. This feature is difficult to use, however, for some of the pages of this volume were placed out of order (p. 239-254) due to a manufacturing error.

Bibliographic Journals

143. **African Book Publishing Record.** Quarterly, 1975- . Oxford: Hans Zell (Bowker-Saur). ISSN 0306-0322.
See also website at **www.hanszell.co.uk/titles.htm**
An important resource for obtaining quality publications produced in Africa. News of the publishing industry and literary world, current directory data for many (sometimes hard-to-find) publishers, and a useful topically-organized bibliography of materials in Western and some African languages, are provided. The entries are indexed by author and by country of publication as well. Each issue also contains brief but informative signed book reviews. An annual feature describes new reference materials on Africa. In addition, a cumulation of these listings appears as *African Books in Print* (Hans Zell, 1993).

144. **Electronic Journal of Africana Bibliography. www.lib.uiowa.edu/ proj/ejab/**
Edited by John Bruce Howell and Yvette Scheven.
"EJAB is a refereed online journal of bibliographies on any aspect of Africa, its peoples, their homes, cities, towns, districts, states, countries, regions, including social, economic sustainable development, creative literature, the arts, and the Diaspora." Includes location codes (not annotated).

145. **International African Bibliography.** Quarterly; 1971- . East Grinstead: Hans Zell. ISSN 0020-5877.
A compilation of current publishing on and about Africa (except Egypt), both monographs and articles in scholarly journals, including some 200 periodicals published in Africa. Some entries have detailed contents notes or abstracts; all articles have at least subject descriptors. A table of contents organizes the entries at a glance, by geographical area and broad topic, and each volume includes indexes by subject, author, ethnic group, language and other names or special vocabulary. The work is edited by David Hall in association with the Centre of African Studies at the SOAS library in London.

Dissertations and Theses

146. **Dix Ans de Recherche Universitaire Française sur le Monde Arabe et Islamique de 1968-89 à 1979.** Paris: Éditions Recherche sur les Civilisations, 1982. 438 p. ISBN 2-86538-019-X.

This publication of the Association Française des Arabisants (in conjunction with the French education and foreign ministries) compiles the titles of theses written in French universities on topics pertaining to the Arab world, Turkey, Iran and Muslim populations elsewhere, including Europe. The entries are organized topically, but one may need the Table des Matières at the end of the book to find specific subjects. There is no index.

147. Selim, George Dimitri. **American Doctoral Dissertations on the Arab World, 1883-1968.** Washington: Library of Congress, 1970. xvii, 103 p.

This compilation includes dissertations in science and technology, the humanities, and social sciences. All Arabic-speaking countries of the Middle East and North Africa are included, plus minorities living in Arabic-speaking countries. Materials relating to Islam are also listed, regardless of geography. Each entry provides source data, and the volumes searched are also noted, so there is no need to reduplicate the effort if no relevant dissertations are listed. The entries are alphabetized by author, and a workable subject index is supplied.

148. Sims, Michael and Alfred Kagan. **American and Canadian Doctoral Dissertations and Master's Theses on Africa, 1886-1974.** Waltham, MA: African Studies Association, 1976. 365 p.

An updated edition of the retrospective bibliography of dissertations by Anne Schneller and Michael Bratton, expanded to include master's theses and works submitted to Canadian universities. Entries are organized by geography: first Africa generally, then by region, then by individual country. Within these categories they are subdivided by broad topic (e.g., agriculture, literature, religion). This volume covers North Africa as a region and each of the northern states as well. An author index and a limited subject index are provided.

149. Sluglett, Peter. **Theses on Islam, the Middle East and North-West Africa 1880-1978 Accepted by Universities in the United Kingdom and Ireland.** London: Mansell, 1983. xii, 147 p. ISBN 0-7201-1651-1.

Over 3000 citations, topically arranged, make up this reference. The citations are grouped into major sections on Islamics, Arabic language and literature, Christianity in the region since the 7th century, and area studies. A sub-section on Islam in Africa lists some titles pertaining to Niger, Somalia, the Tuareg and Hausa, Mauritania and the spread of Islam in the area generally. Materials on North-West Africa include Libya, Algeria, Morocco and Tunisia, while Egypt and Sudan have large blocs of citations under the Middle East heading.

A section of addenda contains titles appearing between 1978 and 1983. An author index is provided, but the subject index is quite primitive; use of the table of contents is likely to be more successful.

Archive Collections and Guides

150. **Middle East Materials in UK and Irish Libraries: a Directory.** Edited by Ian Richard Netton. London: Library Association Publishing, for the Centre for Arab Gulf Studies, University of Exeter, 1983. 136 p. ISBN 0-85365-526-X.

The Middle East Libraries Committee (MELCOM) sponsored the preparation of this directory "of libraries and institutions in Britain and Ireland with large or small collections of Middle East books, manuscripts and materials" (Preface). Entries for these institutions provide addresses and phone numbers, contact information, hours, conditions of access, and a carefully-written brief summary of the holdings.

The entries are organized by location, from Aberdeen to Todmorden; a general index helps somewhat in locating specific subject materials. The bibliography of collection catalogs and other bibliographies is useful. In addition, the editor notes which libraries provided no information, stated that they had no relevant holdings, or did not wish to be included.

151. **Quellen zur Geschichte Nordafrikas, Asiens und Ozeaniens in der Bundesrepublik Deutschland bis 1945.** Bearbeitet von Ernst Ritter. Munich; New York: K.G. Saur, 1984. xlvi, 382 p. ISBN 3-598214-80-4

International Council of Archives. *Guides to the Sources for the History of the Nations, Third Series*, vol. 6.

This series provides a detailed inventory of the manuscript materials held in many major European libraries and archive collections, including government ministries, organized by the location of each library. Volumes are fully indexed.

See also: Guides to the Sources for the History of the Nations; Second Series, Africa South of the Sahara.

152. **SCOLMA Directory of Libraries and Special Collections on Africa in the United Kingdom and Europe.** Fifth edition. Edited by Tom French. London: Hans Zell, for SCOLMA, 1993. viii, 355 p. ISBN 0-905450-89-2.

The Standing Conference on Library Materials on Africa prepares this directory identifying key collections for African studies. The 1993 edition is the first to include institutions in Eastern Europe. Each entry provides contact information, access conditions, and a description of the nature, purpose and size of the collection, and calls attention to special archives or Africana holdings, including manuscripts, films, photos, maps, etc. The entries are arranged by location and alphabetically by name of institution, so it is easy to browse all relevant collections in Denmark, for example. However, topical access is poor: overly broad categories like "anthropology" or "literature" convey nothing. Entry numbers for individual countries as subjects (e.g., "Morocco") are more helpful.

153. **Sources of the History of North Africa, Asia and Oceania in Denmark.**
Compiled by C. Rise Hansen. Munich; Detroit: K.G. Saur; Gale Research, 1980.
842 p. *Sources of the History of North Africa, Asia and Oceania in Scandinavia;*
pt. 1. ISBN 3-598214-74-X

International Council of Archives: *Guides to the Sources for the History of
the Nations, Third Series*, vol. 3.

This series provides a detailed inventory of the manuscript materials held in
many major European libraries and archive collections, including government
ministries, organized by the location of each library. Volumes are fully indexed.

See also: Guides to the Sources for the History of the Nations; Second Series, Africa South of the Sahara.

154. **Sources of the History of North Africa, Asia and Oceania in Finland,
Norway and Sweden.** Compiled by Berndt et al. Federley. Munich; Detroit:
K.G. Saur; Gale Research, 1981. 233 p. *Sources of the History of North Africa,
Asia and Oceania in Scandinavia;* pt. 2. ISBN 3-598214-75-8

International Council of Archives: *Guides to the Sources for the History of
the Nations, Third Series*, vol. 3.

This series provides a detailed inventory of the manuscript materials held in
many major European libraries and archive collections, including government
ministries, organized by the location of each library. Volumes are fully indexed.

See also: Guides to the Sources for the History of the Nations; Second Series, Africa South of the Sahara.

155. **Sources of the History of North Africa, Asia and Oceania in Yugosla-
via.** Munich; New York: K.G. Saur, 1991. 164 p. ISBN 3-598214-86-3

International Council of Archives: *Guides to the Sources for the History of
the Nations, Third Series*, vol. 10.

This series provides a detailed inventory of the manuscript materials held in
many major European libraries and archive collections, including government
ministries, organized by the location of each library. Volumes are fully indexed.

See also: Guides to the Sources for the History of the Nations; Second Series, Africa South of the Sahara.

156. Baker, Philip. **International Directory of African Studies Re-
search/Répertoire International des Études Africaines.** Third edition. Edited
by the International African Institute. London: Hans Zell, 1994. xxiii, 317 p.
ISBN 1-873836-36-8.

An enlarged and updated edition of the 1987 work. It includes a substantial
number of new entries, and some organizations believed to be inactive have been
removed. There is a new index of international organizations, and the other indexes have been improved and expanded.

157. Baker, Philip. **International Guide to African Studies Research/Études Africaines: Guide International de Recherches.** Second fully revised and expanded edition. Published for the International African Institute. London: Hans Zell, 1987. 264 p. ISBN 0-905450-25-6.

A guide to research centers in Europe, the US and Africa pertinent to African Studies, this book offers at least basic directory data and often detailed entries describing library holdings, publications, staff, contact information, and any courses or degrees offered. The guide uses English and French interchangeably. A helpful symbols key is attached inside the back cover. Four essential indexes provide subject access by area or country, access by ethnonym or language, a list of journals published by these research centers, and an index of the personnel and scholars mentioned (the latter is a bit difficult to use because of the many different possible forms of proper nouns).

158. Bhatt, Purnima Mehta. **Scholars' Guide to Washington D.C. for African Studies.** Daniel G. Matthews, Michael R. Winston, and Julian W. Witherell, consultants. Washington: Smithsonian Institution Press, 1980. xiv, 347 p. *Scholars' Guide to Washington, D.C.;* no. 4. ISBN 0-87474-238-2.

This guide, another in the series created by the Woodrow Wilson International Center for Scholars, is meant to direct visiting researchers to materials in African studies found in the U.S. capital. Libraries and archives, museums and galleries, music, art, map and film collections, research centers, government agencies, embassies, media and cultural-exchange organizations and religious institutions are all included.

Entries provide contact information, access conditions and a description (often quite full and detailed) of the holdings or services. All of the countries of the African continent are taken into account, though the regional designations are sometimes confusing (Sudan, for example, is listed under "West Africa"). Some practical information for visiting scholars on housing and getting around Washington is also provided. There is a somewhat awkward subject index.

159. Collison, Robert. **Directory of Libraries and Special Collections on Asia and North Africa.** London: Crosby Lockwood, 1970. x, 123 p. ISBN 0-258-967897

Prepared by the Standing Conference of National and University Libraries (SCONUL), Sub-Committee of Orientalist Libraries.

An annotated directory of collections in Britain with important holdings in area studies on Asia and North Africa. The contact information is now no doubt obsolete, but the descriptions of special archives, photo collections and other noteworthy features may be useful.

160. Cook, Chris. **The Making of Modern Africa: a Guide to Archives.** New York: Facts on File, 1995. v, 218 p. ISBN 0-8160-2071-X.

This unusual and impressive work offers a description and location information for the personal papers and correspondence of leading figures in African history from about 1889 to 1980. It does not repeat references to governmental or official archives of the former colonial powers or newly-independent states available elsewhere; instead, it concentrates on "the myriad private papers of those persons involved in the unfolding history of modern Africa" (Preface). These include governors and viceroys, senior civil administrators and military officers, and other public figures, including African politicians and opposition leaders.

The entries are alphabetically arranged for ready reference, with a very accurate and detailed subject index. There is also an index of archives, showing at a glance relevant holdings in a particular location. Each concise entry provides a full name, dates of birth and death, a brief identification and resume of the individual's roles or offices in Africa, a note describing the nature and subject of the existing papers and the archive where they can be found.

161. Dorr, Steven R. **Scholars' Guide to Washington D.C. for Middle Eastern Studies.** George N. Atiyeh, consultant. Washington: Smithsonian Institution Press, 1981. xiii, 540 p. *Scholars' Guide to Washington D.C.;* no. 7. ISBN 0-87474-372-9.

A project sponsored by the Woodrow Wilson International Center for Scholars, this series of guides is meant to help some of the 20,000 or more visitors who come to Washington each year with serious research interests that can be served by the city's rich resources. Washington's libraries, archives, museums, galleries, collections of music, maps and films, organizations, embassies and government agencies, etc., with holdings or services in Middle East studies are listed here. Entries include directory and contact information, access and circulation policies, and a brief description of the relevant materials. Names and subjects indexes are provided, along with a "subject strength index" showing levels of coverage for various general topics in area libraries. Of the northern Africa countries, only Egypt and Sudan are within the scope of this work. One hopes that an updated edition is in preparation.

162. Gebhardt, Marion. **Institutionen der Afrika-Forschung und Afrika-Information in der Bundesrepublik Deutschland und Berlin (West): Forschungsinstitute, Bibliotheken, Dokumentationsstellen, Archive.** Hamburg: Deutsches Übersee-Institut, Dokumentationsdienst Afrika, 1990. xi, 285 p. ISBN 3-922852-28-9; ISSN 0342-0469.

A helpful guide to collections of Africa-related materials throughout the former West Germany; a variety of library and institute collections is included. Basic directory data is given for each institution, with a brief description of the activities of the organization (if it is a research facility), and of the holdings. The strengths or emphases of each collection are characterized in a simple statement.

The entries are arranged by city, with an alphabetical index by name, a basic subject index, and an index by location in Africa, both regions and individual countries. The states of northern Africa are clearly included, though some do not appear on the register (i.e., Mali and Tunisia). Clearly, the time has come for a new edition of this work covering the whole of the reunified Germany.

163. Gosebrink, Jean E. Meeh. **African Studies Information Resources Directory.** Published for the African Studies Association. Oxford: Hans Zell (K.G. Saur), 1986. xiii, 572 p. ISBN 0-905450-30-2 and 3-598-10657-2.

An extensive compilation of directory data and descriptions of the resources of "libraries and special collections, archival repositories, documentation centers and information services located in educational institutions, government agencies, religious and missionary organizations, museums, learned societies, historical societies, professional and academic associations, philanthropic, research, activist and other institutions and organizations ... publishers, book dealers and distributors of Africa-related materials" (p. viii).

The entries are organized alphabetically, but there is an appendix listing them by location. The emphasis is on sub-Saharan Africa; however, it includes the Horn (here defined as Ethiopia, Somalia, Djibouti *and* the Sudan) and quite a bit of information is also reported on North Africa as a region and the individual states of the northern coast and the Sahel. This information is readily located in the index.

Some readers will be especially pleased to discover Chapter Two, "Resources in Church and Mission Organizations," since many of these collections are historically very rich and are seldom included in library directories.

164. Grant, Gillian. **Middle Eastern Photographic Collections in the United Kingdom.** Durham: Middle East Libraries Committee, 1989. vi, 222 p. *MELC Research Guides;* 3. ISBN 0-948889-03-9.

Potentially a very valuable contribution to research on the Middle East, this volume helps to identify and locate the collections of photographs on relevant subjects residing in British libraries. An interesting introduction explains the origin of these materials. The directory of libraries is organized by city, with an index of places and tribal groups and another of individual names. The photographs described were made not only in Egypt and Palestine, but all around northern Africa, including Algeria, Libya, Morocco, Tunisia, Ethiopia and Sudan. Grant takes care to describe the holdings in enough detail to help the scholar substantially.

165. Howell, John Bruce and Yvette Scheven. **Guides, Collections and Ancillary Materials to African Archival Resources in the United States.** Madison: University of Wisconsin, 1996. vi, 108 p. ISBN 0-942615-32-8

Also available online through University of Iowa Libraries: **www.lib.uiowa. edu/proj/ejab/**

A useful compilation of published guides to archival holdings of Africana. Entries are organized topically and geographically; contents notes and location data are provided. There is a general index. The states of northern Africa (except Djibouti), and North Africa as a region, are included. An important resource for the research scholar or historian.

166. Matthews, Noel and M. Doreen Wainwright. **A Guide to Manuscripts and Documents in the British Isles Relating to the Middle East and North Africa.** Edited by J. D. Pearson. Oxford: Oxford University Press, 1980. xvii, 482 p. ISBN 0-19-713598-6.

An important guide, using the same structure and approach as Matthews and Wainwright's work encompassing Africa as a whole (succeeded by Pearson's 1993 edition).

167. McIlwaine, John. **Writings on African Archives.** London: Hans Zell, 1996. xviii, 279 p. ISBN 1-873836-66-X.

Published for the Standing Conference on Library Materials on Africa, this reference provides access to studies, reports, conference papers, books and articles on archive holdings and their management.

Part 1 presents materials on archives in Africa itself: a section on North Africa refers to Algeria, Egypt, Morocco, and Tunisia, while the nations of the Sahel and Horn are covered in other regional groupings (with the exception of Djibouti).

Part 2 covers archives relating to Africa located in Europe and the United Kingdom, North America, South America and Asia. All relevant European languages are included (as well as some non-European ones). Some of the entries are briefly annotated. A substantial index is provided.

168. Otchere, Freda E. **African Studies Thesaurus: Subject Headings for Library Users.** Westport, CT: Greenwood, 1992. xxvii, 435 p. *Bibliographies and Indexes in Afro-American and African Studies;* no. 29. ISBN 0-3132-7437-1.

A convenient digest of Library of Congress subject headings for African topics, which are not always self-explanatory. Typically-used subdivisions are listed. Headings are also linked with LC classification numbers, and the DT classification outline (where African History is to be found) is spelled out as well.

169. Pearson, J. D. **A Guide to Manuscripts and Documents in the British Isles Relating to Africa.** London: Mansell, 1993. 2 v. ISBN 0-7201-2167-1 (set).

An extensive and detailed guide to manuscripts and documents in the possession of institutions throughout Britain. Vol. 1 deals with London alone, Vol. 2 all collections outside London.

This thorough compilation covers not only major collections like SOAS or University College, but dozens of specialized societies with unusual holdings: Lambeth Palace, the Leprosy Mission, the Post Office Archives, the Royal Entomological Society, etc. This version succeeds the Matthews and Wainwright guide published in 1971, and reflects the changes and "migrations of collections" that have occurred since then (p. vii); it is vastly expanded as well, since a great deal of archival material has recently become available to researchers.

Entries provide an overview of each collection, then very specific notices for every document. Generally speaking, entries are organized by location, then chronologically or by source (e.g., the Peel Papers, the Collins Papers). A substantial general index is provided, and is quite helpful in locating materials on individual countries, persons or topics. Even so, this reference is prepared with the research scholar in mind, and assumes a familiarity with the subject matter.

170. South, Aloha. **Guide to Federal Archives Relating to Africa.** Waltham, MA: African Studies Association (Crossroads Press), 1977. xx, 556 p. *Archival and Bibliographic Series.*

Organized by department or agency of government, this reference lists and describes the archival holdings in detail and indicates their relevance to research on Africa. The materials in these collections cover every topic from diplomacy to soil conservation, to lantern slides of Egyptian pyramids, to reports on the export of coconut oil. The volume is indexed by subject, place name, personal name, ethnic group, and even by the names of ships referred to in logbooks and cargo manifests.

171. South, Aloha. **Guide to Non-Federal Archives and Manuscripts in the United States Relating to Africa.** Published for the National Archives and Records Administration, Washington. London: Hans Zell, 1988. 2 v. ISBN 0-905450-55-8 (set).

A valuable annotated compilation of archives and their holdings throughout the US, organized by state. The reference does not describe every item (like Pearson), but the annotations give the reader a good idea what is included in each collection. More than 100 pages of indexing provide access by subject, name of person or institution, or by the title or heading of individual sources. This is an important reference for the research scholar.

General Journals

172. **Africa Confidential.** 25 issues/year; 1967- . London: Africa Confidential. ISSN 0044-6483.

Descriptive website, current headlines and summaries of certain articles available online at **www.africa-confidential.com** or at **www.blackwellpublishers.co.uk**

A fortnightly newsletter filled with brief but detailed articles going well beyond the level of coverage of African news in most general papers and periodicals. The use of a bold typeface makes it possible to skim articles looking for particular personal names or countries. Northern Africa falls within the scope of this publication; recent issues offered several reports on rising tensions between Ethiopia and Eritrea, and political strife in Algeria. The format is compact and text-rich; there are no photos or advertising.

173. **Africa: Journal of the International African Institute.** Quarterly, 1928- . London: Oxford University Press. ISSN 0001-9720.

Also titled: *Revue de l'Institut African International.* Contents pages available online at **www.oneworld.org/iai/pubs.htm**

Published by the IAI at the School of Oriental and African Studies (SOAS) in London, this journal contains lengthy scholarly articles with full bibliographical references and abstracts. Maps and tables of data are sometimes included. The articles deal with a range of political, social and cultural topics. There is a substantial section of detailed, signed book reviews. The emphasis is on sub-Saharan Africa, but the Sahel and Horn are well represented. An effective index to each volume offers good subject access (much better than many electronic indexes) and access to the year's book reviews. An important resource for the university library.

174. **Africa Report.** Bimonthly, 1960-1995. New York: African-American Institute. ISSN 0001-9836.

An informative, colorful news magazine focused on current events in Africa, apparently the only one of its kind published in the United States. News items of about a page in length and feature articles of 4-5 pages are presented with attractive graphics and photos. A typical recent issue contained features about Somalia, Chad, Sudan, Ethiopia and Eritrea, and news items about Algeria and Libya, the content of which is rarely found in American reporting. The journal is particularly keen on problems of press freedom on the continent. Unfortunately, publication was suspended in 1995 to seek more secure funding, and it is not clear whether the serial will resume.

175. **Africa Research Bulletin: Political, Social and Cultural Series.** Monthly; 1964- . In this form since 1992. Oxford: Blackwell. ISSN 0001-9844.

Also available online through certain service providers; see **www.blackwellpublishers.co.uk**

A news and current-events source reporting and analyzing in considerable detail the pressing concerns and developments in Africa generally, regionally and in specific countries or localities. A great deal of information is presented in a concise and objective fashion. This source provides the distilled essence of more than 80 local and international news agencies, intergovernmental and non-governmental organizations, United Nations departments, media organizations (including the BBC), and newspapers or magazines, from the *Times* of London to *La Nation* (Djibouti).

The entire African continent is covered. Maps, tables of data and other small graphics are printed as needed. Every issue supplies a convenient country index on the back cover; an annual subject index is also provided. The division of the subject matter into two series works well, but may necessitate subscribing to both.

176. **Africa Today.** Quarterly; 1954- . Bloomington: Indiana University Press. ISSN 0001-9887.

Descriptive website at **www.indiana.edu/~iupress/journals/afr.html**

Themed issues, featuring scholarly articles in social sciences and the humanities in English and French. This journal provides "an alternative forum for serious analysis and discussion but offers positive solutions to the problems facing Africa today." A new publisher and editorial staff promise changes. Book reviews and notices are also included. Covers all regions of Africa.

177. **African Affairs: Journal of the Royal African Society.** Quarterly; 1944- . Oxford: Oxford University Press. ISSN 0001-9909.

Contents and abstracts available online at **www.oup.co.uk/jnls/list/ afrafj/contents/**

Focusing on political, economic and international affairs, this academic journal publishes 4-5 articles in each issue, notes or news pertaining to the Royal African Society, a 30-page section of book reviews (not itemized in the table of contents) and a bibliography subdivided by region.

178. **African Research and Documentation.** Three issues/year; 1973- . London: African Studies Association and SCOLMA. ISSN 0305-826X.

SCOLMA website at **www.brad.ac.uk/acad/dppc/dppclib/SCOLMA.html**

Produced by the Standing Conference on Library Materials on Africa, this journal focuses on the research and information needs of African Studies scholars, the African book and publishing trade, and the collection and management of archival materials on African history in world libraries. The editor is respected authority John McIlwaine; supplements to his important reference *Writings on African Archives* will appear in this journal regularly.

179. **African Studies Review.** Three times/year; 1970- . Atlanta: African Studies Association. ISSN 0002-0206.

Contents pages available online at **www.sas.upenn.edu/African_Studies/ ASA/MASR.html**

An academic journal featuring 5-8 research articles with full notes and bibliographical references, one or two lengthy review essays, and up to 40 or so brief but informative book reviews. The reviews may be grouped into topical categories, but they are not indexed by author or title. Often, two or more works are reviewed simultaneously and comparatively: an interesting approach, but it makes individual titles even harder to find.

180. **Afrika Spectrum: Zeitschrift für Gegenwartsbezogene Afrikaforschung.** Three times/year; 1966- . Hamburg: Institut für Afrika-Kunde. ISSN 0002-0397.

Descriptive website available online at **www.rrz.uni-hamburg.de/duei/publ/ afrika/afrika-spectrum.html**

A publication of the Deutsches Übersee-Institut, this interdisciplinary journal studies general and development-related problems in Africa today: political, economic and social. Lengthy research articles (four or five per issue) appear with briefer reports of timely events, such as elections in Mali or a recent conference on Ethiopian studies. Recent issues have dealt with the problems of Ethiopia, Eritrea, Niger and Somalia. Book reviews and occasional bibliographies are also presented. Each year's articles are indexed by country or region.

181. **Afrique Contemporaine.** Three issues/year; 1962- . Paris: Documentation Française; Centre d'Information et de Documentation Internationale Contemporaine (CIDIC). ISSN 0002-0478.

Research articles, reflection and policy papers, often collected in themed issues, comprise this substantial journal. Writers may be diplomats, administrators, business leaders or information specialists as well as academics. The Sahel (including Mauritania) and the Horn are within the scope of this periodical. An interesting feature is the chronology of current events in each issue, and the "retro-chrono" of events 10, 20 or 30 years in the past. Many brief book notices are provided.

182. **American-Arab Affairs.** Quarterly, 1982-1992. Washington: American-Arab Affairs Council. ISSN 0731-6763.

Continues as: *Middle East Policy*. See **www.mepc.org/mep.htm**

This journal provides a venue for discussion of political issues in the Middle East, particularly with a view to U.S. diplomacy. Each issue includes essays, analysis, interviews and/or opinion pieces, substantial signed book reviews, and "documentation": the text of important current speeches, studies, press conferences, releases by the U.S. Department of State or foreign ministries, agreements or joint communiques, etc. The states of northern Africa fall within the scope of this journal.

183. **Arab Studies Journal.** Semiannual; 1993- . Washington: Georgetown University. ISSN 1083-4753.

Contents page available online at **www.georgetown.edu/sfs/programs/ ccas/asj/asj.htm**

The Center for Contemporary Arab Studies produces this journal, which intends to depart from conventional categories of thought on Middle East subjects and "explore new or unexhausted avenues of research and creative writing" (vol. IV, no. 1, p. 1). Northern Africa appears to be within the scope of what the journal refers to as "the Arab World"; Egypt and the Sudan are the focus of articles in recent issues. Political and social-science approaches (especially gender studies) underlie most of this work. Articles are published in English or Arabic. Each issue features just two or three major book reviews.

184. **Arab Studies Quarterly.** Quarterly; 1979- . Lake Forest, IL: AAUG and the Institute of Arab Studies. ISSN 0271-3519.

Available on CD-ROM or microform from UMI.

Studies of social and economic issues such as labor unions or water scarcity, political challenges (the Middle East peace process), history and literature are all within the scope of this journal. An article in a recent issue studied the memoirs of Egypt's Huda Sha'rawi; another recent issue was devoted entirely to the theme "Beyond Colonialism and Nationalism in North Africa" (vol. 20, no. 2).

185. **Aramco World.** Bimonthly, 1987- . Washington: Aramco. ISSN 1044-1891; 0003-7567.

Online version in preparation; descriptive website at **www.aramcoserv-ices.com/**

Published by Saudi Aramco, this glossy, beautifully-produced public relations magazine often contains articles of considerable cultural and human interest. Folk arts, cooking, calligraphy and book design, music and architecture may be featured, along with articles about Islam and the history of the Arab world. Notices of current cultural events and exhibitions are included, and each volume provides an index.

Aramco maintains a collection of photographs of the Middle East, particularly of Saudi Arabia and Islamic culture, that may be made available to non-profit institutions. The magazine itself is distributed free to libraries and schools. Taking the source into account, this is an attractive publication for the high school or college library.

186. **British Journal of Middle Eastern Studies.** Semiannual; 1991- . Abingdon: Carfax. ISSN 1353-0194; 0305-6139.

Description and contents page available online at **www.carfax.co.uk/bjm-ad.htm**

The British Society for Middle Eastern Studies is responsible for this scholarly journal, which stresses current political affairs in the region but also considers historical subjects. Four to six lengthy research articles and as many as 40 book reviews are presented. An article by Fauzi M. Najjar, "Islamic Fundamentalism and the Intellectuals: the Case of Naguib Mahfouz" appeared in a recent issue (vol. 25, no. 1).

187. **Cahiers d'Études Africaines.** Quarterly; 1960- . Paris: Mouton (Éditions de l'École des Hautes Études en Sciences Sociales). ISSN 0008-0055.

One of the most important scholarly journals in the field of African studies, with a long and notable publishing history. This journal tends to be planned as themed issues, and those numbers are published with individual ISBNs. A recent issue was entirely devoted to "La Corne dans tous ses États" (vol. XXXVII, no. 2, 146), with eight major articles on Ethiopia, Djibouti, Somalia and the Horn as a region. Articles appear in English or French, and a sizable section of book reviews and notices is included in each issue. There is annual indexing as well.

188. **Les Cahiers de Tunisie: Revue de Sciences Humaines.** Quarterly; 1953- . Tunis: Université Tunis. ISSN 0008-0012.

Published in Tunisia, this journal does not confine itself to concerns characteristic of the Maghreb, the Middle East or Africa generally. The six or seven scholarly articles in each issue may address historical, cultural and anthropological topics of broader interest, in Arabic, French or English. Book reviews appear in some issues.

189. Current History: a Journal of Contemporary World Affairs. Monthly; 1941- . Philadelphia: Current History. ISSN 0011-3530.

Descriptive website, contents pages with abstracts, and selected full-text articles available online at **www.currenthistory.com/**

Current-events commentary, analysis and interpretation is the aim of this magazine, in which scholars discuss world problems. These are not meant to be research articles with footnotes and bibliographical references, but thought-provoking viewpoint essays. A news feature, "The Month in Review," summarizes recent developments. Themed issues are the rule; May focuses upon Africa, January upon the Middle East.

190. Focus on Africa. Quarterly; 1990- . London: BBC. ISSN 0959-9576.

Official title: *BBC Focus on Africa Magazine.* Description, contents and subscription information available online at **cgi.bbc.co.uk/worldservice/focus/index.htm**

A colorful current events magazine, filled with unique and dramatic news photos, interviews, firsthand correspondents' reports and other special features. A "briefing" section is composed of news clips, with a helpful map. Longer news stories, analysis and commentary cover cultural and social issues, business, development, politics and sports. Announcements about BBC Africa coverage (radio and TV) and a "programme guide" are provided. An unusual and fascinating section prints contributions from the public: photos, letters, essays, drawings, even short stories.

The publication is of such quality that one only wishes it appeared more frequently; monthly, at least. Appropriate for the high school or college library.

191. Harvard Middle Eastern and Islamic Review. Semiannual; 1994- . Cambridge, MA: Harvard University. ISSN 1074-5408.

A publication of Harvard's Center for Middle Eastern Studies, this new academic journal covers history, culture and current affairs with a broad geographic scope. A recent issue contained an article by Eve Troutt Powell, "Egyptians in Blackface: Nationalism and the Representation of the Sudan in Egypt, 1919" (vol. 2, no. 2). Signed book reviews (1-5 pages in length) are included.

192. International Journal of Middle East Studies. Quarterly; 1970- . New York: Cambridge University Press. ISSN 0020-7438.

Also publishes a reference supplement: *International Directory of Middle East Specialists.* Descriptive website available at **www.cup.cam.ac.uk/scripts/webjrn1.asp?mnemonic=mes**

The journal of the Middle East Studies Association of North America, featuring interdisciplinary articles in the social sciences and humanities, pertaining to the widest geographical span of the Middle East from the seventh century to the present. Each issue contains about five scholarly articles with complete bibliographical references, and some 25 signed book reviews of 2-4 pages in length. The reviews are categorized by topic and listed in each issue's table of contents.

193. **Jeune Afrique.** Weekly; 1980- . Paris: Éditions Jeune Afrique. ISSN 0021-6089.
   Also available online at **www.jeuneafrique.com/**
   A very useful weekly news magazine, covering current events all over the African continent. Regional and national news and features about politics, the economy, science and health, culture and lifestyle issues are included. Several related publications are available, while others have now terminated or been combined (Library of Congress cataloging records are helpful in tracing the complex publication history of *Jeune Afrique* periodicals).

194. **Journal des Africanistes.** Semiannual; 1976- . Paris: Société des Africanistes (CNRS). ISSN 0399-0346; each issue has a separate ISBN.
   The arts and cultures of Africa, history and anthropology occupy this scholarly journal. Research articles with footnotes and bibliographical references appear with reflection pieces or essays, book reviews, and news of the Société des Africanistes and notices of their publications.

195. **Journal of African Cultural Studies.** Semiannual; 1998- . Abingdon: Carfax. ISSN 1369-6815.
   Formerly: *African Languages and Cultures*. Descriptive website and contents available online at **www.carfax.co.uk/jac-ad.htm**
   Founded at SOAS in London in 1988, this scholarly journal is concerned with "perceptions of African culture from inside and outside Africa, with a special committment to the fostering of African scholarship" (verso). The languages and literature (including oral tradition), theatre and dance, art, music, the media, anthropology and folklore studies are considered; however, since it was redesigned under a new name, the journal will no longer feature technical studies of African linguistics.

196. **Journal of African Law.** Three times/year; 1957- . London: Oxford University Press for SOAS. ISSN 0021-8553.
   Descriptive website available online at **www.oup.co.uk/jnls/list/jaflaw/scope/**
   A current-events journal studying problems of law (criminal, civil, constitutional) in African states. Though the emphasis in on sub-Saharan Africa, a recent issue contained an article by Jon Abbink, "Ethnicity and Constitutionalism in Contemporary Ethiopia" (vol. 41, no. 2).
   Major concerns of modern Africa are dealt with in these articles, cases and statute notes: human rights, petroleum revenue, refugees, environmental pollution, property and investment, labor laws, etc. In addition, there are notices of recent changes in law and policy in African states and internationally. Some issues also contain book reviews.

197. **Journal of Asian and African Studies.** Quarterly, but with some combined issues; 1966- . Leiden: E.J. Brill. ISSN 0021-9096.

Contents and abstracts available online at **www.yorku.ca/faculty/academic/ ishwaran/jaas.htm**

An academic journal in the social sciences, concentrating on anthropology, sociology and history. A large number of contributions come from scholars of Asian and African origins. Some issues are organized around a theme, such as "Democracy and Democratization in Africa" (vol. XXXI, no. 1-2). A substantial section of 1-2 page book reviews appears in each volume (these are unfortunately neither ordered nor indexed).

198. **Journal of Islamic Studies.** Semiannual; 1990- . Oxford: Oxford University Press. ISSN 0955-2340.

Contents and search page available online at **www.oup.co.uk/islamj/**

Published by the Oxford Centre for Islamic Studies, this scholarly journal is meant to be interdisciplinary, covering history and the humanities but also social science, economics and international relations as they pertain to the Islamic world. A typical issue will contain three lengthy and technical articles with extensive bibliographical references, and 30 or more detailed, signed book reviews.

199. **Journal of Modern African Studies.** Quarterly; 1963- . Cambridge: Cambridge University Press. ISSN 0022-278X.

Descriptive website at **www.journals.cup.org/cup/jrn_info/moa.html.** Further information and online version available only to subscribers.

Substantial interdisciplinary articles with full bibliographical references are meant to appeal to "the political scientist and the practical politician, the administrator and the advocate, the economist and the educator, the banker and the businessman, the diplomat and the technocrat, the civil servant and the nationalist leader" (cover). The political and economic realities of the present are of primary concern. The editors particularly welcome contributions from scholars in African universities. Recent issues featured an article by Anthony Pazzanita on politicial pluralism in Mauritania (vol. 34, no. 4) and two articles on transitional Ethiopia and Eritrea (vol. 34, no. 1). Each issue contains book reviews: sometimes one lengthy literature survey, sometimes as many as 12 brief signed reviews. Articles may be accompanied by maps or tables of data.

200. **Journal of North African Studies.** Three times/year; 1996- . London: Frank Cass. ISSN 1362-9387.

Contents and abstracts available online at **www.frankcass.com/jnls/nas.htm**

A new scholarly journal defining the region to include the Maghreb states (Tunisia, Algeria, Morocco), Mauritania, Libya, Egypt and Sudan. Research covers each of these nations individually, as well as regional concerns. The area's economic, diplomatic, historical and cultural links to both Africa and the Middle East are studied, as well as relations with Europe, the United States and the rest of the world. Recent issues have presented Anna Bozzo's "Islam and

Civil Society in Algeria and France in the Age of Globalization" and "The United States and Conflict in the Maghreb" by Yahia H. Zoubir and Daniel Volman (vol. 2, no. 3). Issues include a lengthy review article or several brief book reviews.

201. **Maghreb Machrek.** Quarterly; 1973- . Paris: Documentation Française. ISSN 1241-5294; 0336-6324.

Also titled: *Monde arabe Maghreb Machrek.*

A journal of current events featuring reporting, study and analysis of major challenges confronting the Arab world, often in themed blocs or themed issues. No. 151 contained seven articles and essays on Islamic fundamentalism in Egypt, particularly its impact upon modern society and law. No. 152 devoted four articles to "la politique musulmane de la France sous la IIIe République." The articles provide ample footnotes and bibliographical references. In addition, a country-by-country chronology offers a record of recent events, mainly in politics and government—a very interesting feature. One or two signed book reviews and many brief annotated notices also appear in each issue.

202. **Maghreb Review: Quarterly Journal on North African and Islamic Studies.** Quarterly; 1976- . [London, s.n.] ISSN 0309-457X.

Also titled: *Majallat al-Maghrib.*

A journal of scholarly work focused upon the history, culture and society of northern Africa, not restricted to Algeria, Tunisia and Morocco. A recent issue featured articles on Mauritania and Libya as well. Articles and reviews may be published in English or French; they include ample footnotes and bibliographical references. Social-science studies may also provide tables of statistical data.

203. **Middle East.** Monthly; 1985- . London: IC Publications. ISSN 0305-0734.

Descriptive website at **dialspace.dial.pipex.com/icpubs**

A news magazine covering current political and economic developments in the region, plus some sports, entertainment and social features. Includes black-and-white and color photos.

204. **Middle East International.** Monthly; 1971- . London: Middle East International. ISSN 0047-7249 .

A monthly bulletin of news, analysis and editorial comment. Its central concern is the Israeli-Palestinian conflict, but it offers detailed and timely coverage of events in a much wider area, including northern Africa. Recent issues included articles on political events in Egypt, Algeria and Sudan. The publication has a strong human-rights emphasis and reports specific events much more thoroughly than the general news media. Also includes some book reviews.

205. **Middle East Journal.** Quarterly; 1947- . Washington: Middle East Institute ISSN 0026-3141.

Descriptive website, contents, abstracts and a sample article available online at **www2.ari.net/mei/**

A journal of scholarly research and analysis on "the area from the Western Sahara to ... the Caucasus" (including the Maghreb, Egypt and Sudan). Articles, a chronology, book reviews and a bibliography of periodical literature cover "the region's political and economic development, cultural heritage, and ethnic and religious diversity." Recent articles have dealt with Islamic fundamentalists in Egypt's professional associations, and the future of the Middle East and North Africa as two regions (vol. 52, no. 4).

206. **Middle East Policy.** Quarterly, 1992- . Washington: Middle East Policy Council. ISSN 1061-1924.

Continues: *American-Arab Affairs*. Contents page with the full text of selected articles available online at **www.mepc.org/mep.htm**

A venue for discussion of political issues in the Middle East (including northern Africa), particularly with a view to U.S. diplomacy. Each issue includes essays, analysis, interviews and/or opinion pieces, substantial signed book reviews, and "documentation": the text of important current speeches, studies, press conferences, releases by the U.S. Department of State or foreign ministries, agreements or joint communiques, etc. Recent issues included articles on USAID assistance in Somalia and Morocco, structural adjustment, the oil industry, Islam and democratization. Issues also contain several 2-3 page book reviews.

207. **Middle East Quarterly.** Quarterly; 1994- . Philadelphia: Middle East Forum. ISSN 1073-9467.

Descriptive website at **www.allenpress.com/mieq/index.html**

A journal of current events, analysis and opinion, sharply focused upon US ties with Israel.

208. **Middle East Report.** Quarterly (bimonthly until 1996); 1988- . Washington: Middle East Research and Information Project (MERIP). ISSN 0899-2851.

Contents page and selected full-text articles or editorials from the current issue available online at **www.merip.org/**

A current-events magazine offering a wide variety of articles, discussion, analysis and correspondents' reports on the political, economic, social and cultural life of the Middle East today. The Mediterranean states of Africa, the Horn and Sudan are covered in detail by this publication. Recent issues focused upon urbanization in Cairo, gender and civil rights in Algeria, and the states of minorities in the Middle East (Berbers, Copts, non-Muslims in the South Sudan). Readable, informative articles, maps and black-and-white news photos are featured.

209. **Middle East Studies Association Bulletin.** Semiannual; 1967- . [New York]: Middle East Studies Association of North America. ISSN 0026-3184.

Descriptive website, select full-text articles, contents and indexing available online at **www.mesa.arizona.edu/Bulletin/welcome.htm**

Not a newsletter, this scholarly journal presents editorial comment, reflection and opinion essays and a huge number of brief but informative signed book reviews, topically organized. Most of these are books published in English, but coverage is expanding.

210. **Middle Eastern Studies.** Quarterly; 1964- . London: Frank Cass. ISSN 0026-3206.

Description, contents pages and subscription information available online at **www.frankcass.com/jnls/mes.htm**

Research articles on literature, history, religions, economics and society in the Middle East form the core of this scholarly journal. Israel and Palestine are important but do not overshadow other concerns in the region. A recent issue contained articles on privatization and tourism in Egypt, and on the history of the slave trade in Sudan (vol. 34, no. 2). Book reviews are included.

211. **New African.** Monthly; 1978- . London: IC Publications. ISSN 0142-9345; 0140-833X.

Also available on microfilm from UMI; full-text online to subscribers through Information Access; contents pages and selected stories online at **dialspace.dial.pipex.com/town/terrace/lf41/**

A monthly news magazine full of correspondents' reports, color photos, columns and features. Much space is afforded to readers' letters, sports coverage, commentary and advertising. The Sahel and Horn are included, but not Mediterranean Africa.

212. **PAIS International in Print.** Monthly edition; 1991- . New York: Public Affairs Information Service. ISSN 1051-4015.

Also available on CD-ROM or tape; available online through DIALOG, OCLC and other vendors to subscribers only. See also **www.pais.org**

Published in this form and in an annual cumulation, this is a massive compilation of social science literature, with abstracts. Books, articles, government documents, statistical publications, research and conference reports are all included. Languages covered are English, German, Spanish, French, Italian and Portuguese. The entries are topically arranged, with specific countries as separate headings, making it possible quickly to browse the current literature on Chad, for example. A basic information source.

213. **Periodica Islamica: an International Contents Journal.** Quarterly; 1991- . Kuala Lumpur, Malaysia: Periodica Islamica. ISSN 0128-3715.

Descriptive website available online at **www.ummah.net/dranees/**

"An international contents journal ... reproducing tables of contents from a wide variety of serials, periodicals and other recurring publications worldwide, selected for indexing on the basis of their relevance to the religious, cultural, socioeconomic and political affairs of the Muslim world." The journal also offers original articles, features, bibliographies and book reviews.

214. **Politique Africaine.** Quarterly; 1981- . Paris: Karthala. ISSN 0244-7827.

Descriptive website available online at **www.cean.u-bordeaux.fr/polaf.html**

A publication of the Centre d'Étude d'Afrique Noire at Bordeaux. Themed issues are the norm for this journal, which includes both scholarly research and current-events analysis. Detailed articles with bibliographical references, reflection/opinion pieces or essays, book reviews and abstracts of forthcoming publications are included. The emphasis is on sub-Saharan Africa (not necessarily francophone).

215. **Princeton Papers: Interdisciplinary Journal of Middle Eastern Studies.** Semiannual; 1996- . Princeton: Markus Wiener. ISSN 1084-5666.

Continues: *Princeton Papers in Near Eastern Studies* (1992-1994). A website is in preparation.

Edited by Charles Issawi and Bernard Lewis, this scholarly journal is published by the Near Eastern Studies Department at Princeton. It covers a broad scope geographically and in terms of subject matter, but emphasizes lengthy articles of analysis and reflection, often arranged in themed issues.

216. **Review of African Political Economy.** Quarterly; 1974- . Sheffield: ROAPE (Carfax). ISSN 0305-6244.

Contents pages available online at **www.carfax.co.uk/rap-con.htm**

A scholarly social-science journal stressing reflection on and evaluation of current trends in African political, economic and social life. Rethinking of issues like globalization, structural adjustment, democracy and the environment is a basic concern of this publication. Book reviews and review articles are featured, and a section called "Current Africana" serves as an annual topically-subdivided bibliography of significant publications in the field.

217. **Review of International Studies.** Quarterly; 1981- . Cambridge: Cambridge University Press for the British International Studies Association. ISSN 02602105.

Also available from the publisher on microfiche. Descriptive website available at **www.cup.cam.ac.uk/journals/jnlscat/ris/ris.html**

According to its publisher, this journal presents "substantial articles and review articles which survey and analyse the literature of relevant fields and disciplines ... debate and discussion on areas of topical concern ... [and] serves the needs of scholars in politics, law, history, economics, and all other areas of social science in the international arena." Each issue contains only five or six lengthy theoretical articles; occasionally a book review in the form of a scholarly essay is featured.

218. **Revue du Monde Musulman et de la Méditerranée.** Quarterly; 1988- . Aix-en-Provence: Éditions ÉDISUD. ISSN 0997-1327; each issue also has a separate ISBN.

This publication of the Association pour l'Étude des Sciences Humaines en Afrique du Nord et au Proche-Orient (in collaboration with IREMAM) functions as a series of edited volumes, each on a specific theme.

Nos. 77-78, for example, appear as a volume of 21 essays and articles entitled *L'Humour en Orient* (ISBN 2-85744-871-6), presented by editors Irène Fenoglio and François Georgeon. Folk humor, jokes and caricatures from Ottoman sources, Tunisia, Egypt and Algeria are represented. The scholarly articles include footnotes and bibliographical references, often extensive, and brief book notices appear in each volume.

219. **World Policy Journal.** Quarterly; 1983- . New York: World Policy Institute ISSN 0740-2775.

Descriptive website, contents and abstracts available online at **worldpolicy. org/index.html**

An eclectic policy review featuring essays, analysis and opinion papers on current problems in foreign affairs. Some have bibliographical references; others are reflection pieces or personal views, and occasionally a photo collection is presented. One major book review article is included in each issue.

Electronic Reference Sources

Databases

Some of these information sources are meant for retail purchase by consumers; others are more likely to be owned or subscribed to by research libraries, other institutions or corporations. Where subscriptions are required, site licenses may limit access to certain groups of users.

220. **Access UN** (InfoWeb Newsbank). **infoweb.newsbank.com**
A searchable database of current and archived United Nations documents and publications, back to 1961. Full access for subscribers only.

221. **Arab Press Service Organization.** Available online through PTS/Information Access
Covers news, foreign policy, defense and economics, especially the oil industry, as "APS Diplomat" and "APS Review."

222. Britannica Book of the Year. Sales information and description at **www.eb.com/bookstore/OVERVIEW/GO_BBOY.html**

Available on CD-ROM.

Very useful for area studies, this annual publication covers politics, business, science, the arts, society and popular culture. Regional and country articles, topical articles and essays.

223. Britannica Online. Descriptive website at **www.britannica.com/** or **www.eb.com/bookstore/index.htm**

Available online to subscribers, or on CD-ROM in standard and multimedia editions.

Full-text encyclopedia database with articles, illustrations, maps, etc.

224. DIALOG. For full information see **library.dialog.com/bluesheets/**

Over 450 searchable full-text databases containing articles from newspapers and periodicals, news agencies, trade and industry sources, directories, scientific and technical journals. Many of these are relevant to area studies, including the Africa News Service, EIU Country Analysis and other services, Middle East News, and Kompass business directories for the Middle East/Africa/Mediterranean.

Because DIALOG search techniques require some training, and because accounts may be charged by time connected, many libraries offer mediated DIALOG searches only. A web-based version is now available.

225. Global Newsbank (InfoWeb Newsbank)**.** For further information see **www.newsbank.com/global/**

Full text of articles and broadcast reports from: Libyan TV (Tripoli), BBC Worldwide Monitoring, press services (InterPress, Reuters, Agence France Presse), US Department of State Background Notes, specific newspapers (including *The Washington Post*), etc. Searchable by keyword. The database covers two years at a time.

226. Infotrac Searchbank. Expanded Academic ASAP. *See also* the Information Access Company website at **library.iacnet.com/libhome.html**

Indexes recent periodical articles. Citations, sometimes with abstracts; full-text document delivery may be arranged. The database includes periodicals like *Petroleum Times Energy Report*, *World Development*, *Arab Studies Quarterly*, *Research in African Literatures*, and *The Middle East*. Searchable by subject or keyword.

227. Infotrac Searchbank. General Reference Center Gold. *See also* the Information Access Company website at **library.iacnet.com/libhome.html**

Encyclopedia and reference book articles and excerpts, newspaper and periodical citations. Some full-text retrieval. Searchable by subject or keyword.

228. **Jane's Sentinel. North Africa.** Available on CD-ROM.
    Part of *Jane's Geopolitical Library*, this resource offers "a one-stop threat assessment for the North Africa region." Geography, map data, military and political science information.

229. **League of Arab States Documentation and Information Center.** (ALDOC) in Cairo.
    Indexing and subject thesaurus in Arabic, English and French. A catalog of the Arab League's own collection and databases they maintain (trade statistics, population data, etc).

230. **LEXIS/NEXIS Academic Universe.** For further information see the Congressional Information Service page at **www.cispubs.com/acaduniv/**
    Searchable full-text database. Country profiles (general encyclopedia-style reference); news classified into "top news" (today only), company, industry and market, government and political, legal news. Also available are directories, biographical data, medical materials, law reviews, etc.
    LEXIS/NEXIS maintains other relevant online services, including the LEXIS Country Information Service (Middle East and Africa) and the Energy Library. Access to these services is password-protected and limited to students, faculty, employees and other authorized members of a company or institution, through site licenses.

231. **Microsoft Encarta Africana.** Description online at **encarta.msn.com/africana** or **office.microsoft.com/magazine/oct1998/ce/history.htm**
    Available on CD-ROM.
    Encyclopedia-style reference covering "the historical and cultural achievements of Africa and people of African descent from prehistoric times to the present." The reference is very attractively presented, with use of interactive and multimedia techniques. Noted authorities Henry Louis Gates Jr. and Kwame Appiah directed this project.

232. **World News Connection.** National Technical Information Service (NTIS). **wnc.fedworld.gov/**
    WNC "offers time sensitive information gathered from thousands of foreign media sources, including political speeches, television programs, radio broadcasts, and articles from newspapers, periodicals, and books. Users get the most extensive and in-depth collection of unclassified military, political, environmental, sociological, scientific and technical data and reports from around the world (U.S. information is not included). All the material is translated into English." Among the regions covered are "Near East and South Asia" and "Sub-Saharan Africa." Full access to subscribers only.

233. **OCLC FirstSearch.** For further information see **www.oclc.org**
    Databases of abstracts, articles, contents pages. Other services include a collection of electronic journals online, and WorldCat, a union catalog of library holdings.

234. **Periodicals Contents Index.** For further information, see the Chadwyck-Healey website at **pci.chadwyck.com/**

Humanities and social sciences. Area studies data covers Africa and the Middle East. Subject areas include history, architecture, anthropology, economics, education, geography, law, music, and religion. The database includes many older sources that are not easy to find in electronic indexes. Citations only.

235. **Readers' Guide Abstracts.** For more information, see **www.hwwilson. com/rdgrga.HTM**

A Wilson database of popular periodicals. Search by subject or keyword. Citations with abstracts are provided, and a full-text version is available.

236. **WebSPIRS.** (SilverPlatter). For more information, see the SilverPlatter website at **www.silverplatter.com/erl/webspirs4.htm**

A collection of centrally-loaded databases, including Ulrich's International periodicals, Current Contents and MLA Bibliography. Extensive science and medicine coverage. Citations only (a full-text option is available).

Search Engines and Links Pages

Many websites exist mainly for the purpose of directing the searcher to other sources of information. Search engines allow the user to enter terms and call up corresponding records, like library public access catalogs. Links pages consist of hypertext links to information pages on a given topic. For an explanation of selection criteria, see the Preface.

237. AdmiNet Africa. **www.adminet.com/africa/**

Links to a variety of information sources, including many in French. Organized by country, with additional links to Arab resources.

238. Africa Dot Com. **www.africa.com/**

Commercial site with links pertaining to business, entertainment, sports, tourism, etc.; a somewhat southern-Africa emphasis.

239. AfricaLand: Focus International. **www.focusintl.com/afriland.htm**

Many links covering business, culture, statistics and themes such as "Gender and Development" or "Pan-Africanism." Offers a "Data by Country" index, with all of northern Africa represented, including Western Sahara. In both French and English.

240. African Governments on the WWW. **www.gksoft.com/govt/en/africa.html**

Links to official ministry and embassy websites for each country, plus those of opposition groups or parties. Includes all the nations of northern Africa except Eritrea and Somalia.

241. African Perspective. **www.public.asu.edu/~aowxll/**
News and culture links.

242. African Politics Classroom. **abacus.cgu.edu/spe/ppp/africa/coun_indx.html**
Basic links, very easy to use.

243. African Studies Association and Stanford University Libraries. Africa South of the Sahara: Selected Internet Resources. **www-sul.stanford.edu/depts/ssrg/africa/guide.html**
Covers the Sahel and Horn (including Sudan and Mauritania).

244. Africances. Société de services Internet. **www.africances.fr/**
Link to « L'Afrique sur Internet », "le site de référence pour trouver des informations à propos d'Internet en Afrique francophone."

245. AfricaServer. **www.africaserver.nl/front_uk.htm**
Many links, organized thematically and geographically. In English.

246. Africa-Index. **www.africa-index.com**
Primarily southern Africa.

247. Al-Murshid. Countries and Regions. **www.murshid.com/Countries_and_Regions/Countries**
Links to pages concerned with Arab and Arab-related countries in the Middle East and Africa: many personal, commercial and entertainment sites.

248. Arab Internet Directory. **www.1001sites.com/**
Commercial search engine.

249. Arabia Online. Links Info Arabia. **www.arabia.com/arabworld/countries.html**
Links to many websites and newsgroups for Tunisia, Sudan, Morocco, Libya, Egypt and Algeria.

250. ArabNet. Online Resource for the Arab World in the Middle East and North Africa. **www.arab.net/welcome.html**
Contains links to helpful pages on Mauritania, Morocco, Algeria, Tunisia, Libya, Egypt, Sudan, Somalia and Djibouti.

251. ArabView Network. **www.arabview.net/**
A links page featuring news, entertainment, culture, cuisine, business and personal sites. Includes nine countries in the Maghreb, Sahel and Horn.

252. H-Africa Home Page. Humanities and Social Sciences Online. **www.h-net.msu.edu/~africa/**
General but helpful links site.

253. Harvard Center for Middle Eastern Studies. Internet Resources on the Middle East. **fas-www.harvard.edu/~mideast/inMEres/inMEres.html**
Valuable academic and cultural resources links page.

254. Internet Africa. Africa's Premier Content Hub. **www.iafrica.com/**
Emphasis on South Africa.

255. Middle East and North Africa Studies Group. North Africa and Middle East Resources on the Internet. **mena.binghamton.edu/Midea.htm**

256. Middle East Internet Pages. **www.middle-east-pages.com/**
General information is topically organized; some is relevant to northern Africa, but the only African country covered under its own heading is Egypt.

257. Middle East Network Information Center (MENIC). Center for Middle East Studies, University of Texas at Austin. **menic.utexas.edu/mes.html**
Very useful links page for all aspects of area studies.

258. Norwegian Council for Africa. Index on Africa: a comprehensive guide to the continent on the Net. **www.africaindex.africainfo.no:80/index.html**

259. Political Resources on the Net. **www.agora.stm.it/politic/**
"Listings of political sites available on the Internet sorted by country, with links to parties, organizations, governments, media and more from all around the world." Africa page, with links for each country (including Western Sahara).

260. SynapseNet. Contemporary Conflicts in Africa. **www.synapse.net/~acdi20/country/**
Searchable database and links to related pages; coverage of Eritrea, Ethiopia, Somalia, Sudan and Algeria.

261. TAMTAM. L'Afrique vous Accueille. **www.pagel.com/tamtam/**
"C'est le premier répertoire virtuel de l'économie et des affaires en Afrique sur Internet. C'est le carrefour de promotion d'affaires et des informations sur le continent africain." Searchable by region (Afrique du Nord, Ouest, Centre, Est), with separate pages for each country.

262. University of Kentucky. World-Wide Web Resources: Africa. **www.uky.edu/Subject/africa.html**

263. University of Pennsylvania, African Studies Center. African Studies WWW. **www.sas.upenn.edu/African_Studies/AS.html**
A great deal of assembled information – particularly the Country pages.

264. University of Utah Department of Political Science. The Middle East North Africa Internet Resource Guide. **www.cc.utah.edu/~jwr9311/MENA.html**
Many links to newsgroups, listservs and other academic and professional contacts.

265. Web of True Blue. Middle Eastern and Arab Resources on the Internet. **www.ionet.net/~usarch/WTB-Services/MiddleEast/WTB-MiddleEast.shtml**
Idiosyncratic personal website.

266. WoYaa! Your Window to Africa on the Internet. **www.woyaa.com/**
Search engine, Africa-related. In English and French.

267. WWW Virtual Library. African Studies. **www.vibe.com/History/AfricanStudies/africanWWW.html**

268. WWW Virtual Library. Columbia University: Middle East Studies. **www.columbia.edu/cu/libraries/indiv/area/MiddleEast/**
See also the **area/Africa** page.

269. Yellow Window. Links to Information Sources on Mediterranean Countries. **www.yellowwindow.be/linkmed.htm**

Reference Websites and Electronic Publications

These sites are for the most part designed as destinations in their own right; in some cases, sites of this nature are now the only form in which this information is published. For selection criteria, see the Preface.

270. African Studies Quarterly. **web.africa.ufl.edu/asq/**
ISSN 1093-2658
A scholarly journal published online by the Center for African Studies at the University of Florida, presenting articles on the economic, political and cultural life of Africa. Indexed by PAIS.

271. Africa International. **www.focusintl.com/pilypily.htm**
"Mensuel No. 1 d'information en Afrique francophone. Fondé en 1958." Online description page for this periodical. The Maghreb is included within the scope of this publication.

272. Africa: One Continent, Many Worlds. **www.lam.mus.ca.us/africa/**
Designed specifically for classroom teachers.

273. Africa Research Central. A Clearinghouse of African Primary Sources. **africa-research.csusb.edu/**
"Africa Research Central is your gateway to the archives, libraries, and museums with important collections of African primary sources."

274. AfricaNet. Information, History and Fact Sheets on Africa. **www.africanet. com/**
   Primarily southern Africa.

275. Afrique Asie. (Le Nouvel Afrique-Asie). **www.afrique-asie.com/**
   Descriptive website for this periodical, with contents and some full-text articles and editorials.
   "Le Nouvel Afrique Asie, avec plus de 100.000 lecteurs en Afrique au Nord et au Sud du Sahara, au Moyen-Orient, en Europe, en Asie, en Amérique latine Amérique du Nord est aujourd'hui le plus lu et le plus influent mensuel de langue française du tiers monde."

276. Agence de la Francophonie. **www.francophonie.org/**
   Pages on Djibouti, Egypt, Mali, Morocco, Mauritania, Niger, Chad and Tunisia.

277. Arab and Muslim NetWork Information. **www.arabinfo.org/**
   General and geographical information, news and links.

278. Arab Countries. Countries of the Arab World. **www.arabbiz.com/ arab_countries.html**
   A basic directory of names and addresses for embassies and chambers of commerce. Includes Algeria, Chad, Djibouti, Egypt, Libya, Mauritania, Morocco, Somalia, Sudan and Tunisia.

279. Arab World Factbook. **www.arabworld.com/**
   Basic description and data about Egypt, Libya, Algeria, Tunisia, Morocco, Mauritania, Western Sahara, Somalia, Djibouti, and Sudan.

280. Arab World and Islamic Resources and School Services. **www.dnai.com/~gui/ awairproductinfo.html**
   Books and other materials for students of all ages.

281. Arab World Online. **www.awo.net/**
   Online magazine, with full-text articles, background features and country profiles (for Mauritania, Morocco, Algeria, Tunisia, Libya, Egypt, Sudan and Somalia).

282. Arabic Electronic Mail Journal. **www.ibmpcug.co.uk/~ajournal/**
   News, opinion and advocacy, on issues important to the Arab world.

283. Arabies - Trends. **www.arabies.com/**
   "The first and only magazine in French dealing with the whole Arab world, under the three headings of politics, economics and culture, Arabies can claim to have contributed for what will soon be 12 years to the French-speaking world's enhanced understanding of the Middle East and the Maghreb." Descriptive website with subscription information.

284. ArabSeek Home Page. **www.arabseek.com/**
    Coverage of the Middle East and North Africa; topically organized.

285. Atlapedia Online. Countries A to Z. **www.atlapedia.com/online/country_
index.htm**
    Basic encyclopedia or almanac articles, with maps.

286. Central Intelligence Agency. World Factbook. **www.odci.gov/cia/publications/
factbook/**
    A great deal of basic information on every country, with a certain point of view.

287. Centre d'Étude d'Afrique Noire. **www.iep.u-bordeaux.fr/cean/index.html**
and **www.cean.u-bordeaux.fr/**
    With links to their collections and publications.

288. Encyclopaedia of the Orient. **i-cias.com/e.o/index.htm**
    Searchable database; includes the Middle East and North Africa.

289. Fourth World Documentation Project. African Documents. **www.halcyon.
com/FWDP/africa.html**
    Special coverage of Morocco, the Western Sahara, the Tuareg, the Nuba Mountains and the South Sudan.

290. International Committee of the Red Cross/Red Crescent (ICRC). **www.icrc.
ch/unicc/icrcnews.nsf/DocIndex/home_eng?OpenDocument**
    Text also available in French and Spanish. Go to the "Site Tree" for links to pages detailing ICRC operations in sub-Saharan Africa, the Middle East and North Africa.

291. L'Cahiers de l'Orient. Revue d'Étude et de Reflexion sur le Monde Arabe et Islamique. **www.sfiedi.fr/cahiers/**
    Descriptive website, with links to full-text articles from recent issues, including recent special issues on Algeria, Egypt and water resources in the Maghreb and Machrek. In French.

292. Library of Congress. African and Middle Eastern Reading Room. **lcweb.loc.
gov/rr/amed/**

293. Library of Congress. Country Studies/Area Handbook Program. **lcweb2.
loc.gov/frd/cs/cshome.html**
    Full text online of the current and very useful Country Studies series.

294. Middle East Research and Information Project. **www.merip.org/**
    A nonprofit organization providing independent, critical, detailed news and feature coverage of events and issues in the region through the current-events magazine *Middle East Report* and other activities. Commentary and reflection on policy concerns is a primary interest.

295. Miftah Shamali. The Largest Website on on North Africa. **i-cias.com/m.s/ index.htm**
   Travel guide, country and culture information on Mauritania, Morocco, Algeria, Tunisia, Libya, Egypt and Sudan.

296. Rulers of the World. **www.geocities.com/Athens/1058/rulers.html**
   Lists heads of state chronologically for each country, and administrators for organizations like the Arab League and the OAU.

297. University of Bradford (UK). Internet Journal of African Studies. **www.brad. ac.uk/research/ijas/**
   Full text of current and recent issues.

298. US Department of State. Bureau of Near Eastern Affairs. **www. state.gov/www/regions/nea/index.html**
   Policy statements, press releases, news articles, remarks, testimony and briefings; also links to "Core State Department Reports," country information, travel advisories, etc., pertaining to the Middle East and North Africa.

299. USAfrica Online. The Authoritative Link for the US and Africa. **www. usafricaonline.com/**
   Intended "to serve as the primary, professional news medium for Africans and Americans; promote and support establishing of pro-development structures and ideas; foster pro-democracy and free market networks inside the African continent and within African communities in the U.S., the Americas and across the world; argue through editorial opinion and reporting such common economic interests of Americans and Africans in investing and trade matters, export and import, public policy and current issues, cultural awareness, sports, and arts reviews." Full text of articles and features in the current issue.

300. WorldViews. **www.igc.apc.org/worldviews/index.html**
   "WorldViews gathers, organizes, and publicizes information and educational resource materials that deal with issues of peace and justice in world affairs." Pages on Africa and the Middle East.

Electronic News Sources

301. Africa Intelligence. Country Channels. **www.indigo-net.com/channels/ ai/countries-AI.htm**
   News and features from the local and international press and media; links to businesses, organizations, government ministries and websites.

302. Africa Intelligence. In French. **www.indigo-net.com/afrique.html**
   News and features from the local and international press and media; links to businesses, organizations, government ministries and websites. Includes *Maghreb Confidenciel* (full text for subscribers only).

303. AfricaNews: News and Views on Africa from Africa. **www.peacelink. it/an_curr.html**
"AFRICANEWS is a feature and news service owned and managed by African journalists. It deals with culture, peace, justice, ecology, religion, gender issues, sustainable development. All topics are seen from the perspective of the common people. In AFRICANEWS Africans speak about Africa." Monthly electronic journal. The focus is mainly on the southern half of the continent, but recent issues have contained articles on Sudan.

304. AfricaNews Online. North Africa. **www.africanews.org/north/**
Country pages with links to abstracts and full-text news articles on Algeria, Egypt, Tunisia, Morocco, Libya and Western Sahara.

305. Afrique Tribune. Actualités et Affaires Internationales. **www.africances. fr/afrint/** or **www.pagel/com/afriquetribune/** (reachable through the Africances or Pagel pages)
"Le magazine AFRIQUE TRIBUNE confirme son positionnement sur Internet et se donne de plus en plus une grille de magazine électronique. Notre ambition: avec vous, assurer une présence efficace d'une Afrique en mouvement sur l'autoroute de l'information."

306. Agence France Presse. Worldwide News Agency. **www.afp.com/**
In French, English, German, Spanish and Portuguese.

307. Al Ahram Weekly. **www.ahram.org.eg/weekly**
Considered by many to be the newspaper of record for the Arab world, *Al Ahram* (Cairo) is now published in English on a weekly basis. Full text of articles and editorials, photos (in color) and political cartoons are posted on this website.

308. Arab News and Media. **www.fares.net/news/**
News of the Arab world and Islam; sports, music, weather.

309. Arabic Newsstand. **www.leb.net/~hajeri/newsstand/arab-news.html**
Links to news sources dealing with the Arab world; newspapers and magazines from Jordan, Lebanon, Palestine and the Gulf. In Arabic and English.

310. ArabicNews. **www.arabicnews.com/ansub/index.html**
News briefs and links to full-text articles. Coverage of the Middle East and North Africa. In English.

311. BBC Online Network. News. **news.bbc.co.uk/hi/english/world/**
With audio and video. Special coverage of Africa and the Middle East. Also available in Spanish, Russian, Welsh, Arabic, Mandarin and Cantonese.

312. BBC World Service. Africa & Middle East. **www.bbc.co.uk/worldservice/ africa/**
Includes broadcast news in Arabic, Somali and Hausa.

313. Center for Research Libraries (CRL). Foreign Newspaper Project. **wwwcrl.uchicago.edu/DBSearch/ForeignNews.asp**
Searchable database of more than 6200 foreign newspapers in the CRL collections.

314. CNN Interactive. **www.cnn.com/**

315. Global Newsbank (InfoWeb Newsbank). For further information see **www.newsbank.com/global/**
Full text of articles and broadcast reports from: Libyan TV (Tripoli), BBC Worldwide Monitoring, press services (InterPress, Reuters, Agence France Presse), US Department of State Background Notes, specific newspapers (including *The Washington Post*), etc. Searchable by keyword. The database covers two years at a time.

316. Le Monde Diplomatique. Afrique. **www.monde-diplomatique.fr/index/ pays/afrique.html**
Archived articles.

317. Le Monde Diplomatique. Maghreb. **www.monde-diplomatique.fr/index/ pays/maghreb.html**
Archived articles.

318. Middle East Times. Egypt Edition (English). **metimes.com/issue98-40/ methaus.htm**
Full text, plus related links.

319. Muslimedia. **muslimedia.com/mainpage.htm**
Full-text news stories relevant to the Islamic world.

320. New York Times on the Web. **www.nytimes.com/**

321. OneWorld News. News by Country. **www.oneworld.org/news/africa/ index.html**
Links to full-text news, features and press releases; search engine.

322. PANA . Agence Panafricaine d'Information. **www.rapide-pana.com/**
Daily news reports. Full text available online, in French.

323. PANA. Panafrican News Agency. **www.nando.net/ans/pana/**
Daily news reports. Full text available online, in English.

324. Radio Africa. La Première Radio Africaine Live sur le Net. **www.radioafrica. com/radioafricaFR.html**
   Requires RealAudio.

325. US Information Agency. Foreign Media Commentary: Daily Digest. **www.usia.gov/usiahome/medreac.htm**

326. Washington Post. Middle East and Africa. **www.washingtonpost. com/wp-srv/inatl/mideast.htm** and **www.washingtonpost.com/wp-srv/inatl/ africa.htm**
   News briefs and links to full-text articles.

327. Washington Report on Middle East Affairs. **www.washington-report.org/**
   "Online magazine published eight times per year providing detailed coverage and extensive commentary. Each issue also contains a catalog of educational books and videotapes about the Middle East, Islam, Islamic countries ranging from Morocco to Bangladesh and beyond to Malaysia and Indonesia, and the relations between those countries and their major non-Islamic neighbors such as Ethiopia, Israel and India" (MENIC). Clearly-stated political point of view.

PART TWO

Area Studies References by Subject

History and Antiquities

Chapter 2

The cultures and societies of Northern Africa may have the richest recorded history in the world. Some of the reference resources relevant to this aspect of area studies are listed here.

Please note that the historical eras used here as subdivisions do overlap to a large degree. The primary interest or concern of a work is the criterion for its classification. For example, Hopkins' *Letters from Barbary* pertains mainly to British foreign policy and will be found under "Colonialism," while Justin McCarthy's works are focused upon Ottoman administration and will be found in that section, even though they deal with a later period chronologically.

For ancient Pharaonic history and culture, see Part Three, "Egypt." For more information on the structures, artifacts and monuments of these eras, see also Part Two, "Art and Architecture," and travel guidebooks for specific locations. For historical maps, see Part Two, "Maps and Atlases."

Prehistory and Archaeology

328. **Encyclopedia of Precolonial Africa: Archaeology, History, Languages, Cultures and Environments.** Edited by Joseph O. Vogel. Walnut Creek, CA: Alta Mira, 1997. 605 p. ISBN 0-7619-8902-1.

A one-volume collection of signed articles describing the early history of the African continent. Physical geography and climate, evolution and hominid origins and the development of hunting/foraging, agriculture, stone age and iron age societies all receive attention. Articles are 4-10 pages in length and include brief bibliographies. Illustration is quite restrained, with 70 small monochrome maps or drawings and a few photos. A detailed index is provided.

329. **International Dictionary of Historic Places.** Vol 4: Middle East and Africa. Chicago: Fitzroy Dearborn, 1996. xvii, 766 p. ISBN 1-884964-03-6 (vol. 4).

Volume 4 of this five-volume set is composed of alphabetized, signed encyclopedia-style articles about sites of archaeological and historical interest in widely-scattered places. Algeria, Egypt, Eritrea, Ethiopia, Libya, Morocco, Sudan and Tunisia are represented here. Each article begins with a capsule description of the site and its location, plus contact data for tourism authorities for further information. The article about Kairouan (or Qairwan) in Tunisia offers four pages of historical detail and two large black-and-white photos, one of the Punic ruins and one of the Great Mosque. A small bibliographic note ("Further Reading") is added. The volume is curiously short of maps, though the end papers provide two good ones. There is a general index.

330. **Oxford Encyclopedia of Archaeology in the Near East.** Editor in chief, Eric M. Meyers. New York: Oxford University Press, 1997. 5 v. ISBN 0-19-506512-3.

The American Schools of Oriental Research created this extensive collection of specific, alphabetically-arranged signed articles to serve a variety of ready-reference and study purposes. The core of the work is Syro-Palestinian archaeology, but the geographic range extends west to Morocco and south to Ethiopia. Chronological coverage includes prehistoric sites through the Crusades; occasionally, later periods are mentioned. The work is meant to present important texts as well as physical objects or realia.

Each article provides a bibliography, but these may range from one citation for AXUM to 17 references in several European languages for CARTHAGE. (Oddly, there is no cross-reference from "Punic," though the term can be found in Vol. 5's detailed and well-organized index.) Also in Vol. 5 are several important appendices: 13 tables of data identifying texts on papyrus, stone, ceramic, etc.; chronological bar-charts or time-lines showing the approximate contemporaneity of civilizations; 12 maps locating ancient sites; a synoptic outline of the work's conceptual scheme. Many articles are illustrated with sharp black-and-white photos or drawings.

331. **Past Worlds: the Times Atlas of Archaeology.** Maplewood, NJ: Hammond, 1988. 319 p. ISBN 0-7230-0306-8.

The design of this attractive, well-illustrated large-format atlas is unusually comprehensive and thematic, with geography a subordinate consideration. The aim is an overall archaeology of the world. It begins with a five-column comparative chronology of the continents, then supplies a substantial chapter on the business of archaeology itself: how information is collected and analyzed, and the significance of various remains and artifacts.

The rest of the chapters are formed conceptually and chronologically: materials pertaining to prehistoric Africa, to Egypt, Axum, the Sahara, Rome and Carthage, Iron Age Africa, early Islam, the Songhay and other trading powers, etc., can be found with a little searching of the table of contents and the index/gazetteer. A glossary and a subdivided bibliography are provided.

332. **Temples and Tombs of Ancient Nubia: the International Rescue Campaign at Abu Simbel, Philae and Other Sites.** General editor Torgny Säve-Söderbergh. London: Thames and Hudson for UNESCO, 1987. 256 p.

A record of the extraordinary international effort to save the antiquities of Nubia threatened by the construction of the High Dam at Aswan, starting in 1954. A full narrative account of the project is accompanied by 43 vivid color plates and 48 black-and-white photos, plus 20 figures, including a number of unusual historical maps showing Nubia during the Old, Middle and New Kingdoms of ancient Egypt, during the Meroitic and Roman Empires, and Christian Nubia. Also, detailed plans and cross-sections of the Temples of Abu Simbel and Philae show the stages of cutting and moving, and some of the methods used in the salvage operation.

In addition, several important appendices are included: lists of the contributions made by various nations and a chronology of the salvage effort, and a brief archaeological description of the two major temples. There is a subdivided, annotated and detailed bibliography, and an adequate index.

333. Canby, Courtland. **A Guide to the Archaeological Sites of Israel, Egypt and North Africa.** With Arcadia Kocybala. New York: Facts on File, 1990. 278p. ISBN 0-8160-1054-4.

A well-organized guide containing descriptive and historical entries on the most important archaeological sites and monuments of Egypt and the Maghreb. Each of the book's three divisions provides a map, an historical summary, and alphabetically-arranged entries, many with black-and-white photos. The work covers the history of the area from the Paleolithic age to the Byzantine, with some early and medieval Islamic monuments. Cross-references are made from the names of sites and monuments to the larger article in which they are discussed: for example, RAMESSEUM see Thebes. An index is also provided. This volume could serve as a convenient ready reference for students or as a field manual for the traveller.

334. Hawkes, Jacquetta. **Atlas of Ancient Archaeology.** New York: McGraw-Hill, 1974. 272 p. ISBN 0-07-027293-X.

An introductory encyclopedia or atlas of the ancient world, illustrated with many plans, maps and drawings. There is an entry for the Tassili N'Ajjer site in eastern Algeria, three sites in the Sudan (Semna, Kerma and Meroe), and a chapter on the major Pharaonic monuments of Egypt.

335. Haywood, John. **The Illustrated History of Early Man.** New York: Smithmark (Brompton Books), 1995. 160 p. ISBN 0-8317-1754-8.

This colorful general introduction to palaeo-archaeology and anthropology is relevant to northern Africa mainly on account of the dramatic discovery of the fossil remains of "Lucy" or *Australopithecus afarensis* in Hadar, Ethiopia in 1974. Some material on ancient Egyptian civilization is included as well.

336. MacKendrick, Paul. **The North African Stones Speak.** Chapel Hill: University of North Carolina Press, 1980. xxi, 434 p. ISBN 0-8078-1414-8.

A scholarly history and description of sites and artifacts from prehistoric and classical Tunisia, Libya, Algeria and Morocco. The book is illustrated with scores of black-and-white photos, maps and plans. Most valuable for reference work is the bibliography section, comprising about one-fifth of the volume; many of the entries are briefly annotated. There is a meticulous index.

337. Ridinger, Robert B. Marks. **African Archaeology: a Selected Bibliography.** New York: G.K. Hall, 1993. viii, 311 p. ISBN 0-8161-9086-0.

Fully annotated, very informative entries, organized geographically, make up this reference. Monographs and periodical literature are included, along with many conference proceedings and reports. The materials chosen provide "data on the excavation results from specific sites as well as regional syntheses and discussions on the development of the discipline" (p. viii). The work focuses on "physiographic regions" (e.g., the Horn of Africa, Nubia, Lake Chad Basin) as well as individual countries; northern Africa is well represented. Descriptions of relevant journals originating in Africa are also provided. There is a helpful subject index.

338. Shinnie, P. L. **Ancient Nubia.** London and New York: Kegan Paul International, 1995. xvii, 145 p. ISBN 0-7103-0517-6.

Portrays the history and archaeology of Nubia, as it once straddled Egypt and the Sudan (from the Stone Age until medieval times). Pertinent plans, maps, drawings and black-and-white photos illustrate the volume. Includes a bibliography and index.

Greco-Roman Africa

For specific antiquities sites, see also the tourism handbooks and guides in Part Three.

339. **Atlas of the Classical World.** Edited by A. A. M. von der Heyden and H. H. Scullard. London: Thomas Nelson, 1959. 221 p.

A companion volume to the *Atlas of the Early Christian World*, this valuable reference deals exclusively with pagan antiquity. Large, clear, colorful maps and plans, black-and-white photos and text display the geography, archaeology and history of the Greco-Roman world. The Punic wars and the incursions of the Roman Empire into North Africa are covered (with the exception of Egypt). An interpretive index is provided.

340. **Atlas of the Early Christian World.** Compiled, translated and edited by Frederik van der Meer, Christine Mohrman, Mary F. Hedlund, and H. H. Rowley. London: Thomas Nelson, 1958. 215 p.

Part of a series of historical atlases originally published in Amsterdam by Elsevier, this impressive volume offers 42 large, detailed and colorful historical maps showing the development and spread of the Christian faith from the first to the eighth centuries of the common era. The earliest known churches in North Africa were at Alexandria in Egypt and at Cyrene in the Pentapolis. Maps display the Roman Empire at the time of Diocletian, reaching from ancient western Mauretania (now Morocco) to Thebes. Individual maps feature the dioceses of Egypt, Tripolitana, Numidia etc., sites of martyrdom, monasticism and pilgrimage, and the area of Hippo Regius and Carthage during the time of St Augustine.

The maps, however, comprise only a small part of the volume, which is a fully-illustrated and annotated guide to the antiquities of the region: the artifacts, structures and physical sites. Scrupulous indexes to geographical names, persons, and things (including synods and councils) are provided.

341. **Atlas of the Greek and Roman World in Antiquity.** Edited by Nicholas G. L. Hammond. Park Ridge, NJ: Noyes Press, 1981. viii, 56 p. ISBN 0-8155-5060-X.

The range of this work is from the Neolithic Age to the 6th century A.D. It concentrates of course on Greece and the Aegean, Italy and Sicily, but there is information on Roman North Africa, including Egypt and Aethiopia (now Sudan). The maps are monochrome but exceptionally clear and detailed. An index and three appendices—a chronology of Greco-Roman colonies and two tables linking ancient place names to modern European locations—are provided.

342. **Der Neue Pauly: Enzyklopädie der Antike.** Edited by Hubert Cancik and Helmuth Schneider. Stuttgart; Weimar: Verlag J.B. Metzler, 1996. Ongoing multivolume publication. ISBN 3-476-01470-3 (set).

Publication of this new edition of the comprehensive and authoritative Pauly encyclopedia of Greco-Roman antiquity in German is now underway; six volumes have appeared so far. This massive work is intended for the scholar and specialist with knowledge of primary sources and original languages. The Mediterranean coast of Africa will be covered as appropriate; see for example the entries on "Afrika," "Ägypten" and Greco-Roman Alexandria. Beautifully detailed and very sharply printed maps are included, and there are some graphical timelines or genealogies, plans, and line drawings of artifacts and structures.

343. **Dictionnaire Encyclopedique du Christianisme Ancien.** Edited by Angelo Di Berardino and François Vial. [Paris]: Cerf, 1990. 2 v. ISBN 2-204-03017-1

Translation of: *Dizionario Patristico e di Antichità Cristiane.*

This very heavy two-volume work provides ample coverage of early Christianity in Africa. Signed entries with bibliographical references are dense and detailed: a scholar's knowledge of primary sources and original languages is assumed.

344. **Encyclopedia of Early Christianity.** Second edition. Edited by Everett Ferguson. New York; London: Garland, 1997. 2 v. ISBN 0-8153-1663-1.

A scholarly ready reference relying heavily on original and primary sources, this work presents concise but carefully-written alphabetized entries on the history and theology of the early Church. Christianity along the northern coast of Africa, from Gibraltar to the Nile Valley, is within the scope of this work. Places, persons, antiquities and doctrines are used as headings, and each entry provides at least a few bibliographical references, and often an extensive list (cf. "Cyril of Alexandria") of scholarly sources in various European languages. The Roman history of sites like Carthage is fully covered.

345. Grant, Michael. **Atlas of Classical History.** Fifth edition. New York: Oxford University Press, 1994. Unpaginated. ISBN 0-19-521074-3.

This collection of 91 monochrome historical maps contains no text at all, but the maps are informative and very clearly reproduced. Most of them would make excellent slides or transparencies. Coverage of ancient North Africa and Egypt is incidental here: the main focus is Europe. An index of place names is provided, but for the subjects of these maps one must browse the "List of Maps" or leaf through the book itself.

Byzantine, Medieval and Ottoman Eras

346. **Imperial Legacy: the Ottoman Imprint on the Balkans and the Modern Middle East.** Edited by L. Carl Brown. New York: Columbia University Press, 1996. xvi, 337 p. ISBN 0-231-10304-2.

Not a reference work, this scholarly interpretation of the historical meaning of Ottoman Empire for the modern world nevertheless contains several useful features. In particular, there is a country-by-country table of the dates and duration of Ottoman rule, and a brief summary of each country's conquest and loss by the Ottomans (simplified to account for changes in boundaries over time). There is also a fully-annotated select bibliography (pp. 307-313) and a superior index.

347. Bosworth, Clifford Edmund. **The Islamic Dynasties: a Chronological and Genealogical Handbook.** Edinburgh: Edinburgh University Press, 1967. 245 p. *Islamic Surveys;* 5. ISBN 0-202-15009-7.

Older, much-appreciated edition of Bosworth's *The New Islamic Dynasties.*

348. Bosworth, Clifford Edmund. **The New Islamic Dynasties: a Chronological and Genealogical Manual.** Enlarged and updated edition. New York: Columbia University Press, 1996. xxvi, 389 p. ISBN 0-231-10714-5.

A very welcome new edition of Bosworth's essential reference, *The Islamic Dynasties* (1967). Each chapter provides a capsule chronology of a particular dynasty, a narrative history, and a very sophisticated bibliography based upon primary sources. The work covers 17 noble families of Arab Northwest Africa and Spain, the royal houses of Egypt, Chad and Sudan, the sultans of Harar (Ethiopia), and the Western Sahel dynasties of Mali, Niger and Hausaland (the

Keita, Songhay and Fulani). The volume is organized geographically, with a detailed names index. Bosworth's work is an indispensable reference for medieval and Islamic history.

349. Graf, Georg. **Geschichte der Christlichen Arabischen Literatur.** Vatican City: Biblioteca Apostolica Vaticana, 1944-1953. 5 v. *Studi e Testi;* v. 118, 133, 146, 147, 172.

Like Brockelmann's classic work, this is not a narrative history, but an intricately annotated catalog of manuscripts in Arabic, with important prefatory remarks and background material. Biblical texts and fragments, lectionaries, apocryphal texts and pseudepigrapha, patristics, hagiography, documents of the ecumenical councils and liturgical literature are all included. Coverage extends from antiquity to the 19th century. Vol. 5 is an index to the whole work.

350. Humphreys, R. Stephen. **Islamic History: a Framework for Inquiry.** Revised edition. Princeton: Princeton University Press, 1991. xiv, 401 p. ISBN 0-691-03145-2.

Not simply a bibliography, this complex and ambitious work is conceived as a guide to the subject area of early and medieval Islamic history (AD 600-1500). Political and social history is the lens through which the subject is viewed, while religion and culture are considered "only insofar as they throw light on questions of social structure and political power" (Preface, p. ix).

Part I is a major bibliographical analysis of the reference tools and sources needed in the study of Islamic civilization; Humphreys describes and evaluates these materials at length and discusses how to use them. The important dictionaries and encyclopedias, bibliographies and indexes, grammars and lexicons, atlases, gazetteers and geographies, chronologies and genealogies, textual studies, concordances and commentaries on the Qur'an and Hadith, the catalogs of research libraries and archives, histories and handbooks of literature, numismatics, epigraphy, art, architecture and archaeology studies are all set forth for the reader, with a summary of their contents and an indication of the suitability of each work to various kinds of research undertakings.

This work, written as an extended essay, offers a careful bibliographic index; in addition, a names and subject index is provided.

351. Mantran, Robert. **Great Dates in Islamic History.** New York: Facts on File, 1996. xii, 404 p. ISBN 0-8160-2935-0.

Translation of Mantran's *Les Grandes Dates de l'Islam* (1990), with additional material.

This interesting volume combines a series of event chronologies with some textual interpretation and several fact boxes and almanac-style features (a table of the Islamic calendar, nine historical maps,etc.). The whole work is organized into historical units, then geographically by region within those units; therefore, it is possible to glance through the table of contents, picking out "The Maghrib" or "Sub-Saharan Africa" in various time periods. For more precise factfinding, there is a very tiny but helpful index. A simple glossary of terms is also provided.

352. McCarthy, Justin. **The Arab World, Turkey and the Balkans (1878-1914): a Handbook of Historical Statistics.** Boston: G.K. Hall, 1982. xxx, 309 p. *A Reference Publication in International Historical Statistics.* ISBN 0-8161-8164-0.

A fascinating selection of Ottoman statistical documents, translated into English, detailing economic and administrative activity of all kinds, as well as population, health and education data. The census of the city of Istanbul for the year 1886, divided by religion, sex and age, is reproduced here; exports of wheat, barley, olive oil and mohair over a 30-year period, and recorded temperatures and rainfall in each province, are available. Unfortunately, the work provides data only on the Ottoman provinces east of Egypt, with no material on northern Africa. (By the time period covered, European involvement in the area had eclipsed Ottoman influence.) The volume is very much in need of a better subject index.

353. McCarthy, Justin. **The Ottoman Turks: an Introductory History to 1923.** London; New York: Longman, 1997. xv, 406 p. ISBN 0-582-25656-9.

A comprehensive narrative history of the Ottoman Empire, capable of serving a number of reference functions.

The volume is amply illustrated with black-and-white photos and artwork, and contains many small but clearly-printed monochrome historical maps. The table of contents sets forth the overall plan of the work, and an index is also provided; material on northern Africa is scattered throughout the volume, so quite a bit of time working with the index is required to find it. There is also a helpful glossary.

354. Rahman, H. U. **A Chronology of Islamic History, 570-1000 C.E.** Boston: G.K. Hall, 1989. xvi, 181 p. ISBN 0-8161-9067-4.

Not a tabular chronology, but a fairly detailed and readable narrative history of the early spread and establishment of Islam. The conquest of northern Africa is described here, especially in Egypt. Some useful features for reference work are three simple maps, genealogies of the Umayyads and Abbasids, and a decent index.

355. Sauvaget, Jean. **Introduction to the Study of the Muslim East: a Bibliographical Guide.** Based on the second edition as recast by Claude Cahen. Berkeley: University of California Press, 1965. xxi, 252 p.

A fundamental work still cited by scholars. This English edition of Sauvaget's *Introduction à l'Histoire de l'Orient Musulman* includes editorial enhancements: some additional materials, updated bibliographic data, and corrections of earlier errors. Because of this, the French-speaking reader is also advised to consult this edition.

The scope of the work incorporates the largest extent of the Ottoman Empire, including Mediterranean Africa. The special relevance of North Africa to French scholars is noted (p. 4); Chapter 24, "The Muslim West," is particularly helpful. One should realize that this is not an itemized bibliography, but rather a book-length bibliographic essay. It is less suited to ready reference than to careful study. Unfortunately, there is neither a titles index nor a subject index; a names index is provided.

356. Spuler, Bertold. **The Age of the Caliphs.** Translated by F. R. C. Bagley. Princeton: Markus Wiener, 1995. xxx, 138 p. ISBN 1-55876-095-4 and 1-55876-079-2.

A compact edition in English of Spuler's *Geschichte der islamischen Länder* (1952), part of the massive reference *Handbuch der Orientalistik*. This version will make accessible to many new readers a well-known narrative history of Islam's expansion from the lifetime of Muhammad to the invasion of Baghdad in 1258. Of particular interest is Chapter V, on Islam in Spain and North Africa. The volume has a few maps and photos, an appendix of dynastic tables, a subdivided bibliography of classic Orientalist works, and a two-part names index.

357. Wheatcroft, Andrew. **The Ottomans.** London: Viking, 1993. xxix, 322 p. ISBN 0-670-84412-8.

Not so much a comprehensive history as a reflection of major themes in the Ottoman age. However, the volume contains some features valuable for reference: 45 intriguing plates, some of them in vivid color; a useful bibliography; an index, in which material pertaining to northern Africa may be found; and one very attractive monochrome map showing the farthest extent of Ottoman control into the African continent.

358. Young, M. J. L, J. D. Latham, and R. B. Serjeant. **Religion, Learning and Science in the Abbasid Period.** Cambridge: Cambridge University Press, 1990. xxii, 587 p. *Cambridge History of Arabic Literature.* ISBN 0-521-32763-3.

This volume of the authoritative *Cambridge History of Arabic Literature* concentrates on aspects of culture in which Arab scholars of the medieval age were very important. Grammar and lexicography, law, administration, biography, history, philosophy, theology, mathematics, applied science and technology, astronomy, astrology, geography and navigation, medicine, and Christian and Jewish documents are all covered here. The subdivided bibliography is of considerable value; a good map and glossary are included. Material on the scholars of Abbasid/Umayyad Africa can be found in the very detailed index (though prior knowledge of the field is helpful).

Colonial Africa and the History of Slavery

359. **L'Afrique Française du Nord, Bibliographie Militaire: des Ouvrages Français on Traduits en Français et des Articles des Principales Revues Françaises Relatifs à l'Algérie a la Tunisie et au Maroc.** Reprinted 1975. Paris: Imprimerie Nationale, 1930-1935. 2 v. ISBN 0-404-56206-X (set).

A major source for documentation of the French colonial era in its North African territories. These two thick volumes contain more than 9400 annotated citations. Vol. 1 covers the period from 1830 to 1926; Vol. 2 commences in 1927. The citations are topically organized, and there are no indexes.

360. **Atlas of the British Empire.** New York; Oxford: Facts on File, 1989. 256 p. ISBN 0-8160-1995-9.

A colorful and ambitious volume chronicling the expansion and contraction of British imperial power. Large maps, photos and artwork illustrate the book. Africa and the Middle East are covered, with interesting material on Suez in particular.

361. **British Documents on Foreign Affairs: Reports and Papers From the Foreign Office Confidential Print.** Edited by Kenneth Bourne, D. Cameron Watt, and Michael Partridge. Bethesda, MD: University Publications of America, 1987-1997. 409 v. ISBN 0-89093-616-1.

This extraordinary multivolume reference contains the full text of tens of thousands of documents generated by and for the British government during the decades of the fullest extension of British influence worldwide. These are not simply collections of random correspondence, nor are they propaganda materials for public consumption: they are publications of the Foreign Office Confidential Print, prepared for internal circulation among the policymakers and bureaucrats of various levels and departments of government. Dated and signed memoranda and letters and lengthy narrative or descriptive reports from staff members in the field are reproduced here.

The collection is classified first by historical period: Part I covers from the mid-nineteenth century to the First World War, Part II up to the Second World War, and Part III the war itself, 1940-45. The collection is then divided into series dealing with various areas of the world. Part I, Series B, "The Near and Middle East," uses a fairly broad interpretation of this geographical scope, including North Africa, Egypt and the Sudan, with two volumes documenting the Ottoman Empire in North Africa. The Sahara and the Horn, especially "Abyssinia and Its Neighbours," are found in Series G. In Part II, Morocco is included in Series G (vols. 23-25); Part II also provides no less than twenty volumes on Egypt and "The Soudan" or Sudan, plus two more volumes on the Suez Canal, 1914-1939.

The organization of the documents in each volume is basically chronological. Informative introductions to each volume are provided, but the documents themselves are reproduced in facsimile form without any editorial remarks. A table of contents identifies each document by number and type (report, memo, despatch), by author and date, and by topic in a simple caption. No indexes are provided. Patient searching is required to find material pertaining to specific persons, events or subjects, and a knowledge of each time period is important.

362. **Colonialism in Africa 1870-1960.** General editors Peter Duignan and L. H. Gann. Cambridge: Cambridge University Press, 1969-1973. 5 v. ISBN 0-521-07859-8.

A Cambridge multi-volume history concentrating on the details of the complex interaction of Africa and Europe in the colonial era. Narrative and interpretive scholarly articles attempt to reexamine imperialist assumptions and "write African history in a more Afrocentric fashion" (Preface). The articles rely on a large corpus of research meeting the needs of the specialist rather more than the general reader. The series is intended to resolve the ideological extremes on the subject of imperialism "by reference to concrete facts." The majority of the material deals with sub-Saharan Africa. In Vol. 5—a giant annotated bibliography and guide to reference works—material can be found relating to Mauritania, Mali, Ethiopia, Sudan, Niger and Chad. Vol. 5 also offers information about relevant collections in the libraries, archives and research centers of the United States, Western Europe and parts of Africa; it also provides an unusual subject guide to works on Africa published up to about 1971.

363. **The Historical Encyclopedia of World Slavery.** Edited by Junius P. Rodriguez. Santa Barbara, CA: ABC-Clio, 1997. 2 v. ISBN 0-87436-885-5.

A substantial new reference on the history of slavery worldwide, covering the ancient Near East, Greece and Rome, the Americas, etc. The concentration of slave-trading activities along the western coast of Africa included regions inhabited by the Wolof, Fulani and Songhai peoples, and articles about Mali and Mansa Kankan Musa reflect this.

Signed articles are concise, provide a few bibliographical references and sometimes a black-and-white photo, and are written in a direct prose style that could be accessible to high school students and undergraduates. Vol. 2 includes a 46-page general bibliography (subdivided) and an effective index.

364. Baxter, Colin F. **The War in North Africa, 1940-1943: a Selected Bibliography.** Westport, CT: Greenwood, 1996. vii, 119 p. *Bibliographies of Battles and Leaders;* no. 16. ISBN 0-313-29120-9; ISSN 1056-7410.

This small volume does provide a list of more than 500 titles pertaining to World War II and supplying material on the North Africa campaign. Some 75 pages, however, are occupied by very interesting bibliographic essays on many different aspects of the war and stages of its development. Through the index, the reader can find Baxter's remarks on any particular work, in a context of related works and events.

365. Broc, Numa. **Dictionnaire Illustré des Explorateurs et Grands Voyageurs Français du XIXe Siècle.** Vol. 1: Afrique. Paris: Éditions du Comité des Travaux Historiques et Scientifiques, 1988. xxxi, 346 p.

A fascinating, well-organized and easy-to-use biographical encyclopedia, filled with contemporary photographs and sketch-maps. Even the very brief entries include at least a few bibliographical references, and more substantial entries (e.g., "Foucauld, Charles de") offer several suggestions for further reading.

There is substantial emphasis upon "Afrique du Nord-Sahara" and "Bassin du Nil," and a geographical index makes these entries readily accessible. There is a general index as well. The copy examined included a pocket with five beautiful loose-leaf period maps in full color, showing both physical and political geography in detail.

366. Drescher, Seymour and Stanley L. Engerman. **A Historical Guide to World Slavery.** New York: Oxford University Press, 1998. xxiv, 429 p. ISBN 0-19-512091-4.

Lengthy, signed articles on broad headings summarizing the history of slavery are presented encyclopedia-style in this one-volume reference. Material pertaining to northern Africa may be found under these broad headings (e.g., "Slave Trade: Trans-Saharan") or in the general index.

Each article provides bibliographical references, and some have black-and-white illustrations. The very wide historical and geographical scope may weaken this reference: it tries to encompass everything from Biblical times through African enslavement to Nazi forced labor and present-day human rights abuses. For this reason, it can offer only a thinly-spread overview of each topic.

367. Gann, L. H. and Peter Duignan. **African Proconsuls: European Governors in Africa.** New York: Free Press (Macmillan), 1978. xi, 548 p. ISBN 0-02-922290-0.

A collection of lengthy biographical essays on 16 of the noteworthy colonial authorities in Africa, representing France, Britain, Belgium, Portugal and Germany. In addition, there is an introductory essay on colonial leadership in general for each of these imperial powers. The essays provide extensive bibliographical references. Some tables of data and a small collection of photographic plates are included, but no maps. There is a useful general index.

368. Griffiths, Ieuan Ll. **The African Inheritance.** London; New York: Routledge, 1995. 216 p. ISBN 0-415-01091-8.

African history and political geography in a small one-volume work, concentrating on Africa's colonial experience and its consequences. This is more than a simple handbook or introduction: the work offers thoughtful analysis of many of the key pressures on contemporary African states. Many significant small maps and figures illustrate the text. Much of the information pertains to sub-Saharan Africa, but there is useful material on the Maghreb, Sahel and Horn; e.g., a discussion of the Western Sahara conflict. A careful index helps the reader discover this material.

369. Hogg, Peter C. **The African Slave Trade and Its Suppression: a Classi-fied and Annotated Bibliography of Books, Pamphlets and Periodical Arti-cles.** London: Frank Cass, 1973. xvii, 409 p. ISBN 0-7146-2775-5.

A section on the Sudan begins on page 32; the materials listed are often relevant to Egypt as well. Sources pertinent to Algeria and other coastal states, Chad and other areas of the interior, and specific enslaved peoples (Nubians, Ethiopians, Berbers, Dinkas, etc.) can be found with patient searching. The geographical name index is of some help in locating these materials; an author index and anonymous title index are also provided.

370. Hopkins, J. F. P. **Letters From Barbary, 1576-1774: Arabic Documents in the Public Records Office.** Oxford: Oxford University Press (British Acad-emy), 1982. xvii, 112 p. *Oriental Documents;* VI. ISBN 0-19-726010-1.

A remarkable collection of documents, annotated and translated into Eng-lish, originating "for the most part from British [diplomatic] missions to the Bar-bary States, i.e. Algiers, Morocco, Tripoli and Tunis, from the later half of the 16th century until almost the end of the 18th" (Introduction). A small portion of the documents in the Public Records Office are in Arabic, and they are the ones presented in this volume. An interesting and readable introduction, a glossary that helpfully notes the presumed Arabic radicals of each word, footnotes, a bib-liography and a general index are provided.

371. Hurewitz, J. C. **The Middle East and North Africa in World Politics: a Documentary Record.** Second edition, revised and enlarged. New Haven: Yale University Press, 1975. 3 v. ISBN 0-300-01294-2.

These volumes present the complete text in English of hundreds of docu-ments essential to the political history of the area. These documents may be trea-ties, conference declarations, decrees, legal conventions, mandates, defense or other military alliances, or international economic agreements governing rail-roads, petroleum, banking, fishing, etc. Colonial administrative documents are well represented (e.g., "Law on the Acquisition of French Citizenship by Mus-lims in Algeria, 4 February 1919") as are the relevant portions of major treaties (sections on Morocco and Egypt in the Versailles Peace, for instance). Vol. 1 covers the period of "European Expansion 1914-1945"; Vol. 2 is "British-French Supremacy 1914-1945"; Vol. 3 is "British-French Withdrawal and Soviet-American Rivalry 1945- ." Each volume contains a lengthy bibliography, but no indexes: access is obtained through a table of contents only, listing the documents in chronological order.

372. Jenkins, Everett Jr. **Pan-African Chronology: a Comprehensive Refer-ence to the Black Quest for Freedom in Africa, the Americas, Europe and Asia, 1400-1865.** Jefferson, NC: McFarland & Co., 1996. viii, 440 p. ISBN 0-7864-0139-7.

The geographical scope of this work is extremely broad, but careful disci-pline of the chronology helps keep order in this information-rich work. The writ-er's aim is to chronicle the complex interaction of Africans with the rest of the world during these very eventful years, with special attention to the displace-ment and enslavement of Africans and their efforts to recover their freedom. A not-very-successful names and subject index (subdivided by year) and a brief bibliography are included. The reader longs for source notes to document these events, but perhaps printing them would have swallowed the chronology in bib-liographic detail. The work is nevertheless a valuable contribution to an under-documented field.

373. Maddox, Gregory and Timothy K. Welliver. **Colonialism and National-ism in Africa: a Four-Volume Anthology of Scholarly Articles.** New York: Garland, 1993. 4 v. ISBN 0-8153-1388-8.

A great deal of information and analysis from a variety of viewpoints is pre-sented here. Unfortunately, this collection does not lend itself well to reference work, as there is no evident order or controlling structure, and no helpful schol-arly apparatus, such as an index. It should also be noted that, since these articles are reprinted, they may have appeared considerably earlier than the collection's publication date.

374. Miller, Joseph C. **Slavery: a Worldwide Bibliography, 1900-1982.** White Plains, NY: Kraus International, 1985. xxvii, 451 p. ISBN 0-527-63659-2.

This unannotated bibliography on the whole subject of slavery is not easy to use, but contains much valuable material. A section on the Muslim slave trade includes some sources pertinent to Egypt, North Africa and the Sahara, Sudan and parts of West and East Africa. A section on slave transport across the Sahara and via the Red Sea is also relevant. An author index and not-very-successful subject/keyword index are provided.

375. Miller, Joseph C. **Slavery and Slaving in World History: a Bibliogra-phy, 1900-1991.** Millwood, NY: Kraus International Publications, 1993. xvii, 556 p. ISBN 0-527-63660-6.

This very substantial reference prepared under the guidance of a noted authority in the field is clearly organized, offering access through the table of contents to materials on Africa, on Muslim areas, and on the Saharan slave trade. (There is also a simple keyword index much in need of improvement.)

The distinctive contribution of this work is its collection of reviews, essays, unpublished papers and conference reports, important encyclopedia entries, schol-arly articles in periodicals, "serious journalism," and portions of multi-authored edited collections, all materials that involve time-consuming efforts to locate. En-tries are not annotated, but their content is usually apparent in the titles.

376. Miller, Joseph C. **Slavery and Slaving in World History: a Bibliogra-phy, 1992-1996.** Vol. II. Armonk, NY; London: M.E. Sharpe, 1999. xxi, 244 p. ISBN 0-7656-0280-6.

An addition to Miller's earlier work, similarly organized and formatted.

377. Morsy, Magali. **North Africa 1800-1900: a Survey From the Nile Valley to the Atlantic.** London; New York: Longmans, 1984. 356 p. ISBN 0-582-78376-3.

A narrative history and analysis of events in northern Africa in the nineteenth century. Though densely written, the work is well organized, and an index is provided. The volume offers thirteen clearly-printed monochrome historical maps and 33 dynastic charts, chronologies and tables of data, many of them unusual and interesting (see, for example, "Trans-Saharan Trade Routes" on p. 54). Chapters are devoted to Egypt, Algeria, Tunisia and Sudan, but material on other parts of northern Africa can be located in the index. (Unfortunately, a manufacturing error has left pages 7-22 out of the copy examined.)

378. Olson, James S. and Robert Shadle. **Historical Dictionary of the British Empire.** Westport, CT: Greenwood, 1996. 2 v. ISBN 0-313-27917-9.

A substantial work, providing signed articles ranging from one paragraph to 4-5 pages, alphabetized for ready reference.

Entries for individuals are brief biographical essays, outlining the life and work of the person and giving an indication of his or her significance. Each entry includes at least one bibliographical reference, and cross-references to other relevant entries. There is also a subdivided bibliography of recent scholarly works (1980-95), and a useful general index. Information on Egypt and the Sudan is easily located.

379. Olson, William J. **Britain's Elusive Empire in the Middle East, 1900-1921: an Annotated Bibliography.** With the assistance of Addeane S. Caelleigh. New York: Garland, 1982. xvii, 404 p. *Themes in European Expansion: Exploration, Colonization and the Impact of Empire*, v. 2; *Garland Reference Library of Social Science,* v. 109. ISBN 0-8240-9273-2.

Materials on Egypt and the Sudan are found in Chapters 4-6 of this extensively-annotated work; the best way to locate them is through the subdivided topical index. Coverage of the Sudan is limited. Citations on the Ottoman Empire may be helpful for North Africa. A long introductory essay is provided.

380. Palmer, Alan. **Dictionary of the British Empire and Commonwealth.** London: John Murray, 1996. xviii, 395 p. ISBN 0-7195-5650-3.

Concise entries, informative and objective in tone, compose this ready reference encompassing the whole horizon of Britain's imperial era. Coverage of northern Africa is not extensive, but Egypt and the Sudan are certainly within the scope of this work. The valuable index points to terms not used as headings, such as "Khartoum." Palmer manages to sum up the extraordinary careers of men like "Chinese Gordon" and T.E. Lawrence with one paragraph each. An appendix lists the Commonwealth countries and provides some basic statistics, and a subdivided bibliography with some commentary is provided.

381. Ponko, Vincent Jr. **Britain in the Middle East, 1921-1956: an Annotated Bibliography.** New York: Garland, 1990. liv, 513 p. *Themes in European Expansion: Exploration, Colonization and the Impact of Empire*, v. 9; *Garland Reference Library of Social Science*, v. 357. ISBN 0-8240-8551-5.

An annotated bibliography of materials dealing with the British Empire's engagements in the Middle East. On the African continent, only Egypt is included; Chapters V and X pertain to Suez. One must take issue with an index that does not list the word "Copt" (though there is mention of Christian and other minority groups).

382. Savage, Elizabeth. **The Human Commodity: Perspectives on the Trans-Saharan Slave Trade.** London: Frank Cass, 1992. 279 p. ISBN 0-7146-3469-7.

A collection of serious articles by important scholars concentrating on displaced, deported and enslaved Africans on the Mediterranean coast, the Sahara, the Niger River region and the Nile Valley. The articles provide detailed bibliographies and source notes, and often tables of data, maps, graphs and other reference helps (see especially Ralph A. Austen, "The Mediterranean Islamic Slave Trade out of Africa: a Tentative Census," pp. 214-248).

One of the contributions, by Joseph C. Miller, is itself a sophisticated bibliography of "Muslim Slavery and Slaving" (pp. 249-271). The volume also includes a basic index.

383. Turbet-Delof, Guy. **La Presse Périodique Française et l'Afrique Barbaresque au XVIIe Siècle (1611-1715).** Geneva: Librairie Droz, 1973. 189 p. *Histoire des Idées et Critique Littéraire;* vol. 138.

A guide to historical sources comprising coverage of the Maghreb in the French press during the age of exploration. There is an index of personal names. The work is organized by source, place and theme, but an index of place names and subjects would be helpful.

Independent African States

384. **Africa Since 1914: a Historical Bibliography.** Santa Barbara, CA: ABC-Clio, 1985. ix, 402 p. *Clio Bibliography Series;* no. 17. ISBN 0-87436-395-0.

A substantial one-volume bibliography covering "a decade (1973-1982) of journal literature on modern Africa since 1914" (Preface). Using a keyword index system, the compilers brought together this body of articles with abstracts and organized them geographically, with an initial section relating to Africa generally (organized by topic and historical period). Materials on northern Africa are easy to find, and every nation is represented. In addition, there is a subject index built upon strings of descriptors, and an author index as well.

385. **Foreign Relations of the United States, 1958-1960.** Vol. XIII: Arab-Israeli dispute; United Arab Republic; North Africa. Washington: US Government Printing Office, 1992. xxx, 928 p. Department of State Publication 9929.

This volume and some others in the massive *Foreign Relations of the United States* series contains the verbatim text of correspondence, declassified documents, memos, records, policy directives, etc., reflecting the diplomatic activity of the United States during the Eisenhower administration. The volumes are carefully organized, with a clear table of contents, an index and other reference helps: of particular value is a list identifying persons mentioned in the text.

US relations with the UAR (in which Egypt was a partner with Syria), covering planning for the High Dam and its Cold War implications, North Africa as a region, oil exploration in Libya, Algeria and US policy toward the FLN, and relations with Morocco and Tunisia are documented in this volume. Helpful footnotes identify the source of each document and often provide cross-references to other relevant material or offer a bit of context.

386. **Foreign Relations of the United States, 1958-1960.** Vol. XIV: Africa. Washington: US Government Printing Office, 1992. xxv, 784 p. Department of State Publication 10006.

This volume contains chapters on the Horn (Ethiopia, Somalia) and the Sudan. Helpful footnotes identify the source of each document and often provide cross-references to other relevant material or offer a bit of context.

387. **Foreign Relations of the United States, 1961-1963.** Vol. XXI: Africa. Washington: US Government Printing Office, 1995. xxviii, 682 p. Department of State Publication 10290.

This volume and some others in the massive *Foreign Relations of the United States* series contains the verbatim text of correspondence, declassified documents, memos, records, policy directives, etc., reflecting the diplomatic activity of the United States during the Kennedy administration. The volumes are carefully organized, with a clear table of contents, an index and other reference helps: of particular value is a list identifying persons mentioned in the text.

This volume contains chapters on North Africa as a region, Algeria, Libya, Morocco, Tunisia, and the Horn. Helpful footnotes identify the source of each document and often provide cross-references to other relevant material or offer a bit of context.

388. **The Middle East in Conflict: a Historical Bibliography.** Santa Barbara, CA: ABC-Clio, 1985. ix, 302 p. *Clio Bibliography Series;* no. 19. ISBN 0-87436-381-0.

An index of journal literature studying developments in the Middle East, the Maghreb, Sudan and, to a lesser extent, Ethiopia and Somalia in the 20th century (up to 1982). Entries pertaining to history and related social sciences and humanities are organized topically and geographically; topics include the Western Sahara conflict of 1973-83. More than 2000 journals in 40 languages (both

European and some Middle Eastern and African publications) are covered. Abstracts are provided for every entry. A detailed subject index built upon strings of descriptors offers efficient access to this useful compendium of material.

389. Modernization in the Middle East: the Ottoman Empire and Its Afro-Asian Successors. Edited by Cyril E. Black and L. Carl Brown. Princeton, NJ: Darwin Press, 1992. xviii, 418 p. *Studies on Modernization.* ISBN 0-87850-085-5.

Produced by a team of scholars under the auspices of the Center of International Studies at Princeton, this volume includes Egypt and Tunisia among the countries covered. Unfortunately, this material is distributed throughout the book, and the index leaves quite a bit of room for improvement.

Of importance, however, is the very informative bibliographical essay (pp. 335-356), divided by chapter. There is also a general bibliography, a chronology and three useful maps.

390. The Third World Without Superpowers: the Collected Documents of the Non-Aligned Countries. Edited by Odette Jankowitsch and Karl P. Sauvant. Dobbs Ferry, NY: Oceana, 1978-1993. 12 v. ISBN 0-379-1046-2074.

This substantial collection presents the full text (in facsimile form) of fundamental documents and declarations prepared by the countries of the Non-Aligned Movement at their conferences or summits since 1955, arranged chronologically. Several of the states of northern Africa were active in this movement since its very inception, while others became involved at later stages. These documents constitute a basic resource for research into the movement and its varied history. Editorial contributions are minimal, however, and there is no indexing.

391. Atiyeh, George N. The Contemporary Middle East, 1948-1973: a Selective and Annotated Bibliography. Boston: G.K. Hall, 1975. xxvi, 664 p. ISBN 0-8161-1085-9.

Atiyeh's major work cites more than 6000 monographs and journal articles, chiefly in the social sciences. Materials listed are mainly in English, French, German, Italian and Spanish, but also include some in Arabic, Turkish and Persian.

The compilation is organized geographically, with large sections on the Middle East and Arab countries generally; one section covers the Nile Valley (Egypt and Sudan), and another North Africa (the Maghreb as a region, then Libya, Tunisia, Algeria and Morocco). Within each section, works are organized topically. Atiyeh's annotations would be very valuable to the researcher, identifying the theme and conclusion of each work. An author index and helpful subject index are provided.

392. Bercovitch, Jacob and Richard Jackson. International Conflict: a Chronological Encyclopedia of Conflicts and Their Management, 1945-1995. Washington: Congressional Quarterly, 1997. xxviii, 372 p. ISBN 1-56802-195-X.

Perhaps if one had heard vague reports of a conflict over Lake Chad in 1983 and wanted a capsule two-paragraph account of the dispute, one might try this volume (though it is easy to think of several other references one ought to try first). The tiny snips of narrative strung together in this book cannot begin to do justice to any of the events here recorded. There is a tendentious tone to many entries; accounts here of Suez and the 1967 war seem designed to vilify Nasser and justify Israeli foreign policy. The volume includes a sizable subdivided bibliography and a capable index.

393.   Bourges, Hervé and Claude Wauthier. **Les 50 Afriques.** Paris: Éditions du Seuil, 1979. 2 v. ISBN 2-02-005359-4.

A guide or handbook to the nations of post-colonial Africa, this work provides individual articles describing the geography, economy, population and recent political history of every country on the continent (not only those with ties to France). A clear and detailed small map, a brief bibliography (usually 6-10 entries, but in the case of Algeria, 25) and a ready-reference table accompany each article. Vol. 1 features Le Maghreb, L'Afrique du Nord-Est, La Corne de l'Afrique, and L'Afrique Sahélo-Soudanienne. A names index is provided for each volume, but unfortunately, no subject index.

394.   Cook, Chris. **The Making of Modern Africa: a Guide to Archives.** New York: Facts on File, 1995. v, 218 p. ISBN 0-8160-2071-X.

This unusual and impressive work offers a description and location information for the personal papers and correspondence of leading figures in African history from about 1889 to1980. It does not repeat references to governmental or official archives of the former colonial powers or newly-independent states available elsewhere; instead, it concentrates on "the myriad private papers of those persons involved in the unfolding history of modern Africa" (Preface). These include governors and viceroys, senior civil administrators and military officers, and other public figures, including African politicians and opposition leaders.

The entries are alphabetically arranged for ready reference, with a very accurate and detailed subject index. There is also an index of archives, showing at a glance relevant holdings in a particular location. Each concise entry provides a full name, dates of birth and death, a brief identification and résumé of the individual's roles or offices in Africa, a note describing the nature and subject of the existing papers and the archive where they can be found.

395.   Darch, Colin. **A Soviet View of Africa: an Annotated Bibliography on Ethiopia, Somalia and Djibouti.** Boston: G.K. Hall, 1980. xxxvi, 200 p. *Bibliographies and Guides in African Studies.* ISBN 0-8161-8365-1.

A work that does justice to the extensive and important literature in Russian pertaining to the Horn of Africa. Soviet involvement in the Marxist government of Ethiopia and in the political life of Somalia are only part of the picture. Darch also documents the ongoing activities of explorers and adventurers, diplomats and researchers in every subject area, and Russian clerics and scholars interested in the Ethiopian Orthodox Church.

In addition to the materials published in Russian, those produced in the Soviet Union in a non-Russian language (including Amharic) are collected in an appendix. The citations are organized according to "the Institute of Ethiopian Studies' modified version of Dewey Decimal Classification" (Introduction, p. xix). Many of the entries are annotated, but this is inconsistent: a few words, a cataloging contents note, or a full abstract may be provided. Book reviews and newspaper articles are found in appendices; there is a subject and a names index.

396. Grace, John and John Laffin. **Fontana Dictionary of Africa Since 1960: Events, Movements, Personalities.** London: Fontana Press, 1991. xix, 395 p. ISBN 0-0068-6214-4.

A sort of pocket paperback reference containing brief identifications of persons, places, organizations and vocabulary terms. The volume includes some other reference helps as well: a simple chronology, a bibliography, and a basic data box for each country. This work could be useful to high school or college students.

397. Shimoni, Yaacov and Evyatar Levine. **Political Dictionary of the Middle East in the 20th Century.** Supplement edited by Itamar Rabinovich and Haim Shaked. New York: Quadrangle/New York Times Book Co., 1972. 510 p. ISBN 0-8129-0482-6.

A one-volume ready reference providing "condensed information, alphabetically arranged, on countries and peoples, on national and political movements, parties and leaders, on ideas and ideologies, on disputes and wars, alliances and treaties" (Foreword). Designed for the English-language reader, the work uses a simplified transliteration method resembling that of press reports and newspapers; some cross-references indicate alternate forms of names and vocabulary terms (e.g., GADDAFI see Qaddhafi). The geographical scope is not specified, but seems to include Egypt, Sudan and Libya.

The authors and editors "have striven to present as accurate and objective a picture of the region as possible"; however, all of them are Israelis, some are members of the Israeli foreign service, and the editors note that "most of them are professional Orientalists" (p. 5).

Journals

398. **African Research and Documentation.** Three issues/year; 1973- . London: African Studies Association and SCOLMA. ISSN 0305-826X.

SCOLMA website at **www.brad.ac.uk/acad/dppc/dppclib/SCOLMA.html**

Produced by the Standing Conference on Library Materials on Africa, this journal focuses on the research and information needs of African Studies scholars, the African book and publishing trade, and the collection and management of archival materials on African history in world libraries. The editor is respected authority John McIlwaine; supplements to his important reference *Writings on African Archives* will appear in this journal regularly.

399. **Antiquities Africaines.** Annual; 1967- . Paris: Éditions CNRS. ISSN 0066-4871.

Published by the Centre National de la Recherche Scientifique, this journal presents scholarly research on the archaeology of northern Africa, "l'Afrique du Nord de la protohistoire à la conquête Arabe" (verso). Vol. 31 (1995) contained indexes for vols. 21-30 (1985-94).

400. **Archaeology.** Bimonthly, 1948- . New York: Archaeological Institute of America. ISSN 0003-8113.

Contents and abstracts available online at **www.archaeology.org/**

A glossy, attractive magazine featuring articles of a popular nature describing current excavations and discoveries in archaeology around the world. Articles are amply illustrated with color photos. Notices of some current books, museum exhibits and online resources are included. The important sites of Pharaonic, Nubian and Greco-Roman antiquity in northern Africa receive due attention. Suitable for the high school or college library.

401. **International Journal of African Historical Studies.** Three times/year; 1972- . Boston: African Studies Center, Boston University. ISSN 0361-7882.

Contents page available online at **gopher1.bu.edu/AFR/Journal.TOC.html**

Four or five research articles dealing with some aspect of Africa's history, from prehistoric times onward, appear in each issue of this scholarly journal. Articles are published in English or French. More than half of each issue is occupied by scores of 3-4 page signed book reviews or longer review articles. Oddly, these seem to be presented in no particular order, and issues are not indexed.

402. **Journal of African History.** Three issues/year; 1960- . Cambridge: Cambridge University Press. ISSN 0021-8537.

Descriptive website and contents page available online at **www.cup.org/ journals/jnlscat/afh/afh.html**

Lengthy scholarly articles with extensive bibliographical references make up the core of this journal. In addition, about one-third of each issue consists of at least 25-30 signed book reviews (about 2 pages each). A recent issue contained a major article by John Hunwick on religious vs. secular authority in the Songhay society (vol. 37, no. 2). Occasionally, an article is illustrated with maps, photos, tables of data or document facsimiles.

403. **Journal of the Economic and Social History of the Orient.** Three times/year; 1957- . Leiden: E.J. Brill. ISSN 0022-4995.

Subscription information and back issues available at **www.brill.nl**

The "Orient" in this journal's title refers broadly to any part of Asia, and in any historical period, from ancient Mesopotamia to Edo (Tokyo). The Ottoman Empire and the Middle East generally are well represented. Themed issues are often presented; vol. 40, no. 2 focused on "women's history," while no. 4 studied "modernity" and its impact. Articles are published in English, French or German; they include footnotes and often extensive bibliographical references.

404. **Journal of Near Eastern Studies.** Quarterly; 1884- . Chicago: University of Chicago Press. ISSN 0022-2968.

Descriptive website at **www.journals.uchicago.edu/JNES/home.html**

A scholarly journal "devoted exclusively to an examination of the ancient and medieval civilizations of the Near East. It has contributions in archaeology, art, history, literature, linguistics, religion, law and science. Old Testament and Islamic studies are also featured." A publication of The Oriental Institute.

405. **Libyan Studies.** Annual; 1979- . London: Society for Libyan Studies. ISSN 0263-7189.

Contents and abstracts available online at **britac.britac.ac.uk/institutes/ libya/libstud.html**

Published by the Institute of Archaeology, this journal covers natural science, linguistics and history as well, but no social science or current events concerns. Several book reviews, some Society news and an annual report are included. Vol. 26 (1995) contained indexes for vols. 16-25 (1985-94).

406. **Mediterranean Historical Review.** Semiannual; 1986- . London: Frank Cass. ISSN 0951-8967.

A humanities journal devoted to scholarly work on the history of Mediterranean societies and civilizations, including 20th-century studies. Bibliographical references drawing from primary sources are included. There are also five or six substantial book reviews in each issue.

407. **Revue d'Histoire Maghrebine: Epoque Moderne et Contemporaine.** Quarterly (since 1995); 1974- . Zaghouan: Université de Tunis [sic]. ISSN 0330-8987.

Also titled: *North African Historical Review.*

An organization known as the Fondation Temimi pour la Recherche Scientifique et l'Information produces this journal, which applies itself to "l'histoire ottomane, morisco-andalouse" (cover), among other things. It contains as many as fifty articles in each issue in English, French, Spanish or Arabic, though the English at least is not always idiomatic.

408. **Slavery and Abolition: a Journal of Slave and Post-Slave Studies.** Three times/year; 1980- . London; Portland, OR: Frank Cass. ISSN 0144-039X.

Descriptive website and contents available online at **www.frankcass. com/jnls/sa.htm**

Societies involved in slavery, from ancient times to the present, are the subject of this scholarly journal. Historical articles with footnotes and bibliographical references, book reviews and review artcles are featured. Although North American concerns predominate, recent issues have included an article by Suzanne Miers, "Britain and the Suppression of Slavery in Ethiopia" (vol. 18, no. 3) and others on the central Sudan, Bambara slaves and the Upper Senegal. An annual bibliographic supplement (prepared by noted authority Joseph C. Miller) and an index are provided.

409. **Sudanic Africa: a Journal of Historical Sources.** Annual; 1990- . Bergen, Norway: Centre for Middle Eastern and Islamic Studies. ISSN 0803-0685.

Descriptive website and index page available online at **www.hf-fak.uib. no/smi/sa/sahome.html**

Among the editors of this scholarly journal is John O. Hunwick, one of the leading authorities in the world on the subject, author of *The Writings of Central Sudanic Africa* (in the new *Arabic Literature of Africa* series). This journal is a venue for the discussion of specific texts and sources in historical literature relating to the Sahel and Horn. Some book reviews appear in each issue.

Websites

410. Classics and Mediterranean Archaeology. University of Michigan. **rome. classics.lsa.umich.edu/welcome.html**

Search engine and many specialized links.

411. Clio en Afrique: l'Histoire Africaine en Langue Française. **newsup.univ-mrs. fr/~wclio-af/**

"Cette lettre d'information remplit un triple objectif, qui est celui du GDR (Groupe de Recherche du CNRS) tout entier: faciliter les échanges entre historiens français et francophones de l'Afrique, défendre la profession dans une conjoncture plutôt défavorable qui tient autant à l'afro-pessimisme ambiant qu'aux réorganisations institutionnelles de la carte scientifique, valoriser les recherches en langue française sur une planète où l'anglais est devenu la première langue scientifique." Online journal, published quarterly.

412. Internet African History Sourcebook. **http://www.fordham.edu/halsall/ africa/africasbook.html**

From earliest human origins to today's current issues; many links and full-text documents.

413. Internet Islamic History Sourcebook. **http://www.fordham.edu/halsall/ islam/islamsbook.html**

Many links and full-text documents; contains some material on Islamic Africa and the Maghreb.

414. Lepcis Magna: the Roman Empire in Africa. **www.alnpete.co.uk/ lepcis/porta.html**

Showcases the excavation of a Tripolitanian Roman city.

415. Mali Interactive. **www.ruf.rice.edu/~anth/arch/mali-interactive/index.html**

Information about Mali and archaeology, especially for teachers. Established by the leaders of an excavation by Rice University's anthropology department conducted at Jenné, "the earliest known urban settlement south of the Sahara and a UNESCO World Heritage site."

416. Oriental Institute. University of Chicago. **www-oi.uchicago.edu/OI/default.html**
   Sponsors of Chicago House at Luxor; responsible for important ongoing excavation and documentation projects, especially in epigraphy. Also, this site is home to ABZU, the enormous "Index to Ancient Near Eastern Resources on the Internet."

417. World History Archives. **www.hartford-hwp.com/archives/index.html**
   "A repository for documents for teaching and understanding contemporary world history and the struggle for social progress." Covers Africa as a whole, and by region.

Social Sciences

Chapter
3

The disciplines of anthropology, sociology, human and physical geography together comprise a vast literature. Emphasis is placed in this chapter on sources relevant to the study of Northern Africa. Many reference works would fit easily into more than one of these categories.

Special sections in this chapter are devoted to maps and atlases, and to works chiefly concerned with the economic, social and personal status of women.

Anthropology and Sociology

418. Survey Research in the Arab World: an Analytical Index. Edited by Monte Palmer et al. Outwell, Cambridgeshire; Boulder, CO: Middle East and North African Studies Press; Westview, 1982. 379 p. ISBN 0-906559-08-1.

This reference allows access to social science research based on population sampling, published before 1982. Not likely to be included in current electronic indexes, this material could be very difficult to find. The compilers provide source information and an informative abstract of the research findings and methods. The surveys are organized by country, and Egypt, Algeria, Libya, Morocco, Tunisia and Sudan are included. There are two limited indexes.

419. Banuazizi, Ali. **Social Stratification in the Middle East and North Africa: a Bibliographic Survey.** With the assistance of Prouchestia Goodarzi. London: Mansell, 1984. xviii, 248 p. ISBN 0-7201-1711-9.

This volume is the first in a planned series aiming to collect literature in Western and "local languages" (here, Arabic, Persian, Turkish and Hebrew) dealing with the social class structure of particular societies; i.e., "the problem of institutionalized inequalities in the distribution of life chances and economic resources ... and their political and cultural ramifications" (Introduction). General and comparative studies on the whole region are presented first: the area covered includes the Mediterranean coast of Africa and Sudan.

The work is chiefly concerned with contemporary societies, but adds "historically-oriented works covering the 19th and early 20th centuries" (p. xii); books, reports and monographs, doctoral dissertations, chapters in edited volumes and journal articles appearing between 1946 and 1982 in English and French are included. The citations are organized geographically; subject and author indexes are provided.

420. Eickelman, Dale F. **The Middle East and Central Asia: an Anthropological Approach.** Third edition. Upper Saddle River, NJ: Prentice Hall, 1998. xii, 388 p. ISBN 0-13-123019-0.

A monograph organized around topics in anthropology: village life, pastoral nomadism, cities, tribes, sex roles and family ties, etc. There are two long chapters on religious and political structures. The work includes extensive bibliographical references, several maps and black-and-white illustrations, a glossary and an index.

421. Olson, James S. **The Peoples of Africa: an Ethnohistorical Dictionary.** Westport, CT: Greenwood Press, 1996. xiv, 681 p. ISBN 0-313-27918-7.

An alphabetical ready-reference providing a brief description and, where possible, a population estimate of more than 1800 ethnic communities in Africa. "In terms of cultural diversity, it is the richest of continents, a bewildering kaleidoscope of thousands of discrete ethnic entities whose group identities are focused and distinct" (Preface). The whole range of African peoples is represented, including those in the Maghreb, Sahel and Horn. This compendium of short entries (1-5 paragraphs) is generously cross-referenced, and many of the entries provide some bibliographic notes. In addition, there is a general bibliography in an appendix. A chronology of African history is provided, and an index offering access to ethnonyms and personal or clan names not appearing as separate headings.

422. Salem-Murdock, Muneera and Michael M. Horowitz. **Anthropology and Development in North Africa and the Middle East.** With Monica Sella. Boulder, CO: Westview Press, 1990. xi, 360 p. *Monographs in Development Anthropology.* ISBN 0-8133-7688-2.

A collection of social-science essays on specific issues or case studies in rural development and change in the region, including Morocco, Tunisia, Libya, Egypt and Sudan. The volume offers 37 unusual and specialized graphs and tables and 27 maps or figures in support of the research. For reference purposes, the index is helpful.

423. Skinner, Elliott P. **Peoples and Cultures of Africa: an Anthropological Reader.** Published for the American Museum of Natural History. New York: Doubleday, 1973. xi, 756 p. ISBN 0-385-08345-9.

This volume is meant "for the student and layman interested in obtaining an overview of Africa, its peoples and their traditional cultures and societies" (Preface). It is a collection of essays, arranged topically, by noted authorities like J.S.

Trimingham, "The Phases of Islamic Expansion and Islamic Culture Zones in Africa" (pp. 700-711). A subject index helps locate specific information. Perhaps more suitable for study than for reference.

424. Strijp, Ruud. **Cultural Anthropology of the Middle East: a Bibliography.** Vol. 1. Leiden: E.J. Brill, 1992. xxvi, 565 p. ISBN 9004096043.

Part of the massive reference *Handbuch der Orientalistik* (Erste Abteilung, Zehter Band), this volume covers 1965-1987, listing both books and articles. The annotated entries are organized geographically; the scope includes all of the northern coast of Africa from Mauritania to Egypt, and Sudan (but not the rest of the Sahel or Horn). A large but rather awkward subject index and an author index are provided.

Studies published in English, French and German are included, amounting to more than 3700 entries. The work is divided into two sections: one for anthropology proper, and the other ("Added Studies") for relevant material produced by scholars in other disciplines.

425. Strijp, Ruud. **Cultural Anthropology of the Middle East: a Bibliography.** Vol. 2. Leiden: E.J. Brill, 1997. xx, 259 p. ISBN 9004107452.

A supplement to Strijp's earlier volume; this is *Handbuch der Orientalistik*, Erste Abteilung, 27er Band. This portion covers 1988-1992.

426. Weekes, Richard V. **Muslim Peoples: a World Ethnographic Survey.** Second edition, revised and expanded. Westport, CT: Greenwood Press, 1984. 2 v. ISBN 0-313-23392-6.

An extensive collection of lengthy signed articles (6-10 pages), each with a bibliography offering from three or four sources to as many as 80. Each article gives a general anthropological characterization of a particular ethnic or tribal entity, with a description of physical features, area of settlement, social customs, diet, language, religion, etc. Many of the peoples of northern Africa are included. The entries are alphabetically arranged, but a supplementary subject index is provided. Valuable ready-reference material is organized into three appendices: a table showing the Muslim nationalities of the world by country, another showing all Muslim ethnic groups and their locations, and another table of the 68 largest Muslim groups, with population figures from 1983 (many of these are in Africa). A number of useful demographical maps are included. The survey is "designed primarily for the English-speaking nonspecialist, whether academician or layman" (Introduction). It emphasizes readability and access to information "related to current patterns of living" rather than intense coverage of specialized subject areas.

Geography

Geographic Studies

Additional materials on desertification, water resources, pollution and other environmental concerns will be found in under "Science and Technology." Sources chiefly concerned with sustainable development are included under "Economics."

427. **Dictionary of Human Geography.** Second edition. Edited by R.J. Johnston, Derek Gregory, and David M. Smith. Oxford: Blackwell, 1994. xx, 724 p. ISBN 0-631-18141-5.

Concise, tightly controlled definitions of the vocabulary used in the study of the world's geography and human economic activity are collected here, and ordered alphabetically for ready reference. Abstract concepts freely discussed in scholarly literature are summed up, often in such a concentrated form that the definition itself requires some study. Cross-references to other entries are included, and there is a thorough index as well. Each entry provides at least a few selected bibliographical references. Concepts relevant to African studies, like "desertification" and "sustainable development," are among these entries.

428. **A Geographical Bibliography for American Libraries.** Edited by Chauncey D. Harris. Washington: Association of American Geographers and the National Geographic Society, 1985. xxiii, 437 p. ISBN 0-89291-193-X.

A helpful annotated guide to collection development in geography-related materials. This volume stands out thanks to its meticulous organization and strong set of contributors. Two chapters are particularly pertinent: Chapter 12, "Southwest Asia and North Africa" by Ian R. Manners, and Chapter 13, "Africa South of the Sahara" by Sanford H. Bederman. Other materials on petroleum geology and deserts/water resources are also relevant.

The works cited are not just maps and atlases, but also monographs, essay collections, bibliographies and periodicals useful for area studies, including scholarly works on urbanization, the environment, development, etc.

429. **The Middle Eastern City and Islamic Urbanism: an Annotated Bibliography of Western Literature.** Bonn: Dümmlers Verlag, 1994. 877 p. *Bonner Geographische Abhandlungen;* heft 91. ISBN 3-427-76411-7; ISSN 0373-0468.

Journal articles and books in Western languages pertaining to urbanism in the Middle East and North Africa comprise this bibliography. The most accessible section is Chapter 2, which includes the Mediterranean coast of Africa and the Sudan. The Sahel is included in Chapter 5, under "West Africa," and the Horn under "East Africa." An index of authors and an index of cities and sites provide some assistance; the subject index, however, is an automated nightmare. There is one map and an explanatory introduction to each chapter.

430. **Peoples of North Africa.** The Diagram Group. New York: Facts on File, 1997. 112 p. *Peoples of Africa Series.* ISBN 0-8160-3483-4.

An attractive, abundantly-illustrated introduction to the physical and human geography and folk customs of northern Africa. Special attention is given to the Berbers, Copts, Dinka, Nuer, Nuba, Shilluk and Tuareg peoples, as well as the wider Arab/Islamic societies, and the remaining Jewish communities. The work dips into archaeology as well, mentioning Saharan rock paintings, Pharaonic Egypt, Nubia and Carthage. Charts of North African languages, a useful glossary and an index are provided. Very appropriate reference for a school library.

431. Chapman, Graham P. and Kathleen M. Baker. **The Changing Geography of Africa and the Middle East.** London and New York: Routledge, 1992. xvii, 252 p. ISBN 0-415-05709-4.

This very interesting collection of scholarly essays was produced by the Department of Geography at SOAS to observe their 25th anniversary. This and a companion volume study significant current trends in human geography in Africa and Asia.

Because the work is specifically written with undergraduates in mind, and because it is clearly divided into regional sections with intelligible subheadings, the volume lends itself well to reference work. Chapters are devoted to North Africa and the Nile Valley as regions, while the Horn is included in East Africa, Chad in Central and the rest of the Sahel in West Africa. A good index, plenty of maps and tables, and a bibliography for each chapter increase the work's reference value.

432. Clarke, John Innes and W. B. Fisher. **Populations of the Middle East and North Africa: a Geographical Approach.** New York: Africana Publishing, 1972. 432 p. ISBN 0-340-11513-0.

A collection of informative studies of population distribution and trends in the region, with chapters on Egypt, Libya, Tunisia, Algeria and Morocco. An introductory essay outlines regional population issues (problems collecting and comparing data, population size, density and growth, urbanization, migration). The volume contains more than 70 tables and figures of considerable reference value pertaining mostly to conditions in the mid-20th century (up to about 1966). Each chapter provides a bibliography of sources in English and French; there is a rough index.

433. Drysdale, Alasdair and Gerald H. Blake. **The Middle East and North Africa: a Political Geography.** New York: Oxford University Press, 1985. xiii, 367 p. ISBN 0-19-503537-2.

This scholarly study is equipped with unusual graphic materials very useful for reference purposes: some 70 detailed and clearly-printed maps and figures, and 18 tables of data. These informative figures show oil fields, facilities, pipelines and routes of export, variations in border placement between Libya and its neighbors (especially Algeria and Chad), population density, language areas and the location of major roads and railways, and historical diagrams depicting the

Arab conquest, colonial era and the present up to 1984. In addition, Libya and Sudan are featured as case studies of national integration in Chapter 7. Each chapter offers a sophisticated bibliography and there is a well-organized, detailed index.

434. Griffiths, Ieuan Ll. **The African Inheritance.** London; New York: Routledge, 1995. 216 p. ISBN 0-415-01091-8.

African history and political geography in a small one-volume work, concentrating on Africa's colonial experience and its consequences. This is more than a simple handbook or introduction: the work offers thoughtful analysis of many of the key pressures on contemporary African states. Many significant small maps and figures illustrate the text. Much of the information pertains to sub-Saharan Africa, but there is useful material on the Maghreb, Sahel and Horn; e.g., a discussion of the Western Sahara conflict. A careful index helps the reader discover this material.

435. Groom, Nigel. **A Dictionary of Arabic Topography and Place Names: a Transliterated Arabic-English Dictionary With an Arabic Glossary of Topographical Words and Placenames.** Beirut; London: Librairie du Liban; Longman, 1983. 369 p.

Those who can read the Arabic alphabet even a little will greatly appreciate the fact that this glossary provides the Arabic term in its proper orthography beside each transliterated term. A simple definition in English is also given. Many of these entries represent vocabulary that is unique to desert geography or to Arab cultural practices (e.g., "rajmah") or limited to a local dialect (e.g., "matarah") . An index of the terms in Arabic script and alphabetical order is included.

436. Held, Colbert C. **Middle East Patterns: Places, Peoples and Politics.** With Mildred McDonald Held. Boulder: Westview Press, 1994. xix, 484 p. ISBN 0-8133-8220-3.

An attractive, well-organized, illustrated encyclopedia of geography, covering physical features, climate, vegetation, mineral wealth, and human settlement and activity. Of the North African states, only Egypt is included.

437. Kirchherr, Eugene C. **Place Names of Africa, 1935-1986: a Political Gazetteer.** Metuchen, NJ: Scarecrow, 1987. viii, 136 p. ISBN 0-8108-2061-7.

An updated and enlarged version of the author's *Abyssinia to Zimbabwe: a Guide to the Political Units of Africa in the Period 1947-1978* (3rd edition). This ready reference offers quick access to the place names of the continent, which were in constant flux during the period covered. A "Supplementary Notes" section provides greater detail about many of the more complex regional territorial problems, including Morocco, Mauritania and the Western Sahara, and also the French administration of Algeria and the Saharan Departments. Two tables and 23 well-chosen maps are included. There is a general bibliography, but no index; terms are generously cross-referenced.

438. McIlwaine, John. **Maps and Mapping of Africa: a Resource Guide.** London: Hans Zell, 1997. xxviii, 391 p. ISBN 1-873836-76-7.

Covering the art and science of mapping Africa from the earliest times to the present, this reference includes directories and catalogs of map collections, bibliographies of geography and cartography, atlases and gazetteers, etc. The volume is meticulously organized, and includes the whole of the continent. Individual countries are listed in the names index; an oddly-formatted subject index is also provided.

439. Moss, Joyce and George Wilson. **The Middle East and North Africa: the Culture, Geographical Setting, and Historical Background of 30 Peoples of the Middle East and North Africa.** Detroit: Gale Research, 1992. xix, 435 p. *Peoples of the World.* ISBN 0-8103-7941-4.

This book provides elementary encyclopedia-style entries describing some of the ancient and modern peoples of the region. Pharaonic Egypt, for example, is covered in five pages of large print, with a bibliography of two very general titles; ancient Egyptian religion is dealt with in one paragraph. Articles appear on the three major modern religions of the area, on Algerians, Berbers, Copts, Libyans, Moroccans, Tunisians and "Arabs," with little country profiles as well. There is a glossary and a very simple bibliography and index. For some reason, many of the maps and photos are very poor.

440. Newman, James L. **The Peopling of Africa: a Geographic Interpretation.** New Haven: Yale University Press, 1995. xiv, 235 p. ISBN 0-300-06003-3.

A fascinating study of the geography and anthropology of the African continent, generously illustrated with 50 unusual and informative maps, and many pertinent black-and-white photos. The transparent organization of this scholarly monograph makes it well-suited to reference work.

A great deal of useful material on early human settlement over the whole land mass is found in Part One. In Part Two, Newman concentrates on regional zones: Northern Africa (the Maghreb and Egypt/Nubia, with connections to the Sahara and Upper Nile), Ethiopia and the Horn, the Sahel and Sudan. A carefully-subdivided index helps to locate material that transcends geographic divisions: for example, on the slave trade. Bibliographic notes are provided for each chapter.

441. Room, Adrian. **African Placenames: Origins and Meanings of the Names for Over 2000 Natural Features, Towns, Cities, Provinces and Countries.** Jefferson, NC: McFarland & Co., 1994. x, 235 p. ISBN 0-89950-943-6.

This gazetteer aims to present the whole African continent, but is admittedly strongest in its Southern Africa coverage. Nevertheless, the ancient and classical place-names of the Mediterranean coast are well documented here, and much interesting information is provided on the Berber or Arabic names. This volume clarifies not only the proper names of individual places, but also general geographical or topographical terms (such as *oued* or *wadi* for watercourses, *jabal* or *gebel* for mountains). Names of European origin are also explained. Four appendices provide quick access to a chronology of exploration, lists of official national names, languages and religions, and a handy list of independence dates. A short bibliography of unusual sources is included; there is no index, but the alphabetized entries are cross-referenced.

442. Rumney, Thomas A. **Geographical Studies on North Africa and Southwest Asia: a Selected Bibliography.** Monticello, IL: Vance Bibliographies, 1981. 43 p. *Public Administration Series;* P-2660. ISBN 0-7920-0190-7; ISSN 0193-970X.

The Vance bibliographies on public administration are composed of topically arranged citations—up to about 1000 in each issue—of books and articles, government bulletins and other publications. The entries are sometimes briefly annotated. The area covered by this issue is enormous, and includes Egypt, Libya, Tunisia, Algeria, Morocco and the Western Sahara. The citations are organized by topic: cultural, social and urban geography, economic, historical and political geography, and physical geography.

Maps and Atlases

443. **Africa on File.** Mapping Specialists, Inc. New York: Facts on File, 1995. Two large looseleaf binders, divided into sections. ISBN 0-8160-3288-2 (set).

Like *African History on File,* this is a huge collection of very clear, full-page monochrome maps, graphics and tables of data, covering the African continent. Vol. 1 includes North Africa (Algeria, Egypt, Libya, Morocco, Tunisia and Western Sahara), but only one map and a fact sheet are provided for each country, since a companion volume called *Middle East and North Africa on File* covers them in detail.

Much fuller treatment is given to Ethiopia, Somalia, Djibouti and Eritrea (under East Africa), and to Mali, Mauritania and Niger (West Africa). Chad and Sudan (Central Africa) are found in Vol. 2.

Administrative units, chronology, physical features, demography, economic statistics, industrial and agricultural resources and some cultural data are conveyed in graphical or symbolic form or in tables. Vol. 2 supplies data on a wide array of regional issues or those affecting all of Africa; there is also a bibliography and a detailed index. Permission is given by the publisher to reproduce these sheets for classroom use.

444. **African History on File.** The Diagram Group. New York: Facts on File, 1994. Large looseleaf binder, paginated in sections. ISBN 0-8160-2910-5.

An interesting collection of monochrome maps, timelines and graphics illustrating African history from prehistoric times up to the 1990s. Section 1 "Prehistory," section 2 "Nile Kingdoms," and section 3, "North Africa" are all pertinent, covering Nubia, Axum and Meroe as well as Pharaonic and Greco-Roman sites. Other sections contain materials on the Sahara and the Horn (notably, sections 4 and 5).

Later sections are compiled by chronology and provide important information on northern tribes and trade routes, exploration and colonialism, and 20th-century independence movements and statehood. A simple but useful index helps to locate these materials.

The very clear and sharp graphics are perfect for photocopies, transparencies or slides for classroom use. Permission to reproduce for this purpose is already provided by the publisher.

445. **The Atlas of Africa.** Edited by Regine Van Chi-Bonnardel. Paris and New York: Éditions Jeune Afrique and The Free Press (Macmillan), 1973. 355 p.

A very large-format volume presenting full-page historical, political, physical and thematic maps of the African continent, in color. Although political details are dated now, the geology, climate, vegetation, rainfall and other natural features of Africa are also covered; settlement since prehistoric times, and human activity (especially industry, agriculture and trade) are depicted as well. A section on North Africa includes the whole Mediterranean coast, plus Western Sahara (still "Rio de Oro") . Mauretania and Mali are considered "West Africa," but so are Niger and Chad. Sudan, Ethiopia and Somalia are grouped together as "Northern East Africa."

This volume contains a surprising amount of text, providing an encyclopedia-style descriptive article for each country, region and topic. Statistical data are presented in the form of bar charts and graphs. An index-gazetteer and simply glossary are included.

446. **Atlas of the Middle East.** Prepared by Carta Jerusalem. Edited by Moshe Brawer. New York; London: Macmillan, 1988. 140 p. ISBN 0-02-905271-8.

A simple and convenient topical atlas, with full-page maps highlighted in red. The "Middle East" here includes Egypt and Libya, but often the topical maps cover a much larger area: Sudan, the Horn, Africa above the 10th parallel, sometimes the entire continent. There is an explanatory text and frequent use of bar graphs, pie charts and other graphics to convey additional information. A subdivided bibliographic essay and an index/gazetteer are provided.

447. **Historical Atlas of Africa.** Edited by J. F. Ade Ajayi and Michael Crowder. Cambridge: Cambridge University Press, 1985. Unpaginated. ISBN 0-521-25353-5.

A colorful large-format atlas with encyclopedia-style articles and black-and-white photo illustrations on facing pages. The work is based on a three-fold plan: "event" maps convey historical information (battle sites, trade routes, etc.); "process" maps display development or change over time (migration, spread of cattle farming); "quantitative" maps present economic data, population density and so on. Coverage of the Maghreb in classical and Byzantine times, trans-Saharan trade and transport, the Arab conquest and medieval dynasties, northeast Africa and the Horn, and developments in the colonial and modern eras are all covered. The index includes personal names (e.g., "Alexander the Great") as well as places.

448. **Third World Atlas.** Prepared by Ben Crow and Alan Thomas. Milton Keynes: Open University Press, 1983. 72 p. ISBN 0-335-10259-X and 0-223-15015-2.

This atlas aims to do more than present basic geographical, political or economic information about a certain subset of the world's nations. The intention here is to illustrate and elucidate the concepts of the "Third World" and "development," to define the characteristics that create such categories and concepts, and to reveal the historical forces that have shaped the divisions between industrialized and developing countries.

The authors begin by considering the political assumptions of mapmaking itself, then display a sort of tour de force of multicolored graphics meant to convey comparative statistical information. The Middle East and North Africa are dealt with together for the most part, beginning with "The Rise of Islam" (p. 24). An appendix provides several tables of data; there is no index.

449. **Tübinger Atlas des Vorderen Orients.** University of Tübingen, Sonderforschungsbereich 19. Wiesbaden: Ludwig Reichert Verlag. Loose sheets, 51 x 73 cm. ISBN 3-88226-800-X (index volumes). Each map sheet has a separate ISBN.

Huge, loose-leaf, full-color historical and topical maps of the Middle East region. The series covers the ancient world (including Pharaonic Egypt and Nubia), the Greco-Roman Mediterranean, the Ottoman Empire, and specific areas or cities. There have been 26 leaves published so far. These large maps are very impressive in detail, execution and scholarly authority. A three-volume index and gazetteer is available.

450. **West African International Atlas.** Organization of African Unity: Scientific, Technical and Research Commission, 1968. 2 v.

Also titled: *Atlas International de l'Ouest Africain.*

Vol. 1 of this very large-format work contains a highly technical text in both English and French, and some illustrative maps, conveying geographical and natural-science data. Vol. 2 is a large cased collection of loose, folded leaves, presenting colorful, clearly-printed and extremely detailed maps of political and administrative boundaries, economic and development data (energy and agricultural resources, medical facilities, etc.) and physical geography. This atlas concentrates on the southern coastal states of West Africa and covers Mauritania and Niger only on the periphery.

451. **World Bank Atlas.** Washington: World Bank. Annual, 1967- . ISBN 0-8213-4127-8

For a description and ordering information online, see **www.worldbank.org/html/extpb/atlas98.htm** or **www.worldbank.org/html/extpb/PopularTitles.html#W**

A small, soft-cover digest of selected material from *World Development Indicators*, packaged in an attractive, colorful format, in English, French and Spanish throughout. Brief summary text is interleafed with vivid maps, tables and graphics displaying world population statistics, environmental information (water use, forest coverage, carbon dioxide emissions, etc.), economic data, and a new section added in 1997: states and markets, "presenting new indicators on private investment and infrastructure" (Foreword) and "the respective roles of the state and private sector" (Introduction). Data are sometimes lacking for parts of northern Africa, notably Libya, Western Sahara, Eritrea and Somalia.

452. Blake, Gerald, John Dewdney, and Jonathan Mitchell. **Cambridge Atlas of the Middle East and North Africa.** Cambridge: Cambridge University Press, 1987. vii, 124 p. ISBN 0-521-24243-6.

An attractive volume of concise articles and expert maps, covering the Mediterranean coast of Africa and the Sudan. Information is presented on many aspects of physical geography and the environment, culture and history, demographics, economic resources, trade and development, transport, tourism and communications, and political features like maritime boundaries and disputed frontiers (not including the Western Sahara). A gazetteer and bibliography are provided.

453. Boustani, Rafic and Philippe Fargues. **The Atlas of the Arab World: Geopolitics and Society.** Preface by Maxime Rodinson. New York: Facts on File, 1991. 144 p. ISBN 0-8160-2346-8.

An unusual and well-focused atlas packed with information about the political, social, cultural and economic character of the Middle East, the North Atlantic and Mediterranean coasts of Africa, Sudan and the Horn. Some of the maps incorporate a larger area; normally, Mauritania and Somalia are included, while Mali, Niger, Chad and Ethiopia are not. A helpful text on facing pages interprets the full-color maps.

The volume covers not only the obvious topics, but also specialized information like the occupations of North Africans living in France, remittances sent home by workers abroad, the degree of press freedom in Arab states, per-capita oil income, states observing UN conventions on the status of women, and so forth. These graphics could be extremely effective as visual aids for lectures or lessons. A country-by-country "data bank" pulls together key statistics. A detailed index is provided.

454. Brice, William C. **An Historical Atlas of Islam.** Leiden: E.J. Brill, 1981. viii, 71 p. ISBN 90-04-06116-9.

Produced "under the patronage" of *The Encyclopaedia of Islam*, this very large-format atlas contains beautiful relief maps and plans, but no text, except some introductory pages of map captions. Some of the maps are unusual: the world according to Idrisi in A.D. 1154, or Al-Sharfi in A.D. 1579; the names, shapes and relative positions of stars and constellations as known to medieval Arab astronomers. Part VI of the atlas covers Muslim Spain and the Maghreb, while Part VII provides six views of North Africa. The index-gazetteer includes persons and the names of ethnic groups.

455. Dempsey, Michael W. **Atlas of the Arab World.** New York: Facts on File, 1983. Unpaginated. ISBN 0-87196-138-5.

About two-thirds of this small volume consists of feature maps (strong on color but short on detail) using graphics displays to present information on the geography and natural resources, land use, industry, transport and communications, media and military, religion and civilization of the region. The maps might make excellent slides or transparencies for classroom use. Explanatory notes in the back of the book help to interpret the maps.

The remaining third of the volume consists of 2-page country profiles, with fact boxes, big color photos, a flag, and simple text. The Mediterranean states of Africa from Mauritania to Egypt, Sudan, Somalia and Djibouti are within the scope of this work. There is no bibliography or index.

456. Fage, J. D. **An Atlas of African History.** New York: Africana Publishing, 1978. Unpaginated. ISBN 0-8419-0429-4.

A small-format atlas with 71 monochrome maps (with some highlighting) depicting the continent's history. There is no text as such, though some captions are provided. This volume is interesting because of its unusual thematic maps, often thickly inscribed with surprisingly detailed information. It is especially meticulous in its coverage of tribal settlements and European incursions in specific places, such as Morocco or Ethiopia. A remarkable map (no. 61) shows the names and dates of pioneer Christian mission outposts in Africa, 1792-1914 ... information that would be very tedious to collect from other sources. An index-gazetteer is provided.

457. Freeman-Grenville, G. S. P. (Greville Stewart Parker). **Historical Atlas of the Middle East.** Cartography by Lorraine Kessel. New York: Simon & Schuster, 1993. 144 p. ISBN 0-13-390915-8.

Historical and topical maps with a page of explanatory text convey information about the region from earliest recorded times to the present. Intended for the general reader, this work would also be quite suitable for an undergraduate library. Coverage of northern Africa varies widely by topic: maps of Roman imperial possessions, the spread of Christianity, use of Semitic languages, the Ummayad dynasty, the Idrisids, Fatimids, Almoravids, Almohads, Mamluks, Ottomans, etc. include detailed treatments of Mediterranean Africa. A few maps also include Sudan, Mauritania and/or the Horn. A decent index and a bibliography are provided.

458. Freeman-Grenville, G. S. P. (Greville Stewart Parker). **The New Atlas of African History.** New York: Simon & Schuster, 1991. 144 p. ISBN 0-13-612151-9.

The aim of this small-format atlas is "to illustrate the history of the African continent from prehistoric times to 1990" (Preface). Clear and detailed monochrome maps are highlighted with red or pink to display population distribution, exploration routes, the slave trade, etc. Text on facing pages helps to interpret the theme of each map. The northern third of the continent is fully covered here, from the earliest human settlement through Pharaonic and Roman times, the Arab conquest, colonial and modern eras. Coverage of the North Africa campaigns during World War II is particularly detailed. An index-gazetteer and table of contents are provided.

459. Freeman, Michael. **Atlas of the World Economy.** Consulting editor, Derek Aldcroft. New York: Simon & Schuster, 1991. xv, 167 p. ISBN 0-13-050741-5.

An atlas that takes an historical approach to the world economy since 1945. It was completed just before the collapse of communism in the former Soviet Union and Eastern Europe, creating a beginning and an end point for its chronological scope. The work is organized by theme, discussing population, agriculture, energy, industry, national income, transport and trade, labor and multinational corporations in successive chapters. Maps and figures dominate the pages, with a brief explanatory text. There is a simple bibliography but no index.

460. Hazard, Harry W. **Atlas of Islamic History.** Maps by Lester Cooke Jr. and J. McA. Smiley. Princeton: Princeton University Press, 1951. 48 p. *Princeton Oriental Studies;* vol. 12.

This collection of full-page color maps is of course not current, but provides a valuable resource for historical study of the period from 601 A.D. to 1950. Demographic and political changes in each century are shown according to a color scheme, with a page of explanatory material accompanying each map. Africa is usually displayed from Morocco to the tip of the Horn (often called Zanj). The map key's use of the expression "gained" or "lost" for territory whose population or regime has changed sounds quaint today but is perhaps typical of Orientalist scholarship. A map showing the extent of the Ottoman Empire in North Africa is helpful. An index is provided.

461. Kidron, Michael and Ronald Segal. **The New State of the World Atlas.** Fourth edition. London: Heinemann, 1991. Unpaginated. ISBN 0-435-35494-9.

A collection of 57 colorful subject-specific maps and captions, supported by a Marxist rejection of capitalism and the nation-state. This political and economic orientation is frankly acknowledged and makes this a reference with an interesting point of view. The volume is not indexed. A fifth edition of this work is now available.

462. Kurian, George Thomas. **Atlas of the Third World.** Second edition. New York: Facts on File, 1992. xiv, 384 p. ISBN 0-8160-1930-4.

The maps and charts in this volume use shades of green to highlight information. Part I presents data in graphic form organized by theme: population, land use, agriculture and industry, the environment, trade, health, defense, education, etc. In Part II, country profiles are provided for nations of the developing world, including the states of northern Africa (except Mali and Djibouti). Bar charts and line graphs are used to show changes over time. There is a helpful subject index.

463. McEvedy, Colin. **Penguin Atlas of African History.** New edition. London: Penguin, 1995. 144 p. ISBN 0-14-051321-3.

A tiny reference, perfect for students, composed of simple but clear and informative historical maps showing changes in the physical and human geography of Africa from 175 million years ago to 1994. Each map covers a page, and on the facing page is a brief interpretation. The maps are black and white, with green highlighting. Northern Africa is capably covered right along with the rest of the continent. A helpful index is included.

464. Murray, Jocelyn. **Cultural Atlas of Africa.** New York: Facts on File, 1981. 240 p. ISBN 0-87196-558-5.

An attractive and colorful large-format atlas, organized along traditional lines: first physical geography, then thematic background articles (on language, religion, archaeology, art and music, colonial history, etc.). Part Three concentrates on regions and individual countries, and does so thoroughly; all of Africa's nations and territories are covered.

In addition, there are feature pages focusing on special topics: Yoruba traditional religion, the source of the Nile, masks and bronzes, healing rituals, etc. Cultural rather than economic or political information is the main emphasis. The color photography in this volume is unusually impressive, and the maps are large, subtly-colored and detailed. A subdivided bibliography, gazetteer and well-organized subject index are included.

Databases and Websites

465. Maps of Africa. **www.lib.utexas.edu/Libs/PCL/Map_collection/africa.html**
An extensive library map collection in digital form.

466. Maps of the Middle East.
www.lib.utexas.edu/Libs/PCL/Map_collection/middle_east.html
An extensive library map collection in digital form.

467. National Geographic Society. Xpeditions atlas. **http://www.nationalgeographic. com/xpeditions/main.html**
Archive of 600 maps available for downloading or printing from this site (requires Adobe Acrobat).

468. TerraServer. **www.terraserver.microsoft.com/**
Microsoft's searchable geographic database; aerial and satellite images.

469. **U.S. Geological Survey**. Maps showing geology, oil and gas fields and geological provinces of Africa. Prepared by Feliks Persits, et al. Denver, CO,1997.

Available on CD-ROM; for futher information online, see **energy.cr. usgs.gov/energy/pubs.html**

470. U.S. Geological Survey. World Energy Publications. **energy.cr.usgs. gov/energy/pubs.html**
Maps of petroleum resources and other information (statistics, bibliographies, assessments).

471. Worldatlas.com. Africa Page. **www.graphicmaps.com/aatlas/africa/ af.htm**
Clear, brightly-colored political maps that print well. Not all regions or countries are yet covered. There are also "Facts/Figures/Flags" pages supplying basic almanac-style information.

472. World Water and Climate Atlas. **www.worldbank.org/html/cgiar/ press/water.html**
Also available on CD-ROM.
A new database of agricultural climate data, providing precise precipitation and temperature measurements gathered over a 30-year period; it can be used to predict the success of specific crops on any given parcel of land (down to 2.5 square kilometers). Intended by the World Bank and USAID to benefit farmers attempting to improve food production.

Women and Society

The traditional roles, civil rights, political participation, creative activities, opportunities and contributions of women in the societies of northern Africa occupy the attention of a great many references, research or statistical works and monographs in area studies. The Islamic character of most of these societies makes the issues involved somewhat sensitive. Some of this substantial literature is represented here.

473. **Femmes et Sociétés dans le Monde Arabo-Musulman: État Bibliographique.** Paris: Mireille, 1989. 254 p. *Travaux et Documents de l'IREMAM;* no. 9. ISBN 2-906809-07-1.
A publication of the Institut de Recherches et d'Études sur le Monde Arabe et Musulman (Universités d'Aix-Marseille I & II). Densely printed and alphabetized by author with a hard-to-use "plan de classement thématique," this work is not user-friendly, though there is a lot of valuable information here.
The bibliography is divided into two sections, for Arabic and for European languages. There is an author index—somewhat redundant since the entries are alphabetized by author—and a ludicrously ineffective "index géographique."

474. **International Directory of Women's Political Leadership 1995.** Compiled by Deborah Welborn Poulin. College Park, MD: Center for Political Leadership and Participation (University of Maryland), 1995. iv, 302 p.

Also available online at **www.inform.umd.edu/WomensStudies/ GovernmentPolitics/**

This work is a country-by-country directory of organizations and individuals involved in facilitating participation by women in political activities and the representation of women's concerns in the political arena. It is organized regionally, with sections for Africa and the Middle East; contact data and titles for female office-holders or directors of NGOs are provided.

In addition, this volume contains a collection of reports on the status of women in Africa. Essays include "Legal Aid for Women in Sudan" by Zeinab Abbas, "Rights Not Privileges" by Asma Mohamed Abdel Halim, "The Project for Women to Bring Peace, Democracy and Human Rights to Somalia" by Hibaaq Osman Bas-Bas, and the report of a conference on women's rights in Asmara. The volume needs a far more extensive index, listing at least personal and organization names.

475. **Répertoire des Competences Feminines Tunisiennes.** Edited by Radhia Knani. Tunis: Ministère aux Affaires de la Femme et de la Famille, 1993. xv, 333 p.

An alphabetized directory of more than 450 Tunisian professional women, active in many walks of life: the arts, banking and finance, agriculture, architecture and engineering, education, law, medicine, diplomacy or development, business and trade, scientific research, news media and entertainment, and so on.

Each entry notes the person's education or training, occupation, languages, an office address, awards, field of research or activity. The volume indexes these entries by profession and by institution/organization.

476. **Social Science Research and Women in the Arab World.** Paris: UNESCO, 1984. x, 175 p. ISBN 0-86187-387-4.

A collection of scholarly essays, with bibliographical references, analyzing the challenges of conducting this type of social-science research. There is a chapter on women in North Africa, and individual chapters on Morocco, Algeria and Sudan. The volume has no index.

477. **Statistical Record of Women Worldwide.** Edited by Linda Schmittroth. Detroit: Gale Research, 1991. xxxiv, 763 p. ISBN 0-8103-8349-7.

One of Gale's many statistical handbooks on various subjects. This volume concentrates on issues of particular relevance to women: home and family concerns, educational opportunities and health care for women and girls, crimes against women, income and occupation issues, population statistics, women's sports, etc. Tables of data are provided, many of which pertain to the United States, but with a little persistence one can discover how many sexual assaults were reported in Ethiopia in 1986, the number of working women in Tunisia, or the female life expectancy in Niger. The index gives access to the data by country. The source of each table is identified, and a bibliography of the sources is provided.

478. **Statistics and Indicators on Women in Africa.** Department of International Economic and Social Affairs Statistical Office. New York: United Nations, 1989. xi, 225 p. *Social Statistics and Indicators;* series K, no. 7. ISBN 92-1-061133-0; UN Sales no. E/F.89.XV.11, 02350.

Also titled: *Statistiques et Indicateurs sur les Femmes en Afrique.*

A collection of tables of data derived from the more comprehensive UN publication *Compendium of Statistics and Indicators on the Situation of Women* (1986). Naturally, this information is dated now, but the convenient format might lend itself to the use of this data in historical or comparative research.

All of the African nations are within the scope of this volume, but not every one is represented on every table. Unfortunately, there is no complete index by country indicating where data are available. All of the information in this volume (not just introductory material) is given in both English and French.

479. **The Status of the Arab Woman: a Select Bibliography.** Compiled by Samira Rafidi Meghdessian. London: Mansell, 1980. 176 p. ISBN 0-7201-1517-5.

Prepared under the auspices of the Institute for Women's Studies in the Arab World at the Beirut University College in Lebanon, this work is mentioned because of its effort to include North Africa as a region and its individual states. The Mediterranean coast of Africa, Mauritania, Sudan and Somalia are represented. Books and articles from the popular press as well as scholarly works and materials from United Nations agencies and NGOs may be found here.

480. **The World's Women 1995: Trends and Statistics.** Second edition. New York: United Nations, 1995. xxiv, 188 p. *Social Statistics and Indicators;* series K, no. 12. ISBN 92-1-161372-8; UN Sales no. E.95.XVII.2.

Prepared for the Fourth World Conference on Women in 1995, this volume of statistical data and interpretive material is well organized and documented. Graphs and tables may stand alone or illustrate the text. The work focuses upon population growth and distribution, family patterns, environment and water resources, health concerns, education and work, and political participation by women. The countries of northern Africa are extensively covered. There is no index.

481. Al-Qazzaz, Ayad. **Women in the Arab World: an Annotated Bibliography.** Detroit: Association of Arab-American University Graduates, 1975. 139 p. *Bibliography Series;* no. 2.

Though dated now, this bibliography is so carefully annotated that researchers looking for materials published before 1975 (not likely to be found in electronic indexes) may find it very helpful. There is a basic subject index.

482. Al-Qazzaz, Ayad. **Women in the Middle East and North Africa: an Annotated Bibliography.** Austin: Center for Middle Eastern Studies, University of Texas, 1977. xii, 178 p. *Middle East Monographs;* no. 2. ISBN 0-292-79009-0.

This bibliography is no longer current, but the annotations are so thorough, thoughtful and literate that it may still be of considerable value to researchers. It includes books and articles—mostly scholarly, but some of interest to the general reader—reporting and analyzing their content in detail.

Entries are organized alphabetically by author; there is an index by country and another by very broad topic, but the work is more suitable for those readers with specific authors in mind. The Mediterranean states of northern Africa and Sudan are included.

483. Berrian, Brenda F. **Bibliography of African Women Writers and Journalists.** Washington: Three Continents Press, 1985. 279 p. ISBN 0-89410-226-5.

This reference calls attention to the often-overlooked contributions of African women to literature (poetry, drama, fiction), journalism and broadcasting, essays, letters, biography and criticism, and offers access to these works. The entries are organized by genre, but there is helpful indexing in a number of forms, including authors and journalists by country, and a names index. Entries are not annotated. The scope of this work includes the counties of northern Africa, but no information is available on Libya, Niger, Djibouti, Chad, Somalia and Western Sahara.

484. Bullwinkle, Davis A. **African Women: a General Bibliography, 1976-1985.** New York: Greenwood Press, 1989. xx, 334 p. *African Special Bibliographic Series;* no. 9. ISBN 0-313-26607-7.

The first volume of Bullwinkle's three-part bibliography on the women of Africa includes material not limited geographically to a single country or region. Citations are organized by topic, rather broadly: a subject index or subdivisions of the topical sections would make the work much more useful. An author index is provided, and three appendices: a directory of organizations active in women's programs, a list of the official names and capitals of African countries, and a cross-reference list linking many different forms of African place-names.

485. Bullwinkle, Davis A. **Women of Northern, Western and Central Africa: a Bibliography, 1976-1985.** New York: Greenwood Press, 1989. xxvii, 601 p. *African Special Bibliographic Series;* no. 10. ISBN 0-313-26609-3.

The compiler has brought together "all the English language publications written about women in Africa during the United Nations Decade for Women from 1976-1985," including monographs, government documents and journal articles. The first 30 pages list materials pertaining to more than a single country, organized by topic; the bulk of the volume is arranged geographically, making countries of northern and western Africa (including the Sahel) easy to find. Where many citations exist—dealing with Egypt, for example—they are subdivided topically; the table of contents offers the best access to these areas, since there is no subject index. Some of the headings (e.g., "Cultural Roles in Western

Africa") present a long list of 70-80 dissimilar articles that must be slowly read through. The citations are not annotated, and no abstracts are provided.

486. Byrne, Pamela R. and Suzanne R. Ontiveros. **Women in the Third World: a Historical Bibliography.** Santa Barbara, CA: ABC-Clio, 1986. xii, 152 p. *ABC-Clio Research Guides;* 15. ISBN 0-87436-459-0.

More than 600 citations of journal articles, with informative abstracts, are collected in this small volume. The articles focus on the status and roles of women in developing countries; the volume is organized along broad geographic lines, with chapters on women in Africa and the Middle East. A subject index is built upon strings of descriptors, with an indication of the time period covered (e.g., "Algeria. Assimilation. France. Social Customs. 1930-1970") . An author index is also provided.

487. Camps, Gabriel. **L'Afrique du Nord au Féminin: Héroïnes du Maghreb et du Sahara.** Paris: Perrin, 1992. 333 p. ISBN 2-262-00740-3.

This lively volume is not a typical collective biography, but rather a collection of 20 stories of strong and brave women from traditional tales or the distant past, along with some documented historical persons. Camps points out that "histoire au féminin, histoire de femmes qui, dans ce Maghreb qu'on dit misogyne, ont joué au fil des siècles un rôle non négligeable" (Avant-Propos). The historical links of these women's stories are made clearer by a chronology of events on which their names appear in context; in addition, there is a map showing the places associated with them. (Another map of the region's geography is provided as well.) A glossary defines unfamiliar terms.

488. Chamie, Mary. **Women of the World: Near East and North Africa.** Washington: U.S. Department of Commerce, 1985. vi, 195 p. *Women in Development;* 3.

The U.S. Bureau of the Census and the U.S. Agency for International Development collaborated to produce a series of four regional reports on the status of women. This volume contains graphs and tables of data in several fundamental measurement categories: population figures, literacy and education levels, economic activity (women in the urban workforce, in agriculture, etc.), marital status and fertility rates, life expectancy, and so forth.

Some textual interpretation of these figures is provided in an introduction and conclusion. There is one simple map, and an appendix providing bibliographical references (no index). Of the northern Africa states, only Morocco, Algeria, Tunisia and Egypt are included.

489. Courtney-Clarke, Margaret and Geraldine Brooks. **Mazighen: the Vanishing Traditions of Berber Women.** New York: Clarkson Potter, 1996. xxiv, 191 p. ISBN 0-517-59771-3.

A colorful, large-format "coffee-table" book, full of large, beautiful photographs of the life and arts of Berber women in the Atlas mountains of Morocco and Algeria. A very nice monochrome map, a simple glossary, bibliography and index are provided as well. The pottery and textiles are especially fine.

490. Ghorayshi, Parvin. **Women and Work in Developing Countries.** Westport, CT: Greenwood, 1994. xix, 223 p. *Bibliographies and Indexes in Women's Studies;* no. 20. ISBN 0-313-28834-8.

Books, articles, reports, dissertations, videos and films relating to opportunities and challenges for the working women of Africa are covered in Chapter 2 of this book, and the Middle East in Chapter 5. An index by country and region also speeds access; a basic subject index is provided. Very simple annotations of one or two sentences are included.

491. Gost, Roswitha. **Bibliographie zur Lebenssituation der Frau in den Gesellschaften des Mittleren Ostens.** Bielefeld: Forschungsschwerpunkt Entwicklungssoziologie, 1988. 84 p. *Reihe Dokumentation.*

A brief bibliography of monographs, scholarly articles and essays in collections dealing with women in Middle Eastern societies. The bibliography is not classified, subdivided or annotated. More than half of the slim volume is an *Anhang* composed of reproduced articles and book reviews from reference works and journals. There is no index.

492. Hadraoui, Touria and Myriam Monkachi. **Études Feminines: Répertoire et Bibliographie.** Casablanca: Éditions le Fennec, 1991. 253 p. *Collections Femmes Maghreb.*

Part 1 of this interesting little reference provides brief sketches of prominent women in or from Algeria, Morocco and Tunisia: "fiches bio-bibliographiques." Most of these women are professors or writers, but some work in other fields, such as cinema production, management or clinical psychology. Their age range was about 30-50 at the time of publication, so they are presumably still in the prime of their professional lives. Part 2 is a substantial bibliography of current works by and about women, mostly journal articles. There are no indexes, so access is possible only by name.

493. Kimball, Michelle R. and Barbara R. von Schlegell. **Muslim Women Throughout the World: a Bibliography.** Boulder; London: Lynne Rienner, 1997. ix, 307 p. ISBN 1-55587-680-3.

Books and articles of a scholarly and popular nature coexist in this bibliography. The entries are not topically organized, only listed alphabetically by author, but there is an extensive index to help narrow the search by subject, region or country. Northern Africa is well covered here, as is the Arab world generally. An opening section presents more than 50 selected sources with full annotations; these are major works of lasting value and would provide a student with an excellent starting point for research.

494. Kinnear, Karen L. **Women in the Third World: a Reference Handbook.** Santa Barbara, CA: ABC-Clio, 1997. xv, 348 p. *Contemporary World Issues.* ISBN 0-87436-922-3.

This volume is more than a subject bibliography. It contains an interesting introductory chapter, a chronology of events in the struggle for women's rights since 1919, a collection of brief biographical sketches of prominent women in the developing world, directory data and descriptions of NGOs active in women's issues, and a fully-annotated bibliography of current books and videos on the topic, plus lists of journals, bibliographies and Internet resources. A useful index is provided.

495. Moghadam, Valentine M. **Women, Work and Economic Reform in the Middle East and North Africa.** Boulder; London: Lynne Rienner, 1998. xi, 258 p. ISBN 1-55587-785-0.

Explores the implications of globalization for working women and the patriarchal traditions that have characterized this region. Case studies from Morocco, Tunisia, Egypt and Algeria are included. The work provides ample current bibliographical references, tables of data and a very careful index.

496. Otto, Ingeborg and Marianne Schmidt-Dumont. **Frauenfrage im Modernen Orient: eine Auswahlbibliographie.** Hamburg: Deutsches Orient-Institut, 1982. xv, 247 p. *Dokumentationsdienst Moderner Orient;* Reihe A, 12. ISSN 0342-0434.

Also titled: *Women in the Middle East and North Africa.*

This volume is put together like a union catalog with pages composed of reproduced cards in two columns. It includes journal articles as well as books, with full bibliographic data, location information and usually abstracts. A detailed subject-index-cum-table-of-contents (the "Sachregister") gives access to the entries. Because they are already grouped geographically, it is also possible to browse the sections on the Islamic world and northern Africa (the Maghreb, Egypt and Sudan). This edition is in German only.

497. Otto, Ingeborg and Marianne Schmidt-Dumont. **Frauenfrage im Modernen Orient: eine Ergänzungsbibliographie.** Hamburg: Deutsches Orient-Institut, 1989. xvi, 113 p. *Dokumentationsdienst Moderner Orient;* Reihe A, 16. ISBN 3-922852-29-7; ISSN 0342-0434.

Also titled: *Women in the Middle East and North Africa.*

A supplement to the earlier volume, extended to 1989.

498. Raccagni, Michelle. **The Modern Arab Woman: a Bibliography.** Metuchen, NJ: Scarecrow, 1978. x, 262 p.

Dated now, very lightly annotated and poorly indexed, this bibliography is mentioned only because its coverage of North Africa is unusually strong. Algeria, Egypt, Libya, Morocco, Sudan, Tunisia and the Maghreb as a region all receive considerable attention.

499. Ruud, Inger Marie. **Women's Status in the Muslim World: a Biblio-graphical Survey.** Köln: E.J. Brill, for the Religionswissenschaftliches Seminar der Universität Bonn, 1981. 143 p. *Arbeitsmaterialen zur Religionsgeschichte;* 6. ISSN 0341-8529.

This compilation of books and articles is organized alphabetically by author. There is a clumsy subject index: finding materials on Egypt alone would require looking up 92 different works. The Maghreb and other African countries present the same difficulty. Entries are not annotated.

500. Seager, Joni. **The State of Women in the World Atlas.** Second edition. London: Penguin, 1997. 128 p. ISBN 0-670-10008-0; 0-14-051374-4.

This collection of 34 very colorful maps and captions conveys information about a wide range of issues, from traditional indicators of women's welfare like literacy and fertility, to domestic violence, lesbian rights, sex tourism, female genital mutilation, and women in the armed forces. The preface acknowledges a firmly feminist ideological viewpoint.

501. Tauzin, Aline and Marie Virolle-Souibès. **Femmes, Famille, Société au Maghreb et en Émigration: 700 Travaux et Documents Inédits.** Paris: Éditions Karthala, 1990. 188 p. ISBN 2-86537-262-6.

A compilation of theses, "mémoires" and documents studying issues of importance to the life and health of women in the Maghreb region. Many of these works were submitted for degrees in psychology, sociology or ethnology, though there are some from the fields of education, literature, economics and political science as well. The entries are not annotated, but some are printed with detailed abstracts. The entries are grouped under broad themes; indexes by author, by place or ethnonym, and by subject are provided.

Websites

See also electronic references pertaining to Islam or economic development.

502. Africa Policy Information Center. Strategic Action Issue Area: African Women's Rights. **http://www.africapolicy.org/action/women.htm**

Southern Africa emphasis, but contains useful links to organizations active on this issue worldwide.

503. African Women Global Network. **www.osu.edu/org/awognet/**

"A global organization that networks all men and women, organizations, institutions and indigenous national organizations within Africa, whose activities are targeted towards the improvement of the living conditions of women and children in Africa."

504. Muslim Women's League. **http://www.mwlusa.org/welcome.html**
Links to full-text news articles on world events of importance to Muslim women; plus chat room, listservs, and other background information.

505. NISAA. An Arab Women's Web Site. **http://www.nisaa.org/**
"NISAA offers women in the Arab World the opportunity to exchange experiences and information on gender specific topics in order to intensify their cooperation among each other. NISAA is also provides a means to enter into and enhance the dialogue between women in the Arab world as well as women in other parts of the world." Includes Egypt, Tunisia, Morocco and Algeria. Information on violence against women, reproductive health issues, etc.

506. Women in Development Network (WIDNET). **www.focusintl.com/widr1.htm**
Basic demographic and statistical information. In English and French.

Government, Politics and Law

Chapter 4

The political and legal institutions of independent African nations, foreign relations, affiliations and alliances formed through international organizations, the position of minority groups and refugees and other human rights issues are the concerns of this chapter. Problems of justice and security are especially acute in several of the countries of Northern Africa. The resources listed here offer materials for the study of these issues.

Post-Colonial Government Structures

507. **Economic Crisis and Political Change in North Africa.** Edited by Azzedine Layachi. Westport, CT; London: Praeger, 1998. 185 p. ISBN 0-275-96142-7.

Political reform, democracy and structural adjustment in Algeria, Morocco, Tunisia, Libya and Western Sahara are the concerns of these analytical essays. The work includes a helpful subdivided bibliography and an index.

508. **Government and Politics in Africa.** Second edition. Edited by William Tordoff. Bloomington: Indiana University Press, 1993. xvii, 340 p. ISBN 0-253-36028-5.

Coverage of Mediterranean Africa is not extensive, but there is material in this volume on the under-studied Sahel and the Horn. The extensive bibliographical references and the index are helpful.

509. **Handbook of Political Science Research on the Middle East.** Edited by Bernard Reich. Westport, CT; London: Greenwood, 1998. viii, 392 p. ISBN 0-313-27372-3.

Straightforward organization and attention to detail make this collection of bibliographical essays unusually attractive. Recent trends in the study of political events in the Middle East are analyzed and documented; chapters are devoted to Egypt, Libya, Tunisia, Algeria and Morocco, with further material on regional issues. Extensive notes for each chapter are supplemented by a small reference bibiography in an appendix. A very full subject index is provided, and an author index. Perhaps future editions could include a titles index, and a chapter on the Sudan.

510. **Political Encyclopedia of the Middle East.** Edited by Avraham Sela. New York; Jerusalem: Continuum; Jerusalem Publishing House, 1999. 815 p. ISBN 0-8264-1053-7.

Deliberately encompassing the whole Arab world, the Maghreb, Egypt, Mauritania, Somalia, Eritrea, Sudan and Djibouti, this work was nonetheless prepared entirely by an Israeli team of contributors and editors. Unsigned alphabetized entries range from one paragraph to several pages, and are fully cross-referenced. Small maps are sometimes provided. Some articles offer useful information in a convenient form (e.g., "Water Politics") , but are lacking in objectivity, while others (for example, "al-Azhar") seem almost intentionally offensive in tone.

511. **Political Handbook of the World 1998: Governments and Intergovernmental Organizations.** Annual; 1975- . Edited by Arthur S. Banks and Thomas C. Muller. Binghamton, NY: CSA Publications (SUNY), 1998. viii, 1287 p. ISBN 0-933199-13-9; ISSN 0193-175X.

Appearing in some form since 1927, this useful encyclopedia-style ready reference is now published annually. It provides a concise country-by-country profile of basic data, political history, parties and structures, and names of current office-holders; similar information is compiled on intergovernmental organizations.

A narrative history and description in some detail is included. Political parties, opposition groups and illegal resistance organizations are identified and described. The political composition of legislative bodies is noted. There is basic data on the news and information media, and a comment on press freedom and independence. Two indexes help to track down specific information, especially individual names. Maps are included where significant border disputes exist, as in Western Sahara (see Morocco). All of the countries of northern Africa are covered, including some quasi-national entities (e.g., Somaliland).

512. **Political Liberalization and Democratization in the Arab World.** Vol. 2: Comparative Experiences. Edited by Bahgat Korany, Rex Brynen, and Paul Noble. Boulder; London: Lynne Rienner, 1998. x, 299 p. ISBN 1-55587-590-4.

Prepared in connection with the Inter-University Consortium for Arab Studies at the University of Montreal, this work follows upon a first volume setting forth a theoretical foundation for the study of democratization in Arab states. This volume is far better suited to reference work, as each essay concentrates upon an individual country—among them Algeria, Egypt, Morocco and Sudan. Tables of data and ample, current, specialized bibliographical references are included. The volume also provides a useful index.

513. **Politics and Government in the Middle East and North Africa.** Edited by Tareq Y. Ismael and Jacqueline S. Ismael. Miami: Florida International University Press, 1991. xix, 570 p. ISBN 0-8130-1043-8.

A collection of informative, readable essays, clearly organized by geography. There are chapters on Egypt, the Sudan, Libya, and the Maghreb, with additional material on Islam and nationalism; a detailed index guides the reader to specific topics. However, some of the essays lack bibliographical references, and the volume provides no general bibliography.

514. Ayittey, George B. N. **Indigenous African Institutions.** Ardsley-on-Hudson, NY: Transnational Publishers, 1991. xlvii, 547 p. ISBN 0-941320-65-0.

A compendium of information on traditional African patterns of leadership and social organization. Legal and political authority, kingdoms/governments and economic structures are discussed. Several maps, a general bibliography and an index are provided. Of the nations of northern Africa, Mauritania, Mali, Niger, Chad, Ethiopia, Somalia and Sudan are included; there is some material dealing with Libya and Morocco, and with tribal groups found within these countries (Dinka, Fulani, Nuer, etc.). The work has a tendentious tone and a distinct ideological agenda.

515. Blaustein, Albert P. and Gisbert H. Flanz. **Constitutions of the Countries of the World.** Dobbs Ferry, NY: Oceana Publications. Ongoing. Multivolume set. ISBN 0-379-00467-4 (series).

In most libraries, large looseleaf folders hold these booklets in which the texts of national constitutions from each country are collected. Newer editions can be added right beside older ones; the constitution of Mauritania, for example, has been published in this format at least three times, in 1979, 1981 and 1986.

A chronology of political events leading up to the formation and/or revision of each constitution is provided, then the full text of the document itself, often translated into English. A small bibliography of related primary and secondary sources is supplied as well.

516. Brownlie, Ian. **African Boundaries: a Legal and Diplomatic Encyclo-paedia.** London; Berkeley: C. Hurst & Co.; University of California Press (for the Royal Institute for International Affairs), 1979. xxxvi, 1355 p. ISBN 0-903983-87-7 and 0-520-03795-2.

A large collection of treaties and decrees reproduced verbatim, establishing the boundaries between African territories and states. The documents date from 1845 to 1975, and cover the whole continent in detail. An explanatory introduction and an index are provided. Appropriately, there is a wealth of maps. This volume is an important resource for the historian or specialist.

517. Cook, Chris and David Killingray. **African Political Facts Since 1945.** Second edition. New York: Facts on File, 1991. vii, 280 p. ISBN 0-8160-2418-9.

A handbook of information nuggets, organized topically: a chronology; lists of governors, commissioners, heads of state and ministers; descriptions of the constitutions and parliamentary structures of independent states; brief identifications of political parties, border conflicts and internal struggles; tables of basic population data; some biographical entries. There is an amazingly ineffective index that merely reproduces the order in which entries are found in the book, without adding anything of value. Obviously, it should have reorganized the material by country, with topical subheadings.

518. DeLancey, Mark W. **Handbook of Political Science Research on Sub-Saharan Africa: Trends From the 1960s to the 1990s.** Westport, CT: Greenwood, 1992. viii, 427 p. ISBN 0-313-27509-2.

This collection of scholarly survey articles functions as a series of bibliographic essays on research in the field. Three topical essays on political and social change, development administration and international relations are presented first, then five regional articles and four country studies, including Chapter 8 on the Horn of Africa. Information on some of the nations of the Sahel is also to be found in the very well-organized subject index. An appendix provides some directory data on the social science research centers and libraries of sub-Saharan Africa, including the Sahel and Horn (and even Egypt). Extensive current bibliographies are supplied for each article, as well as a substantial list of published bibliographies and information sources.

519. Drabek, Anne Gordon and Wilfrid Knapp. **The Politics of African and Middle Eastern States: an Annotated Bibliography.** Oxford: Pergamon Press, 1976. x, 192 p. ISBN 0-08-020584-4.

The sources included in this volume focus on political development and the evolution of former colonies into modern states after independence. They deal with the formation of national structures and institutions, competing ideologies and interest groups, and larger political systems and ideas (nationalism, communism, pan-Africanism, etc.). International relations and conflicts are treated as well. Chapter VII is devoted to North Africa, with the Sudan, Sahel and Horn states distributed among other chapters. All entries are annotated (often very briefly). The typescript format and lack of a names or subject index make this bibliography awkward to use.

520. Jreisat, Jamil E. and Zaki R. Ghosheh. **Administration and Development in the Arab World: an Annotated Bibliography.** New York: Garland, 1986. xxx, 259 p. *Public Affairs and Administration Series;* no. 14. ISBN 0-8240-8593-0.

Books, articles and dissertations covering contemporary Arab societies, their administrative structures or "machinery" (p. xvi), use of human resources, socio-political features and approaches to economic planning are gathered in this bibliography. The literature included was published between 1970 and 1985.

Each entry is briefly annotated, indicating the main premise or argument of the work cited. The dissertations often have more detailed abstracts. The Arab world is defined as member countries of the Arab League, but the more subtle aspects of Arab identity are not overlooked: this volume covers Algeria, Libya, Egypt, Morocco, Tunisia, Somalia and Sudan. There is a very crude country index.

521. Long, David E. and Bernard Reich. **The Government and Politics of the Middle East and North Africa.** Second edition, revised and updated. Boulder, CO: Westview Press, 1986. xii, 479 p. ISBN 0-8133-0336-2.

A convenient state-by-state handbook bringing together essays by "a diverse group of Middle East specialists with academic and policy-oriented experience to produce a current, comprehensive and general book that focuses on the politics (and especially political dynamics) of the region known as the Middle East" (Preface, p. xii). This scope includes the North African coast from Morocco to Egypt, plus Sudan. The volume features 22 maps and 7 tables of data. A descriptive bibliographical mini-essay is provided for each chapter; there is a detailed index.

522. Long, David E. and Bernard Reich. **The Government and Politics of the Middle East and North Africa.** Third edition, revised and updated. Boulder, CO: Westview Press, 1995. vii, 487 p. ISBN 0-8133-2125-5.

A welcome new edition of this useful handbook on the political character of Middle Eastern and North African states. The very direct presentation of the material, and the volume's transparent organization (one comprehensive chapter per state) make it quite suitable as a reference; indeed, each article functions as a "short course" on its subject. Chapters on Egypt, Sudan, Libya, Morocco, Algeria and Tunisia are provided. Each article is equipped with a brief bibliographical essay, and there is a useful index.

523. Maddex, Robert L. **Constitutions of the World.** Washington: Congressional Quarterly, 1995. xxi, 338 p. ISBN 0-87187-992-1.

Articles describing the political foundations of many of the world's countries are brought together in this convenient handbook. Unlike Blaustein and Flanz, this reference does not present the actual text of each country's constitution, but presents an informative account and analysis of each political/legal system, its historical roots, structure, and, to some extent, actual application.

A glossary defining specialized political terms (such as "autogolpe" or "amparo") is helpful; bibliographical references and an index are also provided. Of the countries of northern Africa, only Algeria, Egypt, Libya and Ethiopia are covered in this volume.

524. Mallat, Chibli. **Islam and Public Law.** London: Graham & Trotman, 1993. viii, 282 p. *Arab and Islamic Law Series.* ISBN 1-85333-768-4.

One of the most accessible of this series, produced by the Centre of Islamic and Middle Eastern Law at SOAS in London. Egypt is covered here far more thoroughly than any of the other states of northern Africa. Tracking down specific information is difficult due to the entirely inadequate index.

525. Phillips, Claude S. **The African Political Dictionary.** Santa Barbara, CA: ABC-Clio, 1984. xxviii, 245 p. *Clio Dictionaries in Political Science;* no. 6. ISBN 0-87436-036-6.

Intended to clarify the use of vocabulary in the study of African political and social systems, this reference succinctly defines much of the confusing, ambiguous or heavily-loaded language of this field. Terms like "assimilation" or "association" had very specific connotations during French colonial rule in Africa—meanings that would rarely be found in any general English dictionary. In addition, the author supplies a one-paragraph remark in each entry highlighting the significance of each term in its African context, thereby separating text from commentary in a helpful way. The volume is organized by theme, with a geographical table of contents and an index. Tables of political, military and economic data are given in an appendix. A select bibliography is included.

526. Shimoni, Yaacov. **Political Dictionary of the Arab World.** New York, London: Macmillan, 1987. 520 p. ISBN 0-02-916422-2.

This work is composed of rather lengthy encyclopedia-style articles for the most part, rather than brief dictionary identifications. An entry on Algeria, for example, offers an eight-page narrative history of political events there in the twentieth century. Entries on individuals provide biographical data and an analysis of the person's character and achievements. Oddly, there are no bibliographical references. A few small maps and some cross-references are included, but there is no general bibliography or index of terms not used as entry headings. A negative tone toward the Palestinians is perceptible.

527. Shimoni, Yaacov and Evyatar Levine. **Political Dictionary of the Middle East in the 20th Century.** Supplement edited by Itamar Rabinovich and Haim Shaked. New York: Quadrangle/New York Times Book Co., 1972. 510 p. ISBN 0-8129-0482-6.

A one-volume ready reference providing "condensed information, alphabetically arranged, on countries and peoples, on national and political movements, parties and leaders, on ideas and ideologies, on disputes and wars, alliances and treaties" (Foreword). Designed for the English-language reader, the work uses a simplified transliteration method resembling that used in press reports and newspapers; some cross-references indicate alternative forms of names and vocabulary terms (e.g., GADDAFI see Qaddhafi). The geographical scope is not specified, but seems to include Egypt, Sudan and Libya.

The authors and editors "have striven to present as accurate and objective a picture of the region as possible"; however, all of them are Israelis, some are members of the Israeli foreign service, and the editors note that "most of them [are] professional Orientalists" (p. 5).

528. Tachau, Frank. **Political Parties of the Middle East and North Africa.** Westport, CT: Greenwood Press, 1994. xxv, 711 p. *Greenwood Historical Encyclopedia of the World's Political Parties.* ISBN 0-313-26649-2; ISSN 1062-9726.

A detailed, carefully prepared and organized work providing effective access to information suitable for study or ready reference. A useful introductory essay offers an overview of the political party as a force in the region; chapters on individual countries convey "as much information as possible regarding the formation, evolution and impact of these parties, including their interactions with each other as well as with the societies and governments within and under which they have functioned" (Preface). The Mediterranean coast and Sudan are included, but not the Sahel or Horn.

Names of political organizations are given in English or French, and usually in transliterated Arabic (or other nonroman-alphabet language); the volume is generously cross-referenced, and there is a substantial and fully-subdivided index. Each country section supplies a valuable narrative history of the nation's political life, followed by alphabetized entries for individual parties. In addition, a number of tables and two appendices are provided: a chronology of major political events in the region, and an extraordinary "genealogy" of parties, listing them in order of development, with dates.

Military Resources, Risks and Security

529. **International Military and Defense Encyclopedia.** Edited by Trevor N. Dupuy. Washington: Brassey's, 1993. 6 v. ISBN 0-02-881011-2 (set).

A multivolume collection of lengthy signed articles on all aspects of military activity. Articles on countries include large clusters of statistics, bibliographical references, and a concise account of the history, political structure, strategic concerns, defense industry, international alliances and current force strength of each country.

An article on North Africa focuses on regional history. The individual countries of northern Africa are represented, with the exception of Djibouti, Eritrea (still within Ethiopia), Mali and Niger, though some information about them can be found in Vol. 6's very good general index. The index is also the place to look for information about the North African campaign of World War II, including the major commanders involved.

530. **Jane's Sentinel. North Africa.** Available on CD-ROM.

Part of *Jane's Geopolitical Library*, this resource offers "a one-stop threat assessment for the North Africa region." Geography, map data, military and political science information.

531. **Jane's Sentinel: the Unfair Advantage: Regional Security Assessment, North Africa.** Edited by Paul Beaver. [Alexandria, VA]: Jane's Information Group, 1994. Eight sections, separately paginated.

A looseleaf binder containing country-by-country assessments of the defense capability, prospects for stability or conflict and strategic importance of Algeria, Egypt, Libya, Mali, Morocco, Mauritania, Sudan, Tunisia and Western Sahara.

A color map, descriptive material (country profile, history, political structure, international relations) and itemized information on the equipment and force strength of the military services are provided for each section. Some directory data and basic economic and trade information is included as well.

532. **Political Risk Yearbook.** Vol. 2: Middle East & North Africa. Edited by William D. Coplin and Michael K. O'Leary. East Syracuse, NY: Political Risk Services, 1997. Consists of 15 reports, separately paginated. ISBN 1-85271-354-2; ISSN 0897-8530

Also available on CD-ROM and online.

These reports mean to identify current political and economic conditions in each country and to prognosticate changes likely within the next five years. Efforts to promote growth, control inflation and maintain social order are crucial in attracting foreign investment and creating the kind of stability Western governments and business interests are seeking. This volume includes the Maghreb and Egypt only; Sudan is found in Vol. 4. Each report provides a map, current statistical and directory information, brief entries indicating major "political actors" and "risk factors," and narrative sections describing the role of the military, labor, opposition parties and factions, international contacts and various social pressures on the nation. Where the potential for change is judged to be great (e.g., Algeria), 18-month and 5-year forecasts predict the likely impact on market conditions of three different probable future regimes. Political Risk Services notes that this Yearbook is intended mainly for libraries and research, while other PRS publications are designed for businesses and governments.

533. **World Military Expenditures and Arms Transfers.** Washington: US Arms Control and Disarmament Agency. Annual, 1976- . ISSN 0-897-4667; SuDocs AC 1.16:995.

This source is often consulted and quoted in other reference works. It provides substantial data and some explanatory text on levels and trends in military spending, numbers of armed forces, weapons imports and exports, and the ration of defense expenditures to GNP, for 15-20 regions or alliances and about 170 individual countries. The Middle East and North Africa are shown as two separate regions; a sound approach, since their levels of defense spending and readiness are quite different.

Very clear, colorful graphics, fact boxes and prominent use of subheadings and bold type help to make the data accessible. Tables of detailed data cover a ten-year span in each issue, for comparison. There is no index, but a table of contents and alphabetical listings work reasonably well.

534. Babkina, A. M. **Terrorism: an Annotated Bibliography.** Commack, NY: Nova Science Publishers, 1998. 327 p.

This mysterious volume appears to be no more than a printout of a database search on the broad subject of terrorism in general. There are no original annotations—only the contents notes or Library of Congress subject headings present in each catalog record. No attempt was made to organize this material topically or geographically, except by means of a primitive subject index; browsing such a compilation is nearly impossible. It is not clear why this work was prepared or why it was published in this form.

535. Mickolus, Edward F. **Terrorism, 1988-1991: a Chronology of Events and a Selectively Annotated Bibliography.** Westport, CT: Greenwood, 1993. 916 p. *Bibliographies and Indexes in Military Studies;* no. 6. ISBN 0-313-28970-0; ISSN 1040-7995.

The fourth in a sequence of references on this topic prepared by Mickolus, covering terrorist violence since 1968. "The aim of these volumes is to present a comprehensive picture of international terrorist activities for the given period, based solely on publicly available sources" (Introduction). The anecdotal chronology of terror incidents occupies almost 800 pages of the book; the last 120 pages contain the bibliography, subdivided by region and topic. North Africa is poorly represented in the bibliography: Islamic fundamentalist violence in Egypt and Algeria is not mentioned. To compensate for the lack of indexes, Mickolus suggests obtaining a computer version of the material and running textual searches (p. 6).

536. Schmid, Alex P. **Political Terrorism: a Research Guide to Concepts, Theories, Data Bases and Literature.** Amsterdam: North-Holland; Sociaal-Wetenschappelijk Informatie- en Documentatiecentrum (SWIDOC), 1983. xiv, 585 p. ISBN 0-4448-5602-1.

Though published under the auspices of the Centre for the Study of Social Conflicts at Leiden, this is a curiously clumsy and ineffective work. Lengthy theoretical essays and articles occupy half the volume. A "directory" of terrorist organizations, opposition movements and parties actually offers only a simple list for each country, sometimes with descriptive remarks. Such information is bound to age quickly; this 1983 work does not yet reflect the presence of Islamic extremists in Algeria (though it does in Egypt). A large bibliography section was out-of-date when it was published: materials cited on northern Africa appeared in the 1950s and 1960s. There is an author index.

Journals

537. **Journal of African Law.** Three times/year; 1957- . London: Oxford University Press for SOAS. ISSN 0021-8553.

Descriptive website available online at **www.oup.co.uk/jnls/list/jaflaw/scope/**

A current-events journal studying problems of law (criminal, civil, constitutional) in African states. Though the emphasis in on sub-Saharan Africa, a recent issue contained an article by Jon Abbink, "Ethnicity and Constitutionalism in Contemporary Ethiopia" (vol. 41, no. 2).

Major concerns of modern Africa are dealt with in these articles, case and statute notes: human rights, petroleum revenue, refugees, environmental pollution, property and investment, labor laws, etc. In addition, there are notices of recent changes in law and policy in African states and internationally. Some issues also contain book reviews.

Websites

538. African Governments on the WWW. **www.gksoft.com/govt/en/africa.html**
Links to official ministry and embassy websites for each country, plus those of opposition groups or parties. Includes all the nations of northern Africa except Eritrea and Somalia.

539. African Law Today. **www.africanews.org/specials/africanlaw98.html**
Full text of articles from the current and recent issues. Published by the African Law Committee of the American Bar Association's Section of International Law and Practice.

540. African Voices: a Newsletter on Democracy and Governance in Africa. **www.info.usaid.gov/regions/afr/abic/avspr96.htm**
From the Africa Bureau's Office of Sustainable Development in the U.S. Agency for International Development. "A forum for dialogue on democratization in Africa," published quarterly. Full text available online, including back issues.

541. Center of Islamic and Middle Eastern Law. Islamic and Middle Eastern Law Materials on the Web. **www.soas.ac.uk/Centres/IslamicLaw/Materials.html**
Many links to full-text documents, carefully indexed and organized.

542. FindLaw Africa. **www.findlaw.com/search/a10africa.html**
Search engine organized by region or individual country. This regional site includes all of the countries of northern Africa.

543. Library of Congress. Guide to Law Online. **http://lcweb2.loc.gov/glin/worldlaw.html**
Joint project of the Global Legal Information Network and the Law library; convenient links page, searchable by country.

Foreign Relations

544. Africa in the Post Cold War International System. Edited by Sola Akinrinade and Amadu Sesay. London; Washington: Pinter, 1998. xvi, 232 p. ISBN 1-85567-499-8.

An essay collection focusing attention on issues of current interest in African politics, including democratization, human rights and the environment. Bibliographical references and an index are provided.

545. Contact: Africa 1999. Biennial; 1997- . Washington, DC: The Africa-America Institute, 1999. ISSN 1523-8636.

A directory offering descriptions and contact data for many agencies and organizations in the city of Washington involved in African issues. These include NGOs and IOs as well as officials of the United States government (both executive and Congressional), embassies and diplomatic missions, universities and research institutions. An index by country and sector is provided.

546. Bryson, Thomas A. **United States/Middle East Diplomatic Relations, 1784-1978: an Annotated Bibliography.** Metuchen, NJ: Scarecrow, 1979. xiv, 205 p. ISBN 0-8108-1197-9.

This retrospective bibliography covers more than one might expect, not just the history of the Arab-Israeli conflict. There are two chapters on early involvement with the Barbary coast, the effort to protect American sea trade from pirates, and diplomatic contacts with North Africa; a chapter on the Suez crisis; more than one touching upon petroleum exploration and "oil diplomacy." Annotations are very brief, usually one sentence; books, articles and dissertations appear here. An author index is included, but no subject or title indexes. Because of its historical emphasis, the reference is not appreciably dated.

547. DeLancey, Mark W. **African International Relations: an Annotated Bibliography.** Boulder, CO: Westview Press, 1981. xviii, 365 p. *Westview Special Studies on Africa.* ISBN 0-89158-680-6.

A compilation of "more than 2500 citations of books, journal articles and pamphlets in the field of African international relations" (publisher's note). The citations are given very brief (one-sentence) annotations; some are not annotated at all, or with only a few not-very-revealing words. The entries are gathered under 11 rather broad subject headings and are not subdivided geographically, topically or by type of literature; within each section, entries are alphabetized by author. There is a limited subject index.

548. DeLancey, Mark W. **African International Relations: an Annotated Bibliography.** Second edition. With William Cyrus Reed, Rebecca Spyke, and Peter Steen. Boulder, CO: Westview Press, 1997. xxv, 676 p. ISBN 0-8133-8653-5.

A new edition of DeLancey's 1981 work, revised and updated. Books and journal articles are cited, with very brief and sporadic annotations. This edition apparently concentrates on materials published since the first edition was completed, but "the most important earlier works" (p. 677) are repeated here—about 40% of those in the first edition. The states of northern Africa (including Djibouti and Western Sahara) are covered by this reference, and materials cited are relevant to regional issues as well, especially relations with Arab states. The entries are again organized into 11 topical chapters; there is a names index, but not a titles index. A rather clumsy but adequate subject index is provided.

549. Henry, Clement M. **Politics and International Relations in the Middle East: an Annotated Bibliography.** Ann Arbor: University of Michigan Center for Near Eastern and North African Studies, 1980. iv, 107 p. ISBN 0-932098-18-5.

Annotated carefully for the student and instructor, this bibliography covers the larger themes of international relations and comparative politics in the region, then presents country studies of Algeria, Egypt, Libya, Morocco, Sudan and Tunisia (among others). Journal articles and books in English predominate, though other European languages are found here. Unfortunately, not all of the entries are annotated, and there are no indexes.

550. Parker, Richard B. **North Africa: Regional Tensions and Strategic Concerns.** Revised and updated edition. New York: Praeger, 1987. xi, 214 p. ISBN 0-275-92773-3.

A collection of thoughtful essays sponsored by the Council on Foreign Relations and prepared by an experienced career Foreign Service officer, who served as U.S. Ambassador to Algeria and Morocco. The bibliography and well-organized subject index may make the work useful for reference.

551. Schultz, Ann. **International and Regional Politics in the Middle East and North Africa: a Guide to Information Sources.** Detroit: Gale Research, 1977. xiii, 244 p. *International Relations Information Guide Series;* v. 6. ISBN 0-8103-1326-X.

A useful collection of materials published on the Middle East up to 1977. A section is devoted to North Africa, and some individual countries in the region are covered (Algeria, Egypt, Libya, Morocco and Tunisia). Thematic sections may also be relevant, including Chapter 6, "Petroleum." Enties are briefly annotated. Author, title and subject indexes are provided.

552. Shavit, David. **The United States in Africa: a Historical Dictionary.** New York: Greenwood Press, 1989. xxii, 298 p. ISBN 0-313-25887-2.

Not confining itself to official US government activities in Africa, this work has a far broader and more intriguing function: to identify the "slavers ... colonists, ships and officers ... sea captains and traders, missionaries, diplomats, explorers, travellers and adventurers, soldiers, educators, authors and artists, scientists, mining engineers, hunters and other Americans and American institutions, organizations and business firms, which established a whole gamut of relationships between the United States and Africa" (Preface). This volume excludes the northernmost states of Africa, covering the Sahel east from Mauritania, and the Horn.

An interesting bibliographical essay is provided, plus a general index, a list of all chiefs of American diplomatic missions in Africa 1863-1988, and a helpful ordering of biographical entries by profession or occupation.

553. Silverburg, Sanford R. and Bernard Reich. **Asian States' Relations With the Middle East and North Africa: a Bibliography, 1950-1993.** Metuchen, NJ: Scarecrow, 1994. xii, 158 p. *Scarecrow Area Bibliographies;* no. 6. ISBN 0-8108-2872-3.

A work that aids research in and calls attention to a neglected facet of Middle East current events. Economic, cultural, diplomatic and political ties between Asia and the Middle East/North Africa developed enormously during the time period covered in this bibliography, as the rapidly-industrializing nations' need for energy supplies increased. Another linking factor is, of course, Islam: huge Muslim populations in Asia and the Pacific have important reasons to interact with Arab states, especially for pilgrimage and religious education.

The bibliography is organized alphabetically, with paired subject headings indicating the bilateral relationship (for example, JAPAN—KUWAIT) or topical idea (JAPAN—OIL). "Asia" here extends from India to Japan and south to Australia, while "North Africa" means the northern coast from Morocco to Egypt, plus Sudan. Published materials (mostly journal articles) mainly in English and Western languages are included; there is an author index. Entries are not annotated, nor are abstracts provided.

554. Silverburg, Sanford R. and Bernard Reich. **U.S. Foreign Relations With the Middle East and North Africa: a Bibliography.** Metuchen, NJ: Scarecrow, 1994. xvii, 586 p. *Scarecrow Area Bibliographies;* no. 3. ISBN 0-8108-2699-2.

Following on their 1990 work, the compilers have concentrated in this newer volume on recent citations dealing with radical changes in the political climate of the region after the disintegration of the Soviet Union and the Persian Gulf war (1989-1991). It includes books, articles, essays from scholarly publications, dissertations and theses, in paper, microform and multimedia formats. The Introduction explains the use of important U.S. government publications, both executive and legislative. There is no table of contents, thesaurus or subject index, but by looking up Egypt, Sudan, Libya, Algeria and Morocco, one may find at least a few entries, sometimes subdivided by descriptors. Some terms, like "Arab-Israeli Conflict," offer 20 pages of citations with no topical subdivisions. The entries are not annotated, and no abstracts are provided.

555. Silverburg, Sanford R and Bernard Reich. **United States Foreign Policy and the Middle East/North Africa: a Bibliography of Twentieth-Century Research.** New York: Garland, 1990. 407 p. *Garland Reference Library of Social Science;* v. 570. ISBN 0-8240-4613-7.

This bibliography offers access without annotation to current-affairs materials (including monographs, essays and articles), appearing up to early 1989, dealing with the complex role of the United States government in the Middle East. The Maghreb and the Sudan are covered to a lesser extent. Up-to-date sources are stressed; older materials are listed (as far back as the 1920's) if they are considered significant. Unpublished doctoral dissertations and master's theses, and appropriate materials in microform (particularly government publications) are within the scope of this work. Some sources in Western languages other than English are cited. There is a very weak – indeed, unusable – subject index.

Journals

556. **American Journal of International Law.** Quarterly, 1907- . Washington: American Society of International Law. ISSN 0002-9300.

Also available: in microform and CD-ROM from University Microfilms, Ann Arbor; online though Mead Data Central (provider of LEXIS/NEXIS) and West Publishing (WESTLAW). Descriptive website at **www.asil.org/Abtajo.htm**

This scholarly journal is of interest because of its concern for UN Security Council issues and the World Court, international criminal tribunals, the World Trade Organization and GATT, the World Bank and other multilateral development institutions, human rights issues, immigration, refugees and citizenship, water and energy resources and the environment, and the arbitration or negotiation of border disputes, all of which are of crucial importance for the states and peoples of northern Africa.

Major research articles with full bibliographical references, book reviews and studies of current court decisions and their implications appear in each issue. In addition, each volume provides its own detailed subject index, a "table of cases" indicating where specific court proceedings are discussed, and a cumulative guide to international legal materials.

557. **Foreign Affairs.** Six issues/year; 1922- . New York: Council on Foreign Relations. ISSN 0015-7120.

Also available on microfilm from UMI (Ann Arbor). The full text of a featured article, plus summaries and contents of the current issue, are available online at **www.foreignaffairs.org/**

A journal featuring opinion articles, analysis and essays by leading scholars and policymakers, usually intended to offer an original view of the "big picture" within which specific problems in international relations are studied. A recent issue presents an essay by Bernard Lewis, "The West and the Middle East," discussing the impact of Western influences and modernity upon Islamic societies (vol. 76, no. 1). Each issue also contains five or six lengthy, signed book reviews.

558. **International Affairs.** Quarterly; 1944- . Cambridge: Cambridge University Press and the Royal Institute of International Affairs. ISSN 0020-5850.

Also available full-text on CD-ROM through PAIS Select; for information about this service see **www.pais.inter.net/pais/sellst.htm;** descriptive website and contents available online at **www.riia.org/iaffs.html**

A forum for debate on contemporary world affairs, this academic journal generally (but not always) uses themed issues to bring together the views of several scholars on current major topics: e.g., the Middle East, Asia and the Pacific, globalization. Articles are lengthy and detailed, with full bibliographical references and sometimes maps or tables of data. In addition, about one-third of each issue is devoted to a collection of brief signed book reviews, organized by topic: the reader can turn directly to "Middle East and North Africa" or "Sub-Saharan Africa" to see which new books are profiled there.

559. **International Journal on World Peace.** Quarterly; 1984- . St Paul, MN: Professors World Peace Academy. ISSN 0742-3640.

Descriptive website and contents available online at **www.pwpa.org/IJWP/ index.html**

Problems in strategic studies and political science, ethics and economics are discussed in scholarly articles and essays in this journal. A section of news reports and 1-5 signed book reviews are included in each issue. A recent article by Charles Kwarteng studies Africa's stake in the Israeli-Palestinian peace process (vol. XIII, no. 4). A reviewer's comments and the author's response appear with the article.

560. **International Studies Quarterly: Journal of the International Studies Association.** Six times/year; 1967- . Oxford and Cambridge, MA: Blackwell. ISSN 0020-8833.

Also available online through OCLC FirstSearch Electronic Collections; in microform from UMI, Ann Arbor. Descriptive website and contents page available online at **csf.colorado.edu/isa/isapub/isq.html**

Lengthy theoretical articles in political science with full bibliographical references make up this academic journal. Some articles are of an historical or philosophical nature. This work is intended for the scholar and specialist.

561. **Journal of International Affairs.** Semiannual; 1952- . New York: Columbia University School of International and Public Affairs. ISSN 0022-197X.

Also available in microform through UMI (Ann Arbor). Editorial information and contents available online at **www.columbia.edu/cu/sipa/PUBS/ JOURNAL/journal.html**

Lengthy scholarly articles with full bibliographical references discuss key current problems in international politics. The journal's approach is to organize thematic issues, presenting the views of 12 different writers on various aspects of a single topic. A recent issue explored the theme "Religion: Politics, Power and Symbolism," including articles on the role of African churches in social transformation, and four articles pertaining to religion and politics in the Middle East, particularly Islam (vol. 50, no. 1). Some issues include shorter case-study articles, and each issue contains one major book review and several shorter ones by graduate students in this subject area. A cumulative index is also provided.

562. **Mediterranean Politics.** Three times/year; 1996- . London: Frank Cass. ISSN 1362-9395.

Continues an annual with the same title. Descriptive website at **www.frankcass. com/jnls/mp.htm**

Scholarly articles with ample bibliographical references analyze current problems in the Middle East and North Africa, often collected in themed issues. Several 1-2 page book reviews are included.

563. **Mediterranean Quarterly: a Journal of Global Issues.** Quarterly; 1990- . Washington: Duke University Press for Mediterranean Affairs, Inc. ISSN 1047-4552.

Website with links to full-text articles and other information available on-line at **www.erols.com/mqmq/**

Published by a private foundation known as Mediterranean Affairs, Inc., this journal has no particular brief to cover geographically: it includes analysis and commentary on any question of international studies. These are not so much research articles as essays and policy pieces. Book reviews and letters from readers are featured. Some very prominent public figures have contributed work to this journal.

564. **Review of International Studies.** Quarterly; 1981- . Cambridge: Cambridge University Press for the British International Studies Association. ISSN 0260-2105.

Also available from the publisher on microfiche. Descriptive website available at **www.cup.cam.ac.uk/journals/jnlscat/ris/ris.html**

According to its publisher, this journal presents "substantial articles and review articles which survey and analyse the literature of relevant fields and disciplines ... debate and discussion on areas of topical concern ... [and] serves the needs of scholars in politics, law, history, economics, and all other areas of social science in the international arena." Each issue contains only five or six lengthy theoretical articles; occasionally a book review in the form of a scholarly essay is featured.

Websites

565. Middle East Review of International Affairs (MERIA). **www.biu. ac.il/SOC/besa/meria.html**

Electronic journal and newsletter published by the Begin-Sadat Center for Strategic Studies at Bar-Ilan University. Considers strategic, political and social concerns in the region.

566. La Caisse Française de Développement. L'Agence Française de Développement. **www.afd.fr/**

New website, rapidly developing. Includes northern Africa.

567. Council on Foreign Relations. **www.foreignrelations.org/**
Contains many links to transcripts and full-text versions of public addresses, articles, interviews, summaries or texts of forthcoming books, task force reports, study group papers and other staff publications.

568. Department for International Development (UK). **www.dfid.gov.uk/public/ who/who_frame.html**
"Manages Britain's bilateral and multilateral development programmes in poorer countries." Links to British Aid Statistics and other details.

569. In Black and White/Noir sur Blanc. **home.iSTAR.ca/~nbw_mag/index.html**
A monthly magazine covering economic and social relations between Canada and Africa. Features government and NGO activities in development. In French and English.

570. US Agency for International Development. Africa Bureau Information Center. **www.info.usaid.gov/regions/afr/abic/**

571. US Agency for International Development. Asia & Near East. **www.info. usaid.gov/regions/ane/**

572. US Department of State. Bureau of Near Eastern Affairs. **www.state. gov/www/regions/nea/index.html**
Policy statements, press releases, news articles, remarks, testimony and briefings; also links to "Core State Department Reports," country information, travel advisories, etc., pertaining to the Middle East and North Africa.

Intergovernmental Organizations

573. **African International Organization Directory and African Participation in Other International Organizations.** First edition. Prepared by the Union of International Associations. Munich: K.G. Saur, 1984-1985. 597 p. ISBN 3-598-21650-5 and 0-86291-289-0.
An information-rich guide to organizations, both intergovernmental bodies and NGOs, with significant activities in Africa. The nations of northern Africa are included.
The "secretariat" section identifies organizations with their international headquarters in an African location. The "membership" section shows organizations with headquarters elsewhere and a presence in one or more African countries. For example, one can learn from this source that Algeria is blessed with a chapter of the Association of Catholic Esperantists, and of the Water Polo authority.
Each directory entry provides the formal title and acronym of the organization in English and French, the name of the director or president, an address and phone number, a capsule history and description of the organization's aims,

structure, staff and typical activities, and a list of member countries. There is also a statistical appendix showing, for example, trends in membership in IGOs and NGOs since 1960, and indicating relevant information in the *Yearbook of International Organizations* (from which this data is derived).

An index of names and acronymns and a country-by-country subdivided roster help to pinpoint material. Even so, it takes a bit of time to familiarize oneself with the volume's unusual and rather complex structure. Introductory and explanatory material in this volume is presented in both English and French.

574. **Yearbook of International Organizations.** Annual; 1967- . 35th edition. Munich: K.G. Saur, 1998-1999. 4 v. ISBN 3-598-23362-0; ISSN 0084-3814

Also available on CD-ROM.

Also titled: *Annuaire des Organisations Internationales.*

A massive four-volume reference containing descriptive entries—often very detailed—for thousands of international organizations in every field of activity. Entries are alphabetized in Vol. 1, indexed by country in Vol. 2, and indexed by subject and keyword in Vol. 3. The fourth volume provides a very substantial bibliography of the publications of international organizations, and materials about them and their activities.

All of the nations of northern Africa are represented. The editorial material in this reference is presented in both English and French, and cross-references from various forms of names are provided.

575. **Yearbook of the United Nations.** Department of Public Information. The Hague: Martinus Nijhoff, for the United Nations. Annual. ISBN 90-411-0376-7; ISSN 0082-8521; UN Sales no. E.96.I.1.

Not to be confused with the statistical yearbooks published by the UN, this volume is a descriptive (though unofficial) record of the organization's activities over the past year. Articles are arranged in large thematic categories: in 1995 for example, Part Two, "Regional Questions and Peace-Keeping," provided coverage of recent events in Somalia, Libya, Sudan and Eritrea requiring attention from or action by the UN.

References to relevant UN documents are given, and any formal hearings or resolutions by the General Assembly or the Security Council are noted. A well-constructed subject index makes it possible to find all information in the volume pertinent to Sudan, for instance. Up-to-date material on the important intergovernmental organizations related to the UN (FAO, WHO, WIPO, WTO, etc.) and appendices updating the roster, charter, structure and agenda of the UN are included.

576. Clements, Frank A. **Arab Regional Organizations.** Vol. 2. New Brunswick, NJ: Transaction (Rutgers University), 1992. xxxiii, 198 p. ISBN 1-56000-057-0.

A fully-annotated bibliography of books and articles studying the political and economic alliances of countries considered to be Arab states. An informative introduction provides concise descriptions of each organization (of reference value in itself), then the citations are ordered according to the plan set forth clearly in the table of contents. Author and title indexes are included; the subject index could stand to be a bit more complete, as not all of the countries belonging to these organizations are listed. Membership rosters (with dates) would also add to the reference value of this volume.

577. DeLancey, Mark W. and Terry M. Mays. **Historical Dictionary of International Organizations in Sub-Saharan Africa.** Metuchen, NJ: Scarecrow, 1994. lviii, 517 p. *International Organizations Series;* no. 3. ISBN 0-8108-2751-4.

This reference provides very brief identifications of organizations involved in international and regional cooperative activities in Africa. The historical or retrospective character of the reference means that dormant or defunct organizations are included, and those that have changed their names over the years are traced by cross-references.

A chronology and an informative introduction seek to provide context. Entries exist for some persons who have made significant efforts at African cooperation (e.g., Kwame Nkrumah), and for certain relevant vocabulary terms (Non-Aligned Movement, Pan Africanism, etc.). A great deal of space is devoted to a topically-arranged bibliography.

Though the emphasis is on sub-Saharan issues, there is material here pertaining to western and eastern Africa, francophone and Franco-African organizations, and African-Arab organizations.

578. Fredland, Richard. **A Guide to African International Organizations.** London: Hans Zell, 1990. vii, 316 p. ISBN 0-905450-90-6.

The body of this work is a directory of 400-500 intergovernmental organizations that have functioned in Africa during the colonial and independence periods (including those no longer active). A founding date, a list of member states, and some indication of the organization's goals or purpose are given for most of the alphabetized entries. The most important entries (OAU, ECOWAS, ADB, etc.) have descriptive articles of 1-8 pages. A section of maps (often blurry), a bibliography and a general index are provided.

579. Harris, Gordon. **Organization of African Unity.** New Brunswick: Transaction Publishers (Clio Press), 1994. xxxii, 140 p. *International Organizations Series;* vol. 7. ISBN 1-56000-153-4.

Of the states on the African continent, only three did not belong to the OAU in 1994: these were Morocco, Djibouti and South Africa. The rest of the Maghreb, Sahel and Horn nations have had some stake in this organization and its goal of African unity; indeed, President Hosni Mubarak of Egypt invested a great deal of time and effort trying to realize some of the potential of the OAU. This fully-annotated bibliography offers access to many sources dealing with African diplomacy, special issues such as human rights, border conflicts and refugees, and works detailing and evaluating the structure and role of the OAU itself. Author, title and subject indexes, a chronology and lists of OAU officers and assemblies are also provided.

580. Söderbaum, Fredrik. **Handbook of Regional Organizations in Africa.** Uppsala: Nordiska Afrikainstitutet, 1996. 161 p. ISBN 91-7106-400-1.

A guide to the many intergovernmental organizations active in Africa: over 200 at the time of publication. The compiler has derived information from a number of published sources, and attempted to supplement this with up-to-date material. This reference intends to include northern Africa, and provides a two-page description of the Arab Maghreb Union (p. 24-26).

Entries note the stated aims of each organization, an account of its history, its structure or framework of authority, a sketch of its typical activities (sometimes quite detailed), any publications, contact information for its headquarters, and a list of member states. Many forms of regional cooperation are represented here; for example, the Desert Locust Control Organization for Eastern Africa (of which Ethiopia, Djibouti, Somalia and Sudan are members) and the Lake Chad Basin Commission. A subject index of some kind would probably be helpful.

Journals

581. **Index to International Statistics: a Guide to the Statistical Publications of International Intergovernmental Organizations.** Monthly, with quarterly and annual cumulations; 1983- . Bethesda, MD: Congressional Information Service. ISSN 0737-4461; ISBN 0-88692-418-9.

Also available monthly from CIS on microfiche; also available quarterly from CIS on CD-ROM as "Statistical Masterfile" and online as "Statistical Universe": see **www.cispubs.com/statuniv/**

Detailed abstracts of IO statistical publications in paper and electronic formats comprise Vol. 1 of the paper reference, while Vol. 2 provides a huge index by country or geographic area, names and subjects. Entries are abbreviated, but intelligible.

Databases and Websites

582. Access UN (InfoWeb Newsbank). **infoweb.newsbank.com**

A searchable database of current and archived United Nations documents and publications, back to 1961. Full access for subscribers only.

583. Africa Recovery. A United Nations Publication. **www.un.org/ecosocdev/geninfo/afrec/**

Full text of the current issue online. In English or French.

584. Food and Agriculture Organization of the United Nations (FAO). **www.fao.org/**

Descriptive information, with links to FAOSTAT databases.

585. Haynes, Ed (Winthrop University). League of Arab States. **192.203.180.62/index.html**

A personal website packed with information about the member states of the Arab League, the history of the League, and related issues in the Middle East and northern Africa.

586. Organization for Economic Cooperation and Development (OECD). Club du Sahel. **www.oecd.org/sah/**
  Available in French and English.

587. Organization of African Unity (OAU). **www.oau-oua.org/**
  Also in French.

588. ReliefWeb: United Nations Office for the Coordination of Humanitarian Affairs (OCHA). South Sudan Online. **www.state.gov/www/issues/relief/index.html**
  General ReliefWeb site at **wwwnotes.reliefweb.int/**

589. United Nations Development Programme (UNDP). Sustainable Human Development. **www.undp.org/index5.html**
  The latest issue of Human Development Report is available online through this page.

590. United Nations Industrial Development Organization. **www.unido.org/**

591. United Nations World Food Programme. **www.wfp.org/**
  Current special coverage of Sudan.

592. World Bank. Middle East and North Africa. **www.worldbank.org/html/extdr/mena.htm**

593. World Health Organization (WHO). Regional Office for Africa. **www.users.dircon.co.uk/~glenholm/who/Afro.html**

Minority Groups, Refugees and Human Rights

594. **Freedom in the World: the Annual Survey of Political Rights and Civil Liberties, 1996-1997.** Annual; 1978- . New Brunswick, NJ: Transaction (Freedom House), 1997. 591 p. ISBN 1-56000-354-5; ISSN 0732-6610.
  Essays on political freedom worldwide, regional essays and a country-by-country description of the year's developments are featured. Fact boxes and tabulated ratings of "comparative measures of freedom" (p. 579) are given, plus a "Map of Freedom" on which northern Africa comes off rather badly. This reference makes no apology for its ideological viewpoint.

595. **Human Rights in Developing Countries: Yearbook 1995.** Edited by Peter Baehr et al. Oslo; The Hague: Nordic Human Rights Publications and Kluwer Law International., 1985. xi, 416 p. ISBN 90-411-0127-6.

Topical essays on human rights issues and the efforts of European organizations are featured in this annual, along with selected country reports, presented on a rotating basis. A given country will be reported on every 3-5 years, as a rule. In the 1995 edition, there is a detailed article more than 40 pages long on the Sudan, with a map and fact sheet, footnotes and a bibliography.

596. **Human Rights, Refugees, Migrants and Development: Directory of NGOs in OECD Countries.** Paris: Organization for Economic Co-Operation and Development, 1993. 409 p. ISBN 92-64-03869-8.

The organizations listed and described in this directory are, of course, in Europe, Japan and the United States, but their activities and the aid they provide make an impact on a great many nations of the developing world. Entries are written in either English or French, and introductory material is presented in both languages. The volume is indexed.

597. **Human Rights Watch World Report.** New York: Human Rights Watch. Annual, 1990- . ISBN 1-56432-207-6; ISSN 1054-948X.

A successor to the Human Rights Watch organization's *Annual Report,* this publication continually updates its coverage of human rights abuses by governments: murder, abduction, torture, unjustified detention, discrimination, etc. The 1997 issue contains reports on Algeria, Tunisia, Egypt, Sudan and Ethiopia (the Mediterranean coast of Africa is included in the Middle East division). In addition to the regional and country reports, there are special projects in arms proliferation, children's and women 's rights, prison conditions and so on. Appendices provide information about other publications of this NGO, its staff and advisory committees. For some reason, there is no coverage of human rights abuses in the State of Israel.

598. **World Directory of Minorities.** Edited by the Minority Rights Group. Chicago and London: St James Press and Longmans, 1990. xvi, 427 p. *Longman International Reference.* ISBN 0-582-03619-4.

A useful reference offering concise encyclopedia-style descriptive articles on the civil rights status of scores of ethnic and religious minorities around the world. A six-page article on the southern Sudan, for example, provides a large, detailed map, a header of basic facts and a fairly complete explanation of the historical background and current status of persecuted peoples in the area. Coverage of the Middle East, North Africa and sub-Saharan Africa includes the Berbers, Copts, North African Jews, Afars, Issas, Falashas, Tigrayans, Oromo and various groups in Chad, Mauritania and other parts of the Sahel. References to more specialized MRG reports are given, and extracts from the texts of important international treaties and documents appear in an appendix. There is a helpful index.

599. Andrews, J. A. and W. D. Hines. **International Protection of Human Rights.** London: Mansell, 1987. xiii, 169 p. *Keyguide Series.* ISBN 0-7201-1873-5

Also titled: *Keyguide to Information Sources on the International Protection of Human Rights.*

The international protection of individual rights and freedoms has developed since 1945 into a considerable subject area with its own extensive literature. This annotated and well-organized guide seeks to direct the reader to this source material.

The first five chapters also function as an introduction to the whole subject and a bibliographical essay. In addition, an inventory of intergovernmental and non-governmental organizations active in the field provides a very basic description of their aims and activities. There is a general index, but unfortunately no access by geographical area.

600. Blaustein, Albert P., Roger S. Clark, and Jay A. Sigler. **Human Rights Sourcebook.** New York: Paragon House, 1987. xvi, 970 p. ISBN 0-88702-202-2.

This handy volume contains the complete text of scores of documents fundamental to the definition and protection of human rights worldwide. International treaties and conventions, the United Nations charter and its relevant provisions, statements and declarations prepared by a wide variety of intergovernmental and non-governmental organizations form the basis of the book. Pertinent state constitutions, legislation and judicial decisions are also presented here.

Coverage of Africa is not extensive, but useful material can be found in the index under topical headings (asylum, refugees, slavery, women, etc.) and in documents like the *Universal Islamic Declaration of Human Rights* of 1981.

601. Davies, Julian. **Displaced Peoples and Refugee Studies: a Resource Guide.** Edited by the Refugee Studies Programme, Oxford University. London: Hans Zell, 1990. xii, 219 p. *Hans Zell Resource Guides;* 2. ISBN 0-905450-76-0.

A combined bibliography of published materials and a directory of organizations active in study of and services to displaced populations. Reference works, bibliographies, monographs, dissertations and journals are included, often with helpful annotations. Libraries and research centers and service agencies are identified and contact information is provided, with a brief description of the aims or activites of each institution or organization. There is a general index.

602. Farwer, Christine. **Afrikanische Flüchtlinge: Vertriebung und Internationale Migration: eine Auswahlbibliographie.** Hamburg: Deutsches Übersee-Institut, 1993. xii, 106 p. *Dokumentationsdienst Afrika;* Reihe A, no. 28. ISBN 3-933852-47-5; ISSN 0342-0442.

Editorial and introductory material in German, English and French make this work accessible to a large number of readers. Journal articles, monographs and portions of collective works are cited here, with subject descriptors and very often a helpful abstract or annotation. The abstract may be in German even if the article cited is in another language.

Materials cover 1985-1992, with some older titles included. Entries are ordered geographically, and information pertaining to Mali, Mauritania, Niger, Chad, Ethiopia, Djibouti, Somalia and Sudan is obtainable here. Additional reference helps include a list of bulletins and reports from various refugee aid agencies, indexes of authors and corporate bodies, and library holdings codes indicating where in Germany these materials are to be found.

603. Fenton, Thomas P. and Mary J. Heffron. **Human Rights: a Directory of Resources.** Maryknoll: Orbis, 1989. xviii, 156 p. ISBN 0-88344-534-4.

This publication in the Third World Resources series is based upon theme rather than geography. This resource identifies organizations, books, periodicals, pamphlets, articles and audiovisual materials that pertain to such problems as torture, genocide, apartheid, religious, racial or sexual discrimination, child labor, censorship, and improper imprisonment, detention, disappearance or execution. Entries vary, but most provide detailed descriptions or annotations. Countries covered include Egypt, Algeria, Ethiopia, Libya and Sudan.

604. Friedman, Julian R. and Marc I. Sherman. **Human Rights: an International and Comparative Law Bibliography.** Westport, CT: Greenwood, 1985. xxvii, 868 p. *Bibliographies and Indexes in Law and Political Science;* no. 4. ISBN 0-313-24767-6.

There is a great deal of information about Africa in this substantial bibliography, but it is not at all easy to find. Entries are organized topically, and (apart from an author index) they are also indexed topically, but not geographically.

605. Lawson, Edward. **Encyclopedia of Human Rights.** Second edition. Washington: Taylor & Francis, 1996. xli, 1715 p. ISBN 1-56032-362-0

"Published with the cooperation of the United Nations High Commissioner for Human Rights/Centre for Human Rights, as a contribution to the UN Decade on Human Rights Education, 1995-2005" (verso).

This very large, solid volume is composed of alphabetically-arranged entries, many of which are substantial topical articles with cross-references and a bibliography—e.g., REFUGEES. Biographical entries and country reports are included. An important feature is the printing of the text in full of any relevant documents, such as the UN General Assembly resolution on slavery, within the article on this topic. Useful appendices are also provided: a glossary of human rights terms, such as "amnesty" and "migrant worker"; a chronology of international agreements governing human rights since 1921; an update on the ratification of international human rights conventions, naming all signatory states; a carefully-prepared subject index.

606. Minahan, James. **Nations Without States: a Historical Dictionary of Contemporary National Movements.** Westport, CT: Greenwood, 1996. xxiv, 692 p. ISBN 0-313-28354-0.

An interesting and easy-to-use ready reference offering concise three-page encyclopedia-style entries on various peoples who have not yet achieved independent statehood, or who consider themselves a distinct entity within an existing state. A number of these are in northern Africa, such as the Tuareg (see Azawad), the Afar and Saho (see Adal), the people of Darfur, the Kabyles, the peoples of North Chad, the South Sudan and Somaliland, and of course the Sahrawi (Western Sahara).

Basic population statistics, a sort of country profile, a narrative history/description and some bibliographic references are provided in each entry. The volume is indexed, and two helpful appendices supply dates, a table of peoples by nation, and the names of independence groups, factions or parties.

607. Ray, Donald I. **Directory of the African Left: Parties, Movements and Groups.** Aldershot: Dartmouth Publishing Group, 1989. vi, 273 p. ISBN 1-85521-014-2.

This interesting ready reference seeks to provide brief identifications of the political groups, both formal and informal, active on the "left" in the 1980s. Ray includes organizations whose goal is "to exercise power at the level of the state and/or the region" (i.e., not purely local groups) with an orientation or ideology that can be described as "socialist or communist or Marxist or left nationalist or left national liberation or left pan-Africanist or anti-imperialist" (p. 4-5). Chapter 2 explains these terms and provides a concise overview of the literature on this subject. Northern Africa is fully covered by this volume, with at least one organization listed for every country or area (with the exception of Western Sahara). Indexes by acronym and country are helpful.

608. Segal, Aaron. **An Atlas of International Migration.** Maps by Patricia M. Chalk and J. Gordon Shields. London: Hans Zell, 1993. vii, 233 p. ISBN 1-873836-30-9.

A unique new reference covering voluntary migration and the displacement of refugees, from early human history up to 1991. Legal and illegal migrant workers and slavery are included. Monochrome maps illustrate and reinforce the text. Special attention is given to the dispersal of persecuted peoples or "diasporas." Countries of northern Africa are sometimes classed as Middle East, sometimes as Africa, so looking in both places is a good idea. A valuable glossary, an annotated and a general bibliography, and a helpful index are included.

609. Umozurike, U. Oji. **The African Charter on Human and People's Rights.** The Hague: Martinus Nijhoff, 1997. vii, 240 p. *Raoul Wallenberg Institute Human Rights Library;* v. 2. ISBN 90-411-0291-4.

This monograph, detailing and analyzing the process of forming the Charter, contains some useful reference features: the full text of the Charter itself, plus the procedural rules for its application, a directory of all organizations affiliated with the African Commission on Human and People's Rights, instructions for bringing an issue before the Commission, and a record of the sessions of the ACHPR since 1987. There is also a very helpful bibliography, but no index.

610. Verney, Peter. **Sudan: Conflict and Minorities.** London: Minority Rights Group, 1995. 42 p. ISBN 1-897693-65-6; ISSN 0305-6252.

This internationally-active nongovernmental organization does its own re-search to produce reports on minority populations whose human rights are threatened. Six reports per year are published; MRG reports are also available on Chad, Eritrea, the Falashas, Somalia, the Sahel and the Western Sahara.

Thematic reports are also often relevant to northern Africa, such as studies of refugee problems, language rights and female genital mutilation. This issue on Sudan offers two big, clear monochrome maps (which would make excellent slides), a chronology, footnotes and a bibliography. This information source is suitable for a school or college library.

611. Waltz, Susan E. **Human Rights and Reform: Changing the Face of North African Politics.** Berkeley: University of California Press, 1995. xiv, 281 p. ISBN 0-520-20003-9.

A scholarly monograph on agents for change in human rights practices in Morocco, Tunisia and Algeria. Concerns over serious abuses of citizens by gov-ernments have motivated individuals and groups to organize and seek reform. The book includes bibliographical references for each chapter, and a useful names-and-subject index.

Journals

612. **Human Rights Law Journal.** Quarterly; 1980- . Kehl am Rhein: N.P. Engel. ISSN 0174-4704.

Continues: *Human Rights Review.*

Published in association with the International Institute of Human Rights in Strasbourg, this journal is largely occupied with European law, but also devotes attention to other areas. A recent issue covered the latest sessions of the African Commission on Human and Peoples' Rights in detail—including hearings on violations in Chad—and the Arab League's action on the Arab Charter on Hu-man Rights (Vol. 18, no 1-4). Decisions, reports and documentation of specific rulings and case law form the backbone of this periodical.

613. **Human Rights Quarterly: a Comparative and International Journal of the Social Sciences, Humanities and Law.** Quarterly; 1981- . Baltimore: Johns Hopkins University Press. ISSN 0275-0392; E-ISSN 1085-794-X.

Continues: *Universal Human Rights.* Also available online through OCLC FirstSearch Electronic Collections. Descriptive website at **muse.jhu.edu/journals/hrq/index.html;** full text available online to subscribers.

An academic journal composed of research articles on specific current problems in the administration of justice worldwide. The journal offers "scholars in the fields of law, philosophy and the social sciences an interdisciplinary forum in which to present comparative and international research on public policy within the scope of the Universal Declaration of Human Rights" (title page). Each issue also contains one or two substantial, signed book reviews, and each volume provides an author index.

614. **Index on Censorship.** Bimonthly; 1972- . London: Writers & Scholars International. ISSN 0306-4220.

See also their website at **www.indexoncensorship.org**

The concern of this periodical is intellectual freedom and the repression of minority views or beliefs anywhere in the world. Freedom of expression in northern Africa is among the topics covered.

615. **International Migration Review.** Quarterly; 1966- . New York: Center for Migration Studies. ISSN 0197-9183.

Also titled: IMR. Continues: International migration digest. Also available on microfilm from UMI (Ann Arbor). Contents page and links to the Center for Migration Studies available at **cmsny.org/cmspage3.htm**

These scholarly articles study specific local problems in labor migration, the absorption of immigrants and refugee populations, and also present more theoretical arguments or observations affecting the international community as a whole. Full bibliographical references are included, and every issue contains at least 15 brief but informative, signed book reviews. News of important conferences and symposia also appears in each issue, and there is an annual index.

Websites

616. Africa Policy Information Center. Washington Office on Africa. **www.africapolicy.org/index.shtml**

"Recent policy-relevant documents concerning US/African relations and related issues, multilateral institutions, and African grassroots interests in peace, sustainable development, democratization and human rights."

617. African Human Rights Resource Center. University of Minnesota. **www1.umn.edu/humanrts/africa/index.html**

618. Algeria Watch International (human rights organization). **members.tripod.com/~AlgeriaWatch/**

Detailed and current information, with many links to news sources and other NGOs active in this area.

619. Amnesty International Online. "Working to protect human rights worldwide." **www.amnesty.org/**

620. Coalition Against Slavery in Mauritania and Sudan (CASMAS). **members.aol.com/casmasalc/**

621. Homelands. Autonomy, Secession, Independence and Nationalist Movements. **www.wavefront.com/~homelands/index.html**
Special coverage of the South Sudan.

622. Human Rights Watch. Index. **www.hrw.org/research/**
Source from which to order detailed reports on human rights conditions in Africa and the Middle East.

623. INCORE: Initiative on Conflict Resolution and Ethnicity. Regional Internet Guides. **www.incore.ulst.ac.uk/cds/countries/**
Current, well-organized material, featuring Algeria and Sudan.

624. Le Maghreb. Des Droits de l'Homme. **www.mygale.org/~maghreb/**
"Ce site a pour but d'offrir une tribune à des associations démocratiques Maghrébines et Euro-Maghrébines, d'informer sur les violations des droits de la personne humaine dans les pays du Maghreb et de participer à l'avènement d'Etats de droit et d'une véritable citoyenneté dans ces pays." Morocco, Algeria and Tunisia. In French.

625. Muslim Brotherhood Movement Homepage. **www.ummah.net/ikhwan/**
An Islamist organization active in northern Africa.

626. Naval Postgraduate School. Terrorist Group Profiles. **web.nps.navy. mil/~library/tgp/tgpndx.htm**
Includes information on a number of organizations active in the Middle East and North Africa.

627. Tamazgha. Website of the World Amazigh Congress. **www.worldlynx. net/tamazgha/**
"Tamazgha is a collection of resources on North Africa, the Amazigh (Berber) people, their language and culture." In Tamazight, English, French and Spanish.

628. Tamazight. Un Répertoire du Sites Amazighes. **www.physics.mcgill. ca/~karim/tamazight/**
Site in French devoted to Berber culture, Kabyles and Tuaregs; with many links.

629. United Nations High Commissioner for Refugees (UNHCR). Country Index. **www.unhcr.ch/world/alpha.htm**
Links to detailed information on refugee populations in Africa and the Middle East: especially Egypt, Eritrea, Ethiopia, Somalia, Sudan, Libya, Algeria, Mali, Mauritania and Western Sahara.

Economics—Commerce, Industry and Aid

Northern Africa is the location of some of the poorest countries in the world, with serious development needs escalating into famine emergencies. It is also provided with considerable oil reserves, and petroleum exploration, recovery and trade form the backbone of certain economies. Centrally-planned economies are giving way in many places to privatized and restructured ones, with far-reaching consequences. Sustainable development, social justice and environmental concerns are all important issues in the region.

Development and Demographic Statistics

Development Studies and References

Additional materials on desertification, water resources, pollution and other environmental concerns will be found under "Science and Technology." Sources chiefly concerned with physical and human geography are included under "Social Sciences."

630. **Dictionary of Development: Third World Economy, Environment, Society.** Edited by Brian W. W. Welsh and Pavel Butorin. New York: Garland, 1990. 2 v. *Garland Reference Library of Social Science;* 487. ISBN 0-8240-1447-2 (set).

An opening section provides brief country-by-country statistical profiles, called "Developing Country Indicators," compiled from standard sources. The body of the work is an alphabetized compilation of short entries (mostly 1-5 paragraphs in length) identifying terms in their development context: e.g.

CHOLERA, or FREE MARKET ECONOMY. Longer entries are provided for major topics like FAMILY PLANNING or PRIMARY HEALTH CARE; these longer articles often have useful bibliographies. A major contribution of this reference is its listings for hundreds of agencies, NGOs, church-related projects and other organizations involved in development and environmentally-significant work. A list of relevant periodicals is provided in an appendix.

631. **World Development Report 1992: Development and the Environment.** Oxford: Oxford University Press, for the World Bank, 1992. xii, 308 p. ISBN 0-19-520877-3; ISSN 0163-5085

Also available on CD-ROM.

Not just specific problems of industrial and agricultural air and water pollution and energy use, but also larger environmental concerns are discussed here: sustainable development, global "greenhouse gases," hazardous waste, rainforests, and environmental justice. This work is indicative of the World Bank's attitude toward such issues gradually changing in response to pressure and criticism of the old build-dams-cut-trees-pour-asphalt style of development.

632. **World Development Report 1993: Investing in Health.** Oxford: Oxford University Press, for the World Bank, 1993. xii, 329 p. ISBN 0-19-520889-7; ISSN 0163-5085

Also available on CD-ROM.

The World Bank has identified the health sector—like infrastructure—as an area in which "the impact of public finance and public policy is of particular importance" (Foreword). The 16th issue of this annual contains eight articles and two very useful statistical appendices focusing on the role of the state in health services, especially in developing countries.

633. **World Development Report 1994: Infrastructure for Development.** Oxford: Oxford University Press, for the World Bank, 1994. x, 254 p. ISBN 0-19-520991-5; ISSN 0163-5085

Also available on CD-ROM.

The 17th edition of this annual explores the relationship between infrastructure and development. Improving the quality of infrastructure services (safe water, sanitation, electricity, telecommunications and transport) is a high priority in developing countries struggling to modernize their economies and provide for their people.

634. **World Development Report 1995: Workers in an Integrating World.** Oxford: Oxford University Press, for the World Bank, 1995. ix, 251 p. ISBN 0-19-521103-0; ISSN 0163-5085

Also available on CD-ROM.

Labor and conditions for workers around the world is the theme of the 18th edition of this annual. The income and security of workers, risks to their health and safety, and the increasing globalization of the labor pool through migration and relocation of industries is creating tensions in the more advanced and developing world alike.

635. **World Development Report 1996: From Plan to Market.** Oxford: Oxford University Press, for the World Bank, 1996. ix, 241 p. ISBN 0-19-521108-1; ISSN 0163-5085

Also available on CD-ROM.

The theme of the 19th edition of this annual is the transition of centrally planned economies to a market orientation. Though the report concentrates on Central and Eastern Europe, the former Soviet states, China and Vietnam, the subject is also a crucial one for some countries in northern Africa, notably Egypt.

636. **World Development Report 1997: the State in a Changing World.** Oxford: Oxford University Press, for the World Bank, 1997. viii, 265 p. ISBN 0-19-521115-4; ISSN 0163-5085

Also available on CD-ROM.

The twentieth issue of this annual published by the World Bank (International Bank for Reconstruction and Development) is devoted to the theme of the state's role in economic development. Feature articles try to tailor state responsibilities to resources; the approach is theoretical, with examples and case studies.

Graphics boxes and figures illustrate the text. A specialized but not classified bibliography is included. At the core of the book is a 50-page section of tables of current and comparative economic data, selected from the World Bank's *World Development Indicators* annual. Countries are entered individually by income level; regional statistics are also given (Middle East and North Africa, Sub-Saharan Africa). Technical notes explaining the details of the tables are included.

637. **World Development Report 1998/99: Knowledge for Development.** Oxford: Oxford University Press, for the World Bank, 1998. viii, 264 p. ISBN 0-19-521119-7; 0-19-521118-9; ISSN 0163-5085

Also available on CD-ROM. For a description and ordering information, see **www.worldbank.org/wdr/**

As professionals in the field are aware, universal knowledge and information access is both a technical challenge and a justice issue. That is the subject of the twenty-first edition of this report: knowledge access, from advanced telecommunications and information technology to basic health information in remote villages. It represents a new initiative by the World Bank to become a more effective clearinghouse for the knowledge it has accumulated in more than 50 years of development activity; a new data-delivery system is reportedly being prepared to facilitate access to this information.

The *World Development Report* is also published in Chinese, Arabic, French, Italian, Portuguese, Japanese and German.

638. Fontagné, Lionel and Nicolas Péridy. **The European Union and the Maghreb.** Paris: Organisation for Economic Co-Operation and Development, 1997. 103 p. *Development Centre Studies.* ISBN 92-64-15617-8

Also titled: *L'Union Européenne et le Maghreb.*

This OECD study provides a glimpse of the implications of Maghreb development for the economies of the European Union. Two very clear maps and several graphs and tables of data are included, plus a specialized bibliography.

639. Fry, Gerald W. and Galen R. Martin. **The International Development Dictionary.** Santa Barbara, CA: ABC-Clio, 1991. xxxiii, 445 p. *Clio Dictionaries in Political Science.* ISBN 0-87436-545-7.

This ready reference offers concise entries defining important vocabulary terms and identifying persons, organizations and concepts significant in development theory and practice. A brief, objective paragraph is followed by interpretive remarks meant to help the reader grasp the implications of the event or idea defined. There is a compact bibliography ordered by author. A capable index provides access by specific country or region.

640. Ghosh, Pradip K. **Developing Africa: a Modernization Perspective.** Westport, CT: Greenwood, 1984. xx, 435 p. *International Development Resource Books;* no. 20. ISBN 0-313-24156-2; ISSN 0738-1425.

Of the many monographs and essay collections now available on development, structural adjustment and sustainable policies in Africa, this work deserves mention here because of its reference features. In addition to eight essays, the book includes an annotated bibliography of statistical sources (both economic and demographic information) and a substantial section of statistical tables derived from World Bank publications.

There is a 78-page "resource bibliography" containing annotations or abstracts, mainly from indexing sources. Another section provides guides to United Nations information providers, development-related bibliographies, periodicals and research institutions. The Maghreb states and Egypt are mentioned, but the Sahel and the Horn are more fully covered. There is a simple index. Publication date should be taken into account.

641. Savitt, William and Paula Bottorf. **Global Development: a Reference Handbook.** Santa Barbara: ABC-Clio, 1995. x, 369 p. *Contemporary World Issues.* ISBN 0-87436-774-3.

The facts and figures in this volume are organized topically, with articles on imperialism, sustainable development, economic growth with social justice, debt, militarism, hunger, the status of women, refugees and migration, etc. Descriptive articles are reinforced by tables of statistics. There is a handy section of brief biographical sketches identifying "leading figures in the field of development" (p. 111). Three chapters are devoted to sources of information on development: agencies and organizations, print and nonprint materials. A useful glossary of development-related vocabulary and a general index are provided.

642. Tarver, James D. **Urbanization in Africa: a Handbook.** Westport, CT: Greenwood, 1994. xxxii, 484 p. ISBN 0-313-27760-5.

A useful collection of essays focusing on a crucial factor in Africa's development, environment and quality of life. The volume is clearly divided into geographical units, and chapters are devoted to urbanization in Morocco, Algeria, Libya, Egypt, Mali and Ethiopia. Each chapter has its own bibliography, with maps, tables and figures as required. the volume includes additional bibliographical references, a names index and a useful subject index listing individual cities and areas not covered in separate chapters (for example, Eritrea).

Statistics Sources

Citations and annotations for annuals reflect the issue examined; some changes can be expected in later issues or editions of the same work.

643. **African Development Indicators.** Washington: World Bank, 1995. 419 p. ISBN 0-8213-3127-2; ISSN 1020-2927.

Building on the earlier "provisional" publication, *African Economic and Financial Data*, this volume presents a great deal of additional information in a similar format. It now includes an expanded list of environmental indicators, a new chapter on household welfare indicators, and improved coverage of many of the data series. The editors reiterate that problems of missing or inconsistent data from African national statistics services have not been entirely overcome; estimation methods also differ. Technical notes discuss such differences in methodology. Some bibliographical references are provided. Slow searching of the table of contents is the only way to locate specific material; there is no index.

644. **African Development Report 1995.** Seventh edition. Abidjan: African Development Bank, 1995. xi, 449 p.

Reports and policy papers describe and analyze current conditions in African national economies, structural adjustment and sustainable growth, state planning, privatization, monetary policy, debt, food security and other crucial issues on the continent. Statistical tables for individual member nations as well as various regional groupings (the Maghreb, ECCAS, ECOWAS, the Franc Zone, etc.) appear throughout this volume and in particular appendices or sections; all of the countries of northern Africa are represented, though not every one is included in every figure, section or table. Locating all of the information on any given country in this volume would require considerable effort. A subdivided bibliography is provided.

645. **African Economic and Financial Data.** New York; Washington: United Nations Development Programme and World Bank, 1989. xiii, 204 p. ISBN 0-8213-1251-0.

This document "is intended to provide Africans and those interested in Africa a consistent and convenient set of data to monitor development programs and aid flows in the region" (Preface). The volume consists of full-page tables organized by topic, with each country entered as a line of data. In many cases, change can be charted over time, back to about 1975. The tables usually designate Algeria, Egypt, Libya, Morocco and Tunisia as a separate area called "North Africa." Other countries are subdivided by type of economy: oil exporters, "middle-income economies," etc. There are technical notes explaining the use of terms and values in the tables. Access is provided through a tables list, which calls for some rather slow searching; there is no index.

646. **Bibliography of Publications, Africa Region, 1990-97.** Edited by P. C. Mohan. Washington: International Bank for Reconstruction and Development, 1998. v, 62 p. *World Bank Technical Paper;* no. 393. ISBN 0-8213-4089-1.

Potentially a very useful guide to the sometimes bewildering array of studies published by the World Bank on Africa generally and on individual countries and projects. The guide lists technical and discussion papers by number, then organizes entries by topic, then chronologically (by publication date). An index gives access by broad subject headings. Unfortunately, access by country is not provided, except within certain categories. (Electronic access to this material would probably be more efficient.) Abstracts in English or French are printed with most of the entries. Information on ordering these publications from publishers or distributors is included.

647. **Demographic Yearbook.** Prepared by the Department for Economic and Social Information and Policy Analysis, Statistics Division. New York: United Nations. Annual, 1974- . ISBN 92-1-051086-0; UN Doc. ST/ESA/STAT/SER.R/26; Sales no. E/F.97.XIII.1

Also titled: *Annuaire Démographique.*

This fundamental source has been issued in some form since 1948. A special topic is featured in each issue; in 1995, it was household composition (number of family nuclei, headship rates, age, sex and marital status of householder and dependents, etc.). The tables published annually provide a wealth of comparison data. All contents are in English and French throughout.

648. **Human Development Report 1997.** Annual; 1990- . New York; Oxford Oxford University Press for the United Nations Development Programme (UNDP): 1997 xi, 245 p. ISBN 0-19-511996-7; ISSN 0969-4501.

A similar approach to the World Bank's *World Development Report*, but this work focuses entirely on the causes and effects of poverty, and the world's struggling economies. Tables enumerate "HPI" (human poverty index) indicators; text and fact boxes help to interpret these figures. Ten of the nations of northern Africa are among the neediest according to their HPI rank. Three are at the very bottom (Mali, Ethiopia, Niger), but even the relatively secure states of Mediterranean Africa (such as Morocco) rank surprisingly low. Text and statistical tables are clearly organized, but there is no index.

649. **Social Indicators of Development.** Baltimore: John Hopkins University Press; published for the World Bank. Annual, 1965-96. ISBN 0-8108-4788-5; ISSN 1012-8026

Has now been absorbed by *World Development Indicators.*

Country tables showing "priority poverty indicators" cover human and natural resources, and expenditures on or investment in human capital. In 1994, a new element was added: "supplementary poverty indicators," listing basic public services like health care and safe drinking water. Figures for the Middle East and North Africa as one region, and for sub-Saharan Africa (including Chad, Ethiopia, Somalia, Niger, Mali and Sudan) are given, along with more detailed data for individual countries.

650. **The State of Food and Agriculture.** Annual; 1951- . Rome: FAO, 1997. xx, 285 p. *FAO Agriculture Series;* no. 30. ISSN 0081-4539

Computer diskette is provided displaying "time series data" in English, French and Spanish. See also FAOSTAT Database online at **apps.fao.org/ default.htm**.

This annual is a summary of current conditions in food production worldwide, with a greal deal of descriptive and statistical information conveniently presented. Each year's report has a particular theme: the topic for 1997 was "The Agroprocessing Industry and Economic Development," and several special articles and country studies on this topic are featured here. Africa is reviewed as a region, and so is "Near East and North Africa," with Egypt singled out for additional attention.

Fact boxes, tables of data, figures and graphs (called "exhibits") are freely used throughout. Studying the table of contents is important, as there is no indexing. The statistical information on the diskette (databases in menu format for 150 countries) is searchable and can be printed or exported.

651. **The State of World Rural Poverty: a Profile of the Near East and North Africa.** Compiled by Abdelhamid Abdouli. Rome: International Fund for Agricultural Development, 1994. iv, 59 p.

Companion volumes by IFAD focus upon Asia, Latin America, etc.

This report is partly text and partly graphics and statistics, describing and documenting the causes and effects of poverty in the region. The focus here is on rural populations, so information on natural resources, the environment, access to land, water and capital, infrastructure and technology (especially agricultural research), government policymaking and the status of rural women is presented.

Regional issues and those affecting individual countries (Egypt, Tunisia, Morocco, Somalia and Sudan) are discussed; also, some material is found here relating to neighboring states. Fact boxes and tables of data convey some of the information. There are technical notes, but no bibliography or index.

652. **Statistical Record of Women Worldwide.** Edited by Linda Schmittroth. Detroit: Gale Research, 1991. xxxiv, 763 p. ISBN 0-8103-8349-7.

One of Gale's many statistical handbooks on various subjects. This volume concentrates on issues of particular relevance to women: home and family concerns, educational opportunities and health care for women and girls, crimes against women, income and occupation issues, population statistics, women's sports, etc. Tables of data are provided, many of which pertain to the United States, but with a little persistence one can discover how many sexual assaults were reported in Ethiopia in 1986, the number of working women in Tunisia, or the female life expectancy in Niger. The index gives access to the data by country. The source of each table is identified, and a bibliography of the sources is provided.

653. **World Bank Annual Report 1997.** Washington: World Bank, 1997. xiii, 250 p. ISBN 0-8213-3760-2; ISSN 0252-2942.

This annual provides a public-relations vehicle for the World Bank to summarize and illustrate its activities over the past year. Important programs and new initiatives are highlighted; a greal deal of internal budgetary and administrative information is included (a sort of stockholders' report). Section 3, "Regional Perspectives," features the Middle East and North Africa (pp. 84-91): the World Bank had active operations in 1997 in Algeria, Egypt, Morocco and Tunisia. New projects in Chad, Djibouti, Eritrea, Mali, Mauritania and Niger are listed on pp. 42-43, with ongoing programs detailed through many other tables of data. A subject index helps to locate material.

654. **World Debt Tables: External Finance for Developing Countries.** Annual, 197u-1996. Washington: World Bank. ISBN 0-8213-3302-X (2-vol. set, with periodic supplements); ISSN 0253-2859. 2 v.

Continued by *Global Development Finance*, 1997- .

Also available on diskette or CD-ROM.

An essential and highly technical reference detailing the indebtedness of developing countries to international creditors. Vol. 1 provides analysis and explanation of the current situation in global terms, plus summary tables for regions (including the Middle East and North Africa). Vol. 2 contains the statistical tables for each of the 136 countries that respond through the Debtor Reporting System. In 1996, these included all the nations of northern Africa except Eritrea (Libya and Western Sahara do not participate).

655. **World Development Indicators 1998.** Annual; 1997- . Washington: World Bank, 1998. xxv, 388 p. ISBN 0-8213-4124-3 (print) or 0-8213-4125-1 (CD-ROM); ISSN 0163-5085.

Also available on diskette and CD-ROM, with or without *World Development Report*. For descriptive website and other information, see **www.worldbank. org/html/extpb/wdi98.htm** or **www.worldbank.org/html/extpb/PopularTitles. html#W**

"This former statistical appendix to the *World Development Report* has proven to be a great success as a free-standing publication. Enlarged to include more than 80 tables and 600 indicators for the most recent observations with a comparison for earlier decades, the WDI has become an invaluable source to those in the private sector who analyze business opportunities in developing countries and emerging markets. It is also indispensable in the development, academic, business, and NGO communities" (website).

This publication supercedes both *World Tables* and *Social Indicators of Development*, and is now the primary source for current and time-series data (dating back to 1965) published by the World Bank. It is meant to be used in conjunction with the *World Bank Atlas*. Tables are presented in thematic groups: "world view" (global comparison data), population and social indicators, the environment, production and financing, states and markets, trade. Some text and interpretive material is included along with the statistics.

656. Evalds, Victoria K. **Union List of African Censuses, Development Plans and Statistical Abstracts.** Munich: Hans Zell, 1985. xiv, 232 p. ISBN 0-905450-20-5.

A guide to the holdings of large Africana libraries in the US, this work is meant for "librarians and scholars concerned with African primary sources and their bibliographic control" (Introduction). Most of the entries record post-1945 titles; the materials listed were received in participating libraries up to 1984. An explanatory note gives precise coverage information. The location of the documents, exact volume holdings and medium (paper or microform) are provided for each entry.

657. Pinfold, John R. **African Population Census Reports: a Bibliography and Checklist.** Munich: Hans Zell (K.G. Saur), for SCOLMA, 1985. xii, 100 p. ISBN 3-598-10571-1 and 0-905450-19-1.

This work, prepared in connection with the Standing Conference on Library Materials on Africa, creates a record of national population census documents and demographic surveys in Africa, including some regional and urban population counts. Coverage begins, apparently, with the earliest documents extant: for example, a census of Spanish Africa dating from 1787. These documents are organized chronologically, within a basic country-by-country structure. For most of the citations, some location data is supplied, identifying the documents held in European libraries.

Directories

658. **African Development Sourcebook.** First edition. Paris: UNESCO, 1991. 157 p. ISBN 92-3-002736-7

Also titled: *Guide Pratique du Développement en Afrique.*

Networking and information exchange for development is the aim of this directory, which lists institutions and NGOs involved in labor and trade, transport, social services, medicine, agriculture, banking, etc. This volume covers

Djibouti, Ethiopia, Sudan, Chad, Niger and Mali. Entries provide contact data, objectives, membership, funding sources and activities information for each organization.

659. Development Aid: a Guide to National and International Agencies. London; Birmingham: Butterworths; Eurofi, 1988. 587 p. *International Business Intelligence.* ISBN 0-408-009991-8.

Descriptive entries identify and outline the activities of the major multilateral intergovernmental organizations active in development aid, including regional bodies operating in Africa or the Arab world. In addition, entries summarize the bilateral aid programs of many nations, not only in Europe, the United States or Japan but also the Gulf emirates (Abu Dhabi, Kuwait), Libya and Saudi Arabia. Contact information, technical summaries and many tables of data are provided. There is no index, so time must be devoted to mining specific information.

660. The Development Directory: a Guide to the US International Development Community. Edited by Pamela Korsmeyer and George Ropes. Madison, CT: Editorial PKG, 1988. 333 p.

A directory of foundations and organizations – especially NGOs – based in the United States, granting funds or conducting work aimed at "improving the quality of life in every part of the earth" (Preface). Individuals active in this area as well as corporate, religious, political, educational or advocacy groups are listed. Entries provide contact information, staff names and titles, a statement of purpose, and specific interests or involvements worldwide.

Each major section provides a grouping of entries by geographic area: North Africa & Middle East, East Africa, West Africa and Africa generally may list relevant organizations, and the listings often overlap. Topical groupings (agriculture, energy, health, housing, etc.) are also given.

661. Directory of Development Research and Training Institutes in Africa. In cooperation with the International Development Information Network and CODESRIA (Council for the Development of Economic and Social Research in Africa). Paris: OECD, 1992. 248 p. ISBN 92-64-03539-7

Also titled: *Inventaire des Institutes de Recherche et de Formation en Matière de Développement en Afrique.*

A companion volume to the OECD *Register of Development Research Projects in Africa*, this country-by-country reference lists some 640 centers for development-related research. All of the states of northern Africa are included (except Western Sahara). The entries provide basic data, but not descriptions of the research or library holdings of these institutions – only simple subject descriptors.

662. **Register of Development Research Projects in Africa.** In cooperation with the International Development Information Network and CODESRIA (Council for the Development of Economic and Social Research in Africa). Paris: OECD, 1992. 346 p. ISBN 92-64-03699-7

Also titled: *Répertoire des Projects de Recherche en Matière de Développement en Afrique.*

More than 880 ongoing research projects in economic or social development are profiled in this reference. Entries are presented in either English or French, while introductory and editorial material is provided in both languages.

Each entry identifies and locates the project, lists names, dates and any other collaborating institutions, and offers a summary or abstract of the project and its aims. Many of the projects profiled are seeking to solve specific technical problems – e.g., combating desertification in Mali through better plantation techniques for indigenous trees – while others study social phenomena like labor migration in Egypt.

The reference is organized by country, and includes the states of northern Africa except Somalia, Libya and Djibouti (and Western Sahara). Contact information for the various institutions and several rough indexes are provided. See also the OECD companion volume, *Directory of Development Research and Training Institutes in Africa* (1992).

Journals

663. **Africa Index: Selected Articles on Socio-Economic Development.** Quarterly; 1971- . [New York]: United Nations Economic Commission for Africa. ISBN UN no. E/ECA/LIB/SER/E/97-76

Also titled: Catalogue Afrique: articles choisis sur le développement économique et social.

An index of periodical literature devoted to African development, organized by keyword. Citations only are provided. The work is indexed by author, title, subject and geographic unit (country or region).

664. **African Development Review/Revue Africaine de Développement.** Semiannual; 1989- . Abidjan: African Development Bank. ISSN 1017-6772.

Description and contents pages available online at **www.afdb.org/news/publications.html**.

Social-science studies, economics and population statistics occupy this journal, which is mainly but not entirely concerned with Africa. Special issues are sometimes presented; a recent theme was information technology and its impact upon Africa's development (vol. 10, no. 1).

665. **African Rural and Urban Studies.** Three times/year; 1994- . East Lansing, MI: African Studies Center (Michigan State University Press). ISSN 1073-4600.

Merger of: *Rural Africana* and *African Urban Studies*. Descriptive website available online at **www.msu.edu/unit/msupress/journals/jour3.html**.

A social-science journal concentrating on "urbanization, urban and regional planning, and the institutions of the world's most rapidly urbanizing continent" and "rural society and economy, agriculture, and the institutions of the world's most rural continent" (verso). A recent issue contained an article by David T. Pratten of SOS Sahel International UK on migration and rural development in Mali, Ethiopia and Sudan (vol. 3, no. 1).

666. **Afrique et Développement.** Quarterly; 1976- . Dakar: Council for the Development of Social Science Research in Africa. ISSN 0850-3907 and 0378-3006.

Also titled: *Africa Development.*

A recent themed issue of this journal concentrated on gender issues, in schools and universities, intellectual life, reproductive health and politics (vol. XXII, no. 1). Other issues have examined structural adjustment, democracy, social change, HIV/AIDS, and African studies as an academic discipline. The societies of northern Africa do fall within the scope of this journal (cf. Ali El-Kenz, "Maghreb: from One Myth to Another," vol. XXI, no. 2/3, pp. 245-265).

667. **AID Research and Development Abstracts.** Quarterly; 1974-1996. Washington: USAID. ISSN 0096-1507.

Studies, reports and other publications produced or sponsored by the USAID are described and summarized in this periodical. Each issue is indexed. The research cited here pertains to varied aspects of development: private enterprise, agriculture, nutrition and health, population, environment, energy, education, technology, etc. Many of the publications cited are pertinent to Africa. Unfortunately, this publication ceased in 1996, and it is not clear whether it will resume.

668. **Developing Economies.** Quarterly; 1963- . Tokyo: Institute of Developing Economies (Institute of Asian Economic Affairs). ISSN 0012-1533.

Descriptive IDE website at **www.ide.go.jp/English/welcome.html**.

A social-science journal featuring statistical analysis and case studies of development problems worldwide. Themed issues are sometimes used. Articles include bibliographical references, and one or two lengthy book reviews appear in each issue.

669. **Development and Socio-Economic Progress.** Quarterly; 1977- . Cairo: Afro-Asian Peoples' Solidarity Organization.

Also titled: *Tanmiyah wa al-Taqaddum al-Ijtima'i al-Iqtisadi.*

An advocacy vehicle publishing interesting essays, opinion pieces and lectures promoting the rights of developing countries, considering the roles of various intergovernmental and non-governmental organizations, and reporting news of relevant conference events. Articles may by published in Arabic, French or English.

670. **Development: Journal of the Society for International Development.** Quarterly; 1978- . London: SAGE Publications. ISSN 1011-6370.

Continues: *International Development Review.* Also titled: (*Revue du*) *Développement*; (*Revista del*) *Desarrollo* (*Internacional*). Contents and some full-text articles available online at **www.sidint.org/publications/development/ index.htm**.

An academic journal offering articles of 4-10 pages that make a proposal or state an opinion for discussion. The journal is intended to facilitate "dialogue between activists and intellectuals committed to the search for alternative paths of social transformation towards a more sustainable and just world" (cover). The editors make an effort to represent "local and innovative perspectives from the margins of global development discourse." The articles are direct and readable, with abstracts and some bibliographical references; they could be well-suited in length and technical level to college classroom discussion.

671. **Development Policy Review.** Quarterly; 1983- . London: Blackwell. ISSN 0950-6764 and 0078-7116.

Available in microfom. Also available online to subscribers through Blackwell: **www.blackwellpublishers.co.uk**.

A journal published by the Overseas Development Institute, featuring social-science research articles with full bibliographical references and tables of data. A recent issue included "Economic Gains from Integration among Developing Countries: the Case of the North African Maghreb Union" by Abdelaziz Testas (Vol. 15, no. 2). One long book review article and a section of brief reviews are found in most issues.

672. **Economic Development and Cultural Change.** Quarterly; 1952- . Chicago: University of Chicago Press. ISSN 0013-0079.

Also available on microfilm from UMI (Ann Arbor), and on microfiche from J.S. Canner & Co. Contents available online at **www.journals.uchicago. edu/EDCC/home.html**.

A scholarly journal composed of lengthy research articles with tables of demographic or economic data, technical notes and bibliographical references. The articles study specific development projects or economic policies and evaluate their impact on societies from an anthropological perspective. For example, a recent article investigates efforts by African policymakers to increase productive employment to keep up with population growth; another studies the effect of migrant workers from rural areas seeking employment in cities. Each issue contains seven or eight substantial, signed book reviews; each volume indexes the year's articles by author.

673. **Journal of Development Economics.** Quarterly in two issues; 1974- . New York: Elsevier. ISSN 0304-3878.

Table of contents available online at **www.elsevier.com/inca/publications/ store/5/0/5/5/4/6/**.

A social science journal depending heavily upon statistics and case studies. A recent issue included R. Assaad's "Kinship Ties, Social Networks and Segmented Labor Markets: Evidence from the Construction Sector in Egypt" (vol. 52, no. 1) and material on structural adjustment in Africa. Some books reviews are featured, and each volume includes an author index.

674. **Journal of Development Studies.** Bimonthly; 1964- . London: Frank Cass. ISSN 0022-0388.

Descriptive website and contents page available online at **www.frankcass.com/jnls/jds.htm**.

A social-science journal that tends to discuss development aid, lending, policy, etc. on the macro-economic level. Case studies are also featured.

675. **Third World Quarterly: Journal of Emerging Areas.** Quarterly; 1979- . Abingdon: Carfax. ISSN 0143-6597.

Also available online through OCLC FirstSearch Electronic Collections; descriptive website and contents pages available at **www.carfax.co.uk/twq-ad.htm;** full text also available through website to subscribers.

A scholarly journal concerned with international affairs, especially development policy, population concerns, political change and "North-South" power struggles. A recent issue contained articles about democratization and elections in Algeria and Ethiopia (vol. 19, no. 2). Book reviews and notices are included. Each article provides extensive bibliographical references.

676. **World Bank Policy and Research Bulletin.** Five times/year; 1990- . (Online version four times/year.). Washington: World Bank. ISSN 1014-8590.

Description, contents and full text also available online at **www.worldbank.org/html/dec/Publications/Bulletins/home.html**.

Each issue of this bulletin contains one article reporting on a recent conference sponsored by the World Bank, or on some other aspect of the institution's data-gathering and policy support function. Then it presents notices and descriptions of current World Bank publications: research reports, books, technical papers, policy papers, and electronic data releases. Ordering information is included.

677. **World Bank Research Observer.** Semiannual; 1986- . Washington: International Bank for Reconstruction and Development. ISSN 0257-3032.

Descriptive website available at **www.worldbank.org/html/extpb/observer/resobser.htm**.

This journal is intended "for anyone who has a professional interest in development ... contributors examine key issues in development economics, survey the literature and the latest World Bank research, and debate issues of development policy" (cover). Sometimes, several articles are organized around a certain theme, or set opposite one another as a "point-counterpoint." Abstracts, technical notes, bibliographical references, charts and tables of data are included. A recent issue presented a significant article on structural adjustment and family poverty in Africa, studying the results of macroeconomic policy on individual nations, among them Ethiopia (vol. 11, no. 1).

678. **World Development.** Monthly; 1973- . Oxford: Pergamon Press (Elsevier). ISSN 0305-750X.
Descriptive website and ordering information available online at **www. elsevier.com/locate/worlddev/**.
Africa is among the concerns of this scholarly journal, which emphasizes the larger issues of development, such as debt, globalization or food security. Case studies are often included.

Databases and Websites

679. Africa 2000. **www.africa2000.com/**
Many links to advocacy pages dealing with development, population and North-South tensions; link to *Impact International*, online magazine featuring Islamic issues and other Africa-related material.

680. Africa IPM Link. Integrated Pest Management. **www.cals.vt.edu/ail/index. html** in English; **www.cals.vt.edu/ail/findex.htm** in French (note different suffix).
A new approach to agriculture with reduced pesticides; report of a project in environmental protection and sustainable development sponsored by the USAID and Virginia Tech University. The project is active in Mali and Ethiopia.

681. Africa Technical Department, World Bank. Information Bank on African Development Studies (IBADS). **www.worldbank.org/html/ibads/IBADS.html**
Searchable database of documents.

682. African Development Bank. **http://www.afdb.org/**
Reports on projects in Algeria, Morocco and Tunisia; concerns both public and private sector.

683. African Development Institute. **www.africainstitute.com/**
"An independent, non partisan policy research institute aimed at initiating practical solutions to Africa's developmental crisis. Through education, research, and policy analysis ... the organization challenges policies that lead to the stagnation of Africa's development and offers alternative strategies towards continental self sufficiency."

684. The African Water Page. Nile Basin Initiative. **http://www.sn.apc.org/afwater/ nile.htm**
Reports on the progress of this ongoing project; links to other news about water resources and sustainable development.

685. AfriStat. **www.focusintl.com/afristat.htm**
Basic demographic data by country; includes northern Africa. Some information derived from WIDNET (Women in Development Network). Also in French.

686. British Library for Development Studies (BLDS). **www.ids.ac.uk/blds/ blds_abt.html**
Links to their own bibliographic and index databases, Devline and ELDIS.

687. Canadian International Development Agency. Virtual Library on International Development. **w3.acdi-cida.gc.ca/virtual.nsf**
Follow the series of "site tree" links to specific information on northern Africa and the Middle East. Available in French and English.

688. Department for International Development (UK). **www.dfid.gov.uk/public/ who/who_frame.html**
"Manages Britain's bilateral and multilateral development programmes in poorer countries." Links to British Aid Statistics and other details.

689. Food and Agriculture Organization of the United Nations (FAO). **www. fao.org/**
Descriptive information, with links to FAOSTAT databases.

690. HealthNet Africa. **www.healthnet.org/hnet/africa.html**
Links to participating national health centers in Eritrea, Ethiopia, Sudan and Mali.

691. Institute of Development Studies. Electronic Development and Environment Information System (ELDIS). **nt1.ids.ac.uk/eldis/afr/afr.htm**
Africa links include Djibouti, Eritrea, Ethiopia, Somalia, Sudan, Chad, Mali, Niger and Mauritania.

692. International Development Research Centre. Internet Sites Related to International Development. **www.idrc.ca/library/world/index_e.html**
Carefully-organized site featuring many projects in Africa.

693. International Institute for Sustainable Development. Multimedia Resource for Environment and Development Policy Makers. **www.iisd.ca/**

694. International Service for National Agricultural Research (ISNAR). Agricultural Research Organizations on the Web. **www.cgiar.org/isnar/home1/ arow/africa.htm**
Research centers, laboratories and academic departments engaged in agricultural projects in Egypt, Ethiopia, Morocco, Sudan, plus regional organizations like the Institut du Sahel.

695. La Caisse Française de Développement. L'Agence Française de Développement. **www.afd.fr/**
New website, rapidly developing; includes northern Africa.

696. Network for Environment and Sustainable Development in Africa (NESDA). **www.rri.org/nesda/nesda.html**
Also available in French.

697. Overseas Development Council. **www.odc.org/**
With links to full-text articles and research reports dealing with development issues.

698. United Nations Development Programme (UNDP). Sustainable Human Development. **www.undp.org/index5.html**
The latest issue of *Human Development Report* is available online through this page.

699. United Nations World Food Programme. **www.wfp.org/**
Current special coverage of Sudan.

700. United Nations World Food Programme. Food Outlook Online: FAO Global Information and Early Warning System on Food and Agriculture (GIEWS).
www.fao.org/WAICENT/FAOINFO/ECONOMIC/GIEWS/ENGLISH/fo/fotoc.htm
"Published 5 times a year, *Food Outlook* provides a global perspective on the production, stocks and trade of cereals and other basic food commodities, through an analysis of trends and prospects." Full text and data tables from current and recent issues.

701. US Agency for International Development. Africa Bureau Information Center. **www.info.usaid.gov/regions/afr/abic/**
U.S. bilateral development aid programs and other information.

702. US Agency for International Development. Asia & Near East. **www.info.usaid.gov/regions/ane/**
U.S. bilateral development aid programs and other information.

703. US Census Bureau. International Data Base (IDB) Summary Demographic Data. **www.census.gov/ftp/pub/ipc/www/idbsum.html**
Can be searched by country; demographic and socio-economic information downloadable from this site.

704. Women in Development Network (WIDNET). **www.focusintl.com/widr1.htm**
Basic demographic and statistical information. In English and French.

705. World Bank. Africa Live Database. **www.worldbank.org/html/extpb/
aldb.htm**

Available online to subscribers only.

"A comprehensive database of macroeconomic and sectoral indicators ...
for those who collect and analyze data relating to African countries. The most
complete and up-to-date public collection of World Bank statistics and analyses
on the Sub-Saharan countries."

706. World Bank. Africa Region: Findings. **www.worldbank.org/aftdr/findings/
english/findtoc.htm**

Full text of current research and information. "*Findings* reports on ongoing
operational, economic and sector work carried out by the World Bank and its
member governments in the Africa Region."

707. World Hunger Program. HungerWeb. **www.brown.edu/Departments/
World_Hunger_Program/**

"The aim of this site is to help prevent and eradicate hunger by facilitating
the free exchange of ideas and information regarding the causes of, and solutions
to, hunger. It contains primary information, made available by the World Hunger Program – the prime sponsor of this site – and its partners, as well as links to
other sites where information of relevance to hunger can be found."

Industry and Trade Statistics

Citations and annotations for annuals reflect the issue examined; some
changes can be expected in later issues or editions of the same work.

708. **Direction of Trade Statistics Yearbook.** Prepared by the Real Sector Division, IMF Statistics Department. Washington: International Monetary Fund,
1981. ISBN 1-55775-653-8; ISSN 0252-3019.

DOTS is also available in monthly and quarterly issues.

The 1997 issue of this annual presents "for 182 countries, figures on the
value of merchandise exports and imports by trade partners for the years 1990
through 1996, as well as world aggregates showing trade flows between major
areas of the world" (Introduction). The countries are classified into three main
categories: industrial countries, developing countries, and "other." Five geographical divisions are used: the Middle East (including Egypt and Libya), Africa (with the rest of the Maghreb, Sahel and Horn nations), Asia, Europe and the
Western Hemisphere. In addition, statistics for oil-exporting counties are listed
separately.

The tables of data are clear and well-organized, and the volume is supplied
with ample reference helps (table of contents, cross-references, etc.), plus an explanatory introduction in English, French and Spanish. Each issue of the annual
reproduces statistics for the previous seven years, making current comparisons
easy.

709. **Government Finance Statistics Yearbook.** Prepared by the Government Finance Division of the Statistics Department. Washington: International Monetary Fund. Annual, 1977- . ISBN 1-55775-601-5; ISSN 0250-7374.

A reference publication that provides "detailed data on revenue, grants, expenditure, lending, financing, and debt of central governments and indicates the amounts represented by social security funds and extrabudgetary operations ... [plus] data for state and local governments, and information on the institutional units of government" (verso). Statistical tables for individual countries are given, and world tables make it easy to compare the percentages of total government expenditures on defense, for example, or education, housing, transport, etc. for countries within the same region or outside it. Not all countries of northern Africa are included: there are no tables in the 1997 issue for Libya, Algeria, Mauritania, Mali, Niger, Sudan, Eritrea or Djibouti.

710. **International Marketing Data and Statistics 1997.** 21st edition. London: Euromonitor, 1997. x, 613 p. ISBN 0-86338-690-3; ISSN 0308-2938.

A repackaging of vital statistics, trade, industrial, defense, environmental, consumer, retailing, media, transport and other data, by country, topic and region. This resource lacks the clarity of Clio's *World Economic Data*, but serves a similar purpose.

711. **International Trade Statistics Yearbook.** Prepared by the Department for Economic and Social Information and Policy Analysis, Statistics Division. New York: United Nations. Annual, 1985- . ISBN 92-1-061169-1; UN Pub. ST/ESA/ STAT/SER.G/44; Sales No. E/F.97.XVII.2, Vol. 1 and Vol. 2.

Also available on magnetic tapes and diskettes.

An important reference for world trade statistics, showing "external trade performances in terms of the overall trends in current value, as well as in volume and price, the importance of trading partners and the significance of individual commodities imported and exported" (Introduction). Vol. 1 organizes this very detailed data by country; Vol. 2 organizes it by commodity. In 1995, the nations of northern Africa were covered except Chad, Eritrea, Mauritania, Mali, Sudan and Somalia.

712. **International Yearbook of Industrial Statistics 1998.** Annual; 1995- . Vienna: United Nations Industrial Development Organization. Cheltenham: Edward Elgar, 1998. vi, 722 p. ISBN 1-85898-777-6

Formed by the union of: *Industrial Statistics Yearbook* (vol. 1, *General Industrial Statistics*) and *Handbook of Industrial Statistics*.

Also available on magnetic tape or diskettes.

This thick volume of statistical tables covers the manufacturing and processing of every kind of product, organized by country and by type of industry. Not all the countries of northern Africa are included: Djibouti, Eritrea, Libya, Mali, Mauritania, Somalia and Sudan are not represented by country tables.

There is no indexing, no interpretive material except for a brief introduction, and for some reason, the editorial apparatus here is presented only in English.

713. **Principal International Businesses: World Marketing Directory.**
Bethlehem, PA: Dun & Bradstreet. Annual; 1974- . ISBN 1-56203-494-4; ISSN
0097-6288.

Very brief country-by-country listings for companies operating in various
kinds of trade and manufacturing. A second section organizes the listings by
product type (SIC or Standard Industrial Classification codes); a third lists the
businesses by name, alphabetically. Djibouti and Eritrea are not represented in
the 1997 issue; coverage of Libya is minimal.

714. **Statistical Yearbook.** Prepared by the Department for Economic and So-
cial Information and Policy Analysis, Statistical Division. New York: United
Nations. Annual, 1948- . ISBN 92-1-061167-5; UN Doc. ST/ESA/STAT/
SER.S/17; Sales no. E/F.96.XVII.1

Also titled: *Annuaire Statistique.* Also available: *Monthly Bulletin of Statistics* or MBS Online, at **www.un.org/Depts/unsd/.**

The standard compilation of UN statistics on population, economic activity, social conditions, international trade and production, etc. Later chapters provide some data on the environment, intellectual property, science and technology.
There is a basic index.

715. **World Business Directory.** Detroit: Gale Research, 1994. 4 v. ISBN
0-8103-8056-0 (set).

A source of directory data for companies involved in trade or manufacturing worldwide, published with the World Trade Centers Association. The entry
for Algeria provides nine pages of listings, with contact information and a brief
description of each business. In 1994, the countries of northern Africa—with the
exception of Djibouti, Eritrea and Mali—were included.

716. **World Chamber of Commerce Directory.** Loveland, CO: World Chamber of Commerce Directory. Annual, 1989- . ISBN 0-943581-10-9; ISSN 1048-
2849

Former title: *World Wide Chamber of Commerce Directory.*

The portions of the world covered by this directory seem to consist mainly
of the USA and Canada, but there are three sections toward the back giving basic
contact information for tourist bureaus and chambers of commerce facilitating
trade and business relations in other countries. The 1997 issue contains at least
one listing for every nation in northern Africa except Somalia and Libya.

717. **World Economic and Social Survey.** Prepared by the Department for
Economic and Social Information and Policy Analysis. New York: United Nations. Annual, 1994- . UN Document E/1995/50, ST/ESA/243.

This publication superceded the UN's *World Economic Survey* in 1994.

An annual providing articles on the current state of the world's economies,
the effects of political programs, fiscal and monetary policies, and factors of social change (population growth, literacy, the status of women, etc.). The 1995
issue contains reports on OPEC and world crude oil supplies, and on post-Cold-War

military spending (also an important concern in northern Africa). Information boxes, charts and graphics accompany the text. More than 80 figures and tables of data are distributed throughout. In this volume, geographical units vary: the Middle East usually includes Egypt (but not Libya or Sudan), while North Africa sometimes includes Djibouti, Mauritania and Somalia, and so on.

718. **World Economic Data.** Third edition. Santa Barbara: ABC-Clio, 1991. viii, 261 p. ISBN 0-87436-658-5; ISSN 0891-4125.

A reference work in one "convenient, uniform" volume, "written for librarians, teachers, students and those seeking information on a variety of factors affecting the economy ... compiled from documents not readily available to the average reader" (Introduction). This work makes use of several of the standard statistical annuals and reports, and repackages the data into a simplified form. The first 225-page section is composed of 1-2 page country profiles, with easily-compared economic data under large headings. Part Two involves mainly US economic indicators, though currency conversion charts and tables of US foreign trade statistics are relevant to other nations. A glossary of financial terms is especially suited to classroom use.

719. **World Economic Factbook 1996.** Third edition. London: Euromonitor, 1995. 461 p. ISBN 0-86338-6229.

A carefully-organized almanac-style reference meant to maximize the comparison of figures pertaining to the 207 countries covered. Two-page entries on each country are alphabetically arranged: the first page is a textual summary of current economic and political conditions, while the second page presents selected and simplified statistics in a uniform pattern. The uniformity of the volume makes it possible to provide a section of world rankings: physical area, population, population density, birth rates, percentages of children and the elderly, per capital GDP, etc. – all set forth very clearly. For example, one can see at a glance that Libya, Ethiopia, Niger, Egypt, Algeria and Mali are among the youngest populations in the world (percentage of people age 0-14). The simplicity of organization could make it suitable for students. Five maps are included.

720. **World Economic Outlook: a Survey by the Staff of the International Monetary Fund.** Washington: IMF. Annual, 1980-1983; biennial 1984- . ISBN 1-55775-648-1; ISSN 0256-6877.

An analysis of economic developments and policies in IMF member countries and of the global economic system, with some projections (usually 1-2 years, but may be up to five years). This reference provides data on external debt, balance of payments and external financing, payment balances on current accounts, GDP, private capital flows, exchange and interest rates, government fiscal balances and other major economic indicators. The approach is global, though the book does include data on individual countries and regions as needed.

721. **World Tables.** Annual, with semiannual updates; 1976-1995. Baltimore; London: Johns Hopkins University Press for the World Bank. ISBN 0-8108-4789-3; ISSN 1043-5573; 1013-5456

Published also on diskette, tape and CD-ROM.

Formerly, the fundamental compilation of the statistics from which many World Bank reports were derived. Tables presented economic data comparatively by region and by individual country. Essential economic indicators (external debt, balance of payments, foreign trade, manufacturing activity, GNP and GDP, rate of inflation, monetary holdings, etc.) and some social indicators (fertility rate, infant mortality, adult female literacy, school enrollment, life expectancy) were included. This data is now available in print or electronically as *World Development Indicators*.

722. **Yearbook of Labour Statistics.** Geneva: International Labour Office Annual, 1936- . ISBN 92-2-007352-8; ISSN 00-84-3857

Also titled: *Annuaire des Statistiques du Travail*; *Anuario de Estadisticas del Trabajo*.

A fundamental reference source for world labor statistics, presented in large tables of data. Interpretive text is limited to a page at the beginning of each section "briefly indicating the main characteristics of the different types of data published" (Preface). The tables usually present data covering the past 10 years; however, the figures submitted to the ILO by national statistical services or printed in official publications do vary. An important index shows which tables each country is represented on: for example, data for Algeria appear in only eight of the 31 tables pertaining to Africa. Data for Eritrea, Djibouti and Chad are not given at all. But when the information is available, it is set forth clearly in a way permitting comparisons within regions and over a 10-year period.

723. Barbuto, Domenica M. **The International Financial Statistics Locator: a Research and Information Guide.** New York: Garland, 1995. xii, 338 p. *Research and Information Guides in Business, Industry and Economic Institutions*, v. 11; *Garland Reference Library of Social Science*, no. 924. ISBN 0-8153-1483-3.

This volume functions as an index to 22 major sources of financial and statistical information. The entry for an individual country will show, for example, whether the assets and liabilities of Libya's banking institutions are reported in the IMF's *International Financial Statistics*, or in any of the other sources covered. A directory of world securities markets is included in an appendix.

724. Lester, Ray. **Information Sources in Finance and Banking.** London: Bowker Saur, 1996. xxiv, 828 p. *Guides to Information Sources.* ISBN 1-85739-037-7.

This annotated guide brings together efficiently the current publications on finance and banking produced by major organizations and publishers. Other fields, such as law, are also represented if they have an impact on financial activity. An important chapter reports the relevant materials available in electronic form, including online information services. The annotations help one select the publications most likely to be of value to area studies. Indexes of organizations and serials titles are provided.

Journals

725. **Africa Research Bulletin: Economic, Financial and Technical Series.** Monthly; 1964- . In this form since 1992. Oxford: Blackwell. ISSN 0001-9852.

Also available online through certain service providers; see **www. blackwellpublishers.co.uk**

A news and current-events source reporting and analyzing in considerable detail pressing concerns and developments in Africa generally, regionally and in specific countries or localities. A great deal of information is presented in a concise and objective fashion. This source provides the distilled essence of more than 80 local and international news agencies, intergovernmental and non-governmental organizations, United Nations departments, media organizations (including the BBC), and newspapers or magazines, from the *Times* of London to *La Nation* (Djibouti).

The entire African continent is covered. Maps, tables of data and other small graphics are printed as needed. Every issue supplies a convenient country index on the back cover; an annual subject index is also provided. The division of the subject matter into two series works well, but may necessitate subscribing to both.

726. **African Business.** Monthly; 1978- . London; Paris: IC Publications. ISSN 0141-3929; 0162-4059.

Available online through Reuters (Textline). See also website at **dialspace. dial.pipex.com/town/terrace/lf41/**

A glossy news magazine covering current business activities and opportunities in Africa. Though southern Africa receives the greatest attention, a recent issue contained a ten-page supplement on Eritrea (April 1998, no. 231).

727. **Direction of Trade Statistics Quarterly.** Prepared by the Real Sector Division, IMF Statistics Department. Washington: International Monetary Fund. ISSN 0252-306X.

"Quarterly issues of this publication provide, for about 152 countries, tables with current data (or estimates) on the value of imports from and exports to their most important trading partners ... [plus] similar summary tables for the world, industrial countries and developing countries" (verso). Regional units are not included in the DOTS Quarterly, and comparison data for past years is not provided.

728. **IMF Staff Papers.** Quarterly; 1950- . Washington: International Monetary Fund. ISSN 0020-8027.

Also available on microfilm from UMI (Ann Arbor). Search page for IMF publications available online at **www.imf.org/external/pubind.htm**

The articles in this journal are both theoretical and technical, with tables of data, statistics and many bibliographical references. They are intended to provide a research basis for policymaking.

729. **IMF Survey.** 23 issues/year; 1972- . Washington: International Monetary Fund. ISSN 0047-083X.

Also titled: *Bulletin du FMI* (text in French) and *Boletin del FMI* (text in Spanish). Also available on microfilm from UMI (Ann Arbor). Contents and abstracts available online at **www.imf.org/external/pubs/ft/survey/surveyx.htm**

A combination newsletter/news magazine providing current information on the state of member economies, particular loan programs, credit and interest rates, and emerging policy initiatives. News of the organization itself is also featured. Monochrome maps, tables, graphics and photos are used to illustrate.

730. **Journal of African Economies.** Three times/year; 1992- . Oxford: Oxford University Press. ISSN 0963-8024.

Abstracts are available online at **www.oup.co.uk/jafeco**

A scholarly social-science journal, presenting specific case studies and analysis of Africa's economic conditions more generally. A recent issue contained M. Fafchamps and S. Gavian's study, "The Determinants of Livestock Prices in Niger" (vol. 6, no. 2).

731. **Middle East Economic Digest.** Weekly; 1985- . London: Middle East Economic Digest. ISSN 0047-7238 and 0047-7230.

Title often abbreviated MEED.

This news magazine offers coverage of current Middle East banking and finance, stock markets, construction tenders and contract negotiations, legal/judicial developments and, of course, the oil industry. Bilateral and multilateral aid and lending is also discussed, and European trade is a major interest. Includes black-and-white and color photos.

732. **North Africa Journal.** Monthly; 1997- . Boston: North Africa Journal. ISSN 1097-8844.

A sample issue (in Adobe Acrobat or HTML format) and contents page available online; full text available to subscribers at **www.north-africa.com/**

A new current-affairs magazine emphasizing analysis and commentary on events affecting business and the economy in the Maghreb – Algeria, Morocco and Tunisia. Trade and investment between this region and North America is promoted and stressed, but relations with European countries are also reported; recent issues have offered several articles on conditions for North African immigrants in France. Developments in the petroleum/energy industry, agriculture and food commodities, and defense technology receive special attention. Typical concerns include the sale of Boeing aircraft to Maghreb countries, efforts to restrict corruption in government contracts, a new pilgrimage tax in Morocco and housing shortages in Algeria.

733. **Organization of Arab Petroleum Exporting Countries Bulletin.** Monthly; 1986- . Kuwait: OAPEC. ISSN 1018-595X.

OAPEC website at **www.kuwait.net/~oapec/**

Tables of data on oil prices and production, other economic indicators, and news of the policies and activities of member countries (including Algeria, Egypt, Libya and Tunisia) are featured in this current-affairs bulletin. News of OAPEC conferences and related international events is provided.

734. **World Economy.** Seven times/year; 1977- . Oxford: Blackwell. ISSN 0378-5290.

Available online through FirstSearch Electronic Collections. See also **www.blackwellpublishers.co.uk**

International economic relations, both on the broad theoretical level and in individual cases, occupy this scholarly journal. Some issues are organized around a theme, such as global trade policy agreements. Full bibliographical references and often charts or tables of data are included. Each issue normally contains one or two detailed, signed book reviews.

Databases and Websites

735. CenStats. **www.census.gov/apsd/www/censtats.html**

Statistical databases of the United States Bureau of the Census, including "International Trade Data." Full access for subscribers only.

736. Economic Commission for Africa. Serving Africa Better. **www.un. org/Depts/eca/index.htm**

Many news and conference reports and other information; searchable.

737. EnterWeb. The Enterprise Development Website: Africa and Middle East. **www.enterweb.org/africa.htm**

Private-sector development and business-related information.

738. Infotrac Searchbank. Business Index ASAP. See also the Information Access Company website at **library.iacnet.com/libhome.html**

Index includes *Middle East Economic Digest, Privatisation International, Financial Times, Middle East Executive Reports, The Economist.*

739. International Finance Corporation. Africa Business Network. **www.ifc.org/abn/**

"The Africa Business Network is oriented towards the needs of investors in Africa. For small businesses, it provides general business help and 'how-to' information in formulating a business plan, starting a business, financing and managing it. It also includes a variety of information for larger businesses." Among the countries covered are Ethiopia, Eritrea, Mali and Mauritania; some information is available on Niger, Chad, Sudan and Somalia.

740. International Monetary Fund. **www.imf.org/external/index.htm**
News, publications, projects and policies: very current. See "Direction of Trade Data" in particular.

741. MBendi AfroPaedia. Africa's Electronic Encyclopaedia of Business and Commercial Information. **mbendi.co.za/**
Primarily relevant to South Africa.

742. MidEast Net. Arab and Middle East Business Gateway. **www.mideastnet. com/profile.htm**
Private-sector business contacts and promotion.

743. Privatization News. **www.privatization.net/**
Business-oriented online weekly; offers a focus page on the Middle East and North Africa. Full access for subscribers only.

744. TradePort. Commercial News: International Trade Links. **www.tradeport. org/cgi-bin/banner.pl/links/index.html**
The Country Specific Websites page includes all of the states of northern Africa, even Western Sahara. Most of the Country Library sites include detailed Market Research Reports based on US Department of Commerce data.

745. United Nations Industrial Development Organization. **www.unido.org/**

746. US Department of Commerce. Middle East and North Africa Business Home Page. **www.ita.doc.gov/mena/**
Includes links to current Country Commercial Guides, especially for exporters.

747. US Department of Commerce. Stat-USA Internet; Globus and NTBD. **www.stat-usa.gov/**
International business, economic and trade information, market reports, industry analysis; see "Country Commercial Guides" in particular.

Privatization, State Planning and Foreign Investment

This section includes materials on the special topic of Islamic banking, on both the state and commercial levels.

748. **Adjustment in Africa: Reforms, Results and the Road Ahead.** Washington: International Bank for Reconstruction and Development, 1994. xix, 284 p. *World Bank Policy Research Report.* ISBN 0-19-520994-X; ISSN 1020-0851.
A detailed report with chapters explaining the impact of structural adjustment policies on the markets, public sector, population and environment of

developing countries in Africa. (The Mediterranean states, Western Sahara and Eritrea are not included in the scope of this work). The text is supplemented by numerous fact boxes, figures, tables and graphs suitable for ready reference, and the volume includes a 50-page appendix of statistical tables. There is a valuable current bibliography as well, but no indexes.

749. **The Casablanca Report: Results of the Middle East/North Africa Economic Summit Oct 30-Nov 1, 1994.** New York; Geneva: Council on Foreign Relations; World Economic Forum, 1995. ix, 65 p.

The report of this high-powered gathering is interesting, though the communiqués stay mainly on a general level. The value of the report for reference work is in the lists of participants – identifying leaders and policymakers in governments, industry, banking and finance, agriculture, capital and foreign investment, energy, the environment, human resources, infrastructure, press and mass media, information technology and communications, tourism and travel, water resources and regional economic development. Complete directory data is given for contacts in each country who are prepared to provide information to those pursuing business projects in the area.

750. **Consumer Markets in North Africa.** London: Euromonitor, 1984. 244 p. ISBN 0-86338-037-9.

One of a series of business reports intended to identify "growth markets in the Third World and assess their potential as consumer markets drawing on detailed consumer market information unavailable in any other publications" (Foreword). This volume covers Algeria, Egypt, Libya, Morocco and Tunisia. A brief introduction is followed by some 40 pages of tables for each country, showing basic demographic data, industrial output and GDP, trade and commercial data, including the source, nature and consumption levels of imported goods, retail prices of ordinary consumer articles and average household expenditures, and data on transport and tourism. A table of contents, one map and a list of tables by country are also included.

751. **Directory of Islamic Financial Institutions.** Edited by John R. Presley. London: Croom Helm, 1988. ix, 353 p. ISBN 0-7099-1347-8.

Not a directory in the usual sense, this volume explains at length the theories and structures involved in Islamic banking, describes international financial institutions like the Islamic Development Bank, and presents detailed information about the banking laws and systems of four representative Muslim countries (not in northern Africa) as case studies. Conventional directory data, organized by country, is found in Part 2. Of the states of northern Africa, only Egypt is included. The volume has an interesting bibliography (pp. 78-96), but no index.

752. **Economic Research Institutions of the Islamic World.** Prepared by Shahid S. Doha and Abdullah Gul. Jeddah: Islamic Research and Training Institute, 1984. ix, 132 p.

Published by the Islamic Development Bank, this paperback volume serves as "a directory of the IDB's member countries' research and training institutions in the field of economics, finance and banking" (title page). Actually, it does a bit more than this, as similar institutions in some non-member countries are listed as well.

Contact information, a statement of the nature of the institution (government agency, non-governmental organization, academic department), staff size, director's name, library holdings and a brief description of the activities, publications or research interests of each institution are provided. Entries are organized geographically, with indexes providing access by institution, name of director or senior staff, and general subject area. All of the states of northern Africa are represented except Libya, Djibouti, Ethiopia/Eritrea and Chad.

753. **Économie du Monde Arabe et Musulman.** Fourth edition. Paris: Éditions EMAM, 1992. 240 p. ISBN 2-9503-484-3-2.

A concise handbook covering a wide geographic area, from Mauritania to Pakistan. Of the states of northern Africa, only Niger, Mali, Chad, Ethiopia and Eritrea are outside its scope.

The handbook provides some brief descriptive articles on specific economic, historical, legal and technological issues in the region, a macro-economic analysis, a country-by-country data section, tables of comparative statistics, and material concerning trade within and beyond the region. A directory of major French exporters is also included. There is a helpful table of contents, but no index. The articles contain bibliographical references.

754. **Growth and Stability in the Middle East and North Africa.** Compiled by Mohamed A. El-Erian, et al. Washington: International Monetary Fund, 1996. v, 44 p. ISBN 1-55775-565-5.

This small paperback focuses upon policymaking and the restructuring of economies in the region, assuming the private sector as the engine of growth. The analysis remains largely on this theoretical/ideological level and does not discuss specifics in any detail. The scope includes Algeria, Egypt, Morocco, Sudan, Tunisia, Somalia, Mauritania, Djibouti and Libya: basically, African nations that are members of the Arab League.

755. **Logistical Constraints on International Trade in the Maghreb.** Prepared by François Amiot and Ovadia Salama. Washington: World Bank, 1996. 55 p. *Policy Research Working Paper;* 1598.

Working papers produced within the World Bank are meant to report upon research in progress, disseminating findings that could be useful in the formulation of specific development plans and policies. They are not references or periodicals in the traditional sense, but serve this particular information purpose in a way that other sources do not.

This paper is the result of work pursued in the Private Sector Development, Finance and Infrastructure Division for the Middle East and North Africa, aiming to "assist Maghrebian countries in achieving a broad-ranging set of integration arrangements with the European Union that will improve their competitive positions" (cover). Barriers to the region's trade with Europe include tariffs, restricted access to markets, and inadequate transport and communications systems, equipment and technology. This report briefly outlines the problems, proposes solutions, and supplies supporting data (graphs, charts, tables) in a convenient form.

756. **Third World Economic Handbook.** Second edition. London: Euromonitor, 1989. xix, 387 p. ISBN 0-86338-163-4.

This volume is more like a monograph than a reference book, as it is composed of chapters studying the issues of economic growth and structural change, trade policy, industry, agriculture and the service sector, commodity prices, foreign debt, taxes and government revenues in Third World nations in general. Chapters are devoted to regional economic performance trends as well. The book includes Egypt as part of "West Asia" (i.e., the Middle East) and the Maghreb, Sahel and Horn with "Africa" – a debatable approach, since North African economies are difficult to integrate statistically with the rest of the continent.

757. **Trends in Developing Economies 1990.** Washington: World Bank, 1990. viii, 624 p. ISBN 0-8213-1648-6.

This reference "presents brief analytical descriptions of recent economic performance and trends in individual developing countries ... and economic and social data for all borrowing country members" (Foreword). An alphabetized ready reference for "the economic analyst, investor, researcher or businessperson," this book provides readable articles of about five pages summarizing each country's current situation and prospects, then three pages of selected, clearly-presented statistics covering the past six years. The arrangement allows easy comparison of data without sacrificing detail or accuracy, and the descriptive portion puts the information into context and explains its significance. An excellent source for undergraduate libraries in particular.

758. **World Outlook 1997: Forecasts of Political and Economic Trends in Over 180 Countries.** Annual; 1985- . London: The Economist Intelligence Unit. ISSN 0-424-3331.

Also available online through: FT Profile and M.A.I.D./Profound (UK); LEXIS-NEXIS and MarkIntel (USA).

This information service, designed for "companies establishing and managing operations across national borders" (verso), provides forecasts of market conditions and probable government policies and regulatory activities affecting business. An introductory chapter on "The World Picture" is followed by regionally-organized country-by-country reports. Tables of data show trends over several years, while a one-page text explains the most significant events expected in the near future, in a terse "executive summary" style. The Middle East and North Africa here includes the Mediterranean coast of Africa and Sudan; Sub-Saharan Africa includes the rest of the Sahel and Horn.

759. **WorldCasts: Regional.** Foster City, CA: Information Access Co. (Predicasts). Quarterly, 1979- .
Also cataloged as *World Regional Casts.*
A looseleaf printout compiling "forecasts on products, markets, industry and economic aggregates as reported by experts in the trade and business press" (p. B-1). Data on commercial activity are given for the past year, the present, and about three years into the future. Basic commodities and manufactured goods are listed, with some less tangible products as well (e.g., passenger air transport, communications services). "Northern Africa" appears as a region, and Africa generally (including Egypt); individual countries are listed within their regions, in alphabetical order. An index provides access to specific products or services. A separate publication, *World Product Casts* or *WorldCasts: Products* is organized by type of goods exchanged.

760. Blauvelt, Euan and Jennifer Durlacher. **Sources of African and Middle Eastern Economic Information.** Westport, CT: Greenwood, 1982. 2 v. ISBN 0-313-23058-7.
Over 4000 entries in this two-volume work are arranged by source, in two general classes: either as an international publication (by an intergovernmental organization, agency or commercial publisher), or as a publication produced by a given country's statistics department, central bank or planning authority. This is a useful distinction, and essentially results in two separate but complementary works. An index in each volume lists the sources by title, and another by subject. Most of the entries have at least very brief annotations, and sometimes abstracts. This reference covers the whole of Africa. Contact data for the publishing companies or authorities is provided for each volume, but this information is probably now obsolete.

761. Estell, Kenneth. **World Trade Resources Guide: a Guide to Resources on Importing From and Exporting to the Major Trading Nations of the World.** First edition. Detroit: Gale Research, 1992. xxiv, 891 p. ISBN 0-8103-8404-3.
A country-by-country compilation of directory data for business information sources. Banks and financial institutions, chambers of commerce, government agencies and organizations, business-oriented libraries and research centers, relevant publications and statistical sources, and communications/transport services (air cargo carriers, freight forwarders, port authorities) are represented, with names, addresses and phone or fax numbers if available. Regional listing are also compiled, with sections for Africa and the Middle East. Of the countries in northern Africa, only Algeria, Egypt, Libya and Morocco are covered. A name and keyword index is provided.

762. Hodd, Michael. **African Economic Handbook.** London: Euromonitor, 1986. 335 p. ISBN 0-86338-088-3.

Prepared by a lecturer at the School of African and Oriental Studies in London, this work provides a great deal of information on general economic conditions in Africa, then focuses on the more populous nations for detailed treatment. Sudan receives this particular attention; the rest of the Sahel and Horn nations are mentioned, but this material is harder to find (there is no index). The Mediterranean states of Africa are not included. About one-third of the volume is a "statistical fact file" on each country, compiled from World Bank and IMF data and other sources.

763. Hodd, Michael. **The Economies of Africa: Geography, Population, History, Stability, Structure, Performance Forecasts.** Boston: G.K. Hall, 1991. viii, 363 p. ISBN 0-8161-7357-5.

An introductory section on African economies generally is followed by brief, focused profiles of every African nation. The entire continent is covered by this reference. Each article includes some descriptive material and several tables and graphs showing the economic performance indicators of the country in comparison to its region, to the rest of Africa, and to industrialized countries. The graphs also show each country's exchange rate, imports and exports, GDP growth and inflation rate over a 20-year period (1970-1989). The articles are alphabetically arranged, encyclopedia-style; there is no index.

764. Khan, Javed Ahmad. **Islamic Economics and Finance: a Bibliography.** London: Mansell, 1995. xi, 157 p. ISBN 0-7201-2219-8.

A useful and well-organized bibliography compiling some 1600 sources, both theoretical and practical, on the neglected topic of Islamic-oriented financial systems. Khan covers the topic as a whole and also some individual countries, including Egypt and Sudan.

The bibliography encompasses monographs and anthologies, but consists mainly of journal articles of a scholarly or technical nature, not just from Western publications but also many other sources. The entries are not annotated, except for a helpful appendix describing important journals and serials in the field. The volume supplies an author and a subject index.

765. Khan, Muhammad Akram. **Islamic Economics: Annotated Sources in English and Urdu.** Leicester: The Islamic Foundation, 1981. 2 v. *Islamic Economics Series;* vols. 7 and 16. ISBN 0-86037-127-1 and 0-86037-214-6.

Carefully organized according to a unique classification system, this compilation of books and articles is also indexed by author and subject. Many of the sources are unpublished literature presented in conferences and seminars, and many are works published in Pakistan and other parts of the Muslim world.

The author has annotated each entry with a useful summary and an indication of the appropriate audience: e.g., a simple work for laypersons, works suitable for jurists, theologians or other specialists.

766. Neinhaus, Völker. **Literatur zur Islamischen Ökonomik: in Englisch und Deutsch.** Köln: Al-Kitab Verlag, 1982. xi, 149 p. *Forschungsberichte Islamische Wirtschaft.* ISBN 3-88794-002-4

Also titled: *Literature on Islamic Economics.*

A compilation of sources – carefully organized but not annotated – on Islamic studies in general, then Islam and economics in particular. It covers economic theory (capitalism, Marxism, etc.), property ownership, trade, taxes, banking and lending, labor, social justice issues, and so on. Scholarly books and articles are included. The introductory materials are printed in both English and German. There is an author index.

767. Shaban, S. S. A. **A Classified Bibliography on Islamic Economics.** Mashad, Iran: Islamic Research Foundation, 1989. In three parts, paginated separately.

Economics is understood here in a broad sense to include all forms of production and trade, not just banking or the role of formal financial institutions. Browsing the table of contents might help to identify specific material; Egypt, Tunisia and some other African states are mentioned. The entries are not annotated, and are presented in an unedited terminal-printout style; some of the bibliographical information is confusing. There is a strong emphasis here on conference papers and proceedings. Parts 2 and 3 reorder the same entries by author and title.

768. Wilson, Rodney. **The Arab World: an International Statistical Directory.** Boulder, CO: Westview Press, 1984. Unpaginated. ISBN 0-7108-0251-X.

A practical compilation of tables of statistical data on the economies of 18 Arab nations, including Algeria, Egypt, Libya, Morocco, Sudan and Tunisia. The statistics originate in the national or central banks and monetary agencies of each nation, government statistical reports and yearbooks, the work of private economic consultants, and the publications of intergovernmental organizations (the World Bank, IMF, UN) and some departments of the American and Japanese governments. The tables cover a wide range of economic activity, from petroleum to civil aviation, from commercial bank assets to auto imports; tables on individual nations are far more detailed, showing agricultural and industrial production, education levels in the labor force, the number of tourist visits, amounts of tax revenue, the nationalities of foreign workers, sometimes even the exact number of trees.

The Oil Industry

A great deal of information on petroleum exploration, recovery, refining and trade can be found in the descriptive, analytical and statistical sources listed above. In this section are noted only those sources dealing exclusively with minerals and energy concerns. These sources are appropriate for almost any general or academic library; not listed are internal trade information sources that are proprietary and subject to very restricted access.

769. **L'Énergie en Afrique: la Situation Énergétique de 34 Pays de l'Afrique Subsaharienne et du Nord.** Edited by Jacques Girod. Paris: Éditions Karthala, 1994. viii, 467 p. ISBN 2-86537-549-8

Publication of the Environnement et Développement du Tiers-Monde Programme Énergie (Dakar) and Institut d'Économie et de Politique de l'Énergie (Grenoble).

A country-by-country summation of current conditions in the production, consumption and delivery of energy products and services. Morocco, Algeria, Tunisia, Libya, Egypt, Mauritania, Mali, Niger, Chad, and Djibouti are covered.

Each article provides a map, an outline of and directory data for the agencies and enterprises involved in energy, a description of the country's natural resources and industrial capacity (for petroleum, coal, wood, mineral uranium, and electricity), a current bibliography, and several tables of economic data from various statistical sources. The volume also includes several statistical appendices with tables showing data over the previous ten years. The clear organization of text and tables facilitates comparison of data throughout the volume.

770. **International Petroleum Encyclopedia.** Annual; 1986- . Tulsa, OK: PennWell. ISBN 0-87814-358-0; ISSN 0148-0375.

A glossy, colorful trade publication that seems more suited to public relations than to reference work. Graphs and tables of data, maps and photos are abundant. Statistical summaries of drilling, production, processing and refining are provided. There is coverage of Africa in general, and of Algeria, Egypt and Libya in particular. Some directory data (for relevant government agencies) and an index are included.

771. **North Africa Oil and Gas.** Paris: International Energy Agency and the Organisation for Economic Co-Operation and Development, 1996. 170 p. ISBN 92-64-15330-6.

The first IEA study to focus on North Africa, this handbook presents current data on the petroleum industries of Algeria, Egypt and Libya. There is a bit of explanatory text, but the main attraction here is the wealth of clear, attractive graphics, maps and statistics. However, four large, detailed and colorful maps of oil installations are marred by their weak folds, along which the paper easily tears and separates.

Sharing agreements among the three nations and legislation affecting hydrocarbons are discussed. Information on foreign investment, transport and exploration is also presented.

The collection of 28 graphs and figures, and another 28 tables of data, are supplemented by a "statistical annex" of 67 pages of economic information on each country and the region. It seeks to report and document developments in crude oil and natural gas production and export capacity, retrospectively to about 1970. The text offers prognostications as well, to about 2000. The bibliography is a list of annuals and periodicals that everyone interested in this subject should know about. The volume has a directory of OECD document distributors, but no indexes.

772. **Oil and the Economic Geography of the Middle East and North Africa: Studies by Alexander Melamid.** Edited by C. Max Korpeter. Princeton: Darwin Press, 1991. 319 p. ISBN 0-87850-075-8.

Contrary to its title, this work has almost nothing to do with North Africa. There is one short article on Ethiopia, but no information on the petroleum economies of Algeria, Libya or other northern states.

773. **OPEC Official Resolutions and Press Releases, 1960-1983.** Second edition. Oxford: Pergamon Press; published and distributed on behalf of OPEC, Vienna, 1984. x, 216 p. ISBN 0-08-031122-9.

A collection of full-text documents critical to the history of the Organization of Petroleum Exporting Countries, from its inception in 1960, through the oil-price turmoil and embargo of 1973, up to the early 1980s. This very convenient reference follows an earlier edition covering 1960-1980. It is supplied with a names and a subject index.

774. McCarl, Henry N. and Jong Ahn. **Bibliography on International Trade in Mineral Commodities.** Monticello, IL: Vance Bibliographies, 1986. 27 p. *Public Administration Series;* P-2072. ISBN 1-55590-132-8; ISSN 0193-970X.

The Vance bibliographies on public administration are composed of topically arranged citations – up to about 1000 in each issue – of books and articles, government bulletins and other publications. The entries are sometimes briefly annotated. This issue contains material on OPEC and the petroleum industry, but it is not topically subdivided, making specific subject matter very difficult to find.

775. Miller, E. Willard and Ruby M. Miller. **Economic, Political and Regional Aspects of the World's Energy Problems.** Monticello, IL: Vance Bibliographies, 1979. 99 p. *Public Administration Series;* P-360.

This issue of the Vance bibliographies supplies "an up-to-date comprehensive listing of articles, books and other publications to guide individuals interested in the energy situation in the world in the 1970s" (Preface). The bibliography is presented in two parts: the first section is topical, the second geographical, including materials on Africa generally, Libya and Algeria.

776. Nicholas, David. **The Middle East, Its Oil, Economies and Investment Policies: a Guide to Sources of Financial Information.** Westport, CT: Greenwood Press, 1981. xxiv, 199 p. ISBN 0-313-22986-4.

Aimed at providing "information support for the business community," this guide serves to "bring together in a one-volume, ready reference form, the wide variety of sources that one can turn to for information on the Middle East economies and their petroleum-generated wealth" (Introduction). Egypt, Libya, Morocco, Tunisia, Algeria and Sudan are among the nations covered. Information sources include "books and journals ... theses, annual reports, directories, statistics, unpublished documents, reference tools, computerized data bases ... banks, government agencies, publishers, university departments, etc." (p. xiii). Some of the entries are annotated. There are author and title indexes, and a less successful subject index.

777. Schurr, Sam H. and Paul T. Homan. **Middle Eastern Oil and the Western World: Prospects and Problems.** New York: American Elsevier, 1971. xii, 206 p. ISBN 0-444-00094-1.

This study, co-sponsored by the RAND Corporation and Resources for the Future, Inc., was released shortly before the Arab oil embargo of 1973. It documents the increasing economic "interdependence between two groups of countries – the large producing countries of the Persian Gulf region and North Africa, and the large consuming countries of Western Europe and Japan [and the United States]" (Summary). The study is composed of dense, informative encyclopedia-style articles generously supplied with footnotes, tables and figures or maps. About one-fourth of the volume is a statistical appendix presenting projected world energy consumption and trade flows for 1975 and 1980, with background data to 1955. There is a carefully-organized subject index.

778. Sinclair, Stuart W. **Middle East Economic Handbook.** London: Euromonitor, 1986. 487 p. ISBN 0-86338-126-X.

For purposes of this reference, the Middle East is understood to include Morocco, Algeria, Tunisia, Libya and Egypt (as well as the Arabian peninsula and Iran). The first two chapters give a broad understanding of Middle East economic issues in a world context, then in their regional context; the petroleum industry naturally dominates these discussions. Chapters on the individual countries provide a map, some descriptive material, and several tables showing major economic indicators. A statistical "fact file" of comparison data serves as an appendix. A table of contents and list of figures are provided, but no index.

779. Tétreault, Mary Ann. **The Organization of Arab Petroleum Exporting Countries: History, Politics and Prospects.** Westport, CT: Greenwood Press, 1981. xiv, 215 p. *Contributions in Economics and Economic History.* ISBN 0-313-22558-3.

A scholarly treatment of OAPEC and its connections with the more familiar OPEC. The volume contains seven figures and 35 tables of specialized economic data useful for research and reference. An appendix provides the full text of the international agreement founding the organization. A bibliography and rough subject index are included.

780. Waddams, Frank C. **The Libyan Oil Industry.** Baltimore: Johns Hopkins University Press, 1980. 338 p. ISBN 0-8018-2431-1.

This scholarly monograph details the history of Libya's oil-based economy since the 1950s. Petroleum law, taxation and concessions, oil prices and market forces, international relations and internal conditions in the Libyan economy are considered and documented. Three maps, seven charts or diagrams and 55 tables provide useful graphics for reference work. A brief bibliography and index are included.

781. Weaver, Rose. **The Energy Crisis: a Selective Bibliography.** Monticello, IL: Vance Bibliographies, 1982. 12 p. *Public Administration Series;* no. P-1011. ISSN 0193-970X.

This issue of the Vance bibliographies focuses almost entirely on the consumption of fuels (including petroleum), not production.

Databases and Websites

782. Institut de l'Information Scientifique et Technique, Centre Nationale de la Recherche Scientifique (INIST-CNRS). **Oil and Gas.** Available on CD-ROM.

Bibliographic data on "more than 200 serials on oil and gas industries and products." Updated annually.

783. Knight-Ridder Information. PTBN Newsletter Database. For further information see **www.krinfo.ch/www/rs/DS/OLD/PTBN.HTML**

The full text of specialized business and industry newsletters, including many dealing with the Middle East and the oil industry.

784. Middle East Economic Survey. Interactive Version. **http://www.mees. com/dotcom/index.html**

Weekly newsletter covering banking/finance, politics and economics in the Middle East and North Africa, especially the oil industry (see especially MEES Oil News). Useful links. Full access for subscribers only.

785. Organization of Arab Petroleum Exporting Countries. **www.kuwait. net/~oapec/**

786. PennWell. OJG Online (Oil & Gas Journal). **www.pennwell.com/jet.html**

Online version of the publisher's Oil & Gas Journal, a trade periodical covering exploration, drilling, production, gas processing, refining, petrochemical and pipeline technology – both the business and engineering aspects of the industry. Full access to subscribers only.

787. sci.geo.petroleum. Internet Resources. **www.slb.com/petr.dir/index.html**

Many links to information on the petroleum industry, exploration, geology, professional and academic institutions.

788. University of Texas at Austin. Petroleum and Geosystems Engineering Reading Room. **http://brazos.pe.utexas.edu/Dept/Reading/pepb.html**

Useful links page, to public and proprietary information.

789. University of Tulsa (Oklahoma). Petroleum Abstracts. **http://www. pa.utulsa.edu/PA/petroleum.html**

Indexing service for petroleum-related journal literature and research publishing; also electronic databases. Useful links. Full access for subscribers only.

790. US Department of Energy. Energy Information Administration: Country Analysis Briefs. **www.eia.doe.gov/emeu/cabs/contents.html**
Links to informative pages on oil and gas production in Egypt, Libya and Algeria.

791. US Geological Survey. World Energy Publications. **energy.cr.usgs.gov/energy/pubs.html**
Maps of petroleum resources and other information (statistics, bibliographies, assessments).

Arts and Learning

Chapter

6

Fine arts, architecture, music and film occupy the first section of this chapter. The languages and literatures of northern Africa follow, along with the publishing and media industries. Education and science concerns—including technology, medicine, and the environment—are included in this chapter as well. There is also a section featuring electronic information sites for academic and professional organizations engaged in the study of Africa or the Middle East.

Art and Architecture

792. **African Ethnonyms: Index to Art-Producing Peoples of Africa.** Compiled by Daniel P. Biebuyck, Susan Kelliher, and Linda McRae. New York: G.K. Hall, 1996. xxviii, 378 p. ISBN 0-7838-1532-8.

Art librarians, curators, critics or scholars could benefit from this intriguing reference. One may use it to discover which art texts and sources contain material on a given tribal/ethnic or language group. Entries direct the reader to certain volumes in the extensive bibliography. Indexes provide access by country, listing the identity groups for which an entry exists: there are 21 in Algeria alone, and more than 130 in Sudan. All of the countries of northern Africa are included. In addition, there is a toponyms index for other locations: for example, Agadez, Jebel Barkal or Fezzân. The general bibliography can also be used as a compilation of references and monographs on African art and society.

793. Baer, Eva. **Metalwork in Medieval Islamic Art.** Albany: State University of New York Press, 1983. xxiv, 371 p. ISBN 0-87395-602-8.

Often cited, this work represents an important source on the subject of metal crafts in Islamic styles. More than 230 black-and-white photos illustrate the text. The material is organized by theme. Of the North African states, only Egypt is included in this study. A bibliography and an index are provided.

193

794. Burt, Eugene C. **Ethnoart: Africa, Oceania and the Americas: a Bibliography of Theses and Dissertations.** New York; London: Garland, 1988. xix, 191 p. *Garland Reference Library of the Humanities;* v. 840. ISBN 0-8240-7545-5.

Limiting the scope of this bibliography to theses and dissertations gives it a certain comprehensiveness and depth. Entries, however, are very brief, and do not include abstracts—a puzzling omission in a work of this kind. The artwork and aesthetics of many peoples of the Sahel and Horn are covered here. Author, date and degree-granting institution indexes are provided, along with a subject index.

795. Cigar, Norman. **Architecture of the Sahara.** Monticello, IL: Vance Bibliographies, 1981. 4 p. *Architecture Series;* A-463. ISSN 0194-1356.

A very brief list of articles and books in several European languages analyzing the distinctive characteristics of buildings—not only monumental public structures, but small domestic buildings as well—in "the Sahara region of North Africa" (Introduction).

796. Courtney-Clarke, Margaret and Geraldine Brooks. **Mazighen: the Vanishing Traditions of Berber Women.** New York: Clarkson Potter, 1996. xxiv, 191 p. ISBN 0-517-59771-3.

A colorful, large-format "coffee-table" book, full of large, beautiful photographs of the life and arts of Berber women in the Atlas mountains of Morocco and Algeria. A very nice monochrome map, a simple glossary, bibliography and index are provided as well. The pottery and textiles are especially fine.

797. Creswell, K. A. C. (Keppel Archibald Cameron). **A Bibliography of Muslim Architecture in North Africa, Excluding Egypt.** Supplément à HESPERIS 1954, tome XLI. Paris: Librairie Larose, 1954. 65 p.

An excerpt from Creswell's huge bibliography, organized by site.

798. Creswell, K. A. C. (Keppel Archibald Cameron). **A Bibliography of the Architecture, Arts and Crafts of Islam.** Supplement, Jan 1960 to Jan 1972. Cairo: American University Press, 1973. xiii, 366 p., ix.

Creswell's own supplement, organized along the same pattern as the original work.

799. Creswell, K. A. C. (Keppel Archibald Cameron). **A Bibliography of the Architecture, Arts and Crafts of Islam.** Second Supplement, Jan 1972 to Dec 1980 (with omissions from previous years). By J. D. Pearson. Cairo: American University Press, 1984. xvi, 578 p., xxvi.

Another supplement, prepared by the editor of *Index Islamicus.* Maintains the same style as the earlier works, with the addition of a titles index.

800. Creswell, K. A. C. (Keppel Archibald Cameron). **A Bibliography of the Architecture, Arts and Crafts of Islam, to 1st Jan 1960.** Cairo: American University Press, 1961. xxiv, 1330 p., xxv.

An absolutely massive work citing scholarly books and articles on Islamic arts from some time early in the nineteenth century up till the date specified. The work is divided into two parts: architecture, then arts and crafts. Within these sections, organization is geographical. North Africa is well covered in Part I; in Part II, a little less so. An index of authors is provided.

801. Creswell, K. A. C. (Keppel Archibald Cameron). **Early Muslim Architecture.** Reprint of revised edition. New York: Hacker Art Books, 1979. 2 v. ISBN 0-87817-176-2 (Vol. 1, pts. 1-2; Vol. 2).

This work is itself a monument to meticulous scholarship: it describes and depicts in incredible detail every known Islamic monument built up to A.D. 905. A few of these structures are in northern Africa: the Mosque of 'Amr, the Nilometer and the Mosque of Ibn Tulun in Cairo, and the Great Mosque of Tunis. The drawings and plans in these oversized volumes are unsurpassed, and the accuracy of each description extends to exact measurements, numbers of columns and windows, and compass orientations. Each volume also provides a building chronology, an index in several languages (including Greek) and up to 123 pages of sharp, select black-and-white photographs.

802. Elleh, Nnamdi. **African Architecture: Evolution and Transformation.** New York: McGraw-Hill, 1997. xvii, 382 p. ISBN 0-07-021506-5.

A glossy "coffee table" book, but with an interesting and readable text. Line drawings, maps, site and floor plans, elevations, black-and-white and color photos illustrate the work throughout (however, reproduction of these pictures is not always perfect). The work is concerned not only with tribal or contemporary architecture, but with what is more often considered archaeology: the structures of Pharaonic Egypt, Leptis Magna (Roman Libya), medieval mosques and mosaics of Tunisia, and so on.

Part 2 of the work covers "North Africa: the Maghreb and Egypt," while Part 3, "Central and East Africa" includes the Horn, and Part 5, "West Africa" includes Mali, Niger and Chad. In addition, a chapter on Islamic architecture in Africa and a section on urbanization provide a good deal of relevant material. There is a glossary, a chronology, a subdivided bibliography and a useful index.

803. Hamilton, Alastair. **Europe and the Arab World: Five Centuries of Books by European Scholars and Travellers From the Libraries of the Arcadian Group.** Oxford: Oxford University Press (Azimuth Editions), 1994. 207 p. ISBN 0-19-714400-4.

A lavish "coffee table" book, originally published in French to accompany the exhibition *L'Europe et le Monde Arabe* at the Musée de l'Institut du Monde Arabe in Paris in 1993 and 1994. It is not a bibliography, but a history of books—very rare and fine ones, works of art in the Orientalist vein. Some beautiful illustrations are included, and there is a bibliography (but no index).

804. Hutt, Anthony. **North Africa.** London: Scorpion, 1977. ix, 192 p. *Islamic Architecture.* ISBN 0-905906-01-2.

In a small, attractive volume, Hutt has assembled a fine collection of 24 color and 136 black-and-white plates, effectively illustrating the special features of major Islamic buildings and monuments in Morocco, Algeria, Tunisia and Libya. Each plate is clearly identified and supplied with a caption indicating its significance. An introductory essay, basic time chart and glossary, and index of names and subjects increase the book's reference value. Two simple maps are included.

805. Magnin, André. **Contemporary Art of Africa.** With Jacques Souillou. New York: Harry N. Abrams, 1996. 192 p. ISBN 0-8109-4032-9.

An attractive, richly-illustrated volume displaying the work (drawing, painting, sculpture, objects of all kinds) of twentieth-century African artists. The volume excludes the Maghreb and products of its Arab/Islamic culture; there is also very little coverage of the Sahel and Horn, apart from a few artists in Mali, Niger, etc. The volume includes a glossary, bibliography and index.

806. Marçais, Georges. **Manuel d'Art Musulman: l'Architecture Tunisie, Algérie, Maroc, Espagne, Sicile.** Paris: Éditions Auguste Picard, 1926. 2 v.

An important classic work describing in detail the Islamic monumental buildings of the Maghreb, whether religious, civil or military. Illustrative line drawings and plans, and rather faint black-and-white photos, are quite pertinent. Vol. 1 concerns itself with the 9th-12th centuries, Vol. 2 with the 13th-19th. Footnotes and a subdivided bibliography appear in both volumes; in addition, Vol. 2 includes a detailed "index des termes techniques" and a names index.

807. Prussin, Labelle. **African Nomadic Architecture: Space, Place and Gender.** Washington; London: Smithsonian Institution Press; National Museum of African Art, 1995. xxii, 245 p. ISBN 1-56098-358-2.

A scholarly study of the "vernacular architecture"—dwellings of ordinary people, rather than palaces and monuments—of northern Africa, especially the Sahel and Horn. The Trarza, Kunta and Brakna peoples of Mauretania, the Tuareg of Mali, Algeria and Niger, the Tubu of Chad, the Mahria and Beja of Sudan, and the nomadic peoples of Somalia are all featured. A great deal of information about the customs and behavior of these groups is presented, not just their physical structures. The author devotes particular attention to the activities of women, as homes are private family structures and tend to be a female domain.

The volume is primarily text, but is illustrated with black-and-white and color photos and drawings, with informative captions. A worthwhile bibliography and index are provided.

808. Reswick, Irmtraud. **Traditional Textiles of Tunisia and Related North African Weavings.** Los Angeles: Craft and Folk Art Museum, 1985. xvii, 242 p. *Folk Art Monographs;* 1. ISBN 0295-96281-X.

This unusual volume offers a great deal of technical as well as cultural information on handwoven textiles in North Africa. A map of Tunisia includes transparent overlays showing physical geography and tribal groups. Chapters cover the raw materials, hand-processing and dyeing of the fibers, various looms and tools, and knotting (of carpets).

Distinct black-and-white photos and drawings are used to illustrate the text, and a section of 35 full-color plates is provided. There is a glossary of terms, a specialized bibliography, and an index, increasing the work's reference value.

809. Revault, Jacques. **Palais, Demeures et Maisons de Plaisance à Tunis et ses Environs (du XVIe au XIXe Siècle).** Aix-en-Provence: ÉDISUD, 1984. 174 p. ISBN 2-85744-189-2.

Since this study covers a limited number of structures in a fairly small geographical area, the table of contents (sommaire) and maps are probably adequate to orient the reader; still, a detailed index would help. Large photos—often a full page—are featured, some of them in color. Floor plans for many of the larger structures are included. There is a one-page bibliography.

810. Sourdel-Thomine, Janine and Bertold Spuler. **Die Kunst des Islam.** Berlin: Propyläen Verlag, 1973. 426 p. *Propyläen Kunstgeschichte;* Band 4.

An effective organizational scheme controls this thick volume. First, a substantial historical introduction explains the origin and development of Islam as a "Weltreligion," and the appearance of distinctive art forms belonging to it. Then there is a huge collection of 527 photographic plates on glossy paper, 72 of them in color. A third section of more than 250 pages of fine print ("Dokumentation") describes and explains each of these pictures in detail, often providing plans of structures as well.

An extensive bibliography subdivided by subject and a limited but useful index are included. Important art works in and from northern Africa are easily found in the table of contents or index (see especially "Almohaden," "Almoraviden," etc.).

811. Soustiel, Jean. **Le Céramique Islamique.** With Charles Kiefer. Fribourg: Office du Livre, 1985. 427 p. *Le Guide du Connaisseur.* ISBN 2-8264-0002-9.

A splendidly-illustrated large-format volume presenting a history and description of ceramic art from pre-Islamic to Ottoman times. The work is organized both geographically and chronologically: the extensive Table des Matières is the key to assessing the work's coverage. Egypt is discussed separately from "La Méditerranée Occidentale" (North Africa as a region, then Tunisia, Algeria and Morocco) in Chapter V and Chapter VII, respectively. A substantial text and captions both support and receive support from the illustrations.

A chronology specifically for ceramic art, a sizable subdivided bibliography, a general index and location notes for objects displayed in museum collections increase the reference value of this work.

812. Spring, Christopher and Julie Hudson. **North African Textiles.** Washington: Smithsonian Institution Press, 1995. 144 p. ISBN 1-56098-666-2.
A lavishly-illustrated and informative introduction to the textile arts of Morocco, Algeria, Tunisia, Egypt and Libya (some material on other societies, especially Sudan and Ethiopia, is provided as well). Emphasis is on the cultural and anthropological significance of these artifacts. An interesting text and full captions, a general bibliography, a glossary and index are included.

813. Stanley, Janet L. **The Arts of Africa: an Annotated Bibliography.** Atlanta: African Studies Association, 1992-1996. 5 v. ISSN 1044-8640.
The first volume of this compilation of books and articles, covering 1986-87, appeared in 1992. The newest one available at this point is Vol. 5, covering 1991, published in 1996.
The annotated entries pertinent to Africa in general are organized by topic; sections follow for regions and individual countries. All of the nations of northern Africa are represented in Vol. 5, though for some reason the table of contents does not list them in alphabetical order.
Cross-references in the text and a lengthy subject index help to track down material. An author index is also provided. Works cited were published in a variety of European languages and some others (e.g., Afrikaans); a very rich literature is represented here, from scholarly studies of an anthropological nature to museum and exhibition catalogs.

Journals

814. **African Arts.** Quarterly, 1967- . Los Angeles: African Studies Center, University of California. ISSN 0001-9933.
Also titled: *Arts d'Afrique.* Descriptive website and contact information at **www.isop.ucla.edu/jscasc/afrart/about.htm**
Published by the James S. Coleman Center, this magazine features substantial articles with full bibliographical references on the many impressive art forms of Africa. Several lengthy, detailed and signed book reviews are presented in each issue, plus reviews of recent museum and gallery exhibits. In addition to the expected categories of fine art (painting, sculpture, etc.), this resource pays attention to works in all media, including architecture, clothing and jewelry, dolls and masks, worship objects and so on, and touches upon film, drama, dance and music. The splendid photography could draw students to examine and learn from what is mainly a journal for the collector, curator or critic.

815. **Ethnoarts Index.** Quarterly; 1987- . Seattle: Data Arts. ISSN 0893-0129.
Former title: *Tribal Arts Review.*

An index that covers "the visual arts of the indigenous peoples of Africa, Oceania and the Americas," offering "bibliographic access to recently published materials" (cover). These materials include books, journal articles, book reviews, exhibition reviews, conference papers, theses and dissertations, and collection catalogs. Entries are organized by geography and tribal group; under Mali, for example, materials relating to the art of the Bamana, Djenne, Dogon, Tellem and Mande peoples are easily located. The countries of the Horn and Sahel are within the scope of this work (including Sudan). No abstracts are provided; each issue is indexed. An electronic database search service is offered, upon request.

816. **Journal of African Cultural Studies.** Semiannual; 1998- . Abingdon: Carfax. ISSN 1369-6815.

Formerly: *African Languages and Cultures.* Descriptive website and contents available online at **www.carfax.co.uk/jac-ad.htm**

Founded in its original form at SOAS in London in 1988, this scholarly journal is concerned with "perceptions of African culture from inside and outside Africa, with a special committment to the fostering of African scholarship" (verso). The languages and literature (including oral tradition), theatre and dance, art, music, the media, anthropology and folklore studies are considered; however, since it was redesigned under a new name, the journal will no longer feature technical studies of African linguistics.

817. **Revue Noire: Art Contemporain Africain.** Quarterly; 1991- . Paris: Revue Noire. ISSN 1157-4127 (each issue has a separate ISBN).

Attractive website in English and French available at **www.rio.net/revuenoire**

A large-format, generously illustrated periodical covering the current arts scene in Africa. Issues tend to concentrate on certain places or themes, and are organized by artistic medium. This journal is concerned not only with sculpture and painting, but also photography, dance, theater, music and literature. The text of articles, poems, short stories, etc., is presented in English and French, and sometimes Portuguese.

Websites

818. Afric Network. **www.afric-network.fr/homepage.html**
Eclectic French-language page stressing arts and culture (currently limited to Francophone west-central Africa).

819. AfricArt. l'Internet au Service des Artistes d'Afrique . **www.mediaport.net/ AfricArt/Entree/AccueilAfricArt.html**
Website maintained by Afrique en Créations, founded by the French Ministry for Overseas Development and the Ministry for the Arts; its "aim is to encourage contemporary artistic expression in Africa, to keep it alive and to put African arts before a large public." In French and English.

820. Afrique en Scènes. Index Par Pays. **www.mediaport.net/AeS/Cal/Pays/index.fr.html**
Country index, "sélection par pays d'origine des artistes." Part of the Afrique en Créations website. Dance, music and theater are featured. Includes all of northern Africa.

821. Afrique Virtuelle/Virtual Africa. **www.cyberworkers.com/Leonardo/africa/index.shtml**
Arts and culture information (part of the Leonardo Project). In French.

822. Arab Art. The Online Gallery of Arab Art, Design and Architecture. **www.arab.net/arabart/**
So far, features Tunisia, Egypt and Morocco.

823. Islamic and Arabic Arts & Architecture. **islamicart.com/**
Architecture, coins, rugs, calligraphy and more.

824. Mission Archéologique et Ethnoarchéologique Suisse en Afrique de l'Ouest. **anthropologie.unige.ch/~elia/maesao/intro.html**
Featuring an exhibition of "Céramiques traditionnelles du Mali."

825. Toile Métisse. Association des Artistes et Ecrivains Francophones Presents sur Internet. **www.stratocom.fr/toile-metisse/**
"Notre objectif principal est de développer un lieu virtuel et pratique de rencontre et d'information sur la créativité francophone." The vice president of the association resides in Mali.

826. Universes in Universe. Africa Art: Continent and Regions. **www.kulturbox.de/univers/africa/e_kont.htm**
Museums, galleries, exhibitions, new projects and media, plus history of African art. In German, English and Spanish.

Music

827. **Ethnomusicology: an Introduction.** Edited by Helen Myers. New York; London: W.W. Norton, 1992. 2 v. *Norton/Grove Handbooks in Music.* ISBN 0-333-44444-2 (set).
An important introduction to the field of world music research. Vol. 1 includes a guide to reference sources, and Vol. 2 is a collection of detailed, critical bibliographic essays. Africa is not the strongest area of this work, and Arab music is scarcely mentioned, but many of the more general sources are nevertheless relevant.

828. **The Garland Encyclopedia of World Music.** Vol 1: Africa. New York: Garland, 1998. xv, 851 p. ISBN 0-8240-6035-0

Includes a compact disc "selection of recorded examples ... intended to supplement and illustrate the discussions found in the articles" (Preface); also a booklet of notes on the recordings.

This impressive volume contains lengthy signed articles of a serious nature on the history, ethnomusicology and theory of a wide spectrum of African indigenous music, both secular and religious. Each article provides a substantial current bibliography of books and articles, and the volume is nicely illustrated with graphics, photos and musical scores.

The first two parts of the book explain important thematic and historical issues, while Part 3 concentrates on particular regions, among them North Africa (including articles on the Tuareg and Sudan). An article on Somalia is found under "East Africa," and articles on the Hausa and Yoruba (West Africa) are relevant to various parts of the Sahel. The volume includes an important glossary, a thematic bibliography, and a guide to recordings, films and videos. On the CD provided are recordings of Ethiopian liturgical music, two Tuareg songs recorded in Algeria, and a two-part Somalian chorus. The volume also supplies a clear map of the continent and a very competent index—the place to look for specific subjects, places or ethnonyms.

829. **The New Grove Dictionary of Music and Musicians.** Edited by Stanley Sadie. New York; London: Macmillan, 1980. 20 v. ISBN 0-333-23111-2.

The fundamental reference source for music information. Articles on non-Western musical traditions are informative, detailed, and carefully documented. Relevant articles are headed by geographic terms (Africa, North Africa, Morocco, Egypt, Ethiopia, Chad) or by ethnic group (Arab, Berber, Hausa, Fulani, Songhay, Tuareg music).

Small black-and-white photos and examples in musical notation are often included, and there is an emphasis on the definition of technical terms or vocabulary from other languages. Every article offers cross-references and sophisticated (though not current) bibliographical references.

830. **World Music in Music Libraries.** Edited by Carl Rahkonen. Canton, MA: Music Library Association, 1994. xi, 77 p. *MLA Technical Report;* no 24. ISBN 0-914954-49-0; ISSN 0094-5099.

Helpful information on the bibliographic control of world music materials. The bibliographical references with each essay are especially valuable.

831. **World Music: the Rough Guide.** Edited by Simon Broughton, Mark Ellingham, David Muddyman, and Richard Trillo. London: Rough Guides (Penguin), 1994. 697 p. ISBN 1-85828-017-6.

An engaging, informal descriptive handbook of world music, especially from popular and folk origins. Chapter 3, "Mediterranean and Maghreb," covers Morocco, Mauretania and Algeria (including "rai") and discusses the traditional instruments: oud, rabab, kanun, ghaita, etc. Egypt, Ethiopia and Sudan are found in Chapter 4, and Mali in Chapter 6. The volume provides important reference helps: glossaries of special vocabulary, discographies listing selected recordings and recommending representative contemporary works, fact boxes, and a sprinkling of black-and-white photos. A helpful names and subject index is included.

832. Graham, Ronnie. **The Da Capo Guide to Contemporary African Music.** New York: Da Capo Press, 1988. xii, 315 p. ISBN 0-306-80325-9.

Well-suited to reference work, this convenient guide offers concise descriptions of the musical life of each country, maps, bibliographical references and discographies of recorded music originating in each area. Coverage includes the Sahel and Horn. There are also some black-and-white photos and a helpful index. This handbook is a good first stop for specific personal names and titles.

833. Gray, John. **African Music: a Bibliographical Guide to the Traditional, Popular, Art, and Liturgical Musics of Sub-Saharan Africa.** New York: Greenwood, 1991. xii, 499 p. *African Special Bibliographic Series;* no. 14. ISBN 0-313-27769-9; ISSN 0749-2308.

This volume cites materials—books, dissertations, journal, magazine and newspaper articles, unpublished papers, films, videos and audiotapes—on the music of Africa, covering more than a century. Western languages and several African ones are included.

Though the emphasis is on the southern half of the continent, materials can be found here on several peoples living in northern states, among them the Bambara, Dinka, Falasha, Fulani/Peul, Nuba, Nuer, Anuak, Atuot, Dogon, Bajuni, Sara, Songhai, Bari, Bor, Galla, Funj, Hausa, Kotoko, Hadendowa, Hamar, Harari, Mande, Malinke, Teda, Minianka, Toupouri, and Zerma. An "ethnic group index" leads one efficiently to these entries (unfortunately, the subject index is quite useless). Helpful artist and author indexes are provided. The entries in this volume are not annotated.

834. Kaufman, Walter. **Selected Musical Terms of Non-Western Cultures: a Notebook-Glossary.** Warren, MI: Harmonie Park Press, 1990. x, 806 p. *Detroit Studies in Music Bibliography;* no. 65. ISBN 0-89990-039-9.

A ready reference composed of brief identifications of vocabulary characteristic of world music. The cultural source of each term is noted, a simple definition is given, and the reader is referred to a work in the extensive bibliography for more information. Arab and African musical forms from a variety of areas are within the scope of this volume, but assessing the completeness of coverage is difficult, since entries are listed alphabetically and not grouped by ethnic or national origin.

835. Lems-Dworkin, Carol. **African Music: a Pan-African Annotated Bibliography.** London: Hans Zell, 1991. xvii, 382 p. ISBN 0-905450-91-4.

A compilation of over 1700 books, articles, dissertations, essays, conference papers and periodicals on all aspects of African music. Each entry is annotated, and the variety of sources (in a number of European and African languages) is most interesting.

The author, however, has chosen to avoid organizing the citations by topic, or by type of literature: they are simply alphabetized and numbered. The lack of a table of contents makes it impossible to gain an overview of the book's coverage, or to browse the citations by subject. Time-consuming, careful use of the subject index indicates the presence of materials pertaining to most of the nations of northern Africa, with specific references to the traditional music of the Tuareg, Berber, Anuak, Falasha, Galla, Fulani, Bambara, Songhay, Zarma, Berta, Dinka, Nuer and 'Isawiya peoples, and music in the Arabic, Amharic and Coptic languages. There is an author index.

836. Southern, Eileen. **Biographical Dictionary of Afro-American and African Musicians.** Westport, CT: Greenwood, 1982. xviii, 478 p. *Greenwood Encyclopedia of Black Music* ISBN 0-313-21339-9; ISSN 0272-0264.

A very useful ready reference, though of course much stronger on American artists. An appendix listing individuals by place of birth is quite helpful. The powerful musical traditions of West Africa are well represented, but northern Africa as a cultural source is not (one Egyptian composer is among those included).

Websites

837. Africa Music Page. **www.cc.utah.edu/~pks1019/music.html**
Mostly sub-Saharan, but includes Ethiopia and Sudan. Many links.

838. African Music Archive. Institute of Ethnology and African Studies, Johannes Gutenberg University, Mainz. **www.uni-mainz.de/~bender/Welcome.html**
Extensive collection, teaching and research projects. In English and German.

839. African Music Encyclopedia. **africanmusic.org/**
Coverage is uneven; for example, links exist for Mali, but few other countries in northern Africa.

840. Arabica Musica. The Arabic Music Directory. **www.arabica-musica.com/**
Essays on the history of music in various societies, profiles of artists, and audio samples. Includes Mauritania, Morocco, Algeria, Tunisia, Libya, Egypt and Sudan. In English and French.

841. Aramusic. The Online Arabic Music Source. **www.aramusic.com/**
Articles and online discussion about Arab music, sample tracks, and CDs for sale.

842. Music Africa Home Page. **web.idirect.com/~mafrica/**
"MUSIC AFRICA is a non profit community organisation dedicated to the promotion of African music and culture." Based in Toronto.

843. Raicom. Musiques du Maghreb. **www.leweb.com/raicom/fr.html** (French) and **leweb.com/raicom/us.html** (English).

Devoted to music of the Maghreb (chaabi and raï), and "le patrimoine nord africain." Requires RealAudio to listen to music.

844. RootsWorld. African Music Resources. **www.rootsworld.com/rw/africa. html**

Reviews of recordings and books, articles and interviews, and links.

845. Weltmusik. Afrika Iwalewa. **www.weltmusik.de/**

Articles, reviews, concert reports and general information on African music. In German.

Film

846. Ballantyne, James and Andrew Roberts. **Africa: a Handbook of Film and Video Resources.** London: British Universities Film and Video Council, 1986. 120 p. ISBN 0-901299-46-4.

The writers have divided this volume into two sections: one for films and videos held in archival collections (in libraries, public institutions and private or corporate archives) and another for materials available for rent, loan or sale through institutions or distributors.

Detailed entries are provided for major sources, such as the National Film Archive or the Imperial War Museum. At least a brief annotation or contents note is included in every entry.

Subject sections, further subdivided by country, help to organize this material (noted in contents lists) and an index by title is provided. There is contact information for the institutions and distributors, though some may no longer be current. The nations of northern Africa do fall within the scope of this work.

847. Lems-Dworkin, Carol. **Videos of African and African-Related Performance: an Annotated Bibliography.** Evanston, IL: Carol Lems-Dworkin, 1996. xx, 331 p.

A reference listing almost 1400 videos of music, dance, drama, religious festivals and rituals, carnivals, folk ceremonies and customs, daily life, healing techniques, hunting/gathering and food preparation, work and play, women's activities and child-rearing, sports and other themes (p. xiii).

Annotations offer a description or synopsis of the film's content, its video format and running time, the African country or region concerned, and the viewer age level for which the film is appropriate. The entries are alphabetized by title; a names index and a very helpful subject index are provided.

The scope of this reference does include northern Africa: searching the subject index for individual countries (Egypt, Morocco, Chad) or ethnonyms (Berber, Fulani, Kaba) or topics (Islam; Women, Muslim) quickly yields results. This reference would prove valuable to teachers and to school/university libraries.

848. McClintock, Marsha Hamilton. **The Middle East and North Africa on Film: an Annotated Filmography.** New York: Garland, 1982. xxiii, 542 p. *Garland Reference Library of the Humanities;* v. 159. ISBN 0-8240-9260-0.

The astute annotations in this volume are only part of its charm. It also provides an intelligent introduction, beautifully-organized table of contents, and two indexes. Each entry includes the date, running time, sound track type, color/bw and film size, production, release and distribution informations, any identification or catalog numbers, and location data.

The scope of the work is impressive: all films and videotapes produced between 1903 and January 1980 on this broad topic are included. The geographical range encompasses the Middle East and North Africa in general, plus specific North Coast states, Sudan and Ethiopia (but not Mauritania, the rest of the Sahel, Somalia or Djibouti). There are topical sections as well, covering religion, the Arab-Israeli conflict, and Jerusalem.

McClintock's annotations often summarize the film's content, describe its physical condition (some are damaged or deteriorated), suggest an appropriate age level for the audience, comment on the film's quality, and indicate any viewpoint bias or political agenda.

849. Schmidt, Nancy. **Sub-Saharan African Films and Filmmakers, 1987-1992: an Annotated Bibliography.** London: Hans Zell, 1994. ix, 468 p. ISBN 1-873836-21-X.

Continues the coverage of the 1988 edition, relecting the increasing literature on this topic (3200 new entries). Very brief annotations.

850. Schmidt, Nancy. **Sub-Saharan African Films and Filmmakers: an Annotated Bibliography.** London: Hans Zell, 1988. 401 p. ISBN 0-905450-32-9

Also titled: *Films et Cinéastes Africains de la Région Subsaharienne: une Bibliographie Commentée.*

A substantial compilation of published information on African film and filmmakers: books, monographs, theses, articles, reviews and pamphlets. The work covers the Sahel and the Horn, including Mauritania and Sudan. Introductory material is presented in both English and French.

It is not clear how this can be considered an annotated bibliography, since at most one sentence and usually no more than a fragmentary remark is provided for any entry. There are indexes of film titles, filmmakers, actors and actresses and film festivals; unfortunately, the country index and subject index are quite useless.

851. Wiley, David S. **Africa on Film and Videotape: a Compendium of Reviews, 1960-1981.** East Lansing, MI: African Studies Center, Michigan State University, 1982. xxii, 550 p.

A useful and well-organized collection of detailed entries describing films and videos on Africa, mostly of an educational nature. Each entry provides basic film data and distribution information, subject descriptors, an explicit account of the film's content (often down to the minute), a recommended audience level for classroom use, and a frank, well-written critique of the work, enumerating its strengths and shortcomings. Though not now up-to-date, the retrospective material in this reference may still be of value, especially for school media centers.

Websites

852. Filmaker's Library. Global Issues: Middle East Studies. **www.filmakers.com/MID-EAST.html**
Reviews of recently-released films and videos on the Middle East, including Egypt and Arab North Africa.

853. Michigan State University. African Media Program. **http://www.amp.msu.edu/**
New website providing "an online comprehensive reference guide to film, video and other audio-visual materials concerning Africa (Sub-Saharan and North Africa)."

854. Vues d'Afrique. La Salle de Cinema Africaine. **http://www.vuesdafrique.org/**
Information about contemporary Francophone films and film makers, and the annual African and Creole film festival in Montreal.

Languages

Many excellent dictionaries exist for the translation of Modern Standard Arabic, as well as some regional or colloquial dialects. The references listed here are unusual in some way: they are literary or historical resources, or involve specialized vocabulary. Bibliographies, atlases and other references relevant to the study of Arabic and other languages of northern Africa are included here.

855. **Arabic Computer Dictionary.** Edited by Ernest Kay. London: Routledge & Kegan Paul, 1986. 177 p., 127 p. (two sections, separately paginated). ISBN 0-7102-0457-4
Compiled by Multi-Lingual International Publishers, Ltd.
A quick-reference vocabulary for all aspects of computer production, programming and use. Teachers, translators, businesses, clerical staff supervisors and trainers, as well as those specializing in manufacturing and installation of equipment or software development and operation, would be in need of such information on a daily basis.
The entries provide only an equivalent term in English, transliterated Arabic and Arabic script; there are no definitions, on the assumption that the user already knows what these terms mean and is simply seeking an equivalent in the opposite language. This volume is a valuable resource in a specialized area. Frequent new editions will be necessary for currency, however.

856. **Arabic-English and English-Arabic Dictionaries in the Library of Congress.** Compiled by George Dimitri Selim. Washington: Library of Congress, African and Middle Eastern Division, 1992. xi, 213 p. *Near East Series.* ISBN 0-16-036092-7.

A very useful compilation of the relevant bilingual (and in some cases multilingual) lexicons in the Library of Congress collection. The entries are carefully organized to separate general language dictionaries from the wealth of technical and specialized vocabulary in special subject dictionaries, covering all aspects of commerce, industry, natural science and culture, from banking to baking.

Some of the entries have very brief annotations, but normally the cited work's contents can be understood from the title (especially if one is able to decipher transliterated Arabic). A names index and a titles index are provided. This volume is an important resource for research libraries.

857. **Arabic Resources: Acquisition and Management in British Libraries.** Edited by David Burnett. London; New York: Mansell, 1986. xix, 164 p. ISBN 0-7201-1790-9.

Though specifically focused upon libraries in Britain, this collection of essays contains a good deal of information of interest to similar institutions and researchers elsewhere.

Expert contributors offer insight on collection development and management, cataloging and bibliographic control, and on the character and holdings of important British collections of Arabic materials. Four plates representing the photographic archive at the Middle East Centre are included. There is a names and subject index.

858. **Atlas of the World's Languages.** Edited by Christopher Morley and R. E. Asher. London: Routledge Reference, 1994. viii, 372 p. ISBN 0-415-01925-7.

The detailed, informative text is fundamental to this very large-format atlas. In addition, huge, colorful, clearly-printed maps convey a great deal of technical data through intelligible graphics.

Coverage in this atlas of the Middle East and North Africa in Chapter 7 includes not only the Mediterranean coast, but also the entire Sahel and Horn. It extends even to very fine linguistic distinctions and dialects involving only a few thousand speakers. The text is meant to explain the relationships between language families; the maps and graphs reinforce this information.

A very specific index is provided. This impressive volume would be an important addition to a research library.

859. **Bibliography of African Languages.** Edited by Wilma Meier. Wiesbaden: Otto Harrassowitz, 1984. lxxi, 888 p. ISBN 3-447-02415-1

Also titled: *Bibliographie afrikanischer Sprachen.*

An extensive compilation of all sorts of literature "concerning the structure of individual languages as well as works dealing with the history, classification and geographical spread of linguistic phenomena, and the development of national and standard languages" (p. ix).

In addition to scholarly monographs, articles and essays, this bibliography includes historical works of many kinds: early translations of Scripture, accounts by explorers, missionaries, colonial civil servants and others, from the early 16th century up till 1980. About 4000 authors are represented, and some 2000 African languages and dialects are studied here.

A chronological list of travellers to Africa and the central section, organized by author, help to orient the reader. Two big indexes reorganize the material by language, date and subject. Introductory material in this volume is provided in English, German, French and Russian. It constitutes an important resource for the specialist.

860. Dictionnaire Arabe-Français-Anglais: Langue Classique et Moderne. Par Régis Blachère, Moustafa Chouéme, and Claude Denizeau. Paris: G.-P. Maisonneuve et Larose, 1967. 4 v.

An important resource for the interpretation of the Arabic language into either English or French. The work is meant to include "all the vocabulary that constitutes what, for the sake of convenience, has been named 'literary' Arabic ... by 'literary' Arabic we mean the mass of the vocabulary used, to a varying degree, by poets, writers, journalists, publicists, lecturers, orators and university circles from the second half of the sixth century A.D. and the revelation of the Koran in the first century of the Hegira (7th century A.D.) up to the present day" (Foreword, p. v). The basic meaning of each word is presented in both English and French, then any special connotations or idiomatic uses are explained and Arabic verb and substantive forms, objects, etc. are identified.

861. Le Dictionnaire COLIN d'Arabe Dialectal Marocain. Sous la direction de Zakia Iraqui Sinaceur. Institut d'Études et de Recherche pour l'Arabisation. Rabat: Éditions al-Manahil, undated. 8 v., continuously paginated.

This work seems intended to be a glossary of vocabulary characteristic of Moroccan Arabic. The brief entries provide one Arabic term, with a pronunciation equivalent in roman characters, the part of speech, a capsule translation into French, and often a few idioms or variant uses of the term.

862. Grundriss der Arabischen Philologie. Herausgegeben von Wolfdietrich Fischer and Helmut Gätje. Wiesbaden: Dr. Ludwig Reichert Verlag, 1982. 3 v. ISBN 3-88226-144-7; 3-88226-145-5; 3-88226-214-1.

A meticulously-organized collection of scholarly studies on all aspects of Arabic language and literature. Vol. 1 is devoted to "Sprachwissenschaft," first to the origin of the language, development of regional or historical dialects, morphology, syntax and vocabulary, then the written language and its orthography, calligraphy, epigraphy and ancient texts (inscriptions, coins, papyrus, etc.).

Vol. 2 studies various forms of Arabic literature or "Dichtung," including poetry, rhetoric, folk literature, belles-lettres, historiography and geography, scientific and religious literature, both Islamic and other. Chapter 9 is a bibliographic essay by Reinhard Weipert analyzing materials for the study of Arabic (introductions, grammars, lexica, bibliographies, etc.) and includes a section on national or regional bibliographies; for North Africa, see pp. 512-514.

Vol. 3 is a supplement or update to the first two. Every section of all three volumes provides a very serious scholarly bibliography (even citing sources in Latin from the 17th century) and each volume has its own detailed indexes.

863. **Lexique des Termes Juridiques Français-Arabe.** Edited by M. L. Fadhel Moussa. Tunis: Académie Tunisienne des Sciences, des Lettres et des Arts, 1993. vii, 658 p.

A reference for the translation of French into Arabic only, divided into topical sections, each separately alphabetized (and prepared by different contributors): constitutional law, financial, international, civil, penal/criminal law, etc. There are no definitions, only apparent equivalents in Arabic.

864. **Lexique Marocain-Français.** Daniel Ferré. Morocco: Éditions NEJMA, Imprimerie de Fédala, undated. 313 p.

Prepared by a professor at l'École Industrielle et Commerciale de Casablanca, this handbook seems designed to facilitate spoken communication between Moroccans and French visitors. No Arabic script is used: the vocabulary terms are given in transliterated form, with a simple equivalent in French. No grammatical or syntactical information is provided, except noun plurals.

865. **Le Pataouète: Dictionnaire de la Langue Populaire d'Algérie et d'Afrique du Nord.** Edited by Jeanne et al Duclos. Calvisson: Éditions Jacques Gandini, 1992. 246 p. ISBN 2-906431-117.

A convenient one-volume paperback reference providing concise definitions of over 1000 vocabulary terms characteristic of the Maghreb. Many terms are neither standard French nor Arabic, but uniquely created for their environment. Each entry specifies the part of speech, offers one or more quotes showing the use of the term in context, and a definition. Entries are alphabetical, with cross-references from terms not used.

866. **Wörterbuch der Klassischen Arabischen Sprache.** Herausgegeben durch die Deutsche Morgenländische Gesellschaft. Reprint. Wiesbaden: Otto Harrassowitz, 1970. 5 v.

A standard source for medieval Arabic, this five-volume lexicon provides an interpretation into German for each Arabic term, plus complete grammatical information and references to its use in classical manuscripts.

867. Ashiurakis, Ahmed M. **A Complete Course of How to Speak Arabic in Libya.** Second edition. Misrata: Ad-Dar Aj-Jamahiriya for Publishing, Distribution and Advertising, 1985. xv, 164 p.

Basic grammar rules, vocabulary, phrases and polite formulaic expressions are provided in this little introduction. The Arabic words and sentences are spelled out phonetically in the Roman alphabet. The English and Arabic phrases do not always match, and cannot be taken out of their original context. Used in conjunction with a course in colloquial language for expatriates, this book might be effective.

868. Dozy, R. P. A. **Supplément aux Dictionnaires Arabes.** Third edition. Leiden and Paris: E.J. Brill and G.-P. Maisonneuve et Larose, 1967. 2 v.

A reprint of Dozy's classic work of Arabic lexicography, first published in 1882. Dozy interprets Arabic terms into French, but the distinctive contribution of this work is its references to the uses of these terms in original manuscripts and texts. At the time this reference first appeared, Dozy argued that no comprehensive lexicon of the entire Arabic language could be prepared; hence, the work of scholars should be to create specialized or supplementary collections of terms with manuscript documentation.

869. Fagnan, Edmond. **Additions aux Dictionnaires Arabes.** Reprint of 1923 edition. Beirut: Librarie du Liban, 1960. ix, 193 p.

Like Dozy, Fagnan provides not a comprehensive dictionary of the Arabic language, but a guide to the use of particular terms in original texts and manuscripts. Fagnan is still consulted particularly for information about legal terms and their sources.

870. Groom, Nigel. **A Dictionary of Arabic Topography and Placenames: a Transliterated Arabic-English Dictionary With an Arabic Glossary of Topographical Words and Placenames.** Beirut; London: Librairie du Liban; Longman, 1983. 369 p.

Those who can read the Arabic alphabet even a little will greatly appreciate the fact that this glossary provides the Arabic term in its proper orthography beside each transliterated term. A simple definition in English is also given. Many of these entries represent vocabulary that is unique to desert geography or to Arab cultural practices (e.g., "rajmah") or limited to a local dialect (e.g., "matarah"). An index of the terms in Arabic script and alphabetical order is included.

871. Hendrix, Melvin K. **An International Bibliography of African Lexicons.** Metuchen, NJ: Scarecrow, 1982. xxi, 348 p. ISBN 0-8108-1478-1.

This reference brings together a wealth of linguistic and anthropological information in a convenient form. Over 2600 sources pertaining to the languages of the African continent are found here: vocabularies, dictionaries, polyglot editions of important texts with glossaries, grammars and handbooks. Classic works together with modern ones, and studies in a variety of European languages, are cited. Annotations are given when the work's title is less than self-explanatory. An extensive language and dialect index is provided, along with an author and name index.

872. Mann, Michael and David Dalby. **A Thesaurus of African Languages: a Classified and Annotated Inventory of the Spoken Languages of Africa, with an Appendix on Their Written Representation.** London: Hans Zell, 1987. 325 p. ISBN 0-90-5450-24-8

Published for the International African Institute.

An effort to identify, classify, map and relate Africa's spoken languages. The work includes the languages of northern Africa—though even if the reader knows what these are, it is not easy to locate and comprehend the given information about them. The technical detail is obscure and the authors have used a system of writing conventions (a complete absence of capital letters, for instance) that makes comprehension of the material more difficult. There is a dense 43-page bibliography and an index. This reference may be useful to the subject specialist.

873. Mann, Michael and Valerie Sanders. **A Bibliography of African Language Texts in the Collections of the School of Oriental and African Studies, University of London, to 1963.** London: Hans Zell, 1994. xviii, 429 p. *Documentary Research in African Literatures;* no. 3. ISBN 1-873836-31-7.

The rich archival collections of SOAS, the International African Institute and the International Committee on Christian Literature for Africa are represented here. This very carefully-compiled volume orders these published materials by language. Titles are printed in appropriate orthography (Amharic or Ethiopic script, for example), then transliterated into the Roman alphabet, then translated into English.

Of the northern African languages, only Arabic and classical Ethiopic (Ge'ez) are excluded, but scores of others are included among the more than 8000 entries. Title and author indexes are provided, along with a very helpful index of languages by country; there is also a language classification list, and a list of language name cross-references.

874. Meiseles, Gustav. **Reference Literature to Arabic Studies: a Bibliographical Guide.** Tel Aviv: University Publishing Projects, 1978. xiv, 251 p.

A compilation of scholarly works on a very extensive range of Arabic language, history, dialect and literature studies, covering most aspects of Orientalist scholarship for Arabists. This work has the unusual merit of presenting each entry in its actual language of publication, with Arabic and Hebrew entries in their proper alphabets.

Scholarly journals are listed as well as books, with headings indicating their typical subject coverage. The work also includes some unusual appendices: transliteration tables, standard Arabic literary abbreviations (for Qur'anic studies, for instance), chronologies of Arab civilization studies in Arabic and in Western languages, and a collection of plates showing the format and page layout of several important reference books. In addition, there are indexes in the Roman alphabet, in Arabic and in Hebrew.

This work is not current, but emphasizes classical Orientalist sources that are still needed by historians and specialists. In certain research libraries it would have a place at the reference desk.

875. Shaheen, Esber I. **Arabic-English with a Petroleum Accent.** Tulsa: PPC Books, 1977. viii, 172 p. ISBN 0-87814-043-3.

Intended for the employees of oil companies (and their dependents) assigned to positions in the Arab world, this guidebook offers general background information about the life and work of American expatriates abroad, a "brief history of the Arabs," and practical travel advice. The central part of the book is a simple introduction to the Arabic language, a glossary and a phrase book from English to romanized Arabic ("You have serious engine trouble," "Get a doctor quick," etc.). Appendices offer tables of data on oil reserves, production, demand and supply—now dated—and capsule country profiles on the Maghreb states, Egypt and Sudan.

876. Suleiman, Yasir. **Language and Identity in the Middle East and North Africa.** Surrey: Curzon Press, 1996. vii, 192 p. ISBN 0-7007-0410-8.

Not a reference work, this essay collection nevertheless contains hard-to-find material on the use of French and Arabic in Tunisia, and on the Berber language in North Africa. Its value for the bibliographer lies in the references provided with each essay.

877. Unseth, Peter. **Linguistic Bibliography of the Non-Semitic Languages of Ethiopia.** East Lansing, MI: African Studies Center, Michigan State University, 1989. 113 p. *Ethiopian Series;* Monograph no. 20.

A compilation of materials, mostly of a highly technical nature, on all of the languages of Ethiopia except Somali (and any others of the Semitic family). The citations are alphabetized by author, and there is an index offering access by language—more than 100 are listed. The cited works are in a wide variety of European languages; entries are not annotated.

Journals

878. **Journal of African Languages and Linguistics.** Semiannual; 1979- . Berlin: Walter de Gruyter. ISSN 0167-6164.

Description and contents page available online at **www.degruyter.de/ journals/jall/index.html**

Produced by the Department of African Linguistics at Leiden University, this scholarly journal presents technical research articles and several signed book reviews in each issue. Tribal languages of the Sahel and Horn are included.

879. **Journal of Arabic Literature.** Three times/year; 1970- . Leiden: Brill. ISSN 0085-2376.

Subscription information and back issues available at **www.brill.nl**

The studies of Arabic-language materials in this scholarly journal encompass the "classical and modern, written and oral, poetry and prose, literary and colloquial" (verso). A few lengthy, technical articles and some detailed book reviews appear in each issue.

880. **Studies in African Linguistics.** Semiannual; 1970- . Bloomington: African Studies Program, Indiana University. ISSN 0039-3533.

Published until recently by the James S. Coleman African Studies Center and the Department of Linguistics at UCLA, this scholarly journal focuses on technical aspects of indigenous languages, including those of the Sahel and Horn. News of upcoming professional meetings is also provided.

881. **Zeitschrift für Arabische Linguistik.** Semiannual; 1978- . Wiesbaden: Harrassowitz Verlag. ISSN 0170-026X.

Technical studies of classical Arabic texts, the history of the language and its lexicographers, spoken dialects, and Arabic influences upon other languages are featured here. Each article provides a bibliography of primary and secondary sources. Brief book reviews are sometimes included. In German and English.

Databases and Websites

882. Arabic Script Software Map. **user.cs.tu-berlin.de/~ishaq/arabic/asm/asm.html**

Descriptions of software that can handle the Arabic alphabet.

883. Bucknell University. A Web of Online Dictionaries. **www.facstaff.bucknell.edu/rbeard/diction.html**

Not comprehensive, but interesting online materials for Arabic and a number of the other languages of northern Africa: Somali, Berber, Amharic, Algerian colloquial, etc.

884. Ethnologue Database. Languages of the World. **www.sil.org/ethnologue/ethnologue.html**

Useful general resource for reference, with good coverage of minority languages in many countries.

885. Harvard University. The Modern Standard Arabic Page. **arabic.wjh.harvard.edu/index.htm**

Language resources available online and by FTP: vocabulary files, grammar references, texts, and links.

Literature

886. **African Literatures in the 20th Century: a Guide.** New York: Ungar, 1986. x, 245 p. ISBN 0-8044-6362-X.

A readable and easy-to-use handbook introducing readers of English to a broad sampling of African literature. Survey articles of 5-10 pages provide an account of major personalities and events in each country, and a bibliography of 8-10 sources (books and articles, not always current). In addition, brief articles focusing upon the major writers active in each country may be included: four of

Algeria's great writers, four of Egypt's and one of Somalia's are featured. Some countries of northern Africa are not included, where apparently information is lacking (Chad, Libya, Mauritania, Niger). There is a simple author index. This reference is basic enough for use by beginning students at the high school or college level.

887. **Catalogue Collectif des Ouvrages en Langue Arabe Acquis par les Bibliothèque Françaises 1952-1983.** Prepared by Georges Haddad and Mohammed Saïd with the participation of the Institut du Monde Arabe. Paris: K.G. Saur, 1984. 4 v. ISBN 3-598-10510-X.

A published catalog of the old-fashioned National Union Catalog type, made up of photographic reproductions of the actual catalog cards, many of which are barely legible. This is certainly an important record, as electronic catalogs in the Arabic alphabet have lagged well behind online Roman-alphabet resources. However, this format requires a great deal of patience to use, and the editors and publishers offer the reader no assistance—with the exception of a brief preface and introduction in French, Arabic and curiously non-idiomatic English.

888. **Dictionary of Oriental Literatures.** Edited by Jaroslav Prušek. New York: Basic Books, 1974. 3 v. ISBN 465-01649-9.

The third volume of this reference pertains to the literatures of the vast region "most bound up with the Islamic cultural tradition," reaching from the erstwhile Soviet region of central Asia across the Middle East and Africa to Morocco, including Sudan and ancient Egypt. Most of the 1-2 paragraph alphabetized entries are for writers and poets; however, some titles (usually of folk tales, apocryphal books and other materials of unknown authorship) are listed, as are some vocabulary terms needed for the study of Arabic literature (e.g., "adab," "kalam," "maghazi") . Some bibliographical references are provided. A somewhat mysterious list of national literatures is found in an appendix.

889. **Répertoire des Chercheurs sur les Littératures Maghrébines.** Paris: Éditions l'Harmattan, 1990. 62 p. ISBN 2-7384-0707-2.

A compilation of monographs and dissertations in literary criticism, prepared by the Centre d'Études Littéraires Francophones et Comparées, at the Université Paris-Nord, under the direction of Charles Bonn. The literature studied in these works originated in Morocco, Tunisia and Algeria. The entries are organized alphabetically by author, and there is no title or subject index, nor an index of the university faculty to which the work was submitted. The entries are not annotated.

890. Anderson, Margaret. **Arabic Materials in English Translation: a Bibliography of Works From the Pre-Islamic Period to 1977.** Boston: G.K. Hall, 1980. xiii, 249 p. *Reference Publications in Middle East Studies.* ISBN 0-8161-7954-9.

Anderson has compiled a guide to materials that are often very difficult to find. Over 1600 entries are organized first by document type, then by topic. An index of names, titles and subjects is provided. Most of the entries have at least a brief contents note, and sometimes a more complete annotation.

Translations of the *Holy Qur'an* and the *Thousand and One Nights* (or *Arabian Nights*) are not included, as those have been collected elsewhere.

891. Asante, Molefi Kete and Abu S. Abarry. **African Intellectual Heritage: a Book of Sources.** Philadelphia: Temple University Press, 1996. xvi, 828 p. ISBN 1-56639-402-3.

This interesting anthology of texts covers a period from ancient oral tradition through the present. It contains many Pharaonic Egyptian texts, legends of various tribal peoples and a wealth of modern writings, and explores a wide range of topics, including the history of slavery and the African-American experience, all from an Afrocentric viewpoint. It touches lightly upon Arab cultural sources, the Arabic language and Islam. A helpful glossary of names as well as vocabulary terms, a bibliography and a general index are provided.

892. Badawi, M. M. **Modern Arabic Literature.** Cambridge: Cambridge University Press, 1992. xi, 571 p. *Cambridge History of Arabic Literature.* ISBN 0-521-33197-8.

A comprehensive and authoritative history of and guide to the formation of literature in the Arabic language (novels, poetry, short story, drama, other prose, criticism) in the *Nahdah* or modern period, starting with the invasion of Egypt by Napoleon in 1798.

This work assumes considerable knowledge of the history and culture of the Arab world, and of literature in general, and the ability to comprehend names, titles and vocabulary in transliterated Arabic (a translation is rarely offered). Except for a chapter devoted to the extraordinary artistic impact of the Egyptian novel, this volume is organized by genre, not geographically. However, the meticulous index makes it possible to track down material on North Africa, as well as individual countries, writers, works or topics. The Mediterranean coast of Africa and the Sudan are covered.

The volume includes an extensive, sophisticated, detailed, subdivided bibliography that constitutes an important research source in itself.

893. Bonn, Charles. **Bibliographie de la Critique sur les Littératures Maghrébines.** Paris: L'Harmattan, 1996. 155 p. *Études Littéraires Maghrébines;* no. 10. ISBN 2-7384-4760-0.

A compilation of scholarly studies, journal articles, entries in reference books and monographs pertaining to the work of the writers of the Maghreb. Editions of anthologies, collected essays and conference papers, as well as special themed issues of important periodicals, are included. Entries are not annotated, but their subject matter is almost always clearly identified by the titles. A valuable work, but it needs at least a titles index.

894. Brockelmann, Carl. **Geschichte der Arabischen Litteratur.** Zweite den supplementenbänden angepasste Auflage. Leiden: E.J. Brill, 1943-1949. 2 v.

Being reissued by E.J. Brill (1996-); ISBN 9004105468 and 9004104070.

A very valuable reference work that functions as an annotated catalog of Arabic manuscripts, with biographical information about the authors, and bibliographies of works by and about each one. Coverage begins with the pre-Islamic period and extends to the "Gegenwart" or 1940s. The basic organization is chronological: within each time period, material is further organized by genre (mysticism, poetry, philosophy, law, science and medicine, etc.) and geographically. In Vol. 2, sections pertaining specifically to Egypt, North Africa and "Der Magrib" can be found. In addition, there are three huge supplementary volumes. Brockelmann's work is being pursued further by Fuat Sezgin in his *Geschichte des arabischen Schrifttums* (nine volumes of which have appeared so far). In the title, note the use of two t's in *Litteratur.*

895. Cox, C. Brian. **African Writers.** New York: Charles Scribner's Sons (Macmillan Library Reference), 1997. 2 v. ISBN 0-684-19651-4 (set).

A collection of lengthy signed articles describing and analyzing the life and work of major figures in the history of African letters. Northern Africa is included, but coverage is limited to Camus, Mohammed Dib and Kateb Yacine of Algeria, Nuruddin Farah of Somalia, Albert Memmi and Abu al Qasim al-Shabbi of Tunisia, and Egypt's Taha Husayn, Tawfiq al-Hakim, Yusuf Idris, Nawal al-Sa'adawi (the only woman) and of course Najib Mahfuz. The articles are detailed and authoritative, yet readable, and include subdivided and often extensive bibliographies. Vol. 2 also contains a valuable index.

896. Görög, Veronika. **Littérature Orale d'Afrique Noire: Bibliographie Analytique.** Paris: G.-P. Maisonneuve et Larose, 1981. 394 p. ISBN 2-7068-0819-5.

This CNRS project is meant to provide access to scholarly articles and dissertations/theses studying traditional forms of African creativity and knowledge transmitted in oral form: fables, folk tales, proverbs, chants, epic poems, legends, etc. Each entry is briefly annotated, and many works cited were published in English or German.

Mali, Niger, Chad and Sudan are within the scope of this work, but searching by specific tribal group or language is more successful (e.g., Dinka, Hausa, Bambara). The "index ethno-linguistique" is barely adequate and the "index des genres" impossible.

897. Herdeck, Donald E. **African Authors: a Companion to Black African Writing.** Vol.1: 1300-1973. Washington: Black Orpheus Press, 1973. 605 p. *Dimensions of the Black Intellectual Experience.* ISBN 0-87953-008-1.

A literature ready reference comprising biographical entries (and sometimes portraits) of almost 600 African authors, and references to about 2000 literary works in standard Western categories—novels, poems, plays, short stories—and traditional forms, such as tales, proverbs and legends. Mauritania, the Sahel and Horn are included. Arabic and Amharic (as well as 37 African vernacular languages) are represented, along with several European languages. Most but not all of the literature originated in the 20th century.

Twenty valuable appendices offer: critical essays on major themes; very helpful lists of authors by time period, literary genre, country of origin, native language and gender; directory data on publishers, journals, bookshops and distributors specializing in African literature; a bibliography section that includes classified critical studies and anthologies. (The intended series did not continue; apparently, rights were bought by Gale Research.)

898. Hunwick, John O. **The Writings of Central Sudanic Africa.** Edited by J. O. Hunwick and R. S. O'Fahey. Leiden: E.J. Brill, 1995. xxvi, 732 p. *Arabic Literature of Africa;* vol. 2. ISBN 90-04-10494-1; ISSN 0169-9423.

Like O'Fahey's *The Writings of Eastern Sudanic Africa*, this volume is one of a six-part sequence within the *Handbuch der Orientalistik* (Erste Abteiung, Dreizehnter Band) devoted to the Arabic literature of the continent from its earliest stages. Other planned volumes will focus upon Eastern Africa, Western Sudanic Africa, Eastern Sudanic Africa from c. 1900, and the Western Sahara. The whole series will document the literary history of the Muslim societies of the Nile Valley, the Sahel and the Horn, and will no doubt become an indispensable and authoritative reference tool meeting the needs of specialists in the field. This volume is supplied with meticulous indexes: authors, titles in Arabic and in Western and tribal languages, first lines, and a general index.

899. Lindfors, Bernth. **Black African Literature in English, 1987-1991.** London: Hans Zell, 1995. 675 p. *Bibliographical Research in African Literatures;* no. 3. ISBN 1-873836-16-3.

A continuation of earlier editions, with entries numbered consecutively (starting with item 11963). This reference offers access to review articles, biographical materials on authors, critical introductions to literary works, and scholarly studies on a wide range of Anglophone literature and theatre arts. It does not include the Sahel region or the Horn, but sub-Saharan Africa only.

900. Lindfors, Bernth and Reinhard Sander. **Twentieth-Century Caribbean and Black African Writers.** Third Series. Detroit: Gale, 1995. xiii, 461 p. *Dictionary of Literary Biography;* vol. 157. ISBN 0-8103-9352-2.

The scope of *DLB* literary essays includes African writers publishing important novels, plays and volumes of verse in English. The fourteen nations represented here are sub-Saharan and Caribbean countries in which a Western-style higher education in English is available: the Sahel and Horn are not included.

901. Mieder, Wolfgang. **African Proverb Scholarship: an Annotated Bibliography.** Colorado Springs, CO: African Proverbs Project, 1994. 181 p.

The annotations in this volume—citing 279 books, dissertations and journal articles—should be of assistance to "the international community of paremiologists in particular and scholars from other disciplines interested in proverbs in general" (Introduction). The collection specifically excludes Arabic proverbs but seems to incorporate at least some of the other languages and traditions of northern Africa. The entries are alphabetized by author, and there is a very basic name and subject index.

902. Miller, Jeffrey. **Paul Bowles: a Descriptive Bibliography.** Santa Barbara, CA: Black Sparrow Press, 1986. 323 p. ISBN 0-87685-609-1 and 0-87685-609-5.

A lovingly-prepared compilation of the many editions of original works, scores and translations by poet, novelist, composer and journalist Paul Bowles, whose long residence in North Africa strongly influenced his creative work. Miller's notes are detailed physical descriptions of these publications, of importance to collectors—there are no content summaries or annotations. A helpful general index is included.

903. O'Fahey, R. S. **The Writings of Eastern Sudanic Africa to C. 1900.** Edited by J. O. Hunwick and R. S. O'Fahey. Leiden: E.J. Brill, 1994. xv, 434 p. *Arabic Literature of Africa;* vol. 1. ISBN 90-04-09450-4; ISSN 0169-9423.

Part of the massive *Handbuch der Orientalistik* (Erste Abteilung, Dreizehter Band), this volume is one of a planned six-part series dealing with the literature of Saharan Africa in the Arabic language. Its aim is "to provide for Islamic Africa a reference tool comparable with those of Carl Brockelmann and Fuat Sezgin for the wider Islamic world" (Foreword).

This work documents the arrival and spread of the Arabic language through the Nile Valley and across the Sahara. Literary sources are described in Brockelmann's bio-bibliographical style, reporting about the life and activities of each writer and his known works. One must be fairly knowledgeable about the literary history of the Sahara even to begin using this reference, though very precise indexes are provided: authors, titles, first lines and refrains, and a detailed general index.

904. Sezgin, Fuat. **Geschichte des Arabischen Schrifttums.** Leiden: E.J. Brill, 1967- . Incomplete multivolume work.

Continuing in the tradition of Carl Brockelmann's indispensable *Geschichte der Arabischen Litteratur* (1943-49), this massive reference describes and enumerates the work of writers in Arabic from the Umayyad era onward and provides biographical information about them. The organization of the work is chronological. Nine volumes have appeared so far and apparently, others are in preparation.

905. Young, M. J. L, J. D. Latham, and R. B. Serjeant. **Religion, Learning and Science in the Abbasid Period.** Cambridge: Cambridge University Press, 1990. xxii, 587 p. *Cambridge History of Arabic Literature.* ISBN 0-521-32763-3.

This volume of the authoritative *Cambridge History of Arabic Literature* concentrates on aspects of culture in which Arab scholars of the medieval age were very important. Grammar and lexicography, law, administration, biography, history, philosophy, theology, mathematics, applied science and technology, astronomy, astrology, geography and navigation, medicine, and Christian and Jewish documents are all covered here. The subdivided bibliography is of considerable value; a good map and glossary are included. Material on the scholars of Abbasid/Umayyad Africa can be found in the very detailed index (though prior knowledge of the field is helpful).

906. Zell, Hans M., Carol Bundy, and Virginia Conlon. **A New Reader's Guide to African Literature.** Second completely revised and expanded edition. New York: Africana Publishing, 1983. xvi, 553 p. ISBN 0-8419-0639-4.

A handbook of over 3000 very concise entries identifying the work of African writers, and critical studies of their work, through 1981. Reference materials and anthologies are also listed, along with children's books by African authors. Many entries include review extracts (with attribution); many also provide a brief synopsis of the literary work. Ethiopia, Somalia, Sudan, Chad, Mali, Niger and Mauritania are covered, but not the Mediterranean coast. English, French and Portuguese are the languages used. Some entries include photos. Directory information on publishers is supplemented by data on libraries in North America and Europe with extensive holdings in African literature.

North African Literature in French

907. **Dictionnaire des Oeuvres Littéraires Africaines de Langue Française.** Compiled by Pius Ngandu Nkashama. Ivry-sur-Seine: Éditions Nouvelles du Sud, 1994. 745 p. ISBN 2-87931-093-8.

Brief critical entries on the major African writers in French are collected in this substantial reference. The Maghreb countries are not included, but there are entries for authors from the Sahel countries (Mauritania, Mali, Niger, Chad, but not Sudan) and Somalia. The volume is indexed by author and title, but not by country or subject. The entries do not include bibliographical references.

908. Achour, Christiane. **Dictionnaire des Oeuvres Algériennes en Langue Française.** Paris: Éditions l'Harmattan, 1990. 384 p. ISBN 2-7384-0949-0.

A descriptive dictionary of Algerian literary works in the French language from 1834 until 1989. "Essais, romans, nouvelles, contes, récits autobiographiques, théâtre, poésie, [and] récits pour enfants" are all included.

The nature of each work is summed up in 1-5 paragraphs; sometimes excerpts of poetry are included, or a plot synopsis. The research was conducted at the Université d'Alger.

909. Arnaud, Jacqueline and Françoise Amacker. **Répertoire Mondial des Travaux Universitaires de la Littérature Maghrébine de Langue Française.** Paris: Éditions L'Harmattan, 1984. 78 p. ISBN 2-85802-312-3.

A collection of theses and dissertations presented for degrees at universities not only in France, but also elsewhere in Europe, Canada, the US, Australia and in the Middle East and North Africa itself. The student's name and that of the faculty advisor, the title, date, university and degree awarded are noted. There is an index organizing the theses according to the author who is the topic of the work: all the students doing research on Yacine Kateb, for example, are grouped together. A subject index is also provided, and directory data for all of the universities mentioned.

910. Bonn, Charles. **Bibliographie de la Littérature Maghrébine 1980-1990.** With Feriel Kachoukh. Vanves: EDICEF, 1992. 96 p. *UREF Actualités Bibliographiques Francophones.* ISBN 2-850-69587-4.

A quick-reference compilation of significant literary works published in French by North African writers during the 1980s (though some entries are as recent as 1991). Bibliographic information, genre and country of origin are supplied for each entry. Poetry, novels, billets, autobiography and memoir, récits, essais, contes, and drama (théâtre) are all included. An index of titles and perhaps one for countries of origin would make the volume much easier to use.

911. D'Ambrosio, Nicola. **Bibliographie Méthodique de la Poésie Maghrébine de Langue Française, 1945-1989.** Fasano; Paris: Schena-Nizet, 1991. 206 p. ISBN 88-7514-699-3.

This bibliography offers access to volumes of poetry published in French by Algerian, Moroccan and Tunisian writers. In addition, articles and studies in the literary criticism of poetry are cited, organized by year of publication. Entries are not annotated. There is a general index.

912. Déjeux, Jean. **Bibliographie de la Littérature "Algérienne" des Français: Bibliographie des Romans, Récits et Recueil de Nouvelles Écrit par des Français Inspirés par l'Algérie, 1896-1975.** Paris: Éditions du Centre National de la Recherche Scientifique, 1978. 116 p. *Les Cahiers du CRESM;* no. 7. ISBN 2-222-02351-3.

This series produced by the Centre de Recherche et d'Études sur les Sociétés Méditerannéennes (Aix-en-Provence) documents the powerful interest in "l'Orient et l'exotisme dans la littérature française" (p. 7), and shows how it has influenced cultural life in both North Africa and in France. This volume is easy to use, clearly organized, and indexed by name; entries are not annotated.

913. Déjeux, Jean. **Dictionnaire des Auteurs Maghrébines de Langue Française.** Paris: Éditions Karthala, 1984. 404 p. ISBN 2-86537-05-2.

A useful biographical dictionary of authors writing in French in North Africa from 1880 up to the time of publication. Coverage of Algeria is the most extensive, including writers of all forms of fiction, philosophical and political essays, linguistic and literary criticism, histories (chronicles and memoirs), Islamic studies, religious works and social sciences. For Tunisia and Morocco, writers of fiction, essays and histories are included.

Some of the entries are very brief, with no more than a few facts; others extend to a page or more. An index of pseudonyms is included. There is also a very helpful compilation of anthologies and special issues of periodicals devoted to North African literature in French. Several tables of figures showing literary output over time (since 1945) are placed in an appendix.

914. Dugas, Guy. **Bibliographie Critique de Littérature Judeo-Maghrébine d'Expression Française, 1896-1990.** Paris: Éditions l'Harmattan, 1992. 95 p. *Études Littéraires Maghrébines;* no. 2. ISBN 2-7384-1335-8.

A small and highly specialized bibliography offering access to scholarly works studying the Jewish population of North Africa, Jewish literature in general, and the artistic writing of Jews in North Africa in particular. A chronology reaching back to 1886 is provided. An annotated bibliography lists the literature itself by author; the works include poetry, memoirs, novels, stories, drama and mixed genres. This reference was prepared at Université d'Alger and Université Paris-Nord, and was edited by Charles Bonn.

915. Dugas, Guy. **Bibliographie de la Littérature "Marocaine" des Français, 1875-1983.** Paris: Éditions du Centre National de la Recherche Scientifique, 1981. 121 p. *Les Cahiers du CRESM;* no. 18. ISBN 2-222-03786-7.

This series produced by the Centre de Recherche et d'Études sur les Sociétés Méditerrannéennes (Aix-en-Provence) documents the powerful interest in "la littérature française d'inspiration maghrébine" (p. 1), and shows how it has influenced cultural life in both North Africa and in France. This volume is easy to use, clearly organized, and indexed by name; entries are not annotated.

916. Dugas, Guy. **Bibliographie De La Littérature "Tunisienne" Des Français, 1881-1980.** Paris: Éditions du Centre National de la Recherche Scientifique, 1981. 86 p. *Les Cahiers Du CRESM;* no. 13. ISBN 2-222-02979-1.

This series produced by the Centre de Recherche et d'Études sur les Sociétés Méditerrannéennes (Aix-en-Provence) documents the powerful interest in "la littérature française d'inspirée par le Maroc, l'Algérie ou la Tunisie" (p. 1), and shows how it has influenced cultural life in both North Africa and in France. This volume is easy to use, clearly organized, and indexed by name; entries are not annotated.

917. Ngandu Nkashama, Pius. **Les Années Littéraires en Afrique.** Paris: Éditions l'Harmattan, 1993. 455 p. ISBN 2-7384-1459-1.

A thick inventory of literary and critical works produced in francophone Africa, organized chronologically. The original publishing date is the key to its arrangement, but Ngandu helpfully notes recent reissues of older works as well. Two full indexes offer access by author and by title.

Websites

918. African Literature Association. **132.236.36.31/center/ala.html**
Interested in drama and other art forms, scholarship and criticism.

919. Maghrebi Studies Group at Binghamton University. An Introduction to the Francophone Literature of the Maghreb. **maghreb.net/writers/**
Contains many links to other sites concerned with the culture (especially literature) of the Maghreb.

Publishing and Media

This section concerns literary publishing, the popular media and freedom of expression issues in the region.

920. **The African Book World & Press: a Directory.** Fourth edition. Edited by Hans M. Zell. London: Hans Zell (K.G. Saur), 1989. xxi, 306 p. ISBN 0-905450-50-7

Also titled: *Répertoire du Livre et de la Presse en Afrique.*

A very useful guide to the libraries, publishers and periodicals of Africa. Directory data and sometimes a little holdings information is given for academic, public and special libraries (including foreign cultural centers and archaeological institutes), book dealers, state and private publishers, newspapers, magazines and some scholarly journals, and literary societies.

Every nation of northern Africa is represented by at least a minimum of information, and often a great deal. Appendices provide further material on book fairs and publishing trade events, literary prizes and awards, book clubs, news agencies (mass media), and publishers in the Western world producing or handling African studies materials. There are also two subject indexes: one for special libraries, and another for periodicals.

921. **African Books in Print: an Index by Author, Title and Subject.** Fourth edition. Edited by Hans M. Zell. London: Hans Zell, 1993. 2 v. ISBN 1-8738-3611-2

Also titled: *Livres Africains Disponibles.*

These large volumes cover a variety of works in print at the end of 1991: not only books from commercial and state publishing houses, but also publications "from research institutions, learned societies and professional associations ... university departments, libraries or bookshops acting as distributors" (p. ix), including larger pamphlets or reports, and yearbooks or annuals.

Titles in English, French and African languages are included. Despite the considerable difficulty of collecting and updating this information from African sources, over 700 publishers from 45 countries are represented here. A fifth edition is in preparation.

922. **African Newspapers in the Library of Congress.** Second edition. Compiled by John Pluge, Jr. Washington: Library of Congress, Serial and Government Publications Division, 1984. ix, 144 p. ISBN 0-8444-0457-8.

An important resource for dealing with reference queries, this guide identifies each of the newspapers in the Library of Congress collection and specifies their holdings (mostly in microform). The entries are organized by country, then by city of publication. All of the nations of northern Africa are represented, though of course some have more extensive coverage than others. The holdings are for the most part not current, but of historical interest. A titles index is included.

923. **A Book World Directory of the Arab Countries, Turkey and Iran.** Compiled by Anthony Rudkin and Irene Butcher. London; Detroit: Mansell; Gale, 1981. xiv, 143 p. ISBN 0-7201-0830-6.

A country-by-country guide to the libraries, book dealers, commercial and institutional publishers, newspapers and other periodicals in the Middle East. Morocco, Algeria, Tunisia, Libya, Egypt and Sudan are included. There is an attempt to classify the libraries by subject-area strengths and by type (public, national, academic, etc.). Booksellers and publishers too are categorized. Contact information in this volume is now dated.

924. **Editor and Publisher International Yearbook: the Directory of Newspaper Industry Professionals.** 78th edition. Annual; 1959- . New York: Editor & Publisher, 1998. 2 v. ISBN 0-9646364-0-9 (2 v.); ISSN 0424-4923. ISSN for vol. 2 only 1082-6297

Also available from the publisher on CD-ROM.

Although heavily weighted toward the U.S. media, this trade publication also covers some foreign publishing as well. Directory entries with contact and circulation data are included for at least one daily in each of the countries of northern Africa (except Eritrea), and those countries that serve as regional publishing centers (e.g., Egypt) offer many more. Vol. 2 of this reference is a directory ordered by individual's names.

925. **International Book Publishing: an Encyclopedia.** Edited by Philip G. Altbach and Edith S. Hoshino. New York; London: Garland, 1995. xxvi, 736 p. ISBN 0-8153-0786-1.

With special attention to the conditions of publishing in the Third World, the roles of international donor agencies and state information and culture ministries, press freedom and censorship issues and other key concerns, the scope of this encyclopedia is truly international. New technologies and world intellectual property rights are covered as well.

Articles focused upon specific regions and countries offer surveys of the history and current status of publishing in these areas, prepared by such authorities as Hans M. Zell and John Rodenbeck. Chapters on Africa and the Middle East contain much relevant material. A statistical appendix offers tables of comparison data, 1970-1990, on book production by language. The volume includes a useful index.

926. **Willing's Press Guide.** 124th ed. Annual; 1928- . Teddington: Hollis Directories, 1998. 2 v. ISBN 0-900967-62-5 (set); Vol. 2 only 0-900967-64-1; ISSN 0000-0213.

Vol. 1 of this directory pertains only to publications in the UK, but Vol. 2 is international in scope. The "Middle East and North Africa" section orders periodical entries geographically: first the Arab world in general, then individual countries. Basic circulation and directory data is provided for each periodical. The next section covers sub-Saharan Africa. Comprehensiveness seems lacking; some nations are not mentioned at all (Eritrea, Niger, Mauritania), while others are listed but with very few entries.

927. **World Media Handbook: Selected Country Profiles.** 1995 edition. New York: United Nations Department of Public Information, 1995. viii, 337 p. ISBN 92-1-100574-4; UN Sales No. E.95.1.34.

A directory of mass-media organizations (print, radio, television, telecom) with some background data on each country. All of the nations of northern Africa are covered except Somalia.

928. Green, Jonathon. **The Encyclopedia of Censorship.** New York: Facts on File, 1990. x, 388 p. ISBN 0-8160-1594-5.

Concerned with limits upon both artistic and political expression, this reference is composed of alphabetized entries ranging from one paragraph to several pages in length. It concentrates upon intellectual freedom issues in Western societies, but does have some material on Egypt, Libya, Morocco, Somalia and Sudan. Articles on Saudi Arabia, Iran and the Salman Rushdie affair may be indirectly relevant. There is a useful index, but only a very general bibliography.

929. Jeter, James Phillip et al. **International Afro Mass Media: a Reference Guide.** Westport, CT: Greenwood, 1996. xiii, 297 p. ISBN 0-313-28400-8.

The title may sound like a bibliography, but this is a handbook composed of descriptive articles on the press and electronic media in Africa and parts of the world with many inhabitants of African descent. Conditions shaping these media, the influence of government policies, issues of intellectual freedom and the impact of new technologies (especially computer telecommunications) are studied here.

North Africa is defined in this volume as Morocco, Algeria, Tunisia, Libya and Sudan (Egypt is excluded), while a chapter on Africa south of the Sahara covers the Horn and Sahel (with Mauritania). Each section provides a useful list of bibliographical references, and the volume includes a competent general index.

930. Kamalipour, Yahya R. and Hamid Mowlana. **Mass Media in the Middle East: a Comprehensive Handbook.** Westport, CT: Greenwood, 1994. xvii, 330 p. ISBN 0-313-28535-7.

This handbook is composed of descriptive encyclopedia-style articles on the current state of print media, radio and TV, motion pictures/video and satellite technology in 21 countries of this region, among them Tunisia, Libya, Egypt and Algeria (but not Morocco or Sudan). Each article gives circulation statistics for major publications, an account of radio/TV programming and its audience reach, some impression of press freedom conditions, and bibliographical references. It might be desirable for future editions to include online access and the availability of Internet service providers in each location. A glossary, a general bibliography and a careful index are provided.

931. Walsh, Gretchen. **The Media in Africa and Africa in the Media: an Annotated Bibliography.** London: Hans Zell, 1996. xxv, 291 p. ISBN 1-873836-81-3.

As the title suggests, this work concerns itself not only with the press, broadcasting, film and multimedia in Africa itself, but also with images of Africa and how they influence Western and worldwide opinion. Articles and books, reports and official documents are included. The work gives special attention to issues of intellectual freedom and development. The countries of northern Africa are within the scope of this work. Annotations are very brief—usually no more than a sentence. An author index but no title index is provided; there is an inadequate subject index.

932. Zell, Hans M. and Cécile Lomer. **Publishing and Book Development in Sub-Saharan Africa: an Annotated Bibliography.** Revised edition. London: Hans Zell, 1996. x, 409 p. ISBN 1-873836-46-5.

An updated and greatly expanded edition of Zell's 1984 work, this reference offers access to books and articles, reports, essays in collections, official publications and other sources, mostly in English and French, covering all aspects of the book publishing industry. Entries are arranged by type of literature, by region, by country or by topic, with three very basic indexes. Material may be found here relating to the Sahel, Ethiopia and Sudan.

Journals

933. **African Book Publishing Record.** Quarterly, 1975- . Oxford: Hans Zell (Bowker-Saur). ISSN 0306-0322.

See also website at **www.hanszell.co.uk/titles.htm**

An important resource for obtaining quality publications produced in Africa. News of the publishing industry and literary world, current directory data for many (sometimes hard-to-find) publishers, and a useful topically-organized bibliography of materials in Western and some African languages, are provided. The entries are indexed by author and by country of publication as well. Each issue also contains brief but informative signed book reviews. An annual feature describes new reference materials on Africa. In addition, a cumulation of these listings appears as *African Books in Print* (Hans Zell, 1993).

Websites

934. Afric No1. L'Afrique en Direct: le site de Radio Africa n°1. **www.africa1. com/**

News, sports, culture, and information about the frequencies, program listings and network editors and correspondents.

935. Africa World Press Guide. **www.igc.org/worldviews/awpguide/**
Online version of work by Thomas P. Fenton and Mary J. Heffron.

936. Editor & Publisher. Media Info Links: Online Media Directory. **www.
mediainfo.com/emedia/**
Links to online news-industry sources. Organized by region: see Africa and
the Middle East.

937. Electronic African Bookworm. **www.hanszell.co.uk/navtitle.htm**
Maintained by Hans Zell Publishing Consultants: "A quick-access guide
and pick-list to some of the best sites on Africa, African studies, and on African
publishing and the book trade."

Education and Research

938. **European Expertise on the Middle East and North Africa: a Directory
of Specialists and Institutions.** Edited by Emma Murphy, Gerd Nonneman, and
Neil Quilliam. [Durham]: The European Association for Middle Eastern Studies, 1993. ISBN 0-9521849-0-7.
A useful directory, organized alphabetically and by subject area. Institutions are also listed by their location in Europe. Museums as well as academic
departments and research institutes are covered. There is an emphasis on the culture, politics and history of Islam.

939. **Handbook of World Education: a Comparative Guide to Higher Education and Educational Systems of the World.** Edited by Walter Wickre-
masinghe. Houston: American Collegiate Service, 1991. xxxiii, 898 p. ISBN
0-940937-03-4.
A compilation of descriptive country-by-country articles on education that
manages to be verbose and superficial at the same time. The article on Egypt, for
example, sets forth the national education system in theory, without ever ac-
knowledging the calamitous condition of the system or mentioning the emergence of fee-based language schools at the primary and secondary levels, by far
the most significant development in Egyptian education in recent years. The volume offers no statistical data at all, and has very little reference value.

940. **The International Encyclopedia of Education.** Second edition. Edited
by Torsten Husén and T. Neville Postlethwaite. Oxford: Pergamon (Elsevier),
1994. 12 v. ISBN 0-08-041046-4 (set).
A major reference for statistical and descriptive information dealing with
education at all levels. Articles on specific nations set forth the structures and facilities for primary, secondary and higher education, special services (pre-
school, adult literacy, vocational training, programs for the disabled, etc.),
administration, financing (including international aid), teacher training, curricu-
lum development, and student assessment (promotions, examinations, diplomas). A

bibliography accompanies each article. This reference is flawed by certain baffling omissions: no article at all on either Algeria or Somalia, for instance. Vol. 12 provides an index to the whole work.

941. **International Encyclopedia of National Systems of Education.** Second edition. Edited by T. Neville Postlethwaite. Oxford: Pergamon (Elsevier), 1995. xxii, 1105 p. ISBN 0-08-042302-7.

A digest volume containing the articles from *The International Encyclopedia of Education* covering the systems of education in 142 countries. For some reason, Algeria is included in this issue even though it was omitted from the complete 12-volume work; Somalia is still not represented, nor is Eritrea or Djibouti.

942. Kurian, George Thomas. **World Education Encyclopedia.** New York: Facts on File, 1988. 3 v., continuously paginated. ISBN 0-87196-748-0 (set).

A forgettable introductory essay is followed by a section of global education statistics (enrollment, teaching staff, expenditures, etc.) organized regionally; the northernmost countries of Africa are included with "Arab States." The body of the work consists of country articles up to 40 pages in length, divided into three sections: major countries, middle countries, and minor countries—perhaps not the best way to categorize this material.

Each article presents a basic data box, a descriptive account of the history, constitutional and legal foundation of public education, and an overview of the system. Separate descriptions follow of the primary, secondary and higher education structures, administration and research facilities, "nonformal" education opportunities (especially adult literacy), teacher training, and a fairly frank summary statement of the major problems affecting the system.

Tables of important data accompany articles where available: tables for Egypt include subjects studied in secondary schools, teacher salaries in Egyptian pounds, and enrollment numbers over a 10-year span. In addition, there is a glossary of terms with each article defining unique vocabulary, and a substantial—though now dated—bibliography. Coverage of "middle" countries (Chad, Mali, Somalia) and "minor" countries (Niger, Mauritania, Djibouti) is far less complete. Statistical appendices, a general bibliography and an index appear in Vol. 3.

943. Pantelides, Veronica S. **Arab Education 1956-1978: a Bibliography.** London: Mansell, 1982. xvii, 552 p. ISBN 0-7201-1588-4.

Books, journal articles, dissertations, conference papers, government and NGO reports, even photographs and maps relevant to education in the Arab world are included in this unusually comprehensive subject bibliography.

There is a substantial opening section on the Arab world generally, organized by topic, then sizable chapters for each country belonging to the Arab League in 1978 (including the Mediterranean coast of Africa, Mauritania, Sudan, Somalia and Djibouti). Chapters on each country are topically subdivided, making it possible to scan for relevant material. Entries are annotated, but usually with a very few words. The index occupies more than 80 pages, and is carefully prepared.

944. Sitzman, Glenn L. **African Libraries.** Metuchen, NJ: Scarecrow, 1988. 486 p. ISBN 0-8108-2093-5.

A collection of various information about libraries on the African continent, not including the Mediterranean states. The work presents descriptions of 90 public, school, academic and special libraries visited by the writer, often with black-and-white photos. Foreign cultural center libraries are listed as well. There is a chronology of events in the world of libraries and information, especially of literature on the subject.

A "nation-by-nation survey" offers basic statistics on libraries, education and literacy, and names the known institutions (no directory data is given). A "bibliographical essay" on the development of library literature and a bibliography of books and articles on African librarianship (subdivided by country) are also found here. The volume includes a names index only.

Journals

945. **International Review of Education.** Bimonthly; 1955- . Dordrecht: Kluwer Academic and UNESCO. ISSN 0020-8566.

Also titled: *Internationale Zeitschrift für Erziehungswissenschaft*; *Revue Internationale de Pedagogie* (or *Revue Internationale de l'Education*). Sample issue and contents page available online at **www.wkap.nl/journalhome.htm/ 0020-8566**

This scholarly journal is edited by the UNESCO Institute for Education in Hamburg; it is intended "to provide departments and institutes of education, teacher training institutions and professional readers all over the world with scholarly information on major educational innovations, research projects and trends" (cover). Articles are published in English, French or German, and abstracts are printed in Spanish and Russian as well. The bibliographical references are extensive and often include many sources originating outside the US or Western Europe. Some brief articles (called "notes") , bibliographies and brief but informative signed book reviews are found in this journal. Volume contents and an author index are provided.

Academic and Professional Associations and Research Centers

946. African Literature Association. **132.236.36.31/center/ala.html**
Interested in drama and other art forms, scholarship and criticism.

947. African Studies Association. **www.sas.upenn.edu/African_Studies/ASA/ ASA_Menu.html**
Academic and professional organization.

948. American Folklore Society. African Section. **afsnet.org/sections/african/**
Scholarly and professional organization.

949. Boston University. African Studies Center. **web.bu.edu/afr/**
Links to the African Studies Library.

950. British Library. Africa in the British Library. **www.bl.uk/collections/africa/**

951. Center for Strategic and International Studies. Middle East Studies Program. **www.csis.org/mideast/**
Information about the conferences, meetings and publications of CSIS, as well as the approach and assumptions of their Middle East policy analysis. The Maghreb states and Egypt are included (but not Mauritania or Sudan).

952. Classics and Mediterranean Archaeology. University of Michigan. **rome.classics.lsa.umich.edu/welcome.html**
Search engine and many specialized links.

953. College of William and Mary. Reves Center for International Studies. **www.wm.edu/academics/reves/**

954. Columbia University. Institute of African Studies. **www.columbia.edu/cu/sipa/REGIONAL/IAS/**

955. Consortium inter-universitaire pour les études arabes (CIEA)/Inter-University Consortium for Arab Studies (ICAS). McGill University and the Université de Montréal. **www.arts.mcgill.ca/programs/icas/icas3.html**

956. Cornell University. Africana Studies and Research Center. **www.asrc.cornell.edu/**
Links to the John Henrik Clarke Africana Library.

957. Deutsches Orient-Institut (Hamburg). **www.rrz.uni-hamburg.de/DOI/doi-start.html**
A research center for the Middle East, including the Mediterranean coast of Africa, Mauritania and Sudan.

958. Deutsches Übersee-Institut (Hamburg). **www.rrz.uni-hamburg.de/duei/**
Home of the Institut für Afrika-Kunde and the Deutsches Orient-Institut; a major publisher of research literature.

959. Emory University. Institute of African Studies. **www.emory.edu/COLLEGE/IAS/**

960. Georgetown University. Center for Contemporary Arab Studies. **www.georgetown.edu/sfs/programs/ccas/**

961. Harvard University. African Studies at Harvard. **www.fas.harvard.edu/~cafrica/**
Link to the African Humanities Institute.

962. Hieros Gamos: the Comprehensive Legal Site. Law Schools in Africa and the Middle East. **hg.org/africamideast-schools.html**
Basic directory information. Countries without formal law schools have links to the Ministry of Education.

963. Indiana University at Bloomington. African Studies Program. **www.indiana.edu/~afrist/**
Links to the African Studies Library Collections.

964. Institut du Monde Arabe. Histoire et Devenir. **www.imarabe.org/**
Cultural information, a link to the museum in Paris, and publications for scholars.

965. Institut für Afrika-Kunde (Hamburg). **www.rrz.uni-hamburg.de/duei/iak/iak-home.htm**
In English and German.

966. Institute of Development Studies (IDS), University of Sussex. **www.ids.ac.uk/ids/**

967. International African Institute. School of Oriental and African Studies (SOAS). **www.oneworld.org/iai/**

968. International Federation of Library Associations (IFLA). Web-Accessible National and Major Libraries of the World. **ifla.inist.fr/II/natlibs.htm**
So far, none of these are located in northern Africa. These collections will still be very valuable, of course, for research purposes.

969. Kyoto University. Center for African Area Studies. **www.africa.kyoto-u.ac.jp/**

970. Leiden University. International Institute for the Study of Islam in the Modern World (ISIM). **isim.leidenuniv.nl/**

971. Michigan State University. African Studies Center. **www.isp.msu.edu/AfricanStudies/**
Links to the Africana Collection.

972. Middle East Documentation Center (MEDOC). University of Chicago. **www.lib.uchicago.edu:80/LibInfo/SourcesBySubject/MiddleEast/medoc.html**

973. Middle East Institute. **www2.ari.net/mei/**
"The Middle East Institute, founded in 1946, is dedicated to educating Americans about the Middle East." Publishers of *The Middle East Journal*. Areas studied include "Arab Africa" (Morocco, Algeria, Tunisia, Libya, Egypt, and the Sudan).

974. Middle East Network Information Center (MENIC). Center for Middle East Studies, University of Texas at Austin. **menic.utexas.edu/mes.html**
   Very useful links page for all aspects of area studies.

975. Middle East Research and Information Project. **www.merip.org/**
   A nonprofit organization providing independent, critical, detailed news and feature coverage of events and issues in the region through the current-events magazine *Middle East Report* and other activities. Commentary and reflection on policy concerns is a primary interest.

976. Middle East Studies Association of North America. University of Arizona. **www.mesa.arizona.edu/**
   "MESA is a private nonprofit, non-political organization of scholars and other persons interested in the study of the Middle East, North Africa and the Islamic world. MESA is dedicated to promoting high standards of scholarship and instruction, to facilitating communication among scholars through annual meetings and publications, and to promoting cooperation among those who study the Middle East." Informative website with a link to the *MESA Bulletin*.

977. New York University. Department of Middle Eastern Studies. **www.nyu.edu/gsas/dept/mideast/**

978. Nordiska Afrikainstitutet, Uppsala. **www.nai.uu.se/indexeng.html**

979. Northwestern University. Program of African Studies. **nuinfo.nwu.edu/african-studies/**
   Links to the Melville J. Herskovitz Library of African Studies.

980. Oriental Institute. University of Chicago. **www-oi.uchicago.edu/OI/default.html**
   Sponsors of Chicago House at Luxor; responsible for important ongoing excavation and documentation projects, especially in epigraphy. Also, this site is home to ABZU, the enormous "Index to Ancient Near Eastern Resources on the Internet."

981. Oxford University. Centre for the Study of African Economies. **users.ox.ac.uk/~csaeinfo/**

982. School of Oriental and African Studies. University of London. **www.soas.ac.uk/**
   Links to the SOAS library and archive collections.

983. Standing Conference on Library Materials on Africa (SCOLMA). **http://www.brad.ac.uk/acad/scolma/scolma.html**

984. Stanford University. Center for African Studies. **www-leland.stanford.edu/dept/AFR/**

985. Universität Wien. Institut für Afrikanistik. **www.univie.ac.at/afrikanistik/** In German.

986. University of Bergen, Norway. Centre for Middle Eastern and Islamic Studies. **www.hf-fak.uib.no/Institutter/smi/smi.html**

987. University of Bielefeld/Universität Bielefeld. Forschungsschwerpunkt Entwicklungssoziologie/Sociology of Development Research Centre . **www.uni-bielefeld.de/sdrc/homesdrc**
An important publisher in this subject area. In English and German.

988. University of California at Los Angeles. James S. Coleman African Studies Center. **www.isop.ucla.edu/jscasc/welcome/welcome.htm**

989. University of Durham. Centre for Middle Eastern and Islamic Studies. **www.dur.ac.uk/~dme0www/**
Location of MEDUSA, the Middle East Documentation Unit and the Sudan Archive. See also **www.dur.ac.uk/Library/lib/medu.html** and **www.dur.ac.uk/Library/asc/sudan/index.html.**

990. University of Florida. Center for African Studies. **web.africa.ufl.edu/index.html**

991. University of Illinois at Urbana-Champaign. Center for African Studies. **wsi.cso.uiuc.edu/CAS/**
Links to the Africana Reading Room and the rest of the African resources in the Library; well-organized links pages on many topics.

992. University of Michigan. Center for Middle Eastern and North African Studies. **www.umich.edu/~iinet/cmenas/**

993. University of Pennsylvania. African Studies Center. **www.sas.upenn.edu/~africa/**
Maintains a valuable African Studies links page.

994. University of Pennsylvania. Middle East Center. **ccat.sas.upenn.edu/mec/home.html**

Science and Technology

Science references and periodicals—most of them in electronic form—are available for every branch of research, usually organized or indexed by subject. The sources listed here are those with material pertaining specifically to northern Africa, belonging more to the field of area studies than to science per se.

Sources concerned with the environment (desertification, water resources, pollution, etc.) may also be found with materials on the economy and sustainable development. Physical geography sources are found mainly with Geography, under "Social Sciences."

995. Conservation and Environmentalism: an Encyclopedia. Edited by Robert Paehlke. New York: Garland, 1995. xxxiii, 771 p. *Garland Reference Library of Social Science;* v. 645. ISBN 0-8240-6101-2.

A reference that defines the vocabulary and issues of the natural environment, identifies the major individuals, organizations and endangered species, and highlights habitat and sustainable development. Though the concern is decidedly global, information on specific places or countries is not easy to find. A survey article on "Africa" is very broad, and listings in the index for certain nations are few. Topics known to be relevant to northern Africa (e.g., "desertification") can be found.

996. Dictionary of Scientific Biography. Published under the auspices of the American Council of Learned Societies. Edited by Charles Coulston Gillespie. New York: Scribner, 1981. 18 v. (in 10). Vols. 15- issued as supplements. ISBN 0-684-16962-2 (set)

Also published as a one-volume abridged version: *Concise Dictionary of Scientific Biography*, 1981. Select articles also published as: *Biographical Dictionary of Mathematicians*, 1991.

The unique strength of this reference is historical information, and as such it is very useful. Coverage is good of scientific subjects in which Arab scholars have made important contributions—for example, the history of algebra and astronomy. Substantial encyclopedia-style articles appear on the work of medieval Egyptian mathematician Abū Kāmil, and Morocco's Ibn Al-Bannā (also a mathematician), and many others. These articles provide not just a biographical sketch, but examples from these scholars' mathematical work and an analysis of its value. In addition, scholars of other nationalities whose work was carried out largely in northern Africa are covered, such as the French botanist René-Charles Maire. Every article also provides a sophisticated bibliography for further study. The final volume is an extremely helpful index.

997. Environmental Issues and Sources. Washington, DC: Beacham Publishing, 1993. 5 v. ISBN 0-933833-31-8

Also titled: *Beacham's Guide to Environmental Issues and Sources.*

Organized by topic, this reference offers lengthy, descriptive articles on current environmental concerns around the world. The prose is not overly dense or technical; the work would be suitable for a high school or undergraduate library. The emphasis is on North America, but issues relevant to the African continent are included, such as water supply, famine and food security, population, wildlife conservation, and the role of multinational corporations and development banks in environmental issues globally. Vol. 5 provides a cumulative index.

998. **Profiles of African Scientific Institutions, 1992.** African Academy of Sciences and Network of African Scientific Organizations. Nairobi: Academy Science Publishers, 1992. xiii, 282 p. ISBN 9966-831-11-8.

A country-by-country guide to state organizations or academic institutions engaged in scientific research or activity throughout Africa. Each entry provides basic directory data and a broad description of the institution's work and interests, plus publications if any.

In addition to fundamental research, institutions working in any area of technology or applied engineering are included, such as irrigation, solar power, statistics and data storage/retrieval, agriculture, wildlife and livestock, food and health, forestry, industrial design, or development. All of Africa is included, though some countries have no entries, presumably due to reporting shortfalls (Libya, Mauritania, Somalia). An alphabetical list of institutions is provided.

999. **Profiles of African Scientists.** Second edition, revised and expanded. Nairobi: African Academy of Sciences, 1991. xi, 661 p. ISBN 9966-831-07-X.

A "who's who" organized by country, profiling 600 of the continent's scientists, academicians and researchers. The database is expanding and now covers 40 African nations, among them Morocco, Algeria, Tunisia, Egypt, Mali, Niger, Sudan, Ethiopia and Somalia.

Each entry (in either English or French) provides the academic and professional history of the individual, current research interests, membership in relevant organizations, awards or honors, publications, public service contributions or activities, contact information, and often a small black-and-white photo.

"Science" is broadly construed to include, for example, Mohamed El-Sayed Said, political science and strategic studies analyst in Arab and African affairs at *Al-Ahram* newspaper in Cairo. The volume is indexed by subject and by the individual's names.

1000. **Technology and Transition: the Maghreb at the Crossroads.** Edited by Girma Zawdie and Abdelkader Djeflat. London; Portland, OR: Frank Cass, 1996. 200 p. ISBN 0-7146-4745-4.

This collection of scholarly articles offers focused information, analysis and reflection upon science and technology-based development and change in Algeria, Tunisia, Morocco, Libya and Mauritania. This "geo-economic entity" accounts for 35% of the production of the whole African continent, and is "relatively advanced in terms of the development of infrastructure, industrialization and ... technological capability" (p. v). Yet growth is slowing and technological obsolescence is becoming a major problem.

These essays and articles provide articulate studies of the situation, tables of data and current bibliographical references. The volume includes a helpful index.

1001. **The Water Encyclopedia.** Second edition. Edited by Frits van der Leeden, Fred L. Troise, and David Keith Todd. Chelsea, MI: Lewis Publishers, 1990. xii, 808 p. ISBN 0-87371-120-3.

A large volume of graphs, tables of data, maps and other graphics quantifying the use of water resources. The most detailed data concern North America, but there is information here on water use in Africa; table 5-79, for example, shows the number of hectares of land under irrigation in Africa's countries during a 15-year period (1971-1986). There is a basic index.

1002. Al-Hassan, Ahmad Y. and Donald R. Hill. **Islamic Technology: an Illustrated History.** Cambridge; Paris: Cambridge University Press; UNESCO, 1986. xiv, 304 p. ISBN 0-521-26333-6 and 92-3-102294-6.

A project sponsored by UNESCO to create "adequate reference material for use by engineering educators and students in the region involved in introductory courses dealing with the history of science and technology and the contribution of earlier Arab and Islamic civilizations thereto" (UNESCO Preface).

The book covers mechanical engineering (including water and wind power), civil engineering, military technology, ships and navigation, chemicals (alcohol, petroleum, glass, ceramics, inks and dyes, etc.), textiles, paper and leather, agriculture and food processing, mining and metallurgy. Each chapter is illustrated with photos, drawings and diagrams, complete with informative captions. The bibliography is subdivided by topic, and there is a useful index.

1003. Binns, Tony. **People and Environment in Africa.** Chichester: John Wiley & Sons, 1995. xi, 274 p. ISBN 0-471-95530-2.

A collection of scholarly essays studying "people-environment relationships in the African continent" (Introduction), from family wood-gathering to the level of global climate change. Articles on Egypt, Sudan, Ethiopia and the Sahel generally are included; many are illustrated with maps, black-and-white photos, charts, graphs and tables of data. The volume supplies bibliographic notes and a useful index.

1004. Boulos, Loutfy. **Medicinal Plants of North Africa.** Illustrated by Magdy El-Gohary. Algonac, MI: Reference Publications, 1983. 286 p. *Medicinal Plants of the World.* ISBN 0-917256-16-6.

A dictionary of herbs used for therapeutic purposes along the Mediterranean coast of Africa. In remote areas where health-care facilities are few, many people rely on traditional remedies for common illnesses.

This reference covers 369 species of vascular plants, organized by their technical names. An index of common names for these plants is provided; in addition, there is an index of medical conditions for which these plants are typically used, and a glossary of medical terms. The volume is rich in precise line drawings, usually a full page in size.

1005. Collins, Robert O. **The Waters of the Nile: an Annotated Bibliography.** London: Hans Zell, 1991. xiii, 315 p. ISBN 0-90540-84-1.

Exploring a fascinating topic, this bibliography gathers books, articles, dissertations and government documents pertaining to the Nile River basin. Much more than geography or hydrology is involved: the life of the Nile Valley incorporates concerns "from anthropology to zoology," including what Collins calls "hydropolitics" (p. vii).

The material collected here is impressive, but the organization of the volume itself is less so. Entries are collected in great chunks—110 pages of articles, for example—and ordered by author's name only. The very general subject index cries out for topical subdivision.

1006. Feierman, Steven. **Health and Society in Africa: a Working Bibliography.** Waltham, MA: African Studies Association (Brandeis University), 1979. x, 210 p. *The Archival and Bibliographic Series.*

Sponsored by the Joint Committee on African Studies of the Social Science Research Council and the American Council of Learned Societies.

A compilation of more than 2800 entries—mostly journal articles—detailing the "relations among medicine, disease and social organization in Africa" (p. vii). Settlement patterns, herbal and traditional medicine, economic development and public health and other issues all have an impact upon physical and social welfare. A twelve-page section on relevant bibliographies is fully annotated. The body of the work, however, is neither annotated nor subdivided by topic, but only alphabetized by author. The subject index is quite useless, making this work a sort of historical record of the literature but nothing more, as its information is inaccessible. There is no titles index, nor abstracts, nor any keyword or descriptor system (these would have been hard to manage in 1979). Ondisc and online journal indexes dealing with medicine and social science would be more satisfactory.

1007. Nasr, Seyyed Hossein. **An Annotated Bibliography of Islamic Science.** Tehran: Imperial Iranian Academy of Philosophy, 1975. 3 v.

A rather remarkable relic of pre-revolutionary Iran, this reference seeks to document the contribution of Islamic peoples to civilization and knowledge throughout the centuries. "Science" is broadly construed to incorporate philosophy, mathematics, and areas of the humanities or social sciences that have a bearing on the study of nature or creation.

Many of the entries are briefly annotated; there is an author index. The comprehensive or retrospective emphasis of the bibliography, with its emphasis on early sources, means that though it lacks currency, the early references are still valid.

1008. Otto, Ingeborg and Marianne Schmidt-Dumont. **Die Wasserfrage im Nahen und Mittleren Osten: Literatur seit 1985, eine Auswahlbibliographie.** Hamburg: Deutsches Übersee-Institut, 1995. xlv, 162 p. *Dokumentationsdienst Vorderer Orient;* Reihe A, 23. ISSN 0937-5945

Also titled: *Water in the Middle East and North Africa.*

Literature on water issues published between 1985 and 1995 is compiled in this volume. Entries include bibliographic information, subject descriptors, location data and often an abstract. German and English are used interchangeably throughout the volume, while introductory material is offered in both languages. A chapter on the northern coast of Africa and Sudan is easily found in the table of contents. Water use and management, agriculture, environmental issues, conflicts over water rights, international agreements and legal concerns are involved here. There is an author index.

1009. Swearingen, Will D. and Abdellatif Bencherifa. **The North African Environment at Risk.** Boulder, CO: Westview Press, 1996. xiv, 286 p. *State, Culture and Society in Arab North Africa.* ISBN 0-8133-2127-1.

A collection of scientific studies and scholarly essays on the physical environment of the North African states (here, Morocco, Algeria and Tunisia, and sometimes Libya and Mauritania). This volume is part of an important series, the first in English to focus exclusively on this area. It combines extraordinary detail with careful reflection on the issues. Its reference value lies in its well-written introductory essay, unusual tables and figures, very helpful bibliographies and competent index.

1010. Woillet, J. C. and M. Allal. **Directory of African Technology Institutions.** Geneva: International Labour Office, 1985. 2 v. ISBN 92-2-103662-6 (set).

A country-by-country directory of national and regional research centers, universities, technical departments of government ministries, rural development agencies and other organizations working to promote or create "appropriate technology" (p. xi)—that is, equipment and processes that can be used to improve the standard of living in developing countries at low cost and with minimal pollution and undesirable social impact. Four basic sectors are included in this reference: the manufacture of agricultural implements and machinery; the processing of agricultural yield; the production of building materials for low-cost housing; the utilization of renewable energy resources.

Each entry provides basic contact information, characteristics of the institution (including its chain of accountability to government ministries), its staff, facilities and funding, any publications, and a simple description of its research goals and acitivities. All of the states of northern Africa are represented (there is no entry for Western Sahara).

1011. Zahlan, A. B. **Science and Science Policy in the Arab World.** New York: St. Martin's Press, 1980. 205 p. ISBN 0-313-70232-9.

This monograph—with some tables of data—reflects the status of scientific research in the Arab world in the 1970s, and concentrates on Egypt in particular. Some comparative data (especially in science/technology education and training) is included, and each chapter provides bibliographical references. There is a capable index. The work is useful as a summary of state funding, direction and control of scientific activity in countries with strongly centralized systems.

Databases and Websites

1012. African Networking Initiative (ANI). **www.bellanet.org/partners/ani/**
A consortium of international companies and NGOs working to develop telecommunications and information technology in Africa. Links to their Donors Database.

1013. African Technology Forum. **web.mit.edu/africantech/www/**
"The Premier Source of Information on Science and Technology in Africa," particularly from the development and environment points of view. Links to selected full-text features; also related websites.

1014. The African Water Page. Nile Basin Initiative. **http://www.sn.apc.org/afwater/nile.htm**
Reports on the progress of this ongoing project; links to other news about water resources and sustainable development.

1015. Afrique Médecine et Santé. **members.aol.com/joinams/index.html**
Descriptive page with links to full-text articles.

1016. Arab Academy for Science and Technology (Alexandria). **www.aast.egnet.net/**

1017. Center for International Health Information. Country Health Profile Series. **www.cihi.com/hthpub.htm**
Statistical and descriptive reports are now posted for all the countries of northern Africa except Djibouti, Algeria, Tunisia and Libya.

1018. EcoNews Africa. **www.web.apc.org/~econews/**
"EcoNews Africa is an NGO initiative that analyses global environment and development issues from an African perspective and reports on local, national, and regional activities that contribute to global solutions."

1019. Fridtjof Nansen Institute (Norway). Yearbook of International Cooperation on Environment and Development. **www.ngo.grida.no/ggynet/**
Online version of a resource published by Oxford University Press; also known as *The Green Globe Yearbook*.

1020. HealthNet Africa. **www.healthnet.org/hnet/africa.html**
Links to participating national health centers in Eritrea, Ethiopia, Sudan and Mali.

1021. International Institute for Sustainable Development. Multimedia Resource for Environment and Development Policy Makers. **www.iisd.ca/**

1022. Le Réseau Électronique Francophone (REFER). Université Virtuelle Francophone. **www.refer.org/accueil.htm/**

"L'alliance du numérique et de l'informatique change la réalité des choses en matière d'information. La Francophonie doit très rapidement accroître sa présence sur Internet, sinon d'autres langues, actuellement lancées à grande vitesse, lui en interdiront l'accès. Pour ce faire il faut, sans cesser d'améliorer les réseaux physiques existants, brancher rapidement et massivement les pays du Sud afin que l'ensemble francophone dispose d'un maillage serré de structures d'accès à l'inforoute." Focused upon Francophone Africa in particular.

1023. Network for Environment and Sustainable Development in Africa (NESDA). **www.rri.org/nesda/nesda.html**

Also available in French.

1024. PANA. Science and Health News. **www.africanews.org/pana/science/**

Updated weekly.

1025. SOAS Water Issues Group. Middle East and North Africa. **193.63.73.50:80/Geography/WaterIssues/**

1026. US Department of Commerce. National Technical Information Service. **www.fedworld.gov/ntis/ntishome.html**

"The National Technical Information Service is the official resource for government-sponsored US and worldwide scientific, technical, engineering, and business-related information."

Religion

Chapter

7

Perhaps the most powerful social and cultural force in northern Africa, religious faith and practice is the focus of this chapter. Sources cited here are concerned with religion in general, African traditional religion, Christianity, and Islam, with an additional section on "political Islam," or political ideology and activity based upon Muslim identity.

Reference Sources

1027. **Encyclopedia of World Faiths: an Illustrated Survey of the World's Living Religions.** Edited by Peter Bishop and Michael Darton. New York; Oxford: Facts on File, 1987. 352 p. ISBN 0-8160-1860-X.

An attractive volume illustrated with well-chosen color and black-and-white photos, but lacking maps. Coverage of Christian sects is extensive, but the single chapter on Islam is very basic, and material on African indigenous religions is provided only in passing ("New Religious Movements Among Primal Peoples"). The index is fairly helpful in locating terms like *shahada* and *zakat*. There is a limited subdivided bibliography.

1028. **Religion Index One: Periodicals.** Semiannual, with cumulations; 1977- . Chicago: Americal Theological Library Association. ISSN 0149-8429.

Also available as *ATLA Religion Database* on CD-ROM (annual; 1993-). Descriptive website at **www.atla.com/products/products.html**

The essential index to serial publications in religion.

1029. **Religion Index Two: Multi-Author Works.** Annual, with cumulations; 1976- . Chicago: Americal Theological Library Association. ISSN 0149-8436.

Also available as *ATLA Religion Database* on CD-ROM (annual; 1993-). Descriptive website at **www.atla.com/products/products.html**

The essential index to essay collections, festschrifts, etc. in religion.

1030. **The World's Religions.** Edited by Stewart Sutherland, et al. London: Routledge, 1988. xiv, 995 p. ISBN 0-415-00324-5.

A comprehensive reference composed of scholarly essays by noted authorities all packed into one heavy volume, Cambridge-style. Part 3 includes a dense essay by M. Brett of SOAS on "Islam in North Africa." Christianity in the whole of Africa occupies one essay in Part 2, while African traditional religions are dealt with in Part 5. A chapter on new religious movements in Africa by H.W. Turner of Sellyoak is also presented. Each article contains its own bibliographical references; there is also a substantial and helpful index.

1031. Knappert, Jan. **The Encyclopedia of Middle Eastern Mythology and Religion.** Shaftesbury: Element, 1993. 309 p. ISBN 1-85230-427-8.

This reference defines the Middle East as Egypt and lands eastward, though it does include some entries on the fringes of this area (Candace, Queen of Ethiopia, for instance). The coverage is otherwise so broad and the information so thin that it is not clear for what readership this work was intended—possibly world civilization classes in secondary schools.

1032. Mercatante, Anthony. **The Facts on File Encyclopedia of World Mythology.** New York: Facts on File, 1988. xviii, 807 p. ISBN 0-8160-1049-8.

Comprehensive in scope, this ready reference offers brief alphabetized entries identifying names and terms from folklore around the world. There are very few longer descriptive or interpretive articles, making this more of a dictionary than an encyclopedia. Africa, Pharaonic Egypt and the Ancient Near East are within the scope of this work, and a "Cultural and Ethnic Index" is helpful in locating material from particular traditions. A topically-subdivided and annotated basic bibliography is provided.

1033. Mitchell, Robert Cameron and Harold W. Turner. **A Comprehensive Bibliography of Modern African Religious Movements.** With Hans-Jurgen Greschat. Chicago: Northwestern University Press, 1966. xiv, 132 p.

Though dated, this bibliography is mentioned because of its claim to comprehensiveness on a neglected topic. It presents an anthropological view of non-Islamic religious activities known to be current at the time of publication, both "spontaneous popular manifestations" of religion and more organized or stable cults and churches.

The authors note that "an attempt has been made to include every available reference in any language to modern African religious movements that has been published and achieved more than local circulation" (p. ix). This includes some materials published by indigenous groups themselves, among them histories, biographies, constitutions, catechisms, theological works, polemics and hymnals. The authors caution that works of "vastly uneven quality" are represented here.

Most of the entries are briefly annotated. In northern Africa, only Mali, Ethiopia and Sudan are explicitly included, but some of the more general materials are relevant as well. There is an author index and an index of tribal names (including the Dinka, Yoruba, Peul and Nuer).

1034. O'Brien, Joanne and Martin Palmer. **The State of Religion Atlas.** Edited by David B. Barrett. New York: Simon & Schuster, 1993. 126 p. ISBN 0-671-79376-4.

Since this glossy, colorful small-format atlas seeks to present information about all the world's religions at once, coverage of any particular faith or area is not extensive. Apparently, the basic intent is to compare the major faith groups.

Christianity and Islam are depicted together on Map #4 in terms of population. Map #18 shows the collection and distribution of development and aid funds and *zakat* (charity) worldwide; Map #24 shows where legal systems are based upon *sharia* (Islamic religious law), secular law or a combination of the two.

Some other maps also convey information relevant to the religions of northern Africa (for example, an estimation of the status of women in each country). An interpretation of each map and a note about the sources of the data appear in a section at the back of the book.

1035. Turner, Harold W. **Bibliography of New Religious Movements in Primal Societies.** Vol. 1: Black Africa. Boston: G.K. Hall, 1977. x, 277 p. *Bibliographies and Guides in African Studies.* ISBN 0-8161-7927-1.

A densely-packed compilation of sources in Western languages, mainly of a scholarly nature, on new manifestations of religion in Africa, emerging from Islamic, Christian and indigenous or traditional origins. Some of the citations are briefly annotated. The table of contents provides a clear organization of the materials by country. Mali, Niger, Ethiopia and Sudan are included. There is an author and title index (for periodicals), but no workable subject index; a one-page "select thematic guide" is not helpful.

1036. Williams, Ethel L. and Clifton F. Brown. **The Howard University Bibliography of African and Afro-American Religious Studies: With Locations in American Libraries.** Wilmington, DE: Scholarly Resources, 1977. xxi, 525 p. ISBN 0-8420-2080-2.

The emphasis in this volume—which functions as a sort of union catalog of more than 13,000 primary and secondary sources in this subject area—is on the African American religious experience. But Part 1 lists materials pertaining to African civilizations since ancient times, the Christian missionary age (especially the 19th century), and the independence era. Egypt, Sudan, the Sahel and Horn are included, but other mainly Islamic states of northern Africa are outside the scope of this work. Two appendices offer information on biographical and autobiographical sources, and on the location of manuscripts; these sources relate to black Americans only. A helpful names index is provided. Entries are not annotated, except where the title does not indicate the subject matter of the work cited. Every entry provides at least one location symbol.

1037. Young, Josiah U. **African Theology: a Critical Analysis and Annotated Bibliography.** Westport, CT: Greenwood, 1993. xii, 257 p. *Bibliographies and Indexes in Religious Studies;* no. 26. ISBN 0-313-26487-2.

Very thorough and literate annotations enrich this bibliography of books and articles pertaining to Christianity and traditional religions in Africa. (The Arab and Berber peoples of northern Africa are excluded.) Interesting and informative introductory material is also found here. A reader might wish for full coverage of Coptic and Ethiopian Orthodox Christianity and of the history of monasticism, so important in northern Africa; also, for a far more detailed subject index. An author and a title index are provided.

Journals

1038. **International Bulletin of Missionary Research.** Quarterly; 1950- . New Haven, CT: Overseas Mission Study Center. ISSN 0272-6122.

Published under this title since 1981.

A scholarly journal concerned with the history and theology of Christian missions, and the encounter of Christianity with world religions. Edited by respected scholar Gerald H. Anderson, this journal is an important forum for issues that frequently have implications for area studies. The book reviews in particular often cover topics relevant to Islam, African religion and the history of European colonization and evangelization in Africa.

1039. **Journal of Religion in Africa.** Quarterly; 1967- . Leiden: Brill. ISSN 0022-4200.

Subscription information and back issues available at **www.brill.nl**

Edited by eminent authority Adrian Hastings, this scholarly journal is published in cooperation with the African Association for the Study of Religions. The editorial advisory board includes some of the leading figures in the study of comparative religions. Four or five research articles and several substantial, signed book reviews appear in each issue. The journal is chiefly concerned with sub-Saharan Africa.

African Traditional Religions

1040. Ofori, Patrick E. **Black African Traditional Religions and Philosophy: a Select Bibliographic Survey of the Sources From the Earliest Times to 1974.** Nendeln, Liechtenstein: KTO (Kraus-Thomson Organization), 1975. xix, 421 p.

Though not current, this retrospective bibliography aims to cover "all the major publications in the field ... books, pamphlets, periodical articles, theses and dissertations" (p. xv), mainly in English and French. A compilation of earlier bibliographies and materials on indigenous African religions in general are presented first: then the book is organized geographically and by ethnic group.

Mali, Chad, Ethiopia, Somalia and Sudan are included (but not Niger), and materials on specific tribal groups are easy to find, either in the table of contents or the "ethnic index." There is an author index as well.

Websites

1041. African Traditional Religion. **users.iol.it/cdi/**
Full-text articles, bibliography and links.

1042. The African Traditional Religion Community Links Page. **http://spiritnetwork.com/mamisii/links.html**
Personal and idiosyncratic site, with many links; primarily West Africa (Nigeria).

Christianity

Specialized monographs and essay collections on this subject are many, and journal articles are particularly important. Sources detailing the history of Western Protestant and Catholic missionary efforts in northern Africa are relevant here. Access to these materials may be gained through *Religion Index One* and *Religion Index Two* (see above).

1043. **Coptic Encyclopedia.** Edited by Aziz S. Atiya. New York: Macmillan, 1991. 8 v. ISBN 0-02-897025-X (set).
This unique and authoritative reference source offers a wealth of information on one of the world's most distinctive religious traditions. Substantial signed entries provide identifications of the persons, places, concepts and events essential to the history of Christianity in Egypt, Nubia and Ethiopia. Lengthier articles (e.g., "Monasticism") also provide some analysis of the significance of their subjects.
All entries include at least a few bibliographical references, and often the bibliographies are extensive and sophisticated (for example, "Sahidic") . The work is not heavily illustrated, but there are some figures, drawings, plans and black-and-white photos; twelve useful maps are presented together in an appendix. Volume 8 contains a major appendix on the special topic of the Coptic language. Entries are cross-referenced, and there is also a large and detailed index.

1044. **Histoire des Chrétiens d'Afrique du Nord; Libye, Tunisie, Algérie, Maroc.** Edited by Henri Teissier. Paris: Desclée, 1991. 313 p. ISBN 2-7189-0531-X.
A one-volume history prepared by Roman Catholic scholars, covering the Maghreb from antiquity to modern times. The work devotes special attention to Muslim-Christian relations. A bibliography, index and small section of black-and-white photos are included.

1045. **Historical Dictionary of the Orthodox Church.** By Michael Prokurat, Alexander Golitzin, and Michael D. Peterson. Lanham, MD: Scarecrow, 1996. xvii, 437 p. *Religions, Philosopies and Movements;* no. 9. ISBN 0-8108-3081-7.

Includes basic material on Egypt and Ethiopia, especially monasticism, the Coptic Church, and the Greek patriarchate of Alexandria.

1046. **Répertoire Bibliographique des Institutions Chrétiennes (RIC).** Edited by Marie Zimmermann and Jean Schlick. With Francis Messner. Strasbourg: Cerdic Publications (Centre de Recherches et de Documentation des Institutions de Croyance Religieuses). Semiannual (January and July). ISSN 0079-9300.

An extensive compilation of references to current monographs and articles in religious studies (and religion-related materials on psychology, law, sociology, art, medicine, etc.). Access is offered in Part Two through a subject index of terms in English, with an index to the index in French, German, Spanish and Italian. These entries are coded with a system of symbols referring to the citation in Part One.

It may be worth the reader's time to become familiar with the coding system, because it allows one to see at a glance the relative importance of the book or article in the editors' opinion, the country and confession or denomination discussed, and the presence of bibliographical notes. The citations are classified in Part One by country or region, the first being Africa. The journals indexed include many unusual and hard-to-find publications, and a number of African scholars and authors; however, the sources are mainly in southern or sub-Saharan Africa, revealing the strength of Christian publishing in that region.

1047. **World Christian Encyclopedia: a Comparative Survey of Churches and Religions in the Modern World, AD 1900-2000.** Edited by David B. Barrett. Oxford; New York: Oxford University Press, 1982. xv, 1010 p. ISBN 0-19-572435-6.

This volume is basically a country-by-country survey of the history and current status of the Christian faith and its institutions throughout the world, but it also contains many other reference helps.

The primary articles provide country profile data and statistical tables, a small map and sometimes black-and-white photos (often quite interesting as illustrations), and a concise description of the major religious bodies: Catholic, Protestant and Orthodox, but also Muslim and those of African traditional religions. A note about "Church and State" estimating the degree of religious freedom is included.

The volume also offers a chronology of world evangelization (many of the world's fastest-growing churches are in Africa), ethnolinguistic information, a dictionary, bibliography and map collection, biographical notices and a directory, and extensive indexing. Barrett's statistical information is updated every year in the January issue of the *International Bulletin of Missionary Research.* A new edition of this reference is in preparation; it will appear both in print and on CD-ROM.

1048. Bonk, Jon. **An Annotated and Classified Bibliography of English Literature Pertaining to the Ethiopian Orthodox Church.** Metuchen, NJ: Scarecrow and the American Theological Library Association, 1984. xi, 116 p. *ATLA Bibliography Series;* no. 11. ISBN 0-8108-1710-1.

Prepared by an expert bibliographer and authority on the history of missions, this is a fully-annotated, tightly-focused compilation of books and articles covering the life, learning, worship and polity of one of the world's most venerable churches. Coverage extends from the ancient roots of the church to its activities today. Entries are divided into five main topical clusters, though these are not always self-explanatory: e.g., a sizable literature on the archaeology of early church sites is compiled under "Organization and Government." There is a basic keyword index.

1049. Graf, Georg. **Geschichte der Christlichen Arabischen Literatur.** Vatican City: Biblioteca Apostolica Vaticana, 1944-1953. 5 v. *Studi e Testi;* v. 118, 133, 146, 147, 172.

Like Brockelmann's classic work, this is not a narrative history, but an intricately annotated catalog of manuscripts in Arabic, with important prefatory remarks and background material. Biblical texts and fragments, lectionaries, apocryphal texts and pseudepigrapha, patristics, hagiography, documents of the ecumenical councils and liturgical literature are all included. Coverage extends from antiquity to the 19th century. Vol. 5 is an index to the whole work.

1050. Hastings, Adrian. **The Church in Africa, 1450-1950.** Oxford: Clarendon Press, 1994. xiv, 706 p. ISBN 0-19-826921-8.

A narrative and interpretive history of African Christianity, by one of the world's foremost authorities in the field. The prose may be too dense and sophisticated for beginning students, but scholars in the field will find it absorbing.

Medieval Ethiopia opens the work and receives a great deal of attention; two more chapters also concentrate on the Ethiopian church. Coptic Christianity is discussed in its connection with Ethiopia, but the Mediterranean coast of Africa is outside the scope of this work. A great deal of information on the Sahel and Horn may be located in the detailed index.

Appendices supply a chronology of Ethiopian kings and eight very clear, full-page historical maps. The real reference heart of this work, however, is the extremely valuable 65-page bibliographical essay, identifying and expertly evaluating a vast and varied literature, both in general African history and in religious studies.

1051. Isichei, Elizabeth. **A History of Christianity in Africa: From Antiquity to the Present.** Grand Rapids, MI; Lawrenceville, NJ: William B. Eerdmans; Africa World Press Inc., 1995. xi, 420 p. ISBN 0-8028-0843-3.

A lucid and readable narrative history and analysis by a leading authority in the field. The work is organized both chronologically and regionally. Chapter 1, "North African Christianity in Antiquity," is of course most relevant, as is

Chapter 8, "Northern Africa," and parts of other chapters. The index is helpful in locating specific material, and each chapter offers ample bibliographical references. There are also 13 monochrome historical maps.

1052. Kamil, Jill. **Coptic Egypt: History and Guide.** Cairo: American University in Cairo Press, 1987. xiii, 149 p. ISBN 977-424-104-5.
Kamil manages to convey a great deal of information in this small paperback: a brief narrative history of early Egyptian Christianity, an account of the Coptic Church today, and detailed descriptions of the primary Coptic antiquities, churches and monasteries, not only in Cairo, but also at Wadi Natrun, the Red Sea and Upper Egypt. Small maps and black-and-white photos and several small floor plans are provided. There is a bibliography and a useful index.

1053. Ofori, Patrick E. **Christianity in Tropical Africa: a Selective Annotated Bibliography.** Nendeln: KTO Press, 1977. iv, 461 p. ISBN 3-262-00002-7.
Though this work focuses upon equatorial countries (except Ethiopia), a large portion of the bibliography has to do with Africa generally, and these sources are potentially useful. The volume covers many somewhat obscure older books and periodicals, in a variety of languages, which are unlikely to be included in any electronic indexes and will probably be found in archival collections. The volume has an author and title index; despite its subtitle, however, only a few of the entries are annotated.

1054. Watterson, Barbara. **Coptic Egypt.** Edinburgh: Scottish Academic Press, 1988. ix, 187 p. ISBN 0-7073-0556-X.
A comprehensive introductory history of the Copts in Egypt from pre-Christian Greco-Roman times till the present, in one small and readable volume. A simple structure makes it easy to find certain material (on monasticism, language, architecture, etc.), and there is also a basic index. Two clear maps, especially one showing Coptic sites of settlement and pilgrimage, are useful. A two-page bibliography of fundamental sources is included.

Websites

1055. Centre for the Study of Christianity in the Non-Western World. African Christianity Project. **www.div.ed.ac.uk/centre/african.htm**

1056. Christian Coptic Orthodox Church of Egypt. **cs-www.bu.edu/faculty/best/pub/cn/Home.html**
Accessible information on this special topic.

1057. Christian Network Links for Africa. **www.worship.co.za/dir/**
Southern Africa emphasis.

1058. Coptic Museum in Cairo. **www.idsc.gov.eg/culture/cop_mus.htm**
Artifacts of ancient Egyptian Christianity.

1059. Coptic Network. **cs-www.bu.edu/faculty/best/pub/cn/Menu.html**
Liturgical and cultural resources and directory data; links to other Arab Christian materials.

Islam: Faith and Culture

Reference Sources

1060. **The Cambridge History of Islam.** Edited by P. M. Holt, Ann K. S. Lambton, and Bernard Lewis. Cambridge: University Press, 1970. 2 v. ISBN 521-07567-X and 521-07601-3.

A collection of authoritative essays by eminent Orientalist scholars on the history of the Islamic world, organized geographically for the most part; Vol. 1, "The Central Islamic Lands," begins with pre-Islamic Arabia and includes Egypt; Vol. 2, "The Further Islamic Lands," devotes seven chapters to "Africa and the Muslim West." In addition, Vol. 2 includes a major section of 13 chapters on "Islamic Society and Civilization" that is relevant to the Muslim world in general and incorporates a great deal of detail on societies in northern Africa.

Each essay contains footnotes, often referring to primary sources, and each volume provides a sophisticated, sizable, well-organized bibliography (almost all of the materials cited on North Africa are in French; "trans-Saharan Africa" includes classic texts in English). Each volume also provides dynastic lists, a brief glossary of transliterated Arabic terms and a substantial, detailed index.

1061. **E.J. Brill's First Encyclopaedia of Islam, 1913-1936.** Reprint. Leiden: E.J. Brill, 1987. 9 v. ISBN 90-04-08265-4 (set).

A photomechanical reprint of the original *Encyclopaedia of Islam: a Dictionary of the Geography, Ethnography and Biography of the Muhammadan Peoples.* The four large volumes have been split into eight for easier handling, with their original supplementary volume containing corrections, additions and a collection of plates. This edition is gradually being replaced by the new *EI*, but for now it is the only complete form of this reference.

1062. **The Encyclopaedia of Islam.** New edition. Edited by H. A. R. Gibb, et al. Leiden: E.J.Brill, 1960. ISBN 90-04-08114-3, etc. (volumes numbered separately).

The revision of this essential authoritative reference work (first published in 1913) is still under way; eight volumes and a number of additional fascicules have now appeared. The work is an enormous compilation of signed articles by many of the 20th century's "leading Orientalists" on the geography, history, law, philology, archaeology and ethnography of Muslim states, languages and peoples. It is not an appropriate source for current events, but for deep background, especially biographical detail on historical figures and descriptive material on places and tribal groups, it is unsurpassed.

It provides a sophisticated scholarly apparatus: for example, the bibliography of the meticulous article on the Maghrawa tribe of Berbers in Morocco and Algeria refers the reader to primary medieval texts in Arabic and classic Orientalist sources in French. Almost all of the articles are entered under a transliterated form of the Arabic (Persian, Turkish, etc.) name or vocabulary term, with some cross-references from commonly-used versions of these terms (e.g., CASABLANCA see Al-Dar Al- Bayda; JANISSARIES see devshirme, yeñiceri). Some unusual photo plates and folding maps are included. An index to Vols. I-VI was published in 1991, a glossary and index of technical terms through Vol. VII in 1995, and separate indexes for names and subjects through Vol. VIII in 1996.

1063. **Islamic Desk Reference.** Compiled from *The Encyclopaedia of Islam* by E. Van Donzel. Leiden: E.J. Brill, 1994. ix, 492 p. ISBN 90-04-09738-4.

A convenient one-volume ready reference containing brief identifications of persons, places and important objects or concepts associated with the history of Islam. The concise entries and easy-to-read transliterations make this work quite accessible to readers who would find the full *EI* cumbersome and intimidating.

Some articles of 1-3 pages give a direct, non-technical account of major features of the faith (for example, "Pilgrimage to Mecca") . Sixteen clear and legible maps and eight full-page color plates—mostly of architecture—would make excellent classroom slides. A suitable work for advanced high school, undergraduate or seminary libraries ... at least, those that can afford it.

1064. **The Muslim Almanac.** Edited by Azim A. Nanji. New York: Gale Research, 1996. xxxv, 581 p. ISBN 0-8103-8924-X.

This attractive new reference, "on the history, faith, culture and peoples of Islam," emphasizes the contributions of Muslim peoples to the "shared heritage of humankind." The theological and historical background, intellectual and spiritual life, art, literature, society and folklore are all included, with several unusual sections on women, interfaith relations, modern political concerns (displaced populations, human rights, religious fundamentalism, modernist reforms) and the growing Muslim presence in Western nations. Chapter 10 concentrates on Islam in North Africa. The volume supplies many large black-and-white illustrations, bibliographies for each article and a separate general bibliography, a convenient glossary of names and transliterated Arabic vocabulary terms, and an extensive, thorough index.

1065. **Oxford Encyclopedia of the Modern Islamic World.** Edited by John L. Esposito. New York: Oxford University Press, 1995. 4 v. ISBN 0195066138 (set).

This impressive, up-to-date four-volume reference work boasts an extraordinary board of editors, consultants and advisers. Cogent, concise signed articles under English and transliterated Arabic and Persian headings offer very good points of entry into an array of topics.

Meant to complement the classic *Encyclopaedia of Islam,* this work concentrates on the period from the end of the 18th century to the present. Instead of *EI*'s traditional Orientalist approach based upon philology (and requiring at least some familiarity with the original languages), this work uses a more modern social science methodology. It places an emphasis on the analysis or interpretation of the material, more than on heaping up huge amounts of data. The volumes are very sparsely illustrated with black-and-white photographs; there are no maps.

Each article includes cross-references and a select annotated bibliography of important older and newer works from a variety of perspectives. Essential for the undergraduate or research library.

1066. Al-Faruqi, Ismail R. and Lois Lamya' Al-Faruqi. **The Cultural Atlas of Islam.** New York: Macmillan, 1986. xv, 512 p. ISBN 0-02-910190-5.

An attempt to compile an atlas of Islam using neither a geographical nor a chronological approach, but a phenomenological one. Islam is depicted as something more than the sum of historical events and developments taking place in certain locations and at certain times; the authors wish to communicate something of the ideal or essence, or vision, of Islam, then explain the way this vision has been manifested through cultural phenomena: theology and learning, arts, law and sciences, literature, calligraphy, music, architecture, etc. A number of maps, monochrome photos, fact boxes and other illustrations accompany the text. A names/subject index and a map index are provided.

1067. Ali, S. Amjad. **The Muslim World Today.** Islamabad: National Hijra Council, 1985. 627 p.

A one-volume encyclopedia-style reference, illustrated with many maps and color photos. The "Muslim Middle East," Part 3, includes Djibouti and Somalia; Part 4, "Muslim North Africa," includes Egypt, Sudan, Libya, Algeria, Tunisia, Morocco and Mauritania; in Part 5, "Muslim Sub-Saharan Africa," are found Chad, Niger and Mali. This is an interesting and unusual division of regional categories. The religion of Islam is understood as the basis for each of these societies. The whole reference has a travelogue or public-relations tone; there is no bibliography or other scholarly apparatus.

1068. Bär, Erika. **Bibliographie zur Deutschsprachigen Islamwissenschaft und Semitistik vom Anfang des 19. Jahrhunderts bis Heute.** Wiesbaden: Dr Ludwig Reichert Verlag, 1985. 3 v. ISBN 3-88226-258-3.

This compilation of scholarly writing (essays, articles and monographs) on Islamics and Semitic studies is organized by author: about 250 scholars publishing in German are represented. Vol.1 contains the work of living scholars, while those in Vol. 2 are deceased. For those scholars whose primary work is in another discipline (geography, political science, history, medicine, etc.), only their publications in Semitics or Islamics are included. Works cited date from the beginning of the 19th century up to 1985.

1069. Ede, David. **Guide to Islam.** Boston: G.K. Hall, 1983. xxiv, 261 p. *Asian Philosophies and Religions Resource Guide.* ISBN 0-8161-7905-0.

A well-organized and fully-annotated bibliography of scholarly books and journal articles pertaining to many aspects of Islamic history, philosophy and civilization, for the beginning and advanced student. Coverage goes well beyond theological topics to include Islamic law and institutions, art and architecture, painting, calligraphy and bookbinding, textiles and crafts. Author and subject indexes are provided; materials specifically on north or northwest Africa are easily found in the table of contents. Despite its publication date, however, most of the materials cited were published before 1976.

1070. Geddes, Charles L. **Books in English on Islam, Muhammad, and the Qur'an: a Selected and Annotated Bibliography.** Denver: American Institute of Islamic Studies, 1976. vii, 68 p. *Bibliographic Series;* no. 5.

A carefully-annotated guide to reference works, monographs and other research helps relating to Islamic studies. This small volume provides valuable information on serious literature in English in this field up to the mid-1970s.

1071. Geddes, Charles L. **Guide to Reference Books for Islamic Studies.** Denver: American Institute of Islamic Studies, 1985. xiii, 429 p. *Bibliographic Series;* no. 9. ISBN 0-933017-00-6.

Concentrating on Islamic civilization, history and faith, this bibliography does *not* concern itself with "reference materials on the contemporary politics, modern states, and related subjects of the Middle East and North Africa" (p. vii). Since these concerns are important to area studies, the reader should be aware of the self-imposed limits of this work's scope.

However, for material on classical and Ottoman Islam up to 1924 (the end of the Caliphate), it still offers a valuable collection of books and articles in a range of European languages, works in Arabic, Farsi, Turkish and Urdu (with titles printed in the original scripts). Entries include annotations or a brief contents note. A clear table of contents and general index are provided. This work assumes the ability of the reader to cope with transliterated names and titles, particularly in the index.

1072. Glassé, Cyril. **The Concise Encyclopedia of Islam.** San Francisco: Harper & Row, 1989. 472 p. ISBN 0-06-06313-6.

A convenient one-volume reference consisting of brief alphabetized entries on persons, concepts and historical events in the world of Islam generally. It relies to a large extent on transliterated Arabic vocabulary terms, making it a bit challenging for the novice to use; there are some cross-references. Some entries relating specifically to North Africa can be found: "Berbers," for instance. There are several pages of color photographs, four attractive maps, and charts showing the various branches of Islam, genealogical tables of some Arab dynasties, and a chronology. Unfortunately, the text of this volume is imperfectly printed, making it somewhat faint and hard to read.

1073. Hughes, Thomas Patrick. **A Dictionary of Islam: Being a Cyclopaedia of the Doctrines, Rites, Ceremonies and Customs, Together With the Technical and Theological Terms, of the Muhammadan Religion.** Reprint. New York: Irvington, 1996. vii, 750 p. ISBN 0-697-00053-2.

Reprint of a classic Victorian Orientalist reference for Semitic studies, first published in 1885. Quaint but still useful for concise identification of persons, place names, concepts and vocabulary terms (and for an encapsulated version of the anthropology of its era). Some complex issues receive much fuller treatment: for example, a five-page article on divorce.

A very helpful feature of this work for ready reference is the presence of each term in standard Arabic or Persian orthography, plus any Hebrew, Chaldee or Hindustani equivalents, along with the transliterated or romanized term. The volume is cross-referenced to connect English vocabulary terms with their counterparts in the original language; an index is also provided. The volume also includes several amusing illustrations (see "turban" or "kulah").

1074. Jawed, Mohammed Nasir. **Year Book of the Muslim World: a Handy Encyclopedia.** New Delhi: Medialine, 1996. 776 p. ISBN 81-86420-00-2.

A one-volume almanac-style reference, with articles of current interest, background material on Islamic religion and history, features on society, economics, science and technology and sports in various Muslim countries, and a large section on Palestine. The Arabic-speaking states of North Africa, the Sudan, Sahel and Horn (except Ethiopia and Eritrea) are evidently included; also covered are some states that may not strictly speaking be considered Muslim countries, like Nigeria. The printing is dense and unfortunately of very poor quality.

1075. Kassis, Hanna E. **A Concordance of the Qur'an in English.** Berkeley: University of California Press, 1983. xxxix, 1444 p. ISBN 0-520-04327-8.

An authoritative and extremely useful reference tool, intended for those "who have no command of the Arabic language and yet desire to understand the Qur'an" (Foreword). As Fazlur Rahman explains in his prefatory remarks, "The main distinction of Hanna Kassis's concordance, in my view, is that it utilizes the semantic structure of Arabic vocabulary itself in revealing the meaning of the Qur'an ... a reader who looks in the index of this concordance for a word which he has encountered in reading an English translation ... is directed immediately to the roots of the Arabic Qur'anic terms" (ix).

Indeed, the four-part index functions as an introduction to the triliteral basis of the Arabic language. Combined with Section C of the Introduction, "The Language of the Qur'an," this material offers even the inexperienced reader an entry point to the study of the sacred Scripture on its own terms. The body of the concordance makes it possible efficiently to locate all passages in the Qur'an containing a particular vocabulary element and distinguishes roots that look similar in transliteration but are actually composed of different Arabic letters (for example, **byd** "to sell" and **byD** "to perish").

1076. Kreiser, Klaus and Rotraud Wielandt. **Lexikon der Islamischen Welt.** Völlig überarbeitete Neuausgabe. Stuttgart: W. Kohlhammer, 1992. 289 p. ISBN 3-17-011770-X.

The authors intend to inform the user in a clear, readable and reliable way about the basic facts of Islamic culture, particularly religion, law, philosophy, art (architecture, music) and science. This is a new, fully revised edition of a work that first appeared in 1974. The alphabetically-arranged articles are signed, brief but dense with detail, and include bibliographical references. Where relevant, the equivalent vocabulary term in transliterated Arabic, Persian or Turkish is given. Material pertaining to northern Africa is readily found (e.g., Almohaden, Almorawiden).

1077. Mantran, Robert. **Great Dates in Islamic History.** New York: Facts on File, 1996. xii, 404 p. ISBN 0-8160-2935-0.

Translation of Mantran's *Les Grandes Dates de l'Islam* (1990), with additional material.

This interesting volume combines a series of event chronologies with some textual interpretation and several fact boxes and almanac-style features (a table of the Islamic calendar, nine historical maps,etc.). The whole work is organized into historical units, then geographically by region within those units; therefore, it is possible to glance through the table of contents, picking out "The Maghrib" or "Sub-Saharan Africa" in various time periods. For more precise factfinding, there is a very tiny but helpful index. A simple glossary of terms is also provided.

1078. Ofori, Patrick E. **Islam in Africa South of the Sahara: a Select Bibliographic Guide.** Nendeln, Netherlands: KTO Press, 1977. iv, 223 p. ISBN 3-262-00003-5.

A collection of materials in English and European languages pertaining to the spread of Islam in Africa since the Arab conquest. Though the title indicates the emphasis on sub-Saharan Africa, in fact there is considerable attention given to the Almoravids and Almohads, and Mali, Mauretania, Niger, Chad, Ethiopia, Somalia and Sudan are covered. Some of the entries are briefly annotated, and there is a names index.

1079. Paret, Rudi. **Der Koran: Kommentar und Koncordanz.** Fifth edition. Stuttgart: Verlag W. Kohlhammer, 1993. 555 p. ISBN 3-17-013027-7.

Paret's verse-by-verse critical companion to the Qur'an, in a convenient pocket-size paperback edition very suitable for students. Technical notes and interpretive remarks, plus cross-references, are provided. This reference may be used profitably by readers who lack fluency in Arabic but are willing to use a romanized notation system that requires some patience. But, as Paret himself puts it, "Wenn schon jemand in das Offenbarungsbuch des arabischen Propheten Einsicht nimmt, muss er von sich aus bereit sein, über das, was er liest, nachzudenken und die nötigen Querverbindungen herzustellen. Ohne eine solche Bereitschaft sollte er den Koran lieber überhaupt nicht in die Hand nehmen" (Vorwort, p. 6).

1080. Reysoo, Fenneke. **Pèlerinages au Maroc: Fête, Politique et Échange dans l'Islam Populaire.** Paris: Éditions de la Maison des Sciences de l'Homme, 1991. 227 p. *Recherches et Travaux de l'Institut d'Ethnologie;* 10. ISBN 2-88279-003-1 and 2-7351-0407-9; ISSN 1011-2960.

Published under the auspices of the Faculté des Lettres, Université de Neuchâtel, this interesting anthropological study on various manifestations of popular religion is organized in many concise segments suitable for reference work. The table of contents is thoroughly subdivided (there is no index). The text is augmented by several charts and tables of data (mostly statistical), maps or city plans, and a number of distinct black-and-white photos. There is a useful bibliography and a glossary of specialized terms.

1081. Wensinck, A. J. **A Handbook of Early Muhammadan Tradition, Alphabetically Arranged.** Reprint. Leiden: E.J. Brill, 1960. xviii, 268 p.

A fundamental reference index to eight major collections of *hadith*, organized topically. Wensinck subdivides large topics with phrases to help the reader narrow the search. Personal names used as headings lead the reader to *hadith* in which these figures are mentioned. Cross-references to related headings are provided.

1082. Zoghby, Samir M. **Islam in Sub-Saharan Africa: a Partially Annotated Guide.** Washington: Library of Congress, 1978. viii, 318 p. ISBN 0-8444-0183-8.

Though the emphasis here is on sub-Saharan Africa, the very capable subject index reveals good coverage of Egypt, Ethiopia and the Horn, the Sahel and many specific peoples and places in northern Africa (Fezzan, the Fulani or Fulbe, the Songhay, etc.).

Journals

1083. **American Journal of Islamic Social Sciences.** Quarterly; 1985- . Washington: International Institute of Islamic Thought. ISSN 0742-6763; 0887-7653.

Also available in microform from UMI.

Islamic history and society in the present likewise occupy this journal, published also by the Association of Muslim Social Scientists. In addition to research articles, there are essays and reflection pieces considering tradition and modernity, the academic study of Islam, aesthetics, democracy and economics. Several book reviews and conference reports appear in each issue, along with abstracts of recent dissertations and theses in related subject areas.

1084. **Arabica: Journal of Arabic and Islamic Studies.** Three times/year; 1954- . Leiden: E.J. Brill. ISSN 0570-5398.

Subscription information and back issues available at **www.brill.nl**

The states and societies of northern Africa fall within the scope of this scholarly journal, which concerns itself with the language, literature, history and civilization of the Arab world. The approach tends to be consistent with traditional

Orientalism, with lengthy, technical, text-based studies predominating. Book reviews (some very detailed) are featured, and an index to vols. 1-44 (1954-1997) was published as vol. 45, no. 2.

1085. Der Islam: Zeitschrift für Geschichte und Kultur des Islamischen Orients. Semiannual (since 1980); 1910- . Berlin: Walter de Gruyter. ISSN 0021-1818.

Description, contents pages and subscription information available at **www. degruyter.de/**

Two issues of this academic journal are published per year, each containing six lengthy and highly technical articles on pre-Islamic Arabia, the medieval era, Islamic studies, and important texts in literature, philosophy and law. Each article includes full bibliographical references, very often to primary sources. Familiarity with the original languages is assumed. The second issue of the year presents substantial signed book reviews (1-5 dense pages), not indexed or ordered. Articles and reviews are published in German, English or French.

1086. Die Welt des Islams: Internationale Zeitschrift für die Geschichte des Islams in der Neuzeit. Three times/year; new series 1951- . Leiden: E.J. Brill. ISSN 0043-2539.

Also titled: *World of Islam*; *Monde de l'Islam*. Subscription information and back issues available at **www.brill.nl**

A research journal featuring a small number of very detailed, lengthy articles with extensive and highly technical bibliographical references. Much of each issue is devoted to in-depth book reviews. Though the focus is on "modern Islam" ("in der Neuzeit") , this means the past two centuries; a recent issue contained an article on trade in 19th-century Libya. Articles and reviews are published in English or German. Editorial work for this journal is done at the Orientalisches Seminar der Universität Bonn.

1087. Index Islamicus. Three "advance fascicules" per year, with a cumulative annual bound volume; 1994- . East Grinstead: Bowker-Saur. ISSN 1360-0982 and 0308-7395.

Continues previous *Index Islamicus* publications and supplements. Available on CD-ROM from Bowker-Saur; descriptive website available at **www. saur.de/cdislam.htm**

The essential record of current scholarly publishing in all subject areas related to Islamic studies. The entries are organized by topic: a table of contents helps to orient the reader, and every issue includes a names and a subject index. Reviews of a given work are collected and listed together. New books and scholarly articles are included, in a wide range of European languages. Sometimes a few explanatory words appear, though there are no actual annotations or abstracts. This ongoing work continues the original *Index Islamicus* (J.D. Pearson) covering 1906-85, and the serial *Quarterly Index Islamicus* of 1986-93.

1088. **Islamic Law and Society.** Three times/year; 1994- . Leiden: Brill. ISSN 0928-9380.

Subscription information and back issues available at **www.brill.nl**

A scholarly journal dwelling mainly in the realm of classical and Ottoman law and history, but also featuring articles about Islamic law in contemporary societies. Five research articles provide many footnotes and bibliographical references, often to primary sources (a knowledge of Arabic, or at least of transliterated Arabic names and titles, is assumed). In addition, four or five lengthy, very detailed book reviews are featured.

1089. **The Muslim World.** Quarterly; 1911- . Hartford, CT: Hartford Seminary. ISSN 0027-7909.

Founded by Samuel Zwemer as *The Moslem World*. Also available in microform from UMI.

Published by the Duncan Black Macdonald Center at Hartford Seminary since 1948, this venerable journal is concerned with Islamic history as well as Islamic faith and society in the present. It maintains a particular concern for Islam's encounter and dialogue with the Christian faith. Scholarly articles, reflection pieces, lengthy review articles and shorter book reviews fill each issue. While the journal emphasizes theology, literature, philosophy and history, recent articles analyzed the lithographs of Egypt and Nubia by Victorian artist David Roberts (vol. 88, no.1), and the study of the Arabic language in the West (Vol. 88, no. 2).

1090. **Muslim World Book Review.** Quarterly; 1980- . Leicester: Islamic Foundation. ISSN 0260-3063.

Descriptive website at **dialspace.dial.pipex.com/town/street/gbg00/onlinenews.html;** see also Islamic Foundation website at **www.islamic-foundation.org.uk/islamfound**

A bibliographic publication providing an ongoing index of Islamic literature published in English, and a collection of 1-3 page signed book reviews, topically organized. The periodical covers Islamic philosophy and theology, comparative religion and dialogue, history and area studies, the contemporary Muslim world (politics, society, culture) and reference materials.

1091. **Studia Islamica.** Semiannual; 1953- . Paris: G.-P. Maisonneuve-Larose. ISSN 0585-5292; each issue also has a separate ISBN.

Twice a year, this journal presents scholarly articles "from all sections of the vast field of Islamic studies" (cover). Long and complex articles of an historical/literary nature include many technical and bibliographical notes, usually referring to primary sources. Familiarity with the original languages is assumed.

Book reviews are only about one page long, but are dense and detailed. Some topics related to the study of Islam (e.g., Samir Khalil Samir's *Christian Arabic Apologetics during the Abbassid Period*) are included.

Islam and Politics

Specialized monographs and essay collections on this subject are many, and journal articles are particularly important. Access to these materials may be gained through *Religion Index One* and *Religion Index Two*, and through indexes in the social sciences.

1092. **Fundamentalisms and the State: Remaking Polities, Economies and Militance.** Edited by Martin E. Marty and R. Scott Appleby. Sponsored by The American Academy of Arts and Sciences. Chicago: University of Chicago Press, 1993. ix, 665 p. *The Fundamentalism Project; v. 3.* ISBN 0-226-50883-8.

The Fundamentalism Project is an enormous six-volume collection of scholarly essays and analysis covering the political and social agendas of radical religious movements. Some of these—Jewish extremist groups, Islamists—are pertinent to the Middle East and North Africa; emphasis is placed upon Algeria and Egypt (and, to a lesser extent, Sudan). Important material may be found in any of the six volumes, not just this one, though the focus of attention here is the tension and conflict between religious ideologies and political institutions. Each essay provides bibliographical references (often very current and helpful), and each volume is indexed.

1093. **Islam, Democracy and the State in North Africa.** Edited by John P. Entelis. Bloomington: Indiana University Press, 1997. xxv, 228 p. *Indiana Series in Arab and Islamic Studies.* ISBN 0-253-33303-2.

A collection of scholarly essays by leading authorities in the field, discussing crucial aspects of the exercise of power in northern Africa today. The articles are lengthy and analytical, with full bibliographical references, and in some cases figures or tables of data. A careful index helps to locate specific material. Algeria, Egypt, Libya, Morocco and Tunisia are discussed (with some material pertaining to neighboring states), along with North Africa and the Maghreb as regions.

1094. Burgat, François and William Dowell. **The Islamic Movement in North Africa.** Austin: Center for Middle Eastern Studies, 1993. xi, 310 p. *Middle East Monograph Series.* ISBN 0-292-70793-2

First appeared as *L'Islamisme au Maghreb* (Paris: Éditions Karthala, 1988).

This scholarly work lacks the basic apparatus that would suit it to reference use—a bibliography and index—but it does offer four distinct chapters focusing upon individual nations of northern Africa: Libya, Morocco, Tunisia and Algeria.

1095. Eickelman, Dale F. and James Piscatori. **Muslim Politics.** Princeton: Princeton University Press, 1996. xi, 235 p. *Princeton Studies in Muslim Politics.* ISBN 0-691-03184-3.

Not well suited to reference work, this is nevertheless an important volume for careful study. Two noted authorities in the field reflect on ideological politics in the Islamic world. Material on northern Africa can be found in the index.

1096. Esposito, John L. **Islam and Politics.** Fourth edition. Syracuse, NY: Syracuse University Press, 1998 xxii, 393 p. *Contemporary Issues in the Middle East.* ISBN 0-8156-2774-2.

A new edition of this well-known and valuable monograph on the role of Islam in modern political life, including most of northern Africa. The analysis is authoritative and erudite, yet readable for undergraduates. Bibliographical references and a careful index are included.

1097. Haddad, Yvonne Yazbeck and John L. Esposito. **The Islamic Revival Since 1988: a Critical Survey and Bibliography.** Westport, CT: Greenwood, 1997. xx, 295 p. *Bibliographies and Indexes in Religious Studies;* no. 45. ISBN 0-313-30480-7.

An update of the earlier volume, *The Contemporary Islamic Revival* (1991), this compilation of scholarly books and articles is an important source for current literature on the entire world of Islam, including Europe and the Americas.

Chapter II concentrates on Islamic Africa, giving special attention to Algeria, Libya, Morocco and Tunisia; Egypt and Sudan are covered in Chapter VI, "The Middle East." Every entry has at least a brief annotation, any many include a full summary or abstract. Author, title and subject indexes are provided. This reference should be in every academic or research library.

1098. Haddad, Yvonne Yazbeck, John Obert Voll, and John L. Esposito. **The Contemporary Islamic Revival: a Critical Survey and Bibliography.** New York: Greenwood Press, 1991. xiii, 230 p. *Bibliographies and Indexes in Religious Studies;* no. 20. ISBN 0-313-24719-6.

Prepared by three of today's leading authorities in the field, this scholarly study of the literature of contemporary Islam published in English (1970-1988) will be of value to serious students, writers and bibliographers. Three densely-written essays set forth the issues involved. A compilation of sources follows: books and monographs, journal articles and primary sources (not including material from the popular press). Where the title does not indicate a work's content, an annotation is provided; some annotations comment on the significance of a work for current study. The entries are organized geographically, with author and title indexes and a less-than-successful subject index.

1099. Hussain, Asaf. **Islamic Movements in Egypt, Pakistan and Iran: an Annotated Bibliography.** London: Mansell, 1983. xiv, 168 p. ISBN 0-7201-1648-1.

Only the first 40 pages of this volume relate to northern Africa (specifically Egypt), but the quality of the treatment merits attention. There is a coherent and informative introductory essay on the Islamic revival in Egypt in the 20th century (complete with bibliographical references), then a fully annotated compilation of over 100 sources, both books and articles/essays. Though dated now, this is a useful source of materials on this subject up to the early 1980s. There is an author index.

1100. Monshipouri, Mahmood. **Islamism, Secularism and Human Rights in the Middle East.** Boulder; London: Lynne Rienner, 1998. xi, 258 p. ISBN 1-55587-782-6.

A scholarly monograph studying these issues on both the theoretical and practical levels. The ideas and information here pertain to the entire region, but North Africa is mentioned only in passing; the in-depth studies are of Turkey, Pakistan and Iran.

1101. Shahin, Emad Eldin. **Political Ascent: Contemporary Islamic Movements in North Africa.** Boulder, CO: Westview Press, 1997. xii, 275 p. *State, Culture and Society in Arab North Africa.* ISBN 0-8133-2775-X.

Another volume in the exceptional series edited by John P. Entelis and Michael Suleiman. This scholarly work covers a crucially-important topic, the "role of Islam in political development and social change in Muslim societies" (Introduction). The straightforward organization of the work—one chapter on Islam and the state in general, then separate chapters on Tunisia, Algeria and Morocco—increases its value for reference work. A bibliography subdivided by type of material (books and articles in French, English and Arabic, interviews and news sources) and an index are included.

1102. Shaikh, Farzana. **Islam and Islamic Groups: a Worldwide Reference Guide.** Essex: Longman (CIRCA), 1992. x, 316 p. ISBN 0-582-09146-2.

A clear and easy-to-use country-by-country dictionary of Islamic political groups active in countries where Muslims form either a majority or a significant minority of the population. The focus is on "Islam as the political ideology of almost 1,000 million people" (Introduction). An effort is made to include "semi-clandestine" groups, although the author cautions that this information is derivative and possibly less reliable. Useful introductory material is provided for each country; the entries for individual groups usually amount to about one paragraph, though some longer entries appear. The volume includes a decent map and index. All of the countries of northern Africa are included except Somalia (and, of course, Eritrea).

Websites

1103. Islamic Foundation Online. **dialspace.dial.pipex.com/town/street/gbg00/**
Information about their Leicester conference center, publications, library, etc.

1104. Islamic Gateway. **www.ummah.org.uk/**
Information about religion, culture and politics.

1105. IslamiCity. **www.islamicity.org/**
News, culture and devotional information about Islam; many links.

1106. Leiden University. International Institute for the Study of Islam in the Modern World (ISIM). **isim.leidenuniv.nl**

1107. Muslim Brotherhood Movement Homepage. **www.ummah.net/ikhwan/**
An Islamist organization active in northern Africa.

1108. Muslimedia. **muslimedia.com/mainpage.htm**
Full-text news stories relevant to the Islamic world.

1109. Understanding Islam and the Muslims. **darkwing.uoregon.edu/~kbatarfi/
islam.html**
One of the better introductory sites.

1110. Wisdom Fund. The Truth About Islam. **www.twf.org/**
An organization designed to counter negative publicity about Islam.

PART THREE

Reference Sources by Country and Region

The Maghreb—
Arabic-Speaking
North Africa

Chapter 8

As noted in the Preface, regional divisions in northern Africa are by no means universally accepted. For the purposes of this work, this section will focus upon primarily Arabic-speaking Mediterranean Africa, including Egypt.

Reference Sources

1111. **L'Afrique Française du Nord, Bibliographie Militaire: des Ouvrages Français on Traduits en Français et des Articles des Principales Revues Françaises Relatifs à l'Algérie a la Tunisie et au Maroc.** Reprinted 1975. Paris: Imprimerie Nationale, 1930-1935. 2 v. ISBN 0-404-56206-X (set).

A major source for documentation of the French colonial era in its North African territories. These two thick volumes contain more than 9400 annotated citations. Vol. 1 covers the period from 1830 to 1926; Vol. 2 commences in 1927. The citations are topically organized, and there are no indexes.

1112. **Annuaire de l'Afrique du Nord: l'Encyclopédie Annuelle du Maghreb Contemporain, 1995.** Annual; 1962- . Paris: CNRS Éditions, 1997. 1342 p. ISBN 2-271-0544-0; ISSN 0242-7540

Publié par l'Institut de Recherches et d'Études sur le Monde Arabe et Musulman.

An essential source of current information in French on the Maghreb as a region, and on Algeria, Libya, Morocco, Mauritania and Tunisia in particular. Signed articles with bibliographical references, from two to 40 pages in length, report and comment upon developments in law and the economy, international relations, and broad themes like human rights. Annotated bibliographies in French and Arabic, subdivided by topic, occupy more than 300 pages of the 1995 edition (vol. 34).

1113. **Aramco and Its World: Arabia and the Middle East.** Edited by Ismail I. Nawwab, Peter C. Speers, and Paul F. Hoye. Dhahran: Aramco, 1980. xi, 275 p. ISBN 0-9601164-2-7.

An attractive "coffee table" book illustrating basic material about the history, religion and culture of Saudi Arabia and the role of Aramco in developing its oil industry. Contains maps, charts, diagrams, drawings and photographs, mostly in full color. The book focuses on the Arabian peninsula, but material on Algeria, Egypt, Libya, Tunisia and Morocco may be found in the subject index.

1114. **Encyclopédie Berbère.** Incomplete multivolume work. Publication director. Gabriel Camps. Aix-en-Provence: EDISUD, 1984- . ISBN 2-85744-201-7 and 2-85744-948-8.

An ongoing scholarly publication, documenting the ethnology, anthropology, history and prehistory, language and linguistics, religion, antiquities, geography, even the flora and fauna of the Berber-speaking region of North Africa and the Berber people. The editorial team includes specialists in the Tuareg culture, Punic archaeology, Pharaonic history, the medieval period, and Islam.

Vol. 1 presents an introductory essay on Berber origins and the process of Arabization, then begins the alphabetized collection of signed articles, each with 1-10 scholarly bibliographical references; the long article on the important antiquities of Fezzân provides an extensive current bibliography of almost 100 references in various European languages.

Excellent maps and black-and-white photos or expert artifact drawings generously illustrate each volume. Vol. 18 appeared in 1997 and has brought the publication halfway through the letter F, so presumably, many more fascicules are planned.

1115. **Le Maghreb: Hommes et Espaces.** Paris: Armand Colin, 1985. 360 p. ISBN 2-200-31206-7.

An attractive one-volume introduction, on the order of a classroom text, to the human and physical geography of Morocco, Tunisia and Algeria. Natural resources and topography, water resources and irrigation, population distribution, migration and urbanization, industrialization and development, agricultural production and rural life, tourism, and regional issues are all covered. There is an extensive bibliography and a helpful table of contents, but no indexes.

1116. **North Africa: a Lonely Planet Travel Survival Kit.** First edition. By Damien Simonis. et al. Hawthorn, Victoria: Lonely Planet, 1995. 787 p. ISBN 0-86442-258-X.

A thick, detailed handbook stressing practical travel advice. The largest section covers Morocco, but informative chapters are provided on Algeria, Tunisia and Libya as well. Many small but sharp maps and city plans are included; there is also a 20-page "arts and crafts" section of color photos and captions. The volume is indexed.

1117. **North Africa: Development and Reform in a Changing Global Economy.** Edited by Dirk Vandewalle. London: Macmillan, 1996. xviii, 286 p. ISBN 0-333-67345-X.

Nine essays on the tough economic, environmental and social dilemmas of the North African states, especially Morocco, Algeria, Tunisia and Libya. Analysis and reflection are emphasized here, but there is a superior bibliography on the Maghreb economies that could be quite useful for reference work.

1118. **Political Elites in Arab North Africa: Morocco, Algeria, Tunisia, Libya and Egypt.** New York: Longman, 1982. xii, 273 p. ISBN 0-582-28251-9.

An opening chapter on North Africa in general is followed by individual studies of each of the states mentioned in the title. Coverage of Egypt in particular is enriched with tables of data pertaining to the education, profession and origin of the power elites. The information here seems to be frozen in a snapshot of the early 1980s, however; it may or may not be relevant to other points in time. In any event, it would be of interest historically and for purposes of comparison with more current data. Bibliographical references and an index are included.

1119. Brett, Michael and Elizabeth Fentress. **The Berbers.** Oxford: Blackwell, 1996. xvi, 350 p. *The Peoples of Africa.* ISBN 0-631-16852-4.

A thoroughly researched and well-organized study of the archaeology, history and anthropology of the Berbers and their culture since prehistoric times. For reference work, there are some 40 photographic plates, 41 figures (plans, drawings) and six maps, an easy-to-use index and an outstanding bibliography.

1120. Cigar, Norman. **Government and Politics in North Africa.** Monticello, IL: Vance Bibliographies, 1979. 14 p. *Public Administration Series; P-171.*

The Vance bibliographies on public administration are composed of topically arranged citations—up to about 1000 in each issue—of books and articles, government bulletins and other publications. The entries are sometimes briefly annotated. This issue covers monographs and articles in French and English, pertaining to Libya, Morocco, Tunisia and Algeria just after their independence up to the mid-1970s. The "emphasis is on domestic issues, ideologies, institutions and personalities involved in the process of nation-building and modernization" (Introduction).

1121. Devine, Elizabeth and Nancy L. Braganti. **The Travelers' Guide to Middle Eastern and North African Customs and Manners.** New York: St. Martin's, 1991. vii, 244 p. ISBN 0-312-05523-4.

A handy paperback full of direct advice about social customs, business practices and family life, for the foreign visitor. The format of endless bulleted lists of "do's" and "don'ts" becomes tedious, but it is meant for quick reference. An introductory section covers customs and manners generally, plus basic information on Islam, followed by chapters on individual countries and regions. Egypt, Algeria, Morocco and Tunisia are included (but not Libya or Sudan). The advice is of a practical, common-sense nature, concentrating on clothing, using the telephone, exchanging gifts, etc.

1122. Joffé, George. **North Africa: Nation, State and Region.** London and New York: Routledge, 1993. xvii, 304 p. *School of Oriental and African Studies, Contemporary Politics and Culture in the Middle East.* ISBN 0-415-09162-4.

Prepared for a conference held under the auspices of the Centre for Near and Middle Eastern Studies at SOAS, this collection of scholarly essays serves as a source of sharply-focused information and comment on the region's past and present. The pre-colonial and colonial eras (French, British and Spanish), the independence of Algeria, Morocco, Tunisia and Libya, and the Maghreb region today are under discussion. Each essay provides a brief bibliography, and the index is carefully subdivided by topic.

1123. Lawless, Richard I. and Allan Findlay. **North Africa: Contemporary Politics and Economic Development.** London; New York: Croom Helm; St. Martin's Press, 1984. xv, 282 p. ISBN 0-312-57812-1.

This essay collection is "a reader on the politics and economies of the four countries of Northwest Africa—Algeria, Morocco, Tunisia and Libya—for the decade of the 1970s" (Preface). There are two chapters on each nation, one concentrating primarily on political parties and ideologies, the other on economic trends. The volume includes 50 tables of economic data and five maps of reference value. Each essay has its own bibliographical notes, and there is a simple but useful index.

1124. Miller, E. Willard and Ruby M. Miller. **The Third World—North Africa: a Bibliography.** Monticello, IL: Vance Bibliographies, 1990. 32 p. *Public Administration Series;* P-2971. ISBN 0-7920-0681-X; ISSN 0193-970X.

This newer work by the Millers covers Algeria, Tunisia, Libya and Morocco, stressing political, economic and social concerns, particularly foreign relations.

1125. Pazzanita, Anthony G. **The Maghreb.** Santa Barbara, CA: Clio Press, 1998. xxxiv, 328 p. *World Bibliographical Series;* vol. 208. ISBN 1-85109-310-9.

A regional approach within the Clio bibliographical series, covering books and articles, monographs and some reference materials (but not electronic sources). The volume seems to include a number of sources that are neither classical nor current, published 1950-1980. The work is organized thematically and is easy to browse; very well-written, informative annotations are a pleasure to read. A helpful introduction offers access to the documents of the Arab Maghreb Union. Distinguishing materials on specific countries would be facilitated by a much more detailed subject index. Author and title indexes are provided.

1126. Rogerson, Barnaby. **A Traveler's History of North Africa: Morocco, Tunisia, Libya, Algeria.** New York: Interlink Books, 1998. xiii, 393 p. ISBN 1-56656-252-X.

Not a typical guidebook, this work is a well-organized and convenient history of the Maghreb from prehistoric times. Carthage, the Punic Wars, Roman North Africa, Christian North Africa, the Arab conquests, the Fatimids, Almoravids,

Almohads and medieval dynasties, the Barbary pirates, the Ottoman age, European colonialism and the modern era are covered in readable chapters with clear subheadings. Nine historical maps are included, and many small black-and-white illustrations. There is a helpful index.

1127. Ronart, Stephan and Nandy Ronart. **Concise Encyclopaedia of Arabic Civilization: the Arab West.** New York: Praeger, 1966. vii, 410 p.

Though somewhat dated, this basic reference is still consulted thanks to the many densely-written, information-packed entries in its convenient format. Cross-references from abbreviations and alternative spellings help to locate material, but there is no index.

This work covers only the Maghreb proper: Morocco, Algeria, Tunisia and Libya. A companion volume, *The Arab East* (1959), includes Egypt. According to the Preface of the 1959 volume, *The Arab West* was to have included Sudan, but it seems this plan was abandoned.

1128. Shinar, Pessah. **Islam Maghrébin Contemporain: Bibliographie Annotée.** Paris: Éditions du Centre National de la Recherche Scientifique, 1983. xxi, 506 p. *Recherche sur les Sociétés Méditerranéennes.* ISBN 2-222-02703-9.

A meticulously organized and annotated compilation of scholarly works on Morocco, Algeria, Tunisia and Libya, published from 1830 to 1978. The entries are grouped by type of literature, by country, and by theme, in three related parts, then subdivided further within each section. "Islam" is construed rather broadly here to include folklore and ethnography, law and political resistance, but not fine art or architecture.

Five very careful indexes are provided: authors, subjects, names of individuals as subjects, "noms de lieux," and vocabulary terms from the Arabic or Berber languages. In addition, the "Table des Matières" allows browsing of the book's entire contents.

Journals

1129. **Hespéris Tamuda.** Annual; 1960- . Rabat: Université Mohammed V. ISSN 0018-1005.

Formed by the merger of the original *Hespéris*, published in Paris (1921-1959) and *Tamuda*.

Scholarly articles in Arabic, French and English devoted to the culture and society of the Maghreb appear in this journal. For Morocco in particular, this journal is an important source. Signed book reviews up to ten pages long are featured.

Databases and Websites

1130. Afrique Francophone. **www.lehman.cuny.edu/depts/langlit/french/afrique. html**
   Many links; includes a section on the Maghreb.

1131. American Institute for Maghreb Studies. University of Wisconsin-Milwaukee Center for International Studies . **bertie.la.utexas.edu/research/mena/ aims/**

1132. **Institut de Recherches et d'Études sur le Monde Arabe et Musulman** (IREMAM) in Aix-en-Provence.
   A collection of scanned books, periodicals and unpublished literature covering northern Africa, maintained as ARABASE; access provided through reference service. Material relates to Mauritania, Morocco, Algeria, Libya and Tunisia.

1133. Le Maghreb. Des Droits de l'Homme. **www.mygale.org/~maghreb/**
   "Ce site a pour but d'offrir une tribune à des associations démocratiques Maghrébines et Euro-Maghrébines, d'informer sur les violations des droits de la personne humaine dans les pays du Maghreb et de participer à l'avènement d'E-tats de droit et d'une véritable citoyenneté dans ces pays. " Morocco, Algeria and Tunisia. In French.

1134. Maghrebi Studies Group at Binghamton University. An Introduction to the Francophone Literature of the Maghreb. **maghreb.net/writers/**
   Contains many links to other sites concerned with the culture (especially literature) of the Maghreb.

1135. MaghrebNet. **www.maghreb.net/index.html**
   Searchable website with news, arts and culture information, especially about Morocco.

1136. Le Monde Diplomatique. Maghreb. **www.monde-diplomatique.fr/index/ pays/maghreb.html**
   Archived articles.

Algeria

Reference Sources

1137. **Algeria, a Country Study.** Fifth edition. Edited by Helen Chapin Metz. Federal Research Division, Library of Congress. Washington: Department of the Army, 1994. xxxvii, 342 p. *Area Handbook Series.* ISBN 0-8444-0831-X; ISSN 1057-5294; SuDocs no. D101.22: 550-44/994.

Also available online at **lcweb2.loc.gov/frd/cs/cshome.html**

Each book in this series deals with "a particular foreign country, describing and analyzing its ... systems and institutions, and examining the interrelationships of those systems and the ways they are shaped by cultural factors " (Foreword). The books use a similar five-part structure: historical setting, the society and its environment (sociology, anthropology, geography), the economy, government and politics, and national security. Areas studies specialists prepare each of these five parts, rather like signed encyclopedia articles. The volumes include a capsule "Country Profile," some black-and-white photos, maps and figures, several useful tables of population, trade and other data (in an appendix), a bibliography, glossary of terms and an extensive, well-organized index. The tables often provide data that would be difficult to obtain from any other source: e.g., a country's exact or estimated supply of major aircraft, air defense weapons, naval vessels, field artillery and armored vehicles.

1138. **Algeria Post Report.** Revised April 1984. Washington: Department of State Publication 9209, Foreign Service Series 256. 16 p.; some maps and photos. SuDocs S1.127:Al3/984.

Department of State "Post Reports" are pamphlets containing basic information thought to be useful for U.S. government employees and their families being sent to a new location. Each report includes: a brief description of the "host country" — its climate, population, transport, tourist attractions, health services, etc.; specific information on the American Embassy and any consulates, housing, food and clothing, recreation opportunities, education for dependents; basic travel data on customs duties, currency, import restrictions, local holidays. Some issues provide a handy, clear and detailed street map of the area of the capital city surrounding the American Embassy (often hard to find in any other source).

1139. **Les Archives de la Révolution Algérienne.** Rassemblées et commentées par Mohammed Harbi. Paris: Les Éditions Jeune Afrique, 1981. 583 p. ISBN 2-85258-232-5.

A well-organized scholarly edition of materials representing the history of the Algerian revolution. The editor has grouped the verbatim documents basically in order of their dates, with an attempt to define stages in the revolution's development.

An introductory paragraph and source annotation is often provided, and many documents have explanatory footnotes. Three appendices very suitable for reference are included: a chronological table of the names of important government ministers, governors and other office-holders, the composition of FLN leadership, and a tabular chronology of events. There is also a general index.

1140. **Bibliographie de l'Algérie: Periodiques [et] Livres.** Ministère de la Culture et du Tourisme. Alger: Bibliothèque Nationale, 1988-1990. Semiannual.

A topically-organized record of materials received by the Bibliothèque Nationale in the previous "semestre" or half-year. In French and Arabic. Citations include a large number of official publications, documents and reports, along with some scholarly and literary materials.

1141. **Country Profile: Algeria.** Annual; 1986- . London: Economist Intelligence Unit.

This annual supplement to the quarterly EIU *Country Reports* aims to provide more extensive background reading and statistical tables. Each volume serves as a useful reference source.

1142. **Des Chemins et des Hommes: la France en Algérie 1830-1962.** Hélette: Jean Curutchet (Éditions Harriet), 1995. 267 p. ISBN 2-904-348-506.

This interesting reference is a biographical dictionary of the French in Algeria, and a bit more. Alphabetized short entries about individuals (usually one paragraph in length) provide a thumbnail sketch of the person's life, a list of works if he or she has published books, and a bibliography of further information about the person. Sometimes a black-and-white photo is included. Living people appear in the volume, often scholars of North African studies, editors of journals, artists and so on.

One- or two-page articles are interspersed throughout the volume, offering a glimpse of the history of aviation or railways, sports, health care or painting in Algeria. Appendices provide a chronology, a list of colonial administrators, a subdivided bibliography (with current and historical sources) and two not-very-successful maps.

1143. **Imperial Legacy: the Ottoman Imprint on the Balkans and the Modern Middle East.** Edited by L. Carl Brown. New York: Columbia University Press, 1996. xvi, 337 p. ISBN 0-231-10304-2.

Not a reference work, this scholarly interpretation of the historical meaning of Ottoman rule in the modern world nevertheless contains several useful features. In particular, there is a country-by-country table of the dates and duration of Ottoman rule, and a brief summary of each country's conquest and loss by the Ottomans (simplified to account for changes in boundaries over time). There is also a fully-annotated select bibliography (pp. 307-313) and a superior index.

1144. **La Révolution Algérienne par les Textes.** Documents du FLN présentées par André Mandouze. Paris: François Maspero, 1961. 171 p.

A small paperback full of intriguing quotes and excerpts from FLN documents, statements, press conferences, interviews and communiques published in the mass media. The volume has the virtue of immediacy, as these stories were headline news around the time of publication. There is a detailed table of contents (no index), but no editorial remarks at all: the quotes are simply gathered under topical headings by the compiler. This reference could be suitable for stimulating the interest of high school students or undergraduates.

1145. Bouayed, Mahmoud et al. **L'Algérie a Veille de la Guerre de Libération, 1919-1954.** Alger: Bibliothèque Nationale d'Algérie, 1991. 453 p.

A bibliography grouped under broad topical headings, covering a variety of materials in European languages. Entries are not annotated. There is an index of authors' names, one of institutions or collective authors (including government agencies), one of newspapers and journals cited, and one of names referred to in the title of a work (e.g., *L'Expiation: de l'Algérie de Papa à l'Algérie de Ben Bella* by Pierre Laffont).

1146. Bourdrel, Philippe. **La Dernière Chance de l'Algérie Française: du Gouvernement Socialiste au Retour de DeGaulle, 1956-1958.** Paris: Éditions Albin Michel, 1996. 350 p. ISBN 2-226-08823-7.

A scholarly monograph with a number of special features well suited to reference work. About one third of the volume is devoted to documents and appendices spelling out French military policy and procedure in dealing with Algeria, some public decrees, official correspondence and interrogation reports, and some statistics.

Bibliographical references cite current sources. A detailed chronology of events (1954-1962) is provided, as well as a serviceable names index. In addition, there are two unusual monochrome historical maps clearly showing physical and political/administrative features in detail.

1147. Collot, Claude and Jean-Robert Henry. **Le Mouvement National Algérien: Textes 1912-1954.** Paris: Éditions l'Harmattan, [1978]. 347 p. ISBN 2-858-2-064-7.

This text collection concentrates on documenting the development of the French-Algerian conflict up to the revolution. The materials are organized chronologically, with editorial comments and source notes. A table of contents lists the materials included, but there is no index.

1148. Golvin, Lucien. **Palais et Demeures d'Alger à la Période Ottomane.** Aix-en-Provence: ÉDISUD, 1988. 141 p. ISBN 2-85744-307-2.

Many floor plans, detail drawings and black-and-white photos illustrate the text of this volume. In addition, there are 16 pages of large color plates. A one-page bibliography is provided, but no index.

1149. La Hogue, Jeanine de. **Mémoire Écrite de l'Algérie depuis 1950: les Auteurs et leurs Oeuvres.** Paris: Éditions Maisonneuve et Larose, 1992. 231 p. ISBN 2-7068-1056-4.

A brief biographical sketch and a publishing history for each of these "Pieds-Noirs" makes this volume a useful ready reference. Alphabetized entries provide the date and place of publication for each literary work.

1150. Lawless, Richard I. **Algeria.** Santa Barbara, CA: ABC-Clio Press, 1995. lxxv, 309 p. *World Bibliographical Series;* v. 19. ISBN 1-85109-130-0.

The World Bibliographical Series being produced by Clio provides access for the English-speaking reader to a variety of materials: books and monographs, journals, bibliographies and reference works, theses and dissertations, conference proceedings, and sometimes more specialized information (e.g., manuscript catalogs). Fully-annotated entries (some volumes are annotated better than others) cover history, geography, economics and politics, culture, social customs and religion. Attention is paid to language, literature and the arts as well. An introductory essay and map are provided, and an index of authors, titles and subjects. Sometimes other helps (a glossary or chronology, for example) may be included. Each volume covers one individual country, but in some cases closely-related content overlaps: Somalia and Djibouti, Ethiopia and Eritrea, and so on.

1151. Lawless, Richard I. **Algerian Bibliography: English Language Publications 1830-1973.** In association with the Centre for Middle Eastern and Islamic Studies of the University of Durham. London and New York: Bowker, 1976. xvi, 117 p. ISBN 0-85935-047-9.

Lawless' interesting introduction serves as a bibliographical essay commenting on the challenges of documentation of Algerian life during the period covered by this retrospective bibliography. More than 1400 entries (books and periodical articles) are organized topically. The materials range from works in serious scholarly journals to more popular accounts of travel and exploration: e.g., The Honourable Colonel C.S. Vereker's *Scenes in the Sunny South, Including the Atlas Mountains and the Oases of the Sahara in Algeria* (1871). An author index is provided, but there is no titles index.

1152. Maynadies, Michel. **Bibliographie Algérienne: Répertoire des Sources Documentaires Relatives a l'Algérie.** Alger: Office des Publications Universitaires, 1989. 337 p.

The citations in this collection of bibliographic sources are organized according to a complex topical scheme worked out in the *Table des Matières.* Most of the entries have at least a very brief annotation, and some provide a helpful summary or contents note. The criteria for selection are not immediately clear: only 16 citations are offered under religion, ranging from 1885 to 1983, and several are devoted to sectarian groups, or do not apply to Algeria at all (i.e., Zoghby, *Islam in Sub-Saharan Africa*). There are author and title indexes.

1153. Naylor, Phillip Chiviges and Alf Andrew Heggoy. **Historical Dictionary of Algeria.** Second edition. Metuchen, NJ: Scarecrow Press, 1994. xxxix, 443 p. *African Historical Dictionaries;* no. 66. ISBN 0-8108-2748-4.

The first edition of this work, by A.A. Heggoy, has been substantially expanded and updated by Phillip Naylor. In addition to the body of dictionary entries, it offers a number of special reference helps. These include: nine maps (some poorly reproduced); an introductory essay; lists of French colonial administrators, Algerian revolutionary leaders, and the staff of independence-era governments; an annotated list of Algerian newspapers and journals; some tables of economic data. A classified bibliography of sources in English and French is provided. There is no index.

1154. Ruhe, Ernstpeter. **Algerien-Bibliographie: Deutschland, Österreich, Schweiz, 1962-1994.** 2. erweiterte Auflage. Wiesbaden: Harrassowitz, 1995. 283 p. ISBN 3-447-03737-7.

A topically-organized bibliography, especially helpful for sources (mostly monographs and scholarly articles) in German. Even works originally produced in another language are listed here in German translation. Topics generally missing from area studies bibliographies are included here, such as medicine (including psychiatry) and travel literature. The entries are not annotated. There is an author index.

1155. Stora, Benjamin. **Dictionnaire Biographique de Militants Nationalistes Algériens, 1926-1954.** Paris: Éditions l'Harmattan, 1985. 404 p. ISBN 2-8502-543-3 [sic].

This useful reference provides biographical sketches (from a few sentences in length to about one page) of more than 600 important opposition figures in the years leading up to the armed revolution against French rule in 1954. Each entry includes source notes—usually from articles in periodicals, occasionally from other reference sources—to which the reader can turn for further information. Introductory material provides context and explains the organization of the volume, with a helpful schematic on p. 20.

Other helps include a table of pseudonyms adopted by revolutionary leaders, and an index of individuals mentioned who do not have their own separate entry headings.

Journals/Databases

1156. **Country Report: Algeria.** Quarterly; 1986- . London: Economist Intelligence Unit.

Available online through DIALOG, LEXIS/NEXIS, FT Profile and M.A.I.D./Profound; on CD-ROM from Knight-Ridder and Silver Platter; on microfilm from World Microfilms Publications.

Concise information on current political and economic conditions in particular countries, with forecasts of up to two years. All of the countries of northern Africa are covered (except Western Sahara). Profile data and brief executive summaries of current conditions are included.

The EIU annual *Country Profiles* offer more extensive background reading and statistical tables, to summarize and supplement the quarterly reports.

Websites

1157. Algeria Watch International (human rights organization). **members.tripod. com/~AlgeriaWatch/**
Detailed and current information, with many links to news sources and other NGOs active in this area.

1158. FIS Parliamentary Delegation Abroad. Islamic Salvation Front (Front Islamique du Salut) Homepage. **www.fisalgeria.org/**

1159. International Crisis Group. CrisisWeb. **www.intl-crisis-group.org/**
Special coverage of Algeria.

1160. *Liberté:* Quotidien National d'Information. **www.liberte-algerie.com/**
Daily paper, online.

1161. *El Watan*: le Quotidien Indépendant. **www.elwatan.com/**
Daily paper, online.

1162. World Algeria Action Coalition. **www.waac.org/**
Many links to full-text news reports and documents; meant to provide "a balanced and politically non-biased portrayal of the political, social, and economic conditions in Algeria."

Egypt

Reference Sources

1163. **Country Profile: Egypt.** Annual; 1986- . London: Economist Intelligence Unit. ISBN ISSN 0269-5227.
This annual supplement to the quarterly EIU *Country Reports* aims to provide more extensive background reading and statistical tables. Each volume serves as a useful reference source.

1164. **Doing Business in Egypt.** Revised. Cairo: Price Waterhouse, 1995. 124 p. Pamphlet. *Information Guide Series.*
An occasional handbook "for the assistance of those interested in doing business in Egypt" (Foreword). Helpful current material is offered on foreign investment and the business environment, trade opportunities, investment incentives,

regulatory climate, banking and finance institutions, legal business entities, auditing, accounting and taxation, and labor relations and social insurance issues. Several appendices provide quick access to tax rates and treaties, a "checklist" of concerns to be considered when planning investment, and local contact data for sources of business information.

1165. **Egypt, a Country Study.** Fifth edition. Edited by Helen Chapin Metz. Federal Research Division, Library of Congress. Washington: Department of the Army, 1991. xxxv, 428 p. *Area Handbook Series;* 1. ISBN 0-8444-0729-1; ISSN 1057-5294; SuDocs no. D101.22: 550-43/991.

Also available online at **lcweb2.loc.gov/frd/cs/cshome.html**

Each book in this series deals with "a particular foreign country, describing and analyzing its ... systems and institutions, and examining the interrelationships of those systems and the ways they are shaped by cultural factors " (Foreword). The books use a similar five-part structure: historical setting, the society and its environment (sociology, anthropology, geography), the economy, government and politics, and national security. Areas studies specialists prepare each of these five parts, rather like signed encyclopedia articles. The volumes include a capsule "Country Profile," some black-and-white photos, maps and figures, several useful tables of population, trade and other data (in an appendix), a bibliography, glossary of terms and an extensive, well-organized index. The tables often provide data that would be difficult to obtain from any other source: e.g., a country's exact or estimated supply of major aircraft, air defense weapons, naval vessels, field artillery and armored vehicles.

1166. **Egypt Post Report.** Revised April 1990. Washington: Department of State Publication 9293, Publishing Services Division. 28 p.; maps and photos. SuDocs S1.127:Eg9/990.

Department of State "Post Reports" are pamphlets containing basic information thought to be useful for U.S. government employees and their families being sent to a new location. Each report includes: a brief description of the "host country"—its climate, population, transport, tourist attractions, health services, etc.; specific information on the American Embassy and any consulates, housing, food and clothing, recreation opportunities, education for dependents; basic travel data on customs duties, currency, import restrictions, local holidays. Some issues provide a handy, clear and detailed street map of the area of the capital city surrounding the American Embassy (often hard to find in any other source).

1167. **Egyptian Women in Social Development: a Resource Guide.** Cairo: American University in Cairo Press, 1988. xv, 346 p. ISBN 977-424-184-3.

Prepared by the Network of Egyptian Professional Women, this reference is actually a directory of highly skilled and experienced academics and educators, social service providers, policy-makers and advocates, media figures and journalists, volunteer coordinators and other women involved in development work in Egypt. Each personal entry provides contact information, background and training, positions held, development-related work, languages or international activities and publications. The volume includes two indexes, for names and for type of development work.

1168. **Statistical Year Book: Arab Republic of Egypt, 1952-1993.** Cairo: Central Agency for Public Mobilization and Statistics, 1964. 353 p.

An English-language publication that packages statistical data, collected and reported by government agencies, in the form of tables and graphs. Detailed demographic information, production figures for agriculture and industry, transport and communications services, health and social affairs, housing, education, mass media, tourism, climate and various macro-economic indicators are all included.

A full table of contents is provided (there is no index). Some of the tables contain comparative figures dating back to the 1952 revolution; more often, they go back to about 1988. Assuming accuracy in reporting, this is useful data in a convenient form.

1169. Creswell, K. A. C. (Keppel Archibald Cameron). **A Bibliography of the Muslim Architecture of Egypt.** Cairo: Imprimerie de l'Institut Français d'Archéologie Orientale, 1955. 64 p. *Art Islamique;* tome III.

An excerpt from Creswell's huge bibliography, organized by author.

1170. Creswell, K. A. C. (Keppel Archibald Cameron). **The Muslim Architecture of Egypt.** Reprint of 1952 edition. New York: Hacker Art Books, 1978. 2 v. ISBN 0-87817-175-4 (Vol. 1-2).

Continuing the research documented in *Early Muslim Architecture*, Creswell concentrates in these two volumes on the Islamic monuments of Egypt, A.D. 939-1326. Scale drawings and plans, photographs and exact descriptions record the structures and their decoration, some of which has disappeared since these books were first published. Vol. 2 provides an index, and both volumes contain over 100 pages of plates, often close-up photos of unique architectural detail.

1171. Goldschmidt, Arthur. **Historical Dictionary of Egypt.** Metuchen, NJ: Scarecrow, 1994. xix, 369 p. *African Historical Dictionaries;* no. 67. ISBN 0-8108-2949-5.

Unlike Joan Wucher King's 1984 work, which included medieval Egypt (since the Muslim conquest), this volume takes 1760 as its starting point and concentrates on the modern era and contemporary events. There is a straightforward introductory essay, concise and readable alphabetized entries with cross-references, a very simple chronology, two reasonably helpful maps, and two tables offering equivalents for traditional weights and measures, and military ranks. The useful bibliography is organized topically and subdivided, but there is no author or title index.

1172. Huxley, Frederick C. **Development in Egypt: Bibliography and Informative Abstracts of Selected Research, 1970-82.** Berkeley, CA: Development Research Services, 1983. iv, 111 p.

The title seems to indicate that this is an annotated bibliography, but in fact, there is a separate section of materials for which detailed abstracts are provided (considered to be the most significant works). This compilation may be valuable for those doing research on its time period, since these sources are unlikely to be included in electronic indexes. Similar guides were prepared for development issues in Tunisia and Morocco (also Jordan, Yemen).

1173. Kamil, Jill. **Coptic Egypt: History and Guide.** Cairo: American University in Cairo Press, 1987. xiii, 149 p. ISBN 977-424-104-5.

Kamil manages to convey a great deal of information in this small paperback: a brief narrative history of early Egyptian Christianity, an account of the Coptic Church today, and detailed descriptions of the primary Coptic antiquities, churches and monasteries, not only in Cairo, but also at Wadi Natrun, the Red Sea and Upper Egypt. Small maps and black-and-white photos and several small floor plans are provided. There is a bibliography and a useful index.

1174. King, Joan Wucher. **Historical Dictionary of Egypt.** Metuchen, NJ: Scarecrow Press, 1984. xiii, 719 p. *African Historical Dictionaries;* no. 36. ISBN 0-8108-1670-9.

More than the term "dictionary" would imply, this work is a rich source of information, both for ready reference and careful study. It concentrates on Egypt since the Muslim conquest (i.e., not the Pharaonic, Roman or Byzantine eras), with the greatest attention to the present and recent past. A substantial introductory essay provides an overall narrative history and a description of general issues; a chronology of events from the early Roman era (30 BC) to the assassination of Anwar Sadat (1981) is provided. Articles up to 5-6 pages in length explain major topics (agriculture, role of the military, etc.). There is an unusually diverse and interesting bibliography, but no index. Cross-references link many possible forms of names to the actual terms used.

1175. Makar, Ragai N. **Egypt.** Santa Barbara, CA: ABC-Clio Press, 1988. xxxi, 306 p. *World Bibliographical Series;* v. 86. ISBN 1-85109-039-8.

The World Bibliographical Series being produced by Clio provides access for the English-speaking reader to a variety of materials: books and monographs, journals, bibliographies and reference works, theses and dissertations, conference proceedings, and sometimes more specialized information (e.g., manuscript catalogs). Fully-annotated entries (some volumes are annotated better than others) cover history, geography, economics and politics, culture, social customs and religion. Attention is paid to language, literature and the arts as well. An introductory essay and map are provided, and an index of authors, titles and subjects. Sometimes other helps (a glossary or chronology, for example) may be included. Each volume covers one individual country, but in some cases closely-related content overlaps: Somalia and Djibouti, Ethiopia and Eritrea, and so on.

1176. Mikdadi, Faysal. **Gamal Abdel Nasser: a Bibliography.** New York: Greenwood, 1991. ix, 148 p. *Bibliographies of World Leaders;* no. 5. ISBN 0-313-28119-X.

The articles and books compiled here are meant to serve as a comprehensive collection of literature on the life and work of one of the twentieth century's most interesting political leaders. Mikdadi provides a "summary biography" of Nasser; this narrative offers an introduction to the major issues of his lifetime as well. The book is unevenly annotated, but rarely provides more than a terse sentence for each entry. There is a serials list, an author index, and a basic chronology and subject index. Placed in the hands of an undergraduate, this book might be a helpful starting point for research.

1177. Miller, E. Willard and Ruby M. Miller. **The Third World—Egypt: a Bibliography.** Monticello, IL: Vance Bibliographies, 1990. 26 p. *Public Administration Series;* P-2972. ISBN 0-7920-0682-8; ISSN 0193-970X.

The Vance bibliographies on public administration are composed of topically arranged citations—up to about 1000 in each issue—of books and articles, government bulletins and other publications. The entries are sometimes briefly annotated. This issue lists 266 books and articles documenting political and economic conditions in Egypt in the 1980s (and social issues to a lesser extent).

1178. Ronart, Stephan and Nandy Ronart. **Concise Encyclopaedia of Arabic Civilization: the Arab East.** Amsterdam: Djambatan, 1959. ix, 589 p.

Though somewhat dated, this basic reference is still consulted thanks to the many densely-written, information-packed entries in its convenient format. Cross-references from abbreviations and alternative spellings help to locate material, but there is no index.

This work includes Egypt as part of its geographical area. A companion volume, *The Arab West* (1966), focuses on the Maghreb.

1179. Watterson, Barbara. **Coptic Egypt.** Edinburgh: Scottish Academic Press, 1988. ix, 187 p. ISBN 0-7073-0556-X.

A comprehensive introductory history of the Copts in Egypt from pre-Christian Greco-Roman times till the present, in one small and readable volume. A simple structure makes it easy to find certain material (on monasticism, language, architecture, etc.), and there is also a basic index. Two clear maps, especially one showing Coptic sites of settlement and pilgrimage, are useful. A two-page bibliography of fundamental sources is included.

Journals/Databases

1180. **Country Report: Egypt.** Quarterly; 1986- . London: Economist Intelligence Unit.

Available online through DIALOG, LEXIS/NEXIS, FT Profile and M.A.I.D./Profound; on CD-ROM from Knight-Ridder and Silver Platter; on microfilm from World Microfilms Publications.

Concise information on current political and economic conditions in particular countries, with forecasts of up to two years. All of the countries of northern Africa are covered (except Western Sahara). Profile data and brief executive summaries of current conditions are included.

The EIU annual *Country Profiles* offer more extensive background reading and statistical tables, to summarize and supplement the quarterly reports.

Pharaonic Egypt: History and Archaeology

Ancient Egyptian history and civilization are the subject here (not just the New Kingdom). For other sources containing information on Egyptian archaeology, see also Part Two, "History and Antiquities," and the historical maps in "Maps and Atlases."

1181. **Civilizations of the Ancient Near East.** Edited by Jack M. Sasson. New York: Macmillan Library Reference, 1995. 4 v. ISBN 0-684-19279-9.

An unusual collection of signed scholarly articles: not entries in alphabetical order encyclopedia-style, but lengthy articles organized thematically under broad headings like "The Environment" or "Social Institutions." This arrangement may not be the most efficient, but fortunately Vol. 4 contains a very extensive and detailed index to help locate specific material.

The articles themselves are substantial, quite fascinating, and accompanied by valuable bibliographical references. They are often illustrated by black-and-white photos, plans and technical drawings of structures and artifacts. Egypt and Nubia are the only areas on the African continent covered by this work, but the material here on Pharaonic government, culture and society is richly detailed and includes analysis and comment by such authorities as John Baines. Not a ready reference perhaps, but a work that rewards careful study.

1182. **Egypt in Africa.** Edited by Theodore Celenko. Indianapolis: Indianapolis Museum of Art (Indiana University Press), 1996. 134 p. ISBN 0-253-33269-9.

Emerging from an effort by the Indianapolis Museum of Art, this volume seeks to demonstrate, depict and analyze the close cultural ties between ancient Egypt and the continent of Africa. Rejecting the historical paradigm that views Egypt as the precursor to Greece and Rome—and therefore a sort of honorary European entity—these scholars present evidence that Egyptian art, language, faith, social customs and population origins are consistent with Saharan and sub-Saharan societies.

Each essay includes bibliographical references and numerous illustrations (both black-and-white and color), but there is no index.

1183. Baines, John and Jaromír Málek. **Atlas of Ancient Egypt.** Oxford: Phaidon Press, 1984. 240 p. ISBN ISBN 0-7148-1958-1.

A beautiful and informative large-format reference offering much more than a traditional atlas. The emphasis is on Egyptian civilization, not geography; the volume is organized by topic, except for Part Two, "A Journey Down the

Nile," which is composed of descriptive entries for locations and individual ar-chaeological sites.

A serious text prepared by qualified scholars is illustrated with maps, plans, diagrams, drawings, black-and-white and color photos. Unusual pictures show-ing the workmanship of Egyptian boats, or a cross-section of the structure of Dendara temple, or the design of typical tomb stelae, are included. The photos show actual examples of Egyptian art, or technically-accurate epigraphy and drafting work by competent illustrators.

The volume also includes a list of museums around the world with out-standing Egyptian.collections, a glossary, a subdivided bibliography, a gazetteer and an index, and a comparative chronology or timeline showing other ancient civilizations (Nubia, Syria, Mesopotamia, Anatolia, the Aegean). The only drawback to this volume is its dense print: the maps, bibliography and index are printed in such tiny fonts that they are hard to use, and may discourage some readers.

1184. Bunson, Margaret. **Encyclopedia of Ancient Egypt.** New York: Facts on File, 1991. xv, 291 p. ISBN 0-8160-2093-0.

A ready reference—a dictionary at best, certainly not an encyclope-dia—composed of brief, very simple alphabetized entries, offering a basic defi-nition or identification but not much else. Entries do not include bibliographical references or material from primary sources. Statements are often oversimpli-fied, as if intended for young readers, and assertions are made (e.g., about Ak-henaten and the significance of the Amarna period) without any documentation or supporting evidence.

Most disappointing, however, are this volume's poor production values. There are no photographs, no color pictures, crude maps, no site or floor plans. Coverage of architecture is negligible. The black and white illustrations are not accurate reproductions of actual Egyptian art, but instead, simple line drawings and sketches based upon well-known artifacts but greatly inferior in execution (cf. the drawing of three musicians on p. 179). Famous figures are reduced to paper-doll quality, and strange anomalies abound, like a drawing of Queen Hat-shepsut with a modern European face (p. 109). The effect is like reading Shake-speare's dramas in prose paraphrase instead of the original.

It is amazing that any reference relating to a civilization of unsurpassed ar-tistic genius could be so unattractive. When a reference like Shaw and Nicholson is available, it is not clear why any collection would settle for Bunson's work.

Some useful features are included: a basic chronology (but without a complete list of the Pharaohs' names and dates) and an index that groups together similar terms: e.g., the names of gods and goddesses, or the various temples or pyramids.

1185. David, Rosalie (Ann Rosalie). **Discovering Ancient Egypt.** New York: Facts on File, 1993. 192 p. ISBN 0-8160-3105-3.

The simplicity of this introductory history's organizational plan makes it fairly easy to adapt this book to reference work. The first chapter tells the stories of the great travellers, adventurers, writers, archaeologists and philologists, from ancient times up to the 1960s, who explored and documented—and in some cases, plundered—the antiquities of Egypt. Chapter Two describes the sites themselves and relates the circumstances of their discovery. The third chapter "attempts to show how evidence derived from the excavations has helped Egyptologists to reconstruct the main developments and events of the civilization, from predynastic times to the Graeco-Roman Period" (p. 9).

The volume includes a number of simple monochrome maps and a restrained selection of photos (some in color). A useful index is provided. The chronological table, however, is far too basic, and should include the names and dates of the various Pharaohs at least.

1186. David, Rosalie (Ann Rosalie). **Handbook to Life in Ancient Egypt.** New York: Facts on File, 1998. xvi, 382 p. ISBN 0-8160-3312-9.

A quick-reference source suitable for students, providing a convenient window on a vast expanse of historical and cultural information. The table of contents, careful index and generous use of titles and sectional subheadings guide the reader. Clear, simple maps, a gazetteer and 80 black-and-white photos or reproductions of Egyptian artwork are provided. The chronological table in an appendix is inadequate; a much better table is found in Chapter One, "Historical Background."

1187. David, Rosalie (Ann Rosalie) and Anthony E. David. **A Biographical Dictionary of Ancient Egypt.** London: Seaby, 1992. xiii, 179 p. ISBN 1-85264-032-4.

This reference is composed of entries relating to persons in Pharaonic, Ptolemaic/Greco-Roman and Byzantine Egypt (3100 BC - 600 AD), including some foreign figures of importance in Egyptian history: e.g., Darius I of Persia, Augustus Caesar, Moses. Brief articles identify the individual and suggest his or her significance.

In addition, some articles define entities that are not persons, such as the Kingdom of Mitanni. Entries have a few bibliographical references—usually classic sources like Emery or Breasted—but for some reason these are not all brought together as a useful bibliography. There is an index of additional names (with cross-references) and a simple chronology.

1188. Freeman, Charles. **The Legacy of Ancient Egypt.** Abingdon; New York: Andromeda Oxford; Facts on File, 1997. 224 p. ISBN 0-8160-3656-X.

A big, beautiful, glossy "coffee table" book, filled with dramatic color photos. High print quality makes it possible to include several finely-composed color maps as well.

The table of contents sets forth the rather episodic structure of the book, and there is a helpful index; also, a basic glossary and chronology. An attractive section, "The Rediscovery of Egypt," tells the story of scholarly Egyptology, the adventurous age of treasure-hunting (especially the Tomb of Tutankhamun), and the effect of designs and themes inspired by Egypt on Western cinema, fine art, style and fashion, music, architecture and ornament.

1189. Kamil, Jill. **The Ancient Egyptians: Life in the Old Kingdom.** New and completely revised edition. Maps and illustrations by Elizabeth Rodenbeck. Cairo: American University in Cairo Press, 1996. ix, 196 p. ISBN 977-424-392-7.

A concise, readable introduction to Egypt's fascinating Old Kingdom or Age of the Pyramids, 2575-2145 BC, written on a basis of thorough research.

The author traces early Nile Valley settlement through the consolidation of Pharaonic power and the creation of the immense Saqqara and Giza monuments. There are also chapters on more typical daily life: travel, food and drink, clothing, family life, agriculture, shipbuilding, pottery and other crafts, trades, and entertainment, festivals, sports and folk traditions.

The text is illustrated with many small maps and drawings, and with two sections of color plates (landscape and objects). There is a simple bibliography, an index, and a helpful table of contents.

1190. Lepre, J. P. **The Egyptian Pyramids: a Comprehensive Illustrated Reference.** Jefferson, NC: McFarland, 1990. xvii, 341 p. ISBN 0-89950-461-2.

A comprehensive source on the Pyramids may be unattainable, but this reference does cover a lot of ground. Organized chronologically, it provides descriptive information, diagrams, cross-sections, site plans and black-and-white photos documenting the process of pyramid-building from the First Dynasty mastabas to the Middle Kingdom. Other basic reference helps are included: a chronology, hieroglyph lesson, bibliography, list of explorers and excavators, an index.

1191. Málek, Jaromír. **Egypt: Ancient Culture, Modern Land.** Norman, OK: University of Oklahoma Press, 1993. 192 p. *Cradles of Civilization.* ISBN 0-8061-2526-8.

A vividly-illustrated "coffee table" book, with many color maps and paintings as well as photos. Fact boxes feature some distinct aspects of Egyptology: the activities of Auguste Mariette, hieroglyphic writing, Egyptian battle formations, funerary rites, etc. Chapters on daily life by Janine Bourriau and Jac. J. Janssen are especially interesting, and a chapter on modern Egypt by Penelope C. Johnstone is better than those in most big, colorful books. An extensive chronological chart, useful topically-subdivided bibliography and a capable index are provided.

1192. Manley, Bill. **The Penguin Historical Atlas of Ancient Egypt.** London: Penguin Books, 1996. 144 p. ISBN 0-14-0-51331-0.

This soft-cover, small-format volume may not be an atlas in the same sense as Baines and Málek, but it is nevertheless packed with informative maps covering Egypt's history from prehistoric times to Alexander the Great. In addition to the wealth of colorful and detailed maps, there are tiny color photos or site plans on every page.

Quotations from incriptions, papyri and other primary sources head each section. The text is concise, but serious in tone and not oversimplified. It is divided into many focused units (listed in the Contents) that lend themselves well to reference work. In addition, there is a simple but helpful index.

The volume includes a complete list of Pharaohs and their dates, from Narmer through the Persians (very handy), and a coordinated color timeline meant to show the main events of Egypt's history over against contemporary developments in Nubia, Europe, the Near East and biblical lands. The bibliography directs the reader to seven sources of ancient texts as well as a selection of modern references and monographs.

1193. Martin, Geoffrey Thorndike. **A Bibliography of the Amarna Period and Its Aftermath: the Reigns of Akhenaten, Smenkhkare, Tutankhamun and Ay (c. 1350-1321 BC).** London; New York: Kegan Paul International, 1991. 136 p. (unpaginated). *Studies in Egyptology.* ISBN 0-7103-0413-7.

A compilation of more than 2000 sources (mostly scholarly articles, but some from news sources or the popular press) without any annotations, subject subdivisions or indexing of any kind. Indeed, it is not clear how the reader is expected to use this information, since access is provided only by author's name. One can find here a list of 18 publications by Howard Carter, for example, pertaining to this bibliography's time period. But one cannot recover all of the entries relating to Tutankhamun's tomb or Carter's excavation of it. The same material with far better reference helps would be a great deal more useful.

1194. Murnane, William J. **The Penguin Guide to Ancient Egypt.** Harmondsworth; New York: Penguin, 1983. 367 p. ISBN 0-1404-6326-7.

This handbook, by an expert epigrapher with the University of Chicago's Oriental Institute, is both an informative and readable background introduction to ancient Egypt and a site-by-site, room-by-room visitor's guide.

Many very clear small maps and floor plans direct the visitor to individual scenes of carved relief and painting, or important objects in antiquities museums. The text interprets the significance of the artifacts in Egyptian faith and daily life.

The guide covers the most popular tourist destinations in Cairo and Luxor, but also includes at least some information on less-visited sites in Alexandria and the Delta, Memphis, Abusir and Saqqara, Aswan and the antiquities of Coptic Egypt. Appendices provide a handy capsule history of Pharaonic times, a select bibliography, and two helpful indexes.

1195. Shaw, Ian and Paul Nicholson. **The Dictionary of Ancient Egypt.** New York: Harry N. Abrams, 1995. 328 p. ISBN 0-8109-3225-3.

A publication of the British Museum, this large and attractive volume is illustrated with photos (some black-and-white, some color) of antiquities on every page. The entries are not signed and are more concise than full encyclopedia-style articles, yet they include as many as 5-6 bibliographical references, cross-references and quite a bit of description and detail.

The entries offer some interpretation as well, and often contemporary quotes from primary sources (letters, funerary texts, official documents, etc.). Appendices include a complete chronology of rulers, 5500 BC - 395 AD, a list of European and American Egyptologists with dates, tomb numbers for each location in Thebes, and a helpful index.

This volume can serve as an information-rich resource for the high school, university or research library, and is effective as a ready-reference for beginning through advanced students.

1196. Silverman, David P. **Ancient Egypt.** New York: Oxford University Press, 1997. 256 p. ISBN 0-19-521270-3.

Another colorful, glossy "coffee table" introduction to Egyptian civilization. Color photos of artifacts, not very technical but quite artistic maps, time lines, and huge panoramic or aerial photos of scenery are included. The text offers an elegant account of many of the ideas and beliefs, attitudes and practices of this ancient people, rather than stressing physical description of the sites, structures or objects (though these are not neglected; cf. coverage of the Giza pyramid complex). A glossary, a subdivided bibliography and an index are provided.

1197. Weeks, Kent R. **An Historical Bibliography of Egyptian Prehistory.** Winona Lake, IN: Eisenbrauns, 1985. xxii, 138 p. ISBN 0-936770-11-2.

This publication of the American Research Center in Egypt was prepared by a prominent archaeologist and represents his own impressive research experience. The majority of the entries are articles from scholarly journals, and an effort was made to include especially "the obscure publications that ... are worth recalling to historians of Egyptology" (p. v). Weeks' introduction serves as a most informative bibliographical essay and a subject index as well; it deserves close attention.

1198. Wilkinson, Richard H. **Reading Egyptian Art: a Hieroglyphic Guide to Ancient Egyptian Painting and Sculpture.** London: Thames and Hudson, 1992. 224 p.

This interesting reference is meant to be a dictionary of hieroglyphic symbols and their use as motifs in statues and other artifacts.

Organizing the entries poses a challenge, as they cannot be alphabetized. Wilkinson has arranged the symbols in groups of related objects: human figures, parts of the body, mammals, birds, plants, buildings, ships, furniture, articles of clothing, etc., based upon the index or "sign list" in Alan Gardiner's *Egyptian Grammar* (1982 edition), reproduced in an appendix.

The book is generously illustrated with examples, showing the hieroglyph highlighted in red. A glossary, bibliography and simple index are included.

Modern Egypt: Travel and Description

1199. **Cairo.** Second edition. Edited by John Rodenbeck. Singapore; New York: APA Publications; Houghton Mifflin, 1996. 285 p. *Insight Guides.*

Another in the *Insight Guides* "Egypt Series," with stunning color photos and a well-chosen group of writers. This volume includes an appendix of practical information about shopping, restaurants, transport, etc., in the city.

1200. **Egypt.** Cairo: Lehnert & Landrock, 1981. 408 p. *Guide-Poche Univers.* ISBN 2-7131-0030-5.

An English translation of a pocket guide originally published in French: tiny, but containing a good deal of information, primarily descriptive rather than practical. Several small color maps and photos are included. There is a useful index.

1201. **Egypt.** Third edition. By Veronica Seton-Williams and Peter Stocks. London; New York: A&C Black; W.W. Norton, 1993. 753 p. *Blue Guides.* ISBN 0-7136-3590-8.

A detailed site-by-site handbook to the arts and archaeology of Egypt. Pharaonic antiquities as well as the Islamic monuments of Cairo are meticulously documented. Maps, floor plans and site plans are provided, and there is a section of simplified Cairo street maps. Galleries of the Egyptian Museum are cataloged right down to specific objects. A narrative history and related reference helps (chronology of all Pharaohs and kings, royal cartouches, etc.) are included, and there are two indexes. This book is not a source of practical travel advice.

1202. **Egypt.** Second edition. By Eva Ambros. Munich: Nelles Verlag, 1996. 254 p. *Nelles Guides.* ISBN 3-88618-107-3.

Basic descriptive information, with colorful photos and small maps. General travel guidelines are provided, but not detailed data on accommodations, dining, etc. The book is suited to the packaged-tour traveller. It is indexed.

1203. **Egypt.** Third edition. By Dan Richardson. London: Rough Guides, 1996. *Rough Guides.* ISBN 1-85828-188-1.

A practical handbook for getting to, staying in and seeing the sights of most of Egypt's tourist destinations. Many clear maps and street plans, fact boxes and subheadings direct the eye. Transport, accommodation and entertainment opportunities are covered; there is also a glossary, a helpful index and a remarkable annotated bibliography.

1204. **Egypt.** Third edition. By Robert Morkot. Chicago: Passport, 1997. 336 p. *Odyssey.* ISBN 962-217-298-9.

A conventional guidebook with a simple text, large postcard-style photos, many maps and plans, and a smattering of practical travel information. There are interesting boxes with literary excerpts (Flaubert, Mahfouz, E.M. Forster, etc.). A basic index is provided.

1205. **Egypt.** Fifth edition. Edited by John. Rodenbeck. Singapore; New York: APA Publications; Houghton Mifflin, 1998. 352 p. *Insight Guides* ISBN 0-39579-121-9.

Lavishly illustrated with color photos, this guidebook stresses the experience of visiting Egypt rather than practical travel information. The text is supplied by such knowledgeable writers as John Rodenbeck, Jill Kamil and Cassandra Vivian. Useful features include foldout maps of Egypt and of Cairo inside the covers, along with quick-reference tables of contents. Considerable historical and cultural information is included. There is a simple index.

1206. **Egypt: a Lonely Planet Travel Survival Kit.** Fourth edition. By Leanne Logan, et al. Hawthorn, Victoria: Lonely Planet, 1997. 504 p. ISBN 0-86442-395-0.

Clearly organized, basic travel and background information covering most of Egypt's attractions, with a large section on Cairo. Many small maps and plans, and several pages of color photos. The book is indexed.

1207. **The Nile.** Second edition. Edited by Andrew Eames. Singapore; New York: APA Publications; Houghton Mifflin, 1997. 333 p. *Insight Guides.*

This volume of the attractive and well-written *Insight Guides* "Egypt Series" moves along the lower Nile Valley, Upper Egypt, Nubia and, to some extent, the Nile beyond Egypt. Tourists on Nile cruises would find it interesting. History and description are stressed, with an appendix containing practical "travel tips."

1208. Parker, Richard B. and Robin Sabin. **Islamic Monuments in Cairo: a Practical Guide.** Third edition; revised and enlarged by Caroline Williams. Cairo: American University in Cairo Press, 1985. 334 p. ISBN 977-424-036-7.

An indispensable guide, not yet surpassed, for the visitor to medieval Islamic Cairo. The book is planned as a series of walking tours in which notable structures are viewed in sequence; thorough descriptions lead the visitor's eye to the most important features. A group of small but necessary street maps is attached at the end of the book. There are also a small glossary, a bibliography and a useful index. Unfortunately, the black-and-white photos are indifferently reproduced, but the book is meant for a reader who is viewing each site firsthand.

1209. Wayne, Scott. **Egypt and the Sudan: a Travel Survival Kit.** Berkeley, CA; South Yarra, Australia: Lonely Planet, 1987. 389 p. ISBN 0-86442-001-3.

Practical facts for the independent traveler form the basis of this guidebook. It concerns itself with transport, accommodation, restaurants, visas, and so on, with detailed information and directory data (for hospitals, post offices, etc.) Many small but clear and helpful street maps are included.

Advice on visiting monuments, museums and other attractions is offered, and there are some nice color postcard-style photos to get the reader motivated. For both Egypt and the Sudan, the writer provides a great deal of help for visiting outlying areas (distant oases, small towns, even places that require camping gear) not just the typical five-star-hotel destinations of most tour groups.

Websites

1210. *Al Ahram Weekly.* **www.ahram.org.eg/weekly**
Considered by many to be the newspaper of record for the Arab world, *Al Ahram* (Cairo) is now published in English on a weekly basis. Full text of articles and editorials, photos (in color) and political cartoons are posted on this website.

1211. American Research Center in Egypt (ARCE). **www.arce.org/home.html**
Center for scholarly research in archaeology, history and culture.

1212. American University In Cairo. **auc-inf.org/www/main.html**

1213. Arab Republic of Egypt. Social Fund for Development. **www.sfdegypt. org/**

1214. Arab Republic of Egypt, Ministry of Information. State Information Service. **www.sis.gov.eg/**
Friendly site, stressing culture and tourism.

1215. Cairo University. **www.cairo.eun.eg/**

1216. Christian Coptic Orthodox Church of Egypt. **cs-www.bu.edu/faculty/ best/pub/cn/Home.html**
Accessible information on this special topic.

1217. Coptic Museum in Cairo. **www.idsc.gov.eg/culture/cop_mus.htm**
Artifacts of ancient Egyptian Christianity.

1218. Coptic Network. **cs-www.bu.edu/faculty/best/pub/cn/Menu.html**
Liturgical and cultural resources and directory data; links to other Arab Christian materials.

1219. Egypt: Library Catalogues on the Web. **library.usask.ca/hywebcat/ countries/EG.html**
Includes seven academic, public and special libraries with accessible catalogs.

1220. Egyptian Cabinet Information and Decision Support Center (IDCS). Egypt's Information Highway. **www.idsc.gov.eg/**
Egypt's most important public-sector Internet site.

1221. Egyptian Gazette. **www.egy.com/**
Cairo English-language daily, online version. Select feature articles of cultural interest, from current and back issues.

1222. Egyptian Ministry of Tourism. Tour Egypt: Official Internet Site. **touregypt. net/**
Attractive and information-rich site.

1223. Egyptian Museum in Cairo. **www.idsc.gov.eg/culture/egy_mus.htm**
Unparalleled collection of Pharaonic Egyptian antiquities.

1224. Egyptian Organization for Human Rights. **www.eohr.org.eg/**

1225. KMT: a Modern Journal of Ancient Egypt. **www.egyptology.com/kmt/**
Description and sample articles; full access for subscribers only.

1226. Newton Institute, Cambridge University. Egyptology Resources. **www.newton.
cam.ac.uk/egypt/**
Important links page for sites of academic and cultural interest.

1227. University of Memphis. Institute of Egyptian Art and Archaeology.
www.memphis.edu/egypt/main.html

Libya

Reference Sources

1228. **Country Profile: Libya.** Annual; 1986- . London: Economist Intelligence Unit. ISSN 0269-6347.
This annual supplement to the quarterly EIU *Country Reports* aims to provide more extensive background reading and statistical tables. Each volume serves as a useful reference source.

1229. **Focus on Libya, Feb 1984-June 1989: a Resource Compendium.**
Washington: PEMCON Ltd., 1989. 215 p.
Though it may sound like a bibliography, this volume is actually a collection of five years' worth of monthly newsletters on Libya created by a firm known as Political, Economic and Military Consultants. These newsletters aim to describe Libya's resources, activities and strategic goals, for the sake of policymakers and business leaders responsible for "risk assessment," investment analysis and planning. The absence of source notes is disturbing; the hysterical tone is somewhat amusing.

1230. **Index Libycus: Bibliography of Libya 1957-1969, with Supplementary Material 1915-1956.** Compiled by Hans Schlüter. Boston: G.K. Hall, 1972. viii, 305 p. ISBN 0-8161-0939-7.
A first compilation of the *Index Libycus*, topically organized, containing more than 4000 brief entries in a variety of European languages. The work is especially strong in archaeology, geology, economics and politics, bibliographies and library catalogs, Berber studies and Orientalism. None of the entries is annotated; there is an author index.

1231. **Index Libycus: Bibliography of Libya 1970-1975, with Supplementary Material.** Compiled by Hans Schlüter, with the assistance of Kurt Mager and Hans-Peter Marmann. Boston: G.K. Hall, 1979. 2 v. ISBN 0-8161-8076-8 and 0-8161-8534-4.

This edition of *Index Libycus* continues the earlier work, numbering consecutively from 5001. The entries are topically arranged, and not annotated. Vol. 2 provides extensive indexing by author, title and place name, and reaches cumulatively back to 1915.

1232. **Libya, a Country Study.** Fourth edition. Edited by Helen Chapin Metz. Federal Research Division, Library of Congress. *Area Handbook Series.* Washington: Department of the Army, 1989. xxviii, 351 p. SuDocs no. D101.22: 550-85/989

Also available online at **lcweb2.loc.gov/frd/cs/cshome.html**

Each book in this series deals with "a particular foreign country, describing and analyzing its ... systems and institutions, and examining the interrelationships of those systems and the ways they are shaped by cultural factors " (Foreword). The books use a similar five-part structure: historical setting, the society and its environment (sociology, anthropology, geography), the economy, government and politics, and national security. Areas studies specialists prepare each of these five parts, rather like signed encyclopedia articles. The volumes include a capsule "Country Profile," some black-and-white photos, maps and figures, several useful tables of population, trade and other data (in an appendix), a bibliography, glossary of terms and an extensive, well-organized index. The tables often provide data that would be difficult to obtain from any other source: e.g., a country's exact or estimated supply of major aircraft, air defense weapons, naval vessels, field artillery and armored vehicles.

1233. Alawar, Mohamed A. **A Concise Bibliography of Northern Chad and Fezzan in Southern Libya.** Outwell Cambridgeshire, England; Boulder, CO: Arab Crescent Press; Westview, 1983. xxiii, 229 p. ISBN 0-906559-14-6.

Pulling together a widely-scattered literature pertaining to the border zone between Libya and Chad, this bibliography documents the ongoing contention over the "Uzu Strip" and boundary definitions between the two states.

In addition, this bibliography covers the geography and landscape, wildlife, water and natural resources, tribal peoples, history, politics, culture/society, economy and languages of Chad in general, and of the Fezzan area. French and English sources (books and articles) predominate, but other European languages are represented. The entries are topically arranged, with an author index.

1234. Barbar, Aghil M. **Government and Politics in Libya, 1969-1978: a Bibliography.** Monticello, IL: Vance Bibliographies, 1979. 139 p. *Public Administration Series;* no. 388.

The Vance bibliographies on public administration are composed of topically arranged citations—up to about 1000 in each issue—of books and articles, government bulletins and other publications. The entries are sometimes briefly annotated. This issue provides a substantial compilation of research material on Libya, topically arranged. There is a major section on the petroleum industry in the volatile 1970s.

1235. Barbar, Aghil M. **The Population of Libya.** Monticello, IL: Vance Bibliographies, 1980. 6 p. *Public Administration Series;* no. 455.

Barbar includes only about 50 citations on this specialized topic (in English, French and German), but provides helpful annotations for many of them.

1236. Barbar, Aghil M. **Public Administration in Libya: a Bibliography.** Monticello, IL: Vance Bibliographies, 1979. 5 p. *Public Administration Series;* no. 192.

Here, Barbar compiles only about 60 sources (in English, Italian and French), but they are scholarly works for the most part.

1237. Beschorner, Natasha. **Bibliography of Libya 1970-1990.** London: Centre of Near and Middle Eastern Studies at SOAS, 1990. v, 109 p. ISBN 0-7286-0172-9.

A compilation of books, articles and theses on post-revolutionary Libya held in several major academic collections and the Libyan Studies Centre, Tripoli. The entries are organized first by language (English, Arabic, French, German and Italian), then by keyword and keyword strings. Unfortunately, they are not indexed by title or author.

1238. Bleuchot, Hervé. **Chroniques et Documents Libyens, 1969-1980.** Paris: Éditions du Centre National de la Recherche Scientifique, 1983. 270 p. ISBN 2-222-03277-6.

A publication of the Centre de Recherches et d'Études sur les Sociétés Méditerranéennes, this volume brings together important contemporary extracts from the *Annuaire de l'Afrique du Nord*, documenting the Libyan revolution and the regime of Muammar el-Qaddhafi. The material analyzes the political and economic status of the country at each stage. There is a select bibliography (partially annotated) but no index.

1239. Gurney, Judith. **Libya: the Political Economy of Oil.** Oxford: Oxford University Press; published for the Oxford Institute for Energy Studies, 1996. xii, 244 p. *Political Economy of Oil-Exporting Countries*; 4. ISBN 0-19-730017-0.

A scholarly monograph, part of an important series. The detail and objectivity make this a valuable work; its usefulness as a reference derives from its unusual tables and figures, a select bibliography and helpful index.

1240. Harmon, Robert B. **Administration and Government in Libya: a Selected Bibliography.** Monticello, IL: Vance Bibliographies, 1982. 10 p. *Public Administration Series;* P-940. ISSN 0193-970X.

This small issue of the Vance bibliographies cites many popular sources on the order of *Time* and *Newsweek*; the list of books and monographs is very slim for its time span, about 1960-1980.

1241. Lawless, Richard I. **Libya.** Santa Barbara, CA: ABC-Clio Press, 1987. xxi, 243 p. *World Bibliographical Series;* v. 79. ISBN 1-85109-033-9.

The World Bibliographical Series being produced by Clio provides access for the English-speaking reader to a variety of materials: books and monographs, journals, bibliographies and reference works, theses and dissertations, conference proceedings, and sometimes more specialized information (e.g., manuscript catalogs). Fully-annotated entries (some volumes are annotated better than others) cover history, geography, economics and politics, culture, social customs and religion. Attention is paid to language, literature and the arts as well. An introductory essay and map are provided, and an index of authors, titles and subjects. Sometimes other helps (a glossary or chronology, for example) may be included. Each volume covers one individual country, but in some cases closely-related content overlaps: Somalia and Djibouti, Ethiopia and Eritrea, and so on.

1242. McLachlan, Anne and Keith. **Tunisia Handbook: with Libya.** Bath: Passport Books, 1997. 477 p. *Footprint Handbooks.* ISBN 0-900751-91-6; ISSN 1363-7487.

Concise, well-written and clearly printed, this handbook is just what many visitors will want in a pocket guide. Basic practical travel information is provided—with the confidence of personal experience—but the emphasis is on historical/cultural information and description. Fact boxes are frequently used to call attention to specific tidbits of interest, from the use of elephants by Hannibal to couscous and coffee vocabulary.

The guide assumes the visitor will want all possible help in locating and interpreting classical sites and antiquities; small but sharp monochrome maps, site and city plans, floor plans and diagrams are found throughout. The volume includes a simple phrase collection and glossary, and helpful indexes (a general index, and one for the plans and maps).

Because of Libya's political isolation, up-to-date travel information on this country is hard to find. This guide meets that need with 80 pages of useful material.

1243. St. John, Ronald Bruce. **Historical Dictionary of Libya.** Second edition. Metuchen, NJ: Scarecrow, 1991. xix, 192 p. *African Historical Dictionaries;* no. 33. ISBN 0-8108-2451-5.

Updated version of Lorna Hahn's *Historical Dictionary of Libya* (1981). It includes a sizable classified bibliography, a useful introductory essay, two simple maps and a chronology of political events. Some longer entries in the dictionary provide helpful detail on more difficult subjects, such as Qaddafi's "Third Universal Theory" and other tenets of *The Green Book.*

1244. St. John, Ronald Bruce. **Historical Dictionary of Libya.** Third edition. Lanham, MD: Scarecrow, 1998. xlviii, 451 p. *African Historical Dictionaries;* no. 33. ISBN 0-8108-3495-2.

Newly revised edition with greater depth on ancient and medieval Libya, relations with neighboring states, and recent developments such as the "Great Manmade River." The topical bibliography is also updated and expanded, and a set of maps depicts territorial problems like the boundary disputes with Chad and the Gulf of Sidra. Some helpful lists and documents are placed in an appendix. Entries are cross-referenced, but there is no index.

1245. Waddams, Frank C. **The Libyan Oil Industry.** Baltimore: Johns Hopkins University Press, 1980. 338 p. ISBN 0-8018-2431-1.

This scholarly monograph details the history of Libya's oil-based economy since the 1950s. Petroleum law, taxation and concessions, oil prices and market forces, international relations and internal conditions in the Libyan economy are considered and documented. Three maps, seven charts or diagrams and 55 tables provide useful graphics for reference work. A brief bibliography and index are included.

1246. Witherell, Julian W. **Libya, 1969-1989: an American Perspective: a Guide to U.S. Official Documents and Government-Sponsored Publications.** Washington: Library of Congress, African and Middle Eastern Division, 1990. ix, 180 p. *Near East Series.* ISSN 0196-3562.

A view of the two crucial decades following the Libyan revolution, from the perspective of American diplomats and policymakers. The bibliography includes not only materials in the Library of Congress collection, but some other libraries as well. Contents notes or brief annotations identify the provenance of the material and/or specify its coverage. The compilation is carefully organized by topic, and a general index is provided.

Journals/Databases

1247. **Country Report: Libya.** Quarterly; 1986- . London: Economist Intelligence Unit.

Available online through DIALOG, LEXIS/NEXIS, FT Profile and M.A.I.D./Profound; on CD-ROM from Knight-Ridder and Silver Platter; on microfilm from World Microfilms Publications.

Concise information on current political and economic conditions in particular countries, with forecasts of up to two years. All of the countries of northern Africa are covered (except Western Sahara). Profile data and brief executive summaries of current conditions are included.

The EIU annual *Country Profiles* offer more extensive background reading and statistical tables, to summarize and supplement the quarterly reports.

Websites

1248. JANA News Agency—Libya. News Headlines. **www.peg.apc.org/~jamahir/news.htm** Linked full-text articles.

1249. Lepcis Magna: the Roman Empire in Africa. **www.alnpete.co.uk/lepcis/ porta.html** Showcases the excavation of a Tripolitanian Roman city.

1250. Libya: Our Home. **home.earthlink.net/~dribrahim/** Personal links page with a great deal of information about Libya's history, arts and culture, climate, cuisine, tourist attractions, sports, education, agriculture and industry, human rights.

Morocco

Reference Sources

1251. **Bibliographie Nationale Marocaine, Retrospective 1986-1994: Monographies et Périodiques en Langues Étrangères.** Annual; published in various forms since 1962. Rabat: Bibliothèque Générale et Archives, 1995. 387 p. ISSN 1113-6405.

This volume consists of nine annual bibliographies stuck together, without any attempt to coordinate their contents. Each annual segment is individually subdivided by topic, and indexed by author and title. A separate listing of periodicals, with its own index of editors and corporate bodies, is attached at the end.

Another issue covering monographs and periodicals published in 1995 appeared the following year; that issue includes materials in Arabic (about 60% of the volume). Entries are not annotated.

1252. **Country Profile: Morocco.** Annual; 1986- . London: Economist Intelligence Unit.

This annual supplement to the quarterly EIU *Country Reports* aims to provide more extensive background reading and statistical tables. Each volume serves as a useful reference source.

1253. **Doing Business in Morocco.** Revised. Casablanca and Rabat: Price Waterhouse, 1991. 138 p. *Information Guide Series.*

An occasional handbook for the assistance of those interested in doing business in Morocco. Helpful current material is offered on foreign investment and the business environment, trade opportunities, investment incentives, regulatory climate, banking and finance institutions, legal business entities, auditing, accounting and taxation, and labor relations and social insurance issues. Several appendices provide quick access to tax rates and treaties, a "checklist" of concerns to be considered when planning investment, and local contact data for sources of business information.

1254. **Doing Business in Morocco.** Supplement. Casablanca and Rabat: Price Waterhouse, 1994. Pamphlet. *Information Guide Series.*
A supplement updating information in the 1991 issue.

1255. **Frommer's Comprehensive Travel Guide: Morocco '92-'93.** Prepared by Darwin Porter. New York: Prentice Hall Travel, 1992. ISSN 1053-2447.
Contains a concise introduction to modern Morocco and a section covering history and culture, along with practical information about food, prices, transport, lodging, etc. This guide provides some information about the Atlas Mountains and the Western Sahara as well. Fourteen maps are included.

1256. **Morocco.** Edited by Dorothy Stannard. Singapore: APA Publications, 1999. 321 p. *Insight Guides.* ISBN 0-39581-910-5.
In the colorful *Insight Guides* format, this book calls attention to its lavish photos, with an interesting and informative text worked in around them. A sizable history section is casual in tone, unencumbered by source notes or other documentation.
Feature articles on music, literature, food, architecture, etc., appear, followed by specific descriptions of each of the varied physical regions and urban settlements of Morocco; 14 clear and simple maps are provided. A section of practical "travel tips" forms an appendix. An index and quick-reference panels inside the covers could come in handy.

1257. **Morocco, a Country Study.** Fifth edition. Edited by Harold D. Nelson. American University, Foreign Area Studies. Washington: Department of the Army, 1985. xxviii, 448 p. *Area Handbook Series.* SuDocs no. D101.22: 550-49/85
Not yet available online.
Each book in this series deals with "a particular foreign country, describing and analyzing its ... systems and institutions, and examining the interrelationships of those systems and the ways they are shaped by cultural factors " (Foreword). The books use a similar five-part structure: historical setting, the society and its environment (sociology, anthropology, geography), the economy, government and politics, and national security. Areas studies specialists prepare each of these five parts, rather like signed encyclopedia articles. The volumes include a capsule "Country Profile," some black-and-white photos, maps and figures, several useful tables of population, trade and other data (in an appendix), a bibliography, glossary of terms and an extensive, well-organized index. The tables often provide data that would be difficult to obtain from any other source: e.g., a country's exact or estimated supply of major aircraft, air defense weapons, naval vessels, field artillery and armored vehicles.

1258. **Morocco Post Report.** Revised July 1985. Washington: Department of State Publication 9198, Foreign Service Series 245. 24 p.; map and photos. Su-Docs S1.127:M82/985.

Department of State "Post Reports" are pamphlets containing basic information thought to be useful for U.S. government employees and their families being sent to a new location. Each report includes: a brief description of the "host country"—its climate, population, transport, tourist attractions, health services, etc.; specific information on the American Embassy and any consulates, housing, food and clothing, recreation opportunities, education for dependents; basic travel data on customs duties, currency, import restrictions, local holidays. Some issues provide a handy, clear and detailed street map of the area of the capital city surrounding the American Embassy (often hard to find in any other source).

1259. Ellingham, Mark and Shaun McVeigh. **The Rough Guide to Morocco.** London: Routledge & Kegan Paul, 1985. 344 p. ISBN 0-7102-0153-2.

A guidebook stressing practical information for the independent traveller, including the public-transport passenger, camper and youth-hostel user. There are site descriptions and useful historical and cultural information, though not much depth on archaeology or antiquities. Many small maps and city plans are included, but the decision was made to use hand-lettered sketch maps that are not always successful. There is a very simple index.

1260. Findlay, Anne M. and Allan M. Findlay. **Morocco.** Santa Barbara, CA: ABC-Clio Press, 1995. xxxii, 178 p. *World Bibliographical Series;* v. 47. ISBN 1-85109-216-1.

The World Bibliographical Series being produced by Clio provides access for the English-speaking reader to a variety of materials: books and monographs, journals, bibliographies and reference works, theses and dissertations, conference proceedings, and sometimes more specialized information (e.g., manuscript catalogs). Fully-annotated entries (some volumes are annotated better than others) cover history, geography, economics and politics, culture, social customs and religion. Attention is paid to language, literature and the arts as well. An introductory essay and map are provided, and an index of authors, titles and subjects. Sometimes other helps (a glossary or chronology, for example) may be included. Each volume covers one individual country, but in some cases closely-related content overlaps: Somalia and Djibouti, Ethiopia and Eritrea, and so on.

1261. Hargraves, Orin. **Culture Shock! Morocco: a Guide to Customs and Etiquette.** Portland, OR: Graphic Arts Center Publishing Co., 1995. 286 p. *Culture Shock.* ISBN 1-55868-241-4.

A self-help book rather than a travel guide, this work tries to provide what the well-intentioned traveler or expatriate might need in order to adjust to life in Morocco. Cultural background, practical advice, phrases and vocabulary, and emotional encouragement are all delivered in a personal, almost intimate tone. This compendium of clues for the clueless could be a thoughtful gift for someone going to an Arab North African country for the first time.

1262. Huxley, Frederick C. **Development in Morocco: Bibliography and Informative Abstracts of Selected Research, 1970-82.** Berkeley, CA: Development Research Services, 1983. v, 90 p.

The title seems to indicate that this is an annotated bibliography, but in fact, there is a separate section of materials for which detailed abstracts are provided (considered to be the most significant works). This compilation may be valuable for those doing research on its time period, since these sources are unlikely to be included in electronic indexes. Similar guides were prepared for development issues in Egypt and Tunisia (also Jordan, Yemen).

1263. Jadda, M'Hamed. **Bibliographie Analytique: des Publications de l'Institut des Hautes Études Marocaines, 1915-1959.** Rabat: Royaume du Maroc Université Mohammed V, 1994. 495 p. *Thèses et Mémoires;* no. 26. ISBN 9981-825-21-2; ISSN 1113-0342.

A lengthy introduction presents a history of academic publishing in Morocco, explains the role of the IHEM, and plots the bureaucracy of education and the processes of state control of research. The retrospective bibliography occupies most of the volume, organized by publishing source in some sections and by subject area in others. Fortunately, there are four indexes to help in locating material. Studies of Berber language and culture are well represented in this reference.

1264. Park, Thomas K. **Historical Dictionary of Morocco.** New edition. Lanham, MD: Scarecrow, 1996. xxx, 540 p. *African Historical Dictionaries;* no. 71. ISBN 0-8108-3168-6.

This expert work (following on William Spencer's 1980 edition) contains many features not found in other volumes of this series. The author has included a collection of useful reference helps: an appendix showing names and dates for 14 local or imperial dynasties or successions of European leaders; another appendix providing a brief description and directory information for libraries and archives in Europe and Morocco with important holdings for Moroccan studies; 30 historical and political maps (unfortunately, too small and often poorly reproduced); a glossary of Arabic terms. About 260 pages of the volume are devoted to a very valuable bibliography of books and monographs, articles and classic manuscripts, in a variety of European languages and Arabic (in translation). Many of the works cited are not current or in print, but are important for in-depth study.

The author employs a unique romanization system for Arabic names and terms; this system is accurate, well-justified and explained clearly in a prefatory note. Nevertheless, it will prove very daunting to readers who are unable to translate the headings mentally into Arabic orthography or to recognize conventions used in other standard references.

1265. Parker, Richard B. **A Practical Guide to Islamic Monuments in Morocco.** Printed in Lebanon by The Catholic Press. Charlottesville: Baraka Press, 1981. 181 p.

A delightful guide offering a short course in the history, styles and structures of traditional buildings in Morocco. Parker explains the origin and function of basic building features, the type of ornamentation, and the meaning of special vocabulary. Many line drawings or sketches clarify the points made in the text. Guidebook information for visiting scores of sites in nine major locations is set forth, making this book a worthwhile travel companion. Plans of the towns as well as the sites, plus suggested day trips and itineraries, are provided. The book includes a collection of 90 plates, some in color. There is a simple index.

1266. Reysoo, Fenneke. **Pèlerinages au Maroc: Fête, Politique et Échange dans l'Islam Populaire.** Paris: Éditions de la Maison des Sciences de l'Homme, 1991. 227 p. *Recherches et Travaux de l'Institut d'Ethnologie;* 10. ISBN 2-88279-003-1 and 2-7351-0407-9; ISSN 1011-2960.

Published under the auspices of the Faculté des Lettres, Université de Neuchâtel, this interesting anthropological study on various manifestations of popular religion is organized in many concise segments suitable for reference work. The table of contents is thoroughly subdivided (there is no index). The text is augmented by several charts and tables of data (mostly statistical), maps or city plans, and a number of distinct black-and-white photos. There is a useful bibliography and a glossary of specialized terms.

1267. Rogerson, Barnaby. **Morocco.** London; Old Saybrook, CT: Cadogan; Globe Pequot, 1997. 596 p. *Cadogan Guides.* ISBN 1-86011-043-6.

A guide that is at once informative and entertaining, engagingly written by the author of *A Traveler's History of North Africa.* An opening section of practical information is supplemented by relevant data in each chapter on transport, shopping, restaurants, accommodation, etc. The needs of travelers ranging from luxury hotels to campgrounds have been considered. Many small maps offer the most essential information.

Descriptions of sites and structures are general, meant more for pleasure travel than a serious study of Islamic architecture. Historical and cultural background is interesting but not technical. A good index, phrase list, glossary and other reference helps are included.

A chapter on the Western Sahara seems to provide as much about this "desolate ... piece of land" as a casual traveler is likely to require.

Journals/Databases

1268. **Country Report: Morocco.** Quarterly; 1986- . London: Economist Intelligence Unit.

Available online through DIALOG, LEXIS/NEXIS, FT Profile and M.A.I.D./Profound; on CD-ROM from Knight-Ridder and Silver Platter; on microfilm from World Microfilms Publications.

Concise information on current political and economic conditions in particular countries, with forecasts of up to two years. All of the countries of northern Africa are covered (except Western Sahara). Profile data and brief executive summaries of current conditions are included.

The EIU annual *Country Profiles* offer more extensive background reading and statistical tables, to summarize and supplement the quarterly reports.

Websites

1269. Al Akhawayn University. Moroccan Resources on Internet. **www.alakhawayn. ma/morocco/**

1270. Association Scientifique Marocaine (ASMA). **www.ift.ulaval.ca/ ~asma-net/**
Also contains general information, description and photos of Morocco. In French and English.

1271. Kingdom of Morocco. Ministry of Communication. **www.mincom. gov.ma/**
Public-relations information, available in English or French. With special attention to "the history of the reintegration of the Saharian provinces."

1272. *Maroc Hebdo International.* Journal d'Informations Generales. **www. maroc-hebdo.press.ma/**
Full-text weekly, online.

1273. Marocnet. La Vie Économique. **www.marocnet.net.ma/vieeco/**
"Premiere hebdomadaire d'information du Maroc." Full-text articles.

Tunisia

Reference Sources

1274. **Country Profile: Tunisia.** Annual; 1986- . London: Economist Intelligence Unit. ISSN 0269-8129.
This annual supplement to the quarterly EIU *Country Reports* aims to provide more extensive background reading and statistical tables. Each volume serves as a useful reference source.

1275. **Tunisia, a Country Study.** Third edition. Edited by Harold D. Nelson. Foreign Area Studies, The American University. Washington: Department of the Army, 1988. xxvii, 380 p. *Area Handbook Series;* DA Pam 550-89. SuDocs no. D101.22: 550-89/987
Also available online at **lcweb2.loc.gov/frd/cs/cshome.html**
Each book in this series deals with "a particular foreign country, describing and analyzing its ... systems and institutions, and examining the interrelationships of those systems and the ways they are shaped by cultural factors " (Foreword). The books use a similar five-part structure: historical setting, the society and its environment (sociology, anthropology, geography), the economy, government and politics, and national security. Areas studies specialists prepare

each of these five parts, rather like signed encyclopedia articles. The volumes include a capsule "Country Profile," some black-and-white photos, maps and figures, several useful tables of population, trade and other data (in an appendix), a bibliography, glossary of terms and an extensive, well-organized index. The tables often provide data that would be difficult to obtain from any other source: e.g., a country's exact or estimated supply of major aircraft, air defense weapons, naval vessels, field artillery and armored vehicles.

1276. **Tunisia Post Report.** Revised Aug 1986. Washington: Department of State Publication 9187, Foreign Affairs Information Management Center. 20 p.; map and photos. SuDocs S1127:T83/986.

Department of State "Post Reports" are pamphlets containing basic information thought to be useful for U.S. government employees and their families being sent to a new location. Each report includes: a brief description of the "host country" — its climate, population, transport, tourist attractions, health services, etc.; specific information on the American Embassy and any consulates, housing, food and clothing, recreation opportunities, education for dependents; basic travel data on customs duties, currency, import restrictions, local holidays. Some issues provide a handy, clear and detailed street map of the area of the capital city surrounding the American Embassy (often hard to find in any other source).

1277. Cohen, David. **Le Parler Arabe des Juifs de Tunis: Textes et Documents Linguistiques et Ethnographiques.** École Pratique des Hautes Études (Sorbonne). Paris: Mouton & Co., 1964. x, 177 p. *Études Juives;* v. vii.

1278. Cohen, David. **Le Parler Arabe des Juifs de Tunis: Textes et Documents Linguistiques et Ethnographiques.** Tome II: Étude linguistique. Paris and The Hague: Mouton, 1975. 318 p.

The first volume of this fascinating work presents texts originating in the ancient Jewish community of Tunisia, transliterated from Arabic and Hebrew scripts and translated into French, with detailed marginal notes and an index-glossary. These texts include marriage and funeral ceremonies and other religious rites, popular rituals and superstitions, songs, poetry and proverbs, even a recipe. The second volume is a detailed study of the phonology and grammar of the language, with its own index.

1279. Faath, Sigrid. **Tunesien, die Politische Entwicklung seit der Unabhängigkeit, 1956-1986: Kommentar und Dokumentation.** Hamburg: Deutsches Orient-Institut, 1986. viii, 553 p. *Mitteilungen des Deutschen Orient-Instituts;* no. 27. ISBN 3-89173-003-9.

About a third of this volume is a study and analysis of Tunisia's political development since independence in 1956, with a basic bibliography. The remaining two-thirds is composed of reprinted articles from newspapers and magazines (*Le Monde, La Presse, Neue Zürcher Zeitung, Jeune Afrique, The Guardian*, etc.), government publications and documents.

A country profile, tables of government ministers and other introductory material is provided. In addition, there is a detailed chronology of thirty years of political events. The materials are grouped under broad topical headings, but no index is included.

1280. Findlay, Allan M., Anne M. Findlay, and Richard I. Lawless. **Tunisia.** Santa Barbara, CA: ABC-Clio Press, 1982. xxviii, 251 p. *World Bibliographical Series;* v. 33. ISBN 0-903450-63-1.

The World Bibliographical Series being produced by Clio provides access for the English-speaking reader to a variety of materials: books and monographs, journals, bibliographies and reference works, theses and dissertations, conference proceedings, and sometimes more specialized information (e.g., manuscript catalogs). Fully-annotated entries (some volumes are annotated better than others) cover history, geography, economics and politics, culture, social customs and religion. Attention is paid to language, literature and the arts as well. An introductory essay and map are provided, and an index of authors, titles and subjects. Sometimes other helps (a glossary or chronology, for example) may be included. Each volume covers one individual country, but in some cases closely-related content overlaps: Somalia and Djibouti, Ethiopia and Eritrea, and so on.

1281. Golany, Gideon S. **Earth-Sheltered Dwellings in Tunisia: Ancient Lessons for Modern Design.** Newark: University of Delaware Press, 1988. 164 p. ISBN 0-87413-297-5.

A scholarly study of subterranean and earth-built structures and cliff dwellings in Tunisia—in Berber, Arab and ancient Roman settlements.

The volume is supplied with ample sketches, maps and black-and-white photos. There are also tables of temperature measurements to gauge the insulating properties of these structures. Information about the geology and climate is, of course, important to this study and is found throughout. A topically-subdivided bibliography and an index are included.

1282. Hinton, Amanda. **Tunisia.** London; New York: A&C Black; W.W. Norton, 1996. 222 p. *Blue Guides.* ISBN 0-7136-4105-3; 0-393-31419-7.

A condensed, no-nonsense, information-rich guide, specializing in detailed room-by-room descriptions of the Roman antiquities, museum collections and Islamic architecture of Tunisia. An adequate amount of practical travel information is provided as well. Site plans, simplified city street maps and some small drawings appear, along with a central section of nice (but unnecessary) color photos. An index is included.

1283. Huxley, Frederick C. **Development in Tunisia: Bibliography and Informative Abstracts of Selected Research, 1970-82.** Berkeley, CA: Development Research Services, 1983. iv, 141 p.

The title seems to indicate that this is an annotated bibliography, but in fact, there is a separate section of materials for which detailed abstracts are provided (considered to be the most significant works). This compilation may be valuable for those doing research on its time period, since these sources are unlikely to be included in electronic indexes. Similar guides were prepared for development issues in Egypt and Morocco (also Jordan, Yemen).

1284. Khaled, Ahmed. **Documents Secrets du 2ème Bureau, Tunisie-Maghreb: dans la Conjoncture de Pré-Guerre, 1937-1940.** Tunis: Société Tunisienne de Diffusion, 1983. 866 p.

A rather cumbersome volume (with a few printing problems) offering access to archival material documenting French military policy and practice in Tunisia. Some facsimiles and photographs are included (29 pages of large black-and-white plates). A names index, with brief identifications of the individuals, is provided, plus other indexes of tribal names, political parties or associations, print and media sources. The detailed table of contents is essential to this volume.

1285. McLachlan, Anne and Keith. **Tunisia Handbook: with Libya.** Bath: Passport Books, 1997. 477 p. *Footprint Handbooks.* ISBN 0-900751-91-6; ISSN 1363-7487.

Concise, well-written and clearly printed, this handbook is just what many visitors will want in a pocket guide. Basic practical travel information is provided—with the confidence of personal experience—but the emphasis is on historical/cultural information and description. Fact boxes are frequently used to call attention to specific tidbits of interest, from the use of elephants by Hannibal to couscous and coffee vocabulary.

The guide assumes the visitor will want all possible help in locating and interpreting classical sites and antiquities; small but sharp monochrome maps, site and city plans, floor plans and diagrams are found throughout. The volume includes a simple phrase collection and glossary, and helpful indexes (a general index, and one for the plans and maps).

Because of Libya's political isolation, up-to-date travel information on this country is hard to find. This guide meets that need with 80 pages of useful material.

1286. Perkins, Kenneth J. **Historical Dictionary of Tunisia.** Metuchen, NJ: Scarecrow Press, 1989. xxv, 234 p. *African Historical Dictionaries;* no. 45. ISBN 0-8108-222-6-1.

A ready reference conveying a great deal of well-organized information on the history of Tunisia from the founding of Carthage (814 BC) to the present, with emphasis on the colonial and independence eras. Some of the most interesting entries describe relationships with other powers: Rome, Egypt, France, etc. A handy chronology and table of Tunisia's rulers since medieval times, a brief introduction and one not-very-impressive map are included. The strength of the volume is a well-researched and carefully organized classified bibliography. There is no index, but entries are cross-referenced.

1287. Perkins, Kenneth J. **Historical Dictionary of Tunisia.** Second edition. Lanham, MD: Scarecrow, 1997. xxvii, 311 p. *African Historical Dictionaries;* no. 45. ISBN 0-8108-3286-0.

The new edition of Perkins' reference is particularly well-supplied with carefully-written longer articles on the most important persons, places and things: the entry on Habib Bourguiba is a biographical essay one might expect to find in an encyclopedia. The topically-arranged bibliography encompasses a range of West European languages. Oddly, the bibliography is not indexed by author or title.

1288. Rogerson, Barnaby and Rose Baring. **Tunisia.** London; Old Saybrook, CT: Cadogan; Globe Pequot, 1998. x, 469. *Cadogan Guides.* ISBN 1-86011-059-2.

Engagingly written by the author of *A Traveler's History of North Africa*, this guide offers an unusually good balance of practical information and background/description. Sharp, nicely-printed street maps, a chapter of travel advice, and specific information on transport, lodging, dining, shopping, etc. are all built into this book. There is useful material on the Punic wars, classical and Hellenistic sites and structures and Islamic monuments, as well as the contemporary culture and people. A vocabulary, chronology, index and other reference helps are included. The author is reportedly preparing a *Cadogan Guide* to Libya.

1289. Yetiv, Isaac. **1001 Proverbs From Tunisia.** Washington: Three Continents Press, 1987. xiv, 152 p. ISBN 0-89410-615-5.

In possibly the strangest ordering of material ever witnessed in a reference work, this collection of proverbial sayings is alphabetized by the first roman letter of its transliterated Arabic form: in other words, by a symbol that is completely arbitrary and unreal. Entries range from *âdiha* to *zman,* with a thousand equally unhelpful terms in between. If the proverbs had been printed first in actual Arabic script, they could at least be alphabetized accurately. A very simple thematic index without subject subdivisions is the only help offered to the reader.

Each proverb is presented in romanized form, then translated literally, then paraphrased more generally to indicate the gist of it, or occasions for which the saying would be appropriate. Even so, such sayings out of their cultural and conversational context have an absurd fortune-cookie quality that does little to convey the "richness of the popular culture and the folklore" of Tunisia (p. xi). Like volumes of Egyptian proverbs or Goha stories, these sayings were no doubt much more fun to collect than they are to read.

Journals/Databases

1290. **Country Report: Tunisia.** Quarterly; 1986- . London: Economist Intelligence Unit.

Available online through DIALOG, LEXIS/NEXIS, FT Profile and M.A.I.D./Profound; on CD-ROM from Knight-Ridder and SilverPlatter; on microfilm from World Microfilms Publications.

Concise information on current political and economic conditions in particular countries, with forecasts of up to two years. All of the countries of northern Africa are covered (except Western Sahara). Profile data and brief executive summaries of current conditions are included.

The EIU annual *Country Profiles* offer more extensive background reading and statistical tables, to summarize and supplement the quarterly reports.

Websites

1291. Tunisia and the World. Foreign policy of the Republic of Tunisia. **www.tunisiaworld.com/2home.htm**

1292. Tunisia Online. **www.tunisiaonline.com/**
Attractive public-relations site with useful links.

1293. Tunisian Dailies Online (in French). *La Presse de Tunisie* and *d'Essahafa*. **www.tunisie.com/LaPresse/**

1294. TunisieCom. **www.tunisie.com/**
General descriptive information and media links.

1295. Tunisinfo. Net Business Center for Tunisia. **www.tunisinfo.com/ homeengl.htm**

The Sahel Region—
Sahara

Chapter 9

As noted in the Preface, regional divisions in northern Africa are by no means universally accepted. For the purposes of this work, this section will include those countries at or about 20° north latitude, bordering the great Sahara Desert.

Reference Sources

1296. **L'Afrique Noire: Politique et Économique.** 5e édition. Paris: Ediafric la Documentation Africaine, 1983. Thirteen sections, separately paginated.

This country-by-country reference provides concise almanac-style reports on current political and economic conditions, including names of office-holders, agricultural and industrial production, infrastructure, budget, lending and debt, international aid, etc. There is no interpretive or descriptive text, just statistical tables and lists of facts and data. Countries covered include Mali, Mauritania, Niger and Chad.

1297. **Elements for a Bibliography on the Sahelian Countries.** No. 19: 1995/96. Compiled by Amina Zaarrou. Annual; 1986- . Paris: Organisation for Economic Co-operation and Development, 1997. 199 p.

Also titled: *Éléments de Bibliographie sur les Pays du Sahel.*

An annual publication of the OECD's Club du Sahel, this bibliography brings together materials (mostly articles or reports in French or English) detailing current economic, social and political activities in the region. Mauritania, Mali, Niger and Chad are among the countries covered. The entries are topically arranged, with five indexes to improve access.

1298. **West Africa: a Lonely Planet Travel Survival Kit.** Third edition. By Alex Newton and David Else. Hawthorn, Victoria: Lonely Planet, 1997. 923 p. ISBN 0-86442-294-6.

Detailed, practical information for the independent traveler in some of the continent's less-developed areas. Regional descriptions and advice are supplemented by separate chapters for each country—among them Mali, Mauritania and Niger. Cultural and historical information is concise and interesting, with a small section of color photos. A glossary and index are included.

1299. Balandier, Georges and Jacques Maquet. **Dictionary of Black African Civilization.** New York: Leon Amiel, 1974. 350 p. ISBN 0-8148-0480-2.

Translation of: *Dictionnaire des Civilisations Africaines.*

This nicely-illustrated reference deals almost entirely with sub-Saharan Africa, but contains articles on the Fulani, Dogon, Mussoi, Songhai, Bambara, Nubians and other peoples of the Sahel. Many black-and-white photos are included showing tribal customs or artifacts originating with these peoples.

1300. Jenkins, Mark. **To Timbuktu.** New York: William Morrow, 1997. 224 p. ISBN 0-688-11585-3.

Not a guidebook, this is a personal account of exploratory travel along the Niger River Valley, in Mali, Niger and beyond. There is reflection, first-person narrative, and some background description. The author traveled mainly by hiking, kayak or motorbike through very remote village areas. A section of 18 color photos (some of them very attractive) is included. There is a small bibliography, but no index.

1301. Porgès, Laurence. **Sources d'Information sur l'Afrique Noire Francophone et Madagascar: Institutions, Répertoires, Bibliographies.** Paris: Ministère de la Coopération [et] La Documentation Française, 1988. 389 p. ISBN 2-11001787-2.

This important volume combines an institutional directory and a reference bibliography, covering French-speaking Mauritania, Mali, Niger and Chad (among other countries). Directory data and brief descriptions of the activities or holdings of research institutes, universities, archives, libraries and documentation centers, scientific and professional associations are provided.

Briefly-annotated listings of indexes, collection catalogs, "répertoires de thèses," general and specialized bibliographies (including all topics from linguistics to geology to economics) offer access to information on individual countries and on a regional level. There are four careful indexes and a detailed table of contents, quite effective for orienting the reader to the whole work. This reference would be essential for the university or research library.

1302. Staudinger, Paul. **In the Heart of the Hausa States.** Translated by Johanna E. Moody. Athens, OH: Ohio University Press, 1990. 2 v. *Monographs in International Studies;* no. 56. ISBN 0-89680-160-8 (set).

This edition of the Staudinger classic *Im Herzen der Hausaländer* (1889) is mentioned here because it has previously been inaccessible to students reading only English or modern German. The narrative (vol. 1) is interesting to historians, and vol. 2 presents a report of "the expedition's scientific results"—observations on climate, geography, industry, flora and fauna, customs of the people, etc. Some of the Hausa territory existed in what is now Mali and Niger.

1303. Westfall, Gloria D. **French Colonial Africa: a Guide to Official Sources.** London: Hans Zell, 1992. ix, 226 p. ISBN 1-873836-60-0.

Prepared by an authority on French government documents, this valuable guide offers access to many types of publications pertaining to France's colonial possessions in Africa. It covers official manuals and directories, reports, statistics, biographical and personnel information, political, legal and economic/financial documents, and materials in social and cultural affairs, as well as semiofficial publications and those generated by colonial governments. There are explanatory chapters on archival holdings in Africa and in France.

This volume appears to cover Chad, Mali, Mauritania and Niger, but not Algeria, Morocco or Tunisia (consistent with French policy); but due to a manufacturing error, the preface and pages 1-14 are missing, so an exact statement of the volume's coverage is not available.

Websites

1304. Africa Info. **africa-info.ihost.com/**
Descriptive pages about the geography, climate, population, economy, culture, religion, history, tourism of select countries. Will include Mali, Mauritania and Niger. In French and English.

1305. Organization for Economic Cooperation and Development (OECD). Club du Sahel. **www.oecd.org/sah/**
Available in French and English.

1306. US Agency for International Development. Famine Early Warning System (FEWS). **www.info.usaid.gov/fews/fews.html**
Current special reports on Africa, including "The Sahel in Depth" and a link to the Greater Horn Information Exchange.

Chad

Reference Sources

1307. **Chad, a Country Study.** Second edition. Edited by Thomas Collelo. Federal Research Division, Library of Congress. Washington: Department of the Army, 1990. xxiv, 254 p. *Area Handbook Series;* DA Pam 550-159. SuDocs no. D101.22: 550-159/990

Also available online at **lcweb2.loc.gov/frd/cs/cshome.html**

Each book in this series deals with "a particular foreign country, describing and analyzing its ... systems and institutions, and examining the interrelationships of those systems and the ways they are shaped by cultural factors " (Foreword). The books use a similar five-part structure: historical setting, the society and its environment (sociology, anthropology, geography), the economy, government and politics, and national security. Areas studies specialists prepare each of these five parts, rather like signed encyclopedia articles. The volumes include a capsule "Country Profile," some black-and-white photos, maps and figures, several useful tables of population, trade and other data (in an appendix), a bibliography, glossary of terms and an extensive, well-organized index. The tables often provide data that would be difficult to obtain from any other source: e.g., a country's exact or estimated supply of major aircraft, air defense weapons, naval vessels, field artillery and armored vehicles.

1308. **Chad Post Report.** Revised April 1986. Washington: Department of State Publication 9477, Foreign Affairs Information Management Center. 16 p.; map and photos. SuDocs S1.127:C34/986.

Department of State "Post Reports" are pamphlets containing basic information thought to be useful for U.S. government employees and their families being sent to a new location. Each report includes: a brief description of the "host country"—its climate, population, transport, tourist attractions, health services, etc.; specific information on the American Embassy and any consulates, housing, food and clothing, recreation opportunities, education for dependents; basic travel data on customs duties, currency, import restrictions, local holidays. Some issues provide a handy, clear and detailed street map of the area of the capital city surrounding the American Embassy (often hard to find in any other source).

1309. **Country Profile: Cameroon, Central African Republic, Chad.** Annual; 1986- . London: Economist Intelligence Unit.

This annual supplement to the quarterly EIU *Country Reports* aims to provide more extensive background reading and statistical tables. Each volume serves as a useful reference source.

1310. Tchad Bibliographie: Réalisée à Partir de la Banque de Données. 2ème édition. Edited by Catherine Cyrot. Paris: Association IBISCUS (Ministère de la Coopération et du Développement), 1990. 68 p. *Collection Réseaux Documentaires sur le Développement, Références Bibliographiques.* ISSN 1152-0698.

Annotated entries, many with detailed abstracts, compose this bibliography. Even those entries without abstracts do provide keywords or descriptors identifying their basic content. All of the works cited are in French, but they may be published either in Europe or in Chad itself. Books, articles and conference papers are included.

The works cited pertain to development-related issues in agriculture, commerce and finance, the environment, industry, international relations, health, social and demographic factors, transport, urban conditions, housing, etc. There are three rough indexes of authors, subjects and geographic names.

1311. Alawar, Mohamed A. **A Concise Bibliography of Northern Chad and Fezzan in Southern Libya.** Outwell Cambridgeshire, England; Boulder, CO: Arab Crescent Press; Westview, 1983. xxiii, 229 p. ISBN 0-906559-14-6.

Pulling together a widely-scattered literature pertaining to the border zone between Libya and Chad, this bibliography documents the ongoing contention over the "Uzu Strip" and boundary definitions between the two states.

In addition, this bibliography covers the geography and landscape, wildlife, water and natural resources, tribal peoples, history, politics, culture/society, economy and languages of Chad in general, and of the Fezzan area. French and English sources (books and articles) predominate, but other European languages are represented. The entries are topically arranged, with an author index.

1312. Azevedo, Mario J. and Emmanuel U. Nnadozie. **Chad: a Nation in Search of Its Future.** Boulder, CO: Westview, 1998. xvii, 170 p. *Nations of the Modern World: Africa.* ISBN 0-8133-8677-2.

One of the very useful *Nations of the Modern World* series, this readable but scholarly volume is a welcome addition to the slim literature on the land and people of Chad. The work is transparently organized, with a clear table of contents leading the reader directly to desired information. For very specific topical headings, there is also a helpful index.

Some simple black-and-white maps, graphs and tables of figures are provided, along with a political chronology (800-1997) and a subdivided bibliography. In addition, each chapter has its own bibliographical references. This work provides what one would expect from an encyclopedia article, plus knowledgeable analysis and commentary built into the text.

1313. Decalo, Samuel. **Historical Dictionary of Chad.** Third edition. Lanham, MD: Scarecrow, 1997. xlviii, 601 p. *African Historical Dictionaries;* no. 13. ISBN 0-8108-3253-4.

Updating Decalo's 1987 edition, this ready-reference provides considerable biographical and historical information, particularly on Chad's somewhat obscure political life. Brief alphabetized entries (cross-referenced) are enhanced by much longer articles on the more complex topics (e.g., "Armed Forces," "Political Parties") and more prominent persons.

The 150-page bibliography is subdivided by topic; it includes many older works of historical interest. The volume also provides a chronology of events, introductory essay, tables of demographic and economic data, and six disturbingly crude maps.

1314. Joffé, George and Valérie Day-Viaud. **Chad.** Santa Barbara, CA: ABC-Clio Press, 1995. xxviii, 188 p. *World Bibliographical Series;* v. 177. ISBN 1-85109-231-5.

The World Bibliographical Series being produced by Clio provides access for the English-speaking reader to a variety of materials: books and monographs, journals, bibliographies and reference works, theses and dissertations, conference proceedings, and sometimes more specialized information (e.g., manuscript catalogs). Fully-annotated entries (some volumes are annotated better than others) cover history, geography, economics and politics, culture, social customs and religion. Attention is paid to language, literature and the arts as well. An introductory essay and map are provided, and an index of authors, titles and subjects. Sometimes other helps (a glossary or chronology, for example) may be included. Each volume covers one individual country, but in some cases closely-related content overlaps: Somalia and Djibouti, Ethiopia and Eritrea, and so on.

Journals/Databases

1315. **Country Report: Cameroon, Central African Republic, Chad.** Quarterly; 1986- . London: Economist Intelligence Unit. ISSN 0269-4336.

Available online through DIALOG, LEXIS/NEXIS, FT Profile and M.A.I.D./Profound; on CD-ROM from Knight-Ridder and Silver Platter; on microfilm from World Microfilms Publications.

Concise information on current political and economic conditions in particular countries, with forecasts of up to two years. All of the countries of northern Africa are covered (except Western Sahara). Profile data and brief executive summaries of current conditions are included.

The EIU annual *Country Profiles* offer more extensive background reading and statistical tables, to summarize and supplement the quarterly reports.

Websites

1316. Chad. Tschad Evasion. **www.africances.fr/tchadevasion/**
Tourism information.

1317. My Travel Guide. Chad. **http://www.mytravelguide.com/countries/chad/**
Basic tourist information.

1318. US Energy Information Administration. Chad Internet Links. **http://www.eia.doe.gov/emeu/cabs/chadlnks.html**

Simple, convenient links page.

1319. Washington Post. Chad. **http://www.washingtonpost.com/wp-srv/inatl/longterm/worldref/country/chad.htm**

News archive, plus links.

Mali

Reference Sources

1320. **Country Profile: Côte D'Ivoire, Mali.** Annual; 1993- . London: Economist Intelligence Unit. ISSN 0269-4417.

This annual supplement to the quarterly EIU *Country Reports* aims to provide more extensive background reading and statistical tables. Each volume serves as a useful reference source. In 1993, the grouping of these countries into publication units was changed.

1321. **Country Profile: Guinea, Mali, Mauritania.** Annual; 1986-1992. London: Economist Intelligence Unit. ISSN 0269-4417.

The EIU *Country Profile* for Mali was published in one volume with Guinea and Mauritania until 1993.

1322. **Mali Post Report.** Released Mar 1992. Washington: Department of State Publication 9212, Office of Information Services. 24 p.; map and photos. SuDocs S1.127:M29/992.

Department of State "Post Reports" are pamphlets containing basic information thought to be useful for U.S. government employees and their families being sent to a new location. Each report includes: a brief description of the "host country"—its climate, population, transport, tourist attractions, health services, etc.; specific information on the American Embassy and any consulates, housing, food and clothing, recreation opportunities, education for dependents; basic travel data on customs duties, currency, import restrictions, local holidays. Some issues provide a handy, clear and detailed street map of the area of the capital city surrounding the American Embassy (often hard to find in any other source).

1323. Barth, Hans Karl. **Mali: eine Geographische Landeskunde.** Darmstadt: Wissenschaftliche Buchgesellschaft, 1986. xxi, 395 p. *Wissenschaftliche Länderkunden;* Band 25. ISBN 3-534-08157-9; ISSN 0174-0725.

An exhaustive study of every aspect of Mali's geography, natural resources and social/population patterns, considered as a basis for development. There are more than 70 tables of data, a dense and lengthy bibliography (with many unusual sources cited), a names index and a subject index.

1324. Brasseur, Paule. **Bibliographie Générale du Mali, 1961-1970.** Dakar: Institut Fondamental d'Afrique Noire, 1976. 284 p. *Catalogues Et Documents;* no. XVI-2.

This unusually complete, well-organized and wide-ranging bibliography is still in use, as it covers a period of time not accessible by other means. The Niger and Senegal River regions and the Sahara portion of Mali are dealt with in detail as physical environments, including scientific studies of the climate, geology, hydrology, plants and animals. The human civilization and culture, political/legal institutions and economy are fully documented as well. Many of the entries have brief annotations. A general index is included.

1325. Imperato, Pascal James. **Historical Dictionary of Mali.** Third edition. Lanham, MD: Scarecrow, 1996. lxxxv, 362 p. *African Historical Dictionaries;* no. 11. ISBN 0-8108-3128-7.

A lengthy chronology of Mali's history, a brief but information-rich introductory essay and 12 very useful tables of data distinguish this volume of the AHD series. The tables spell out the names and dates of the dynastic rulers, colonial administrators and national leaders of independent Mali, and provide population statistics by region through 1994 and projections through 2050.

The dictionary entries identify persons, places and events and define vocabulary terms from French, Arabic and local languages such as Songhay and Peul. More important entries are 2-3 pages long. A substantial bibliographical essay introduces a topically-arranged 85-page listing of books, monographs and articles. There is no index.

1326. Imperato, Pascal James and Eleanor M. Imperato. **Mali: a Handbook of Historical Statistics.** Boston: G.K. Hall, 1982. xxv, 339 p. *A Reference Publication in International Historical Statistics.* ISBN 0-8161-8147-0.

A compilation of detailed information about Mali's population, climate, geography and wildlife, industry/agriculture and economy, presented mainly in the form of tables of data, but there are also unusual maps and informative introductions with each chapter. Bibliographies of interesting and unusual sources are included with each chapter as well. A helpful index is also provided. Most of the data refers to the 1960s and 1970s, but sometimes data from the 1930s-1950s are available.

Journals/Databases

1327. **Country Report: Côte D'Ivoire, Mali.** Quarterly; 1993- . London: Economist Intelligence Unit.

Available online through DIALOG, LEXIS/NEXIS, FT Profile and M.A.I.D./Profound; on CD-ROM from Knight-Ridder and Silver Platter; on microfilm from World Microfilms Publications.

Concise information on current political and economic conditions in particular countries, with forecasts of up to two years. All of the countries of northern Africa are covered (except Western Sahara). Profile data and brief executive summaries of current conditions are included. In 1993, the grouping of these countries into publication units was changed.

The EIU annual *Country Profiles* offer more extensive background reading and statistical tables, to summarize and supplement the quarterly reports.

1328. Country Report: Guinea, Mali, Mauritania. Quarterly; 1986-1992. London: Economist Intelligence Unit. ISSN 0269-7203.

The EIU *Country Report* for Mali was published in one volume with Guinea and Mauritania until 1993, when the grouping of these countries into publication units was changed.

Websites

1329. Art and Life in Africa. Mali Information and Links. **www.uiowa. edu:80/~africart/toc/countries/mali.html**

From the Art and Life in Africa database, also available on interactive CD-ROM. Specifically covers the Bamana and Dogon peoples.

1330. Mali. Le Site non-officiel du MALI. **www.geocities.com/NapaValley/ 2111/Mali.html**

1331. Mali. Société des Télécommunications du Mali. **www.sotelma.net/**
Public-sector telecom authority.

1332. Mali Interactive. **www.ruf.rice.edu/~anth/arch/mali-interactive/index.html**

Information about Mali and archaeology, especially for teachers. Established by the leaders of an excavation by Rice University's anthropology department conducted at Jenné, "the earliest known urban settlement south of the Sahara and a UNESCO World Heritage site."

1333. Mission Archéologique et Ethnoarchéologique Suisse en Afrique de l'Ouest. **anthropologie.unige.ch/~elia/maesao/intro.html**

Featuring an exhibition of "Céramiques traditionnelles du Mali."

Mauritania

Reference Sources

1334. Country Profile: Guinea, Mali, Mauritania. Annual; 1986-1992. London: Economist Intelligence Unit. ISSN 0269-4417.

The EIU *Country Profile* for Mauritania was published in one volume with Guinea and Mali until 1993.

1335. **Country Profile: The Gambia, Mauritania.** Annual; 1993- . London: Economist Intelligence Unit.

This annual supplement to the quarterly EIU *Country Reports* aims to provide more extensive background reading and statistical tables. Each volume serves as a useful reference source. In 1993, the grouping of these countries into publication units was changed.

1336. **Mauritania, a Country Study.** Second edition. Edited by Robert E. Handloff. Federal Research Division, Library of Congress. Washington: Department of the Army, 1990. xxv, 218 p. *Area Handbook Series;* DA Pam 550-161. SuDocs no. D101.22: 550-161/990.

Also available online at **lcweb2.loc.gov/frd/cs/cshome.html**

Each book in this series deals with "a particular foreign country, describing and analyzing its ...systems and institutions, and examining the interrelationships of those systems and the ways they are shaped by cultural factors " (Foreword). The books use a similar five-part structure: historical setting, the society and its environment (sociology, anthropology, geography), the economy, government and politics, and national security. Areas studies specialists prepare each of these five parts, rather like signed encyclopedia articles. The volumes include a capsule "Country Profile," some black-and-white photos, maps and figures, several useful tables of population, trade and other data (in an appendix), a bibliography, glossary of terms and an extensive, well-organized index. The tables often provide data that would be difficult to obtain from any other source: e.g., a country's exact or estimated supply of major aircraft, air defense weapons, naval vessels, field artillery and armored vehicles.

1337. **Mauritania Post Report.** Released April 1990. Washington: Department of State Publication 9389, Office of Information Services. 15 p.; map and photos. SuDocs S1.127:M44/990.

Department of State "Post Reports" are pamphlets containing basic information thought to be useful for U.S. government employees and their families being sent to a new location. Each report includes: a brief description of the "host country"—its climate, population, transport, tourist attractions, health services, etc.; specific information on the American Embassy and any consulates, housing, food and clothing, recreation opportunities, education for dependents; basic travel data on customs duties, currency, import restrictions, local holidays. Some issues provide a handy, clear and detailed street map of the area of the capital city surrounding the American Embassy (often hard to find in any other source).

1338. Calderini, Simonetta, Delia Cortese, and James L. A. Webb, Jr. **Mauritania.** Santa Barbara, CA: ABC-Clio Press, 1992. xvi, 165 p. *World Bibliographical Series;* v. 141. ISBN 1-85109-152-1.

The World Bibliographical Series being produced by Clio provides access for the English-speaking reader to a variety of materials: books and monographs, journals, bibliographies and reference works, theses and dissertations, conference proceedings, and sometimes more specialized information (e.g., manuscript catalogs). Fully-annotated entries (some volumes are annotated better than others) cover history, geography, economics and politics, culture, social customs and religion. Attention is paid to language, literature and the arts as well. An introductory essay and map are provided, and an index of authors, titles and subjects. Sometimes other helps (a glossary or chronology, for example) may be included. Each volume covers one individual country, but in some cases closely-related content overlaps: Somalia and Djibouti, Ethiopia and Eritrea, and so on.

1339. Gerteiny, Alfred G. **Historical Dictionary of Mauritania.** Metuchen, NJ: Scarecrow Press, 1981. xv, 98 p. *African Historical Dictionaries;* no. 31. ISBN 0-8108-1433-1.

This slim volume provides useful ready-reference information on persons, places, organizations and ideas important in the recent history of Mauritania. An introductory essay offers a helpful overview of early settlement and exploration, the medieval period, French colonial rule and the independence era. A map and several tables of population statistics and economic data are included. Cross-references link search terms with acronyms or technical vocabulary: for example, IRON see MIFERMA. The entry for Islam takes care to define many unfamiliar terms. There is a small classified bibliography, but no index.

1340. Ould Hamody, Mohamed Saïd. **Bibliographie Générale de la Mauritanie.** [s.l.]: Mission de Coopération et d'Action Culturelle Française en Mauritanie, 1995. 580 p. ISBN 2-907888-69-2.

A carefully-organized retrospective or comprehensive bibliography, prepared by an experienced diplomat (Conseiller du Ministre des Affaires Étrangères d'Nouakchott). Entries are not annotated, but appear with keywords or descriptors identifying their basic content.

Journal articles as well as books are included (but without abstracts). There are indexes of authors, geographic names and an automated keyword index, and other reference helps. The bibliography covers the general areas of law, current events, economics and finance, history, culture and humanities, and science (especially geography and geology). Archival materials and maps are cited in separate sections.

1341. Pazzanita, Anthony G. **Historical Dictionary of Mauritania.** Second edition. Lanham, MD: Scarecrow, 1996. xxviii, 315 p. *African Historical Dictionaries;* no. 68. ISBN 0-8108-3095-7.

This ready reference includes longer articles on the most significant persons, historical events and political parties in Mauritania's past and present. Two maps, a chonology, a small bibliography and an introductory essay are provided. The author alphabetizes the entries according to traditional usage (Mohammed Khouna Ould Heydallah under M) but without cross-references or an index.

1342. Robert, Dieter. **Recueils Bibliographiques Concernant la Mauritanie.**
Second edition. Nouakchott: published by author, 1985. Three sections, separately paginated.

This somewhat legible typescript covers for the most part materials in
French (books, articles and portions of collective works) published in Europe,
but there are also many locally-printed materials included. A small section covers cultural matters; the much larger portion of the volume pertains to the economy, health and education, rural development, mineral resources and energy,
transport, urban conditions, banking, tourism, and regional or local development
or administrative issues. There is no indexing of any kind.

Journals/Databases

1343. **Country Report: Guinea, Mali, Mauritania.** Quarterly; 1986-1992.
London: Economist Intelligence Unit. ISSN 0269-7203.

The EIU *Country Report* for Mauritania was published in one volume with
Guinea and Mali until 1993, when the grouping of these countries into publication units was changed.

1344. **Country Report: Senegal, The Gambia, Mauritania.** Quarterly; 1993- .
London: Economist Intelligence Unit.

Available online through DIALOG, LEXIS/NEXIS, FT Profile and
M.A.I.D./Profound; on CD-ROM from Knight-Ridder and Silver Platter; on microfilm from World Microfilms Publications.

Concise information on current political and economic conditions in particular countries, with forecasts of up to two years. All of the countries of northern Africa are covered (except Western Sahara). Profile data and brief executive
summaries of current conditions are included. In 1993, the grouping of these
countries into publication units was changed.

The EIU annual *Country Profiles* offer more extensive background reading
and statistical tables, to summarize and supplement the quarterly reports.

1345. **Institut de Recherches et d'Études sur le Monde Arabe et Musulman**
(IREMAM) in Aix-en-Provence.

A collection of scanned books, periodicals and unpublished literature covering northern Africa, maintained as ARABASE; access provided through reference service. Material relates to Mauritania, Morocco, Algeria, Libya and
Tunisia.

Websites

1346. Mauritania. Office des Postes et de Télécommunications de Mauritanie.
www.opt.mr/
Public-sector telecom authority.

1347. Mauritania. Site Officiel du Gouvernement Mauritanien. **www.mauritania. mr/**

1348. Mauritanie. **www.toptechnology.mr/maurita01.html**
General information page: maps, culture, climate, geography, economy, population, tourism; photos of Nouadhibou and Nouakchott. In French.

1349. University of Nouakchott. **www.univ-nkc.mr/**

Niger

Reference Sources

1350. **Country Profile: Burkina Faso, Niger.** Annual; 1997- . London: Economist Intelligence Unit. ISSN 1366-428X.
This annual supplement to the quarterly EIU *Country Reports* aims to provide more extensive background reading and statistical tables. Each volume serves as a useful reference source. In 1997, the format of this publication unit was changed.

1351. **Country Profile: Niger, Burkina.** Annual; 1986-1996. London: Economist Intelligence Unit. ISSN 0269-8064.
This annual was published in this format until 1997.

1352. **Niger Post Report.** Revised Sept 1985. Washington: Department of State Publication 9147, Foreign Service Series 201. 16 p.; map and photos. SuDocs S1.127:N56/2/985.
Department of State "Post Reports" are pamphlets containing basic information thought to be useful for U.S. government employees and their families being sent to a new location. Each report includes: a brief description of the "host country"—its climate, population, transport, tourist attractions, health services, etc.; specific information on the American Embassy and any consulates, housing, food and clothing, recreation opportunities, education for dependents; basic travel data on customs duties, currency, import restrictions, local holidays. Some issues provide a handy, clear and detailed street map of the area of the capital city surrounding the American Embassy (often hard to find in any other source).

1353. Decalo, Samuel. **Historical Dictionary of Niger.** Third edition. Lanham, MD: Scarecrow, 1997. xxxi, 486 p. *African Historical Dictionaries;* no. 72. ISBN 0-8108-3136-8.
This new edition of Decalo's useful reference includes a chronology current through mid-1996, two maps and nine tables of economic data. A concise introductory essay is followed by the ready-reference portion identifying important persons, places and vocabulary terms. About one-third of the volume consists of an extensive classified (but not annotated) bibliography of books, monographs and articles in English and French.

1354. Zamponi, Lynda. **Niger.** Santa Barbara, CA: ABC-Clio Press, 1994. xl, 233 p. *World Bibliographical Series;* v. 164. ISBN 1-85109-204-8.

The World Bibliographical Series being produced by Clio provides access for the English-speaking reader to a variety of materials: books and monographs, journals, bibliographies and reference works, theses and dissertations, conference proceedings, and sometimes more specialized information (e.g., manuscript catalogs). Fully-annotated entries (some volumes are annotated better than others) cover history, geography, economics and politics, culture, social customs and religion. Attention is paid to language, literature and the arts as well. An introductory essay and map are provided, and an index of authors, titles and subjects. Sometimes other helps (a glossary or chronology, for example) may be included. Each volume covers one individual country, but in some cases closely-related content overlaps: Somalia and Djibouti, Ethiopia and Eritrea, and so on.

Journals/Databases

1355. **Country Report: Burkina Faso, Niger.** Quarterly; 1997- . London: Economist Intelligence Unit. ISSN 1366-4115.

Available online through DIALOG, LEXIS/NEXIS, FT Profile and M.A.I.D./Profound; on CD-ROM from Knight-Ridder and Silver Platter; on microfilm from World Microfilms Publications.

Concise information on current political and economic conditions in particular countries, with forecasts of up to two years. All of the countries of northern Africa are covered (except Western Sahara). Profile data and brief executive summaries of current conditions are included. In 1997, the grouping of these countries into publication units was changed.

The EIU annual *Country Profiles* offer more extensive background reading and statistical tables, to summarize and supplement the quarterly reports.

1356. **Country Report: Togo, Niger, Benin, Burkina.** Quarterly; 1986-1992. London: Economist Intelligence Unit. ISSN 0269-7262.

The EIU *Country Report* for Niger was published in one volume with Togo, Benin and Burkina Faso until 1997, when the grouping of these countries into publication units was changed.

Websites

1357. Camel Express Télématique Issues Online. Weekly Independent News of Niger. **www.txdirect.net/users/jmayer/cet.html**

An attractive and informative site.

1358. Focus on Niger. **www.txdirect.net/users/jmayer/fon.html**

With many illustrations and links, including specialized information on the Tuareg and Hausa. In French and English.

1359. République de Niger. Le Niger. **www.mygale.org/07/hammoudt/**
Personal website: general descriptive information and links. In French.

Sudan

Reference Sources

1360. **Country Profile: Sudan.** Annual; 1986- . London: Economist Intelligence Unit.

This annual supplement to the quarterly EIU *Country Reports* aims to provide more extensive background reading and statistical tables. Each volume serves as a useful reference source.

1361. **The Europeans in the Sudan, 1834-1878: Some Manuscripts, Mostly Unpublished, Written by Traders, Christian Missionaries, Officials and Others.** Translated and edited by Paul Santi and Richard Hill. Oxford: Clarendon Press, 1980. xiv, 250 p. ISBN 0-19-822718-3.

A collection of fascinating first-person documents dating from before the establishment of the Anglo-Egyptian Condominium. A helpful introduction points out primary contrasts between this early period and the later administration. Detailed editorial glosses and footnotes are provided. There is a very clear historical map and a names index.

1362. **Sudan, a Country Study.** Fourth edition. Edited by Helen Chapin Metz. Federal Research Division, Library of Congress. Washington: Department of the Army, 1992. xxxiii, 336 p. *Area Handbook Series.* ISBN 0-8444-0750-X; ISSN 1057-5294; SuDocs no. D101.22: 550-27/992

Also available online at **lcweb2.loc.gov/frd/cs/cshome.html**

Each book in this series deals with "a particular foreign country, describing and analyzing its ... systems and institutions, and examining the interrelationships of those systems and the ways they are shaped by cultural factors " (Foreword). The books use a similar five-part structure: historical setting, the society and its environment (sociology, anthropology, geography), the economy, government and politics, and national security. Areas studies specialists prepare each of these five parts, rather like signed encyclopedia articles. The volumes include a capsule "Country Profile," some black-and-white photos, maps and figures, several useful tables of population, trade and other data (in an appendix), a bibliography, glossary of terms and an extensive, well-organized index. The tables often provide data that would be difficult to obtain from any other source: e.g., a country's exact or estimated supply of major aircraft, air defense weapons, naval vessels, field artillery and armored vehicles.

1363. Sudan: What Future for Human Rights? New York: Amnesty International, 1995. Paperback publication, unpaginated. ISBN 0-939994-96-8.

This Amnesty International briefing report is not a reference work, but it calls attention to an important source of current information on human rights issues worldwide. Many NGOs publish their own bulletins, and AI is among those most respected for impartiality. This publication concentrates on the human rights abuses perpetrated by the Omar Hassan Ahmad al-Bashir regime in the Sudan.

1364. Sudan Year Book. No. 1. Compiled and published by SUDANOW. Khartoum: Sudan Publicity, 1983. 332 p.

A kind of almanac containing descriptive encyclopedia-style articles on life in the Sudan, tables of statistical information, and eight interesting maps. Economic data is matched by material on the arts, sports, climate, etc. Directory data for businesses, professionals and trade organizations, some government bodies and NGOs is included. This information is dated now, but it is not clear whether further issues of this yearbook were published.

1365. Ahmed, Osman Hassan. **A Bibliography of Documentary and Educational Films on Sudan.** Washington: Office of the Cultural Counsellor, Embassy of the Democratic Republic of the Sudan, 1982. xii, 114 p.

A very handy (if dated) compilation of films, in English and French, dealing with traditional and tribal life in the Sudan, archaeology, current political or social problems, wildlife and landscape, agriculture, history, exploration/adventure, etc. Each entry provides technical and distribution information and an abstract or synopsis. Appendices listing archival footage from United Nations and news-agency sources could be of interest to the historian.

1366. Ahmed, Osman Hassan. **Sudan and Sudanese: a Bibliography of American and Canadian Dissertations and Theses on the Sudan.** Washington: Cultural Office, Embassy of the Democratic Republic of Sudan, 1982. viii, 153 p. *Sudanese Publications Series;* no. 9.

An unusual plan guides this bibliography, which compiles two collections of academic writing in one volume: a list of all dissertations and theses written in North America by Sudanese students, on any topic; and a list of works by non-Sudanese students writing on the Sudan as their subject.

Each of these compilations is organized under topical headings. There are only 88 works in the second category (by non-Sudanese), but over 1200 in the first. Many of the Sudanese students wrote about the Sudan, but others did not, so it is difficult to find relevant materials mixed in with papers on genetics, dairy farming or diesel engines. The topical headings do nothing to solve this problem, and there are no indexes.

1367. Asher, Michael. **In Search of the Forty Days Road.** Essex: Longman, 1984. xiii, 179 p. ISBN 0-582-78364-X.

This personal travel narrative is not a guidebook, but is included here because capable firsthand description of the Sudan is hard to find. (The book is not, as the British Library CIP data would have it, about Libya.)

The author describes his encounters with village people in outlying areas reached by camel. Sixteen pages of color plates are included, with candid photos of ordinary people rather than monuments or tourist attractions. There is a small glossary of Sudanese Arabic terms, but no index.

1368. Daly, M. W. **Sudan.** Revised and expanded edition. Santa Barbara, CA: ABC-Clio Press, 1992. xix, 194 p. *World Bibliographical Series;* v. 40. ISBN 1-85109-187-4.

The World Bibliographical Series being produced by Clio provides access for the English-speaking reader to a variety of materials: books and monographs, journals, bibliographies and reference works, theses and dissertations, conference proceedings, and sometimes more specialized information (e.g., manuscript catalogs). Fully-annotated entries (some volumes are annotated better than others) cover history, geography, economics and politics, culture, social customs and religion. Attention is paid to language, literature and the arts as well. An introductory essay and map are provided, and an index of authors, titles and subjects. Sometimes other helps (a glossary or chronology, for example) may be included. Each volume covers one individual country, but in some cases closely-related content overlaps: Somalia and Djibouti, Ethiopia and Eritrea, and so on.

1369. Daly, M. W. and L. E. Forbes. **The Sudan: Photographs From the Sudan Archive, Durham University Library.** Reading: Garnet Publishing, 1994. 205 p. *Caught in Time: Great Photographic Archives.* ISBN 1-873938-94-2.

This fascinating volume reproduces photographs from the period of the Condominium, 1898-1956, creating an "impressionistic" and "subjective" record of those times (Preface). A well-written text and careful captions help to place these images in context. The reader wishes for a keyword index or some means of organizing the images; however, this book is really meant for leafing through at leisure.

1370. Daly, M. W. and Ahmad Alawad Sikainga. **Civil War in the Sudan.** London: British Academic Press, 1993. x, 220 p. ISBN 1-85043-515-4.

This collection of essays aims to clarify the issues and the chronology of events in the Sudan up to 1989. The titles of the individual essays and the index help to direct the reader.

1371. El-Singaby, Talaat. **La République Démocratique du Soudan: Bilan des Recherches en France et en R.F.A. Bibliographie Sélective, 1900-1986.** Aix-en-Provence: Universités d'Aix-Marseille, 1987. 139 p. *Travaux et Documents de l'IREMAM;* no. 4. ISBN 2-906809-020.

The Institut de Recherches et d'Études sur le Monde Arabe et Musulman, and the Centre d'Études et de Recherches sur l'Orient Arabe Contemporain are responsible for this volume, a small but useful retrospective bibliography. A sizable body of scholarly literature is represented here. In addition, there are two unusually clear and detailed maps of the Sudan and the Nile Valley. The citations are not annotated, and are grouped into very broad categories; there is no index. Many works in English are included.

1372. Elbashir, Ahmed E. **The Democratic Republic of the Sudan in American Sources.** Washington: Cultural Office, Embassy of the Democratic Republic of Sudan, 1983. 59 p. *Sudanese Publications Series;* no. 12.

A small compilation of books and articles, some of a general nature but most having to do with the Sudan, topically organized. There is an author index.

1373. Ertur, Omer S. and William J. House. **Population and Human Resources Development in the Sudan.** Ames, Iowa: Iowa State University Press, 1994. xiii, 329 p. ISBN 0-8138-0699-2.

This collection of essays and population studies was compiled in cooperation with the United Nations Population Fund (UNFPA) and the International Labor Organization (ILO). It contains 80 tables and figures, many of them targeting specific data that is not easy to obtain elsewhere (mostly from Sudanese government statistical documents), showing the nutritional status of children, health staffing and facilities, the cost of medical-care visits, the training and skills of workers, school enrolments, internal migration, etc. In addition, each essay or study provides a specialized and fairly current bibliography on these and other issues. Unfortunately, the volume has no index.

1374. Fluehr-Lobban, Carolyn, Richard A. Lobban, Jr., and John Obert Voll. **Historical Dictionary of the Sudan.** Second edition. Metuchen, NJ: Scarecrow, 1992. lxx, 409 p. *African Historical Dictionaries;* no. 53. ISBN 0-8108-2547-3.

A work by three noted authorities detailing the history, politics and cultural complexity of one of Africa's most diverse states. This volume contains a much more substantial chronology, introductory essay and bibliography (the latter extending to almost 150 pages) than most volumes in this series. A number of charts, figures, photographs and seven informative appendices increase the reference value of the work. This edition supplies new interpretive articles and bibliography entries on current issues of importance including the rights of women, refugees, slavery, the civil war and the Sahel drought and famine.

1375. Hulme, Michael. **An Annotated Bibliography of the Climate of Sudan.** Cambridge: African Studies Centre, 1987. iv, 54 p. *Cambridge African Occasional Papers;* 5. ISBN 0-902993-20-8.

A small and specialized volume, but containing a great deal of information on "the surprisingly large literature on this particular aspect of the Sudanese environment" (p. iii). Indeed, any work on the climate of a region where abnormal rainfall can create devastating famine is clearly of importance. This bibliography provides some 240 entries, topically organized and fully annotated. There is an author index, and an index by year (1829-1987).

1376. Kok, Peter Nyot. **Governance and Conflict in the Sudan, 1985-1995: Analysis, Evaluation and Documentation.** Hamburg: Deutsches Orient-Institut, 1996. 382 p. *Mitteilungen des Deutschen Orient-Instituts;* 53. ISBN 3-89173-043-8; ISSN 0177-4156.

The text and documents in this volume are in English, not German, and the "analysis" or scholarly monograph occupies the majority of the pages. There is a 150-page appendix containing 19 verbatim documents representing the establishment and development of the various revolutionary regimes over this unstable ten-year period. These documents are reproduced facsimile-style, without editorial notes or indexing. There is a basic bibliography.

1377. Sidahmed, Abdel Salam. **Politics and Islam in Contemporary Sudan.** New York: St. Martin's, 1996. xiv, 249 p. ISBN 0-312-16144-1.

Not a reference work, this scholarly study of postcolonial Sudan requires careful reading. A good index helps to locate specific information.

1378. Verney, Peter. **Sudan: Conflict and Minorities.** London: Minority Rights Group, 1995. 42 p. ISBN 1-897693-65-6; ISSN 0305-6252.

This internationally-active nongovernmental organization does its own research to produce reports on minority populations whose human rights are threatened. Six reports per year are published; MRG reports are also available on Chad, Eritrea, the Falashas, Somalia, the Sahel and the Western Sahara.

Thematic reports are also often relevant to northern Africa, such as studies of refugee problems, language rights and female genital mutilation. This issue on Sudan offers two big, clear monochrome maps (which would make excellent slides), a chronology, footnotes and a bibliography. This information source is suitable for a school or college library.

1379. Voll, John Obert and Sarah Potts Voll. **The Sudan: Unity and Diversity in a Multicultural State.** London and Sydney; Boulder, CO: Croom Helm; Westview, 1985. xiii, 178 p. *Profiles: Nations of the Contemporary Middle East.* ISBN 0-86531-302-4.

A scholarly monograph whose clarity of organization lends itself to reference work. Distinct chapters are devoted to physical geography, ethnic/tribal identity, language, religion, stages in Sudan's history, the economy, international relations—and within these chapters, the text is broken up with prominent headings that make it easier to find specific information. There is also an index, source footnotes for each chapter, and a helpful bibliographical essay (pp. 167-171). A useful introductory text for the college library.

1380. Wawa, Yosa H. **Southern Sudan: a Select Bibliography.** Khartoum: Institute of African and Asian Studies, Library & Documentation, 1988. iv, 138 p.

Primary source materials, articles and books in English, Arabic and French are cited in this bibliography, which is organized not by topic but by type of materials. A subject index offers some help with topical access. The researcher will be frustrated, even baffled, by the absence of bibliographic data. Many citations provide nothing more than a title and a date. It appears that many hours in the National Records Office, state and university libraries in Khartoum would be needed to locate these works.

1381. Wawa, Yosa H. and Amal Eisa El-Fadil. **Bibliography on Sudan International Relations.** Khartoum: Institute of African and Asian Studies, Library & Documentation, 1990. lii, 277 p.

Brief annotations are included for many of the works cited in this bibliography of English and Arabic materials. Some primary sources (especially correspondence and agreements with various foundations, governments and donor agencies) are found here. Bibliographic data is very sparse, but most entries do include a location code indicating which institution in Khartoum can furnish a copy. The entries are topically organized, and the subject index is helpful.

1382. Wayne, Scott. **Egypt and the Sudan: a Travel Survival Kit.** Berkeley, CA; South Yarra, Australia: Lonely Planet, 1987. 389 p. ISBN 0-86442-001-3.

Practical facts for the independent traveller form the basis of this guidebook. It concerns itself with transport, accommodation, restaurants, visas, and so on, with detailed information and directory data (for hospitals, post offices, etc.) Many small but clear and helpful street maps are included.

Advice on visiting monuments, museums and other attractions is offered, and there are some nice color postcard-style photos to get the reader motivated. For both Egypt and the Sudan, the writer provides a great deal of help for visiting outlying areas (distant oases, small towns, even places that require camping gear) not just the typical five-star-hotel destinations of most tour groups.

1383. Willis, C. A. **The Upper Nile Province Handbook: a Report on the Peoples and Government in the Southern Sudan, 1931.** Oxford: The British Academy, 1995. xx, 476 p. ISBN 0-19-726146-9.

Edited by noted authority Douglas H. Johnson, this volume does more than reproduce a quaint artifact of British administration in the "Anglo-Egyptian Sudan." It provides an historical summary of the area up to 1926, an account of the eventful administration of C.A. Willis as Governor, an analysis of the historical record of the Condominium, and some carefully-evaluated statistical data.

The volume also includes the "handing-over notes" of Willis' predecessor, a very interesting retrospective bibliography, some contemporary maps, an index, a glossary, and an appendix that serves as a handy biographical dictionary identifying the persons (British, Egyptian and Sudanese) significant in this historical period.

1384. Zahlan, A. B. **Agricultural Bibliography of Sudan, 1974-1983: Selected, Classified and Annotated.** London: Ithaca Press, 1984. 325 p. *Middle East Science Policy Series.* ISBN 0-86372-017-X.

A carefully-organized compilation of scholarly sources (books, articles, dissertations, lectures) covering a wide spectrum of economic and social issues in Sudan having to do with food production.

The physical environment and natural resources; geology, climate, groundwater and rainfall, idigenous vegetation, soils, forests, fishing resources, even biomass for energy use are all covered. The social organization of agricultural labor, education in husbandry, agro-industry and mechanization, pest control, human diseases associated with farm work and veterinary medicine are likewise included.

Entries are annotated, and many offer lengthy and detailed abstracts. An author index is provided. The introduction also contains a brief description of the agriculture-related research stations in Sudan and their activities. A new edition of this valuable work is overdue.

Journals/Databases

1385. **Country Report: Sudan.** Quarterly; 1986- . London: Economist Intelligence Unit.

Available online through DIALOG, LEXIS/NEXIS, FT Profile and M.A.I.D./Profound; on CD-ROM from Knight-Ridder and Silver Platter; on microfilm from World Microfilms Publications.

Concise information on current political and economic conditions in particular countries, with forecasts of up to two years. All of the countries of northern Africa are covered (except Western Sahara). Profile data and brief executive summaries of current conditions are included.

The EIU annual *Country Profiles* offer more extensive background reading and statistical tables, to summarize and supplement the quarterly reports.

1386. **Northeast African Studies.** Three times/year; 1979- (new series 1994-). East Lansing, MI: Michigan State University Press. ISSN 0740-9133.

Descriptive website available at **www.msu.edu/unit/msupress/journals/ jour4.html;** contents page available at **h-net2.msu.edu/~africa/toc/neas/ neas2-2.html**

Sponsored by the Northeast African Studies Committee, this interesting and varied journal concentrates upon Eritrea, Ethiopia, Djibouti, Somalia and Sudan. Social science research, policy studies, history, anthropology and folklore, philosophy and literature are all within the scope of this publication. Each issue includes a section of brief but informative signed book reviews. Articles are published in English or French.

Websites

1387. History of the World. Another Sudan Links Page. **historyoftheworld. com/africa/sudan.htm**

1388. Homelands. Autonomy, Secession, Independence and Nationalist Movements. **www.wavefront.com/~homelands/index.html**
    Special coverage of the South Sudan.

1389. ReliefWeb: United Nations Office for the Coordination of Humanitarian Affairs (OCHA). South Sudan Online. **www.state.gov/www/issues/relief/index.html**
    General ReliefWeb site at **wwwnotes.reliefweb.int/**

1390. Sudan Catholic Information Office. Sudan Monthly Report. **www.peacelink.it/ africa/scio/month.html**
    Eyewitness accounts of famine. Full text of current and recent issues.

1391. Sudan News and Views Online. **webzone1.co.uk/www/sudan/snv/ snv29.htm#FORCIBLE29**
    "An independent electronic Newsletter working to advocate peace, human rights and humanitarian aid for the Sudan." Full text of current and recent issues.

1392. Sudan Update. **www.sas.upenn.edu/African_Studies/Newsletters/ menu_SD_Update.html**
    "An international media review, published twice monthly, recording news and comment on Sudanese affairs from all quarters to promote dialogue and education." Full text of current and back issues.

1393. SudanNet. **www.sudan.net/**
    Popular website, with many links.

1394. United Nations World Food Programme. **www.wfp.org/**
    Current special coverage of Sudan.

1395. University of Khartoum. **www.columbia.edu/~tm146/Khar/UofK.html**

1396. World Vision. Cry the Divided Country: Sudan. **www.worldvision.org/ worldvision/pr.nsf/stable/sudaninfokit**
    World disaster relief NGO: special coverage of famine in Sudan.

Western Sahara

Reference Sources

1397. Pazzanita, Anthony G. **Western Sahara.** Santa Barbara, CA: ABC-Clio Press, 1996. xl, 259 p. *World Bibliographical Series;* v. 190. ISBN 1-85109-256-0.

The World Bibliographical Series being produced by Clio provides access for the English-speaking reader to a variety of materials: books and monographs, journals, bibliographies and reference works, theses and dissertations, conference proceedings, and sometimes more specialized information (e.g., manuscript catalogs). Fully-annotated entries (some volumes are annotated better than others) cover history, geography, economics and politics, culture, social customs and religion. Attention is paid to language, literature and the arts as well. An introductory essay and map are provided, and an index of authors, titles and subjects. Sometimes other helps (a glossary or chronology, for example) may be included. Each volume covers one individual country, but in some cases closely-related content overlaps: Somalia and Djibouti, Ethiopia and Eritrea, and so on.

1398. Pazzanita, Anthony G. and Tony Hodges. **Historical Dictionary of Western Sahara.** Second edition. Metuchen, NJ: Scarecrow, 1994. lxxii, 560 p. *African Historical Dictionaries;* no. 55. ISBN 0-8108-2661-5.

Revising the first edition of this work (Tony Hodges' *Historical Dictionary of Western Sahara*, 1982) was necessitated by the violent conflict and UN-monitored ceasefire in in this disputed region since 1981. The chronology, introductory essay and lengthy classified bibliography reflect this development. Some deeper background data on the history and culture of the Saharawi tribes had to be eliminated from this edition; the Preface suggests that the reader search Hodges' original version for more material on those topics.

1399. Sipe, Lynn F. **Western Sahara: a Comprehensive Bibliography.** New York: Garland, 1984. xxxiv, 418 p. *Garland Reference Library of Social Science;* v. 178. ISBN 0-8240-9125-6.

Focusing on the status of the area since Spanish colonial times, this bibliography brings to light a substantial body of literature on the subject, including "books and monographs, journals and periodical articles, newsletters, research reports, conference proceedings, annuals and yearbooks, government publications, maps, dissertations and theses, and ... significant editorial comment, opinion columns and extended feature articles" (Introduction). Materials in Western European languages are included. An entry is briefly annotated if the title does not indicate its content, or if only a certain portion of a larger work is devoted to the Western Sahara, or if the material issues from a highly biased source (Spanish fascist publications, for example). The pattern of organization is set forth in the table of contents; the author-and-subject index is helpful for specific persons.

1400. Zoubir, Yahia H. and Daniel Volman. **International Dimensions of the Western Sahara Conflict.** Westport, CT: Praeger (Greenwood), 1993. xv, 255 p. ISBN 0-275-93821-3.

Ten scholarly essays on the regional and geopolitical aspects of the Western Sahara conflict are collected in this volume, offering access to specific material on this problem. The roles of international law, the United Nations and the World Court, former colonial powers and Cold War antagonists are discussed. Each essay includes bibliographical references; a glossary, a general bibliography and an index are also provided.

Websites

1401. Western Sahara Information Service, Vienna. **www.isoc.vienna.org/ westsahara/**

Information and advocacy links.

1402. Western Sahara/Sahara Occidental. **www.arso.org/index.htm**

Human rights and "struggle for self-determination of the Sahrawi people" emphasis.

The Horn of Africa

Chapter 10

As noted in the Preface, regional divisions in northern Africa are by no means universally accepted. This section will include the countries on the eastern spur of the African continent, known as the Horn (bordered by Kenya and Sudan).

Reference Sources

1403. **Country Profile: Eritrea, Somalia, Djibouti.** Annual; 1997- . London: Economist Intelligence Unit. ISSN 1364-7377.

This annual supplement to the quarterly EIU *Country Reports* aims to provide more extensive background reading and statistical tables. Each volume serves as a useful reference source. In 1997, Ethiopia was set off from the other countries of the Horn in its own profile, and these three nations became a separate publication unit.

1404. **Country Profile: Ethiopia, Eritrea, Somalia, Djibouti.** Annual; 1994-1996. London: Economist Intelligence Unit. ISSN 1352-2957.

1405. **Country Profile: Ethiopia, Somalia, Djibouti.** Annual; 1986-1993. London: Economist Intelligence Unit.

In 1993, with the formation of Eritrea as an independent state, the grouping of countries in these profiles was changed.

1406. **Ethiopia and Eritrea: a Documentary Study.** Compiled with an introduction by Habtu Ghebre-Ab. Trenton, NJ: The Red Sea Press, 1993. xv, 264 p. ISBN 0-932415-87-3.

A collection of verbatim documents (not facsimiles) pertaining to important milestones in the history of the Horn from 1888 to 1955. The activities of the major European colonial powers are documented here, along with United Nations involvement in the post-colonial territorial disputes. The documents (agreements, treaties, conventions, protocols, conference proceedings, declarations, memoranda, statements, messages and constitutional instruments) are ordered and numbered chronologically. There is no index, but the table of contents makes the nature of the material fairly clear.

1407. Darch, Colin. **A Soviet View of Africa: an Annotated Bibliography on Ethiopia, Somalia and Djibouti.** Boston: G.K. Hall, 1980. xxxvi, 200 p. *Bibliographies and Guides in African Studies.* ISBN 0-8161-8365-1.

A work that does justice to the extensive and important literature in Russian pertaining to the Horn of Africa. Soviet involvement in the Marxist government of Ethiopia and in the political life of Somalia are only part of the picture. Darch also documents the ongoing activities of explorers and adventurers, diplomats and researchers in every subject area, and Russian clerics and scholars interested in the Ethiopian Orthodox Church.

In addition to the materials published in Russian, those produced in the Soviet Union in a non-Russian language (including Amharic) are collected in an appendix. The citations are organized according to "the Institute of Ethiopian Studies' modified version of Dewey Decimal Classification" (Introduction, p. xix). Many of the entries are annotated, but this is inconsistent: a few words, a cataloging contents note, or a full abstract may be provided. Book reviews and newspaper articles are found in appendices; there is a subject and a names index.

1408. Freeman-Grenville, G. S. P. (Greville Stewart Parker). **The East African Coast: Select Documents From the First to the Earlier Nineteenth Century.** Second edition. London: Rex Collings, 1975. 314 p.

The documents collected here pertain mainly to the eastern coast south of the Horn, though some references to Ethiopia and Somalia may be found. There are six interesting little maps and a general index.

1409. Gurdon, Charles. **The Horn of Africa.** New York: St. Martin's Press, 1994. 123 p. ISBN 0-312-12063-X and 0-312-12064-8.

A scholarly essay collection issued at the peak of a period of drastic political change in Sudan, Ethiopia/Eritrea and Somalia. Compiled at the Geopolitics and International Boundaries Research Center at SOAS (London), the collection serves as a history and analysis of those eventful years. A map, bibliographies for each essay, tables of the area's political groups and clans, and a careful index increase the book's reference value.

1410. Hanley, Gerald. **Warriors: Life and Death Among the Somalis.** London: Eland, 1993. 179 p. ISBN 0-907871-27-5.

Not a guidebook, this is a personal travel narrative of a literary nature about life in rural reaches of the Horn of Africa, and about the British, French and Italian colonial presence there. It includes a beautiful handlettered historical map of the region.

1411. Marcus, Harold G. **The Modern History of Ethiopia and the Horn of Africa: a Select and Annotated Bibliography.** Stanford: Hoover Institution Press, 1972. xxii, 641 p.

A compilation of over 2000 annotated entries covering Ethiopia's history from the viewpoint of European geographic journals, especially the smaller and more obscure publications of 19th and 20th century geographical and exploration societies. This fascinating material involves ethnology, geology, anthropology, linguistics and other aspects of the physical and cultural environment.

The work is organized by language: materials in English, French, Italian, German, and Russian (et al.) are grouped together. This scheme requires some heavy indexing: indexes of authors, of proper nouns (names of individuals and groups other than authors), of place names, and of subjects are provided. Appendices list the journals and books consulted. The annotations are detailed enough to be of real value to the researcher.

1412. Matthies, Volker. **Äthiopien, Eritrea, Somalia, Djibouti: das Horn von Afrika.** Munich: C.H. Beck, 1997. 186 p. ISBN 3-406-42446-5.

A pocket handbook concentrating on text and description, with a bare minimum of practical travel information or photos. The description serves as a capable and readable introduction to the history, culture, economy and political problems of the region. An appendix provides chronologies, a topically-subdivided, current bibliography of serious reading, a helpful index, and five very clear small maps.

1413. Miller, E. Willard and Ruby M. Miller. **Tropical, Eastern and Southern Africa: a Bibliography on the Third World.** Monticello, IL: Vance Bibliographies, 1981. 82 p. *Public Administration Series;* no. 819.

The Vance bibliographies on public administration are composed of topically arranged citations—up to about 1000 in each issue—of books and articles, government bulletins and other publications. The entries are sometimes briefly annotated. Ethiopia and Somalia are included in this issue.

1414. Prouty, Chris. **A Catalogue of Documentary Films and Film Footage on Ethiopia and Eritrea.** Addis Ababa: Institute of Ethiopian Studies, 1996. 111 p.

A guide to existing film and video works pertaining to Ethiopia, Eritrea, the Oromo, the Falashas, etc. is to be appreciated, as a great deal of this material is ephemeral or fugitive, and otherwise unrecorded. Many of the productions described here were prepared as television news reports or features; many classic movie-theatre newsreels are also carefully listed here.

Works in a variety of languages, held in many European countries, the United States, Israel, Japan and Mexico, have been tracked down and mentioned. They are cited here by country of origin, then by production date. Annotations note when copies are available outside Ethiopia, through distributors or in archival collections. A names and subject index to this catalog would be most welcome.

1415. Prouty, Chris and Eugene Rosenfeld. **Historical Dictionary of Ethiopia and Eritrea.** Second edition. Metuchen, NJ: Scarecrow, 1994. xxvi, 612 p. *African Historical Dictionaries;* no. 56. ISBN 0-8108-2663-1.

This edition, completed just before Eritrea became established as a separate state in 1993, still refers to Eritrea as a region of Ethiopia. This volume contains two maps, a very concise and direct introduction, a chronology of political events, the dictionary itself, and a very substantial, carefully-organized and classified bibliography of materials (books and articles) in English and several European languages.

1416. Sorenson, John. **Disaster and Development in the Horn of Africa.** New York: St. Martin's Press, 1995. xvii, 272 p. *International Political Economy Series.* ISBN 0-312-12538-0.

This collection of essays emerged from papers presented to a conference sponsored by the Eritrean Relief Association in Canada. The topical essays focus on specific problems in Northeast Africa's development: famine, pastoralism, population displacement, public health, international relief efforts and intelligence operations. The introductory essay by John Sorenson serves as an effective capsule description of current conditions in Ethiopia, Eritrea, Sudan, Somalia and Djibouti. Each article provides an up-to-date bibliography of 20-80 sources. The volume includes a carefully subdivided index, some tables of data, and several unusual maps and figures.

1417. Woodward, Peter. **The Horn of Africa: State Politics and International Relations.** London: Tauris, 1996. ix, 226 p. *International Library of African Studies.* ISBN 1-85043-741-6.

A political history and analysis of the area, with a clear organizational plan. Chapters on the Horn in general, then on the individual states, make up Part One; Part Two deals with international developments. Notes and a current bibliography are provided; there is an inferior index.

Journals/Databases

1418. **Country Report: Ethiopia, Eritrea, Somalia, Djibouti.** Quarterly; 1993- . London: Economist Intelligence Unit. ISSN 1352-2922.

Available online through DIALOG, LEXIS/NEXIS, FT Profile and M.A.I.D./Profound; on CD-ROM from Knight-Ridder and Silver Platter; on microfilm from World Microfilms Publications.

Concise information on current political and economic conditions in particular countries, with forecasts of up to two years. All of the countries of northern Africa are covered (except Western Sahara). Profile data and brief executive summaries of current conditions are included.

The EIU annual *Country Profiles* offer more extensive background reading and statistical tables, to summarize and supplement the quarterly reports.

1419. **Northeast African Studies.** Three times/year; 1979- (new series 1994-). East Lansing, MI: Michigan State University Press. ISSN 0740-9133.

Descriptive website available at **www.msu.edu/unit/msupress/journals/ jour4.html;** contents page available at **h-net2.msu.edu/~africa/toc/neas/ neas2-2.html**

Sponsored by the Northeast African Studies Committee, this interesting and varied journal concentrates upon Eritrea, Ethiopia, Djibouti, Somalia and Sudan. Social science research, policy studies, history, anthropology and folklore, philosophy and literature are all within the scope of this publication. Each issue includes a section of brief but informative signed book reviews. Articles are published in English or French.

Websites

1420. Abyssinia Cyberspace Gateway. Community Resource on the Web. **www. cs.indiana.edu/hyplan/dmulholl/acg.html**

Links to attractive and informative pages on Djibouti, Ethiopia, Eritrea, Somalia and Somaliland.

1421. Centre for Environment and Development, University of Bern. **www. giub.unibe.ch/cde/**

With reference specifically to Ethiopia and Eritrea.

1422. NomadNet. The Homepage for Somalia, Peacekeeping, Relief and Economic Development Issues. **www.netnomad.com/**

Relevant to the Horn in general.

1423. The Hornet. News from the Horn of Africa. **www.sas.upenn.edu/ African_Studies/Hornet/menu_Hornet.html**

A collection of links and full-text documents about the Horn of Africa, including the monthly UNDP Emergencies Unit for Ethiopia report, and other material on Northeast Africa.

1424. US Agency for International Development. Greater Horn Information Exchange. **www.info.usaid.gov/HORN/DJIBOUTI**

Djibouti

Reference Sources

1425. **Djibouti Post Report.** Revised Dec 1996. Washington: Department of State Publication 10369, Office of Information Services. 14 p.; photos. SuDocs S1.127:D64/996.

Department of State "Post Reports" are pamphlets containing basic information thought to be useful for U.S. government employees and their families being sent to a new location. Each report includes: a brief description of the "host country"—its climate, population, transport, tourist attractions, health services, etc.; specific information on the American Embassy and any consulates, housing, food and clothing, recreation opportunities, education for dependents; basic travel data on customs duties, currency, import restrictions, local holidays. Some issues provide a handy, clear and detailed street map of the area of the capital city surrounding the American Embassy (often hard to find in any other source).

1426. **Djibuti: an Open Gate on a Market of Over 80,000,000 Inhabitants.** Djibouti: Chambre Internationale de Commerce et d'Industrie, 1992. 50 p.

The text of this publication is in English, presumably in the service of investment by companies from the United States and Britain. There are some colorful maps and pictures, directory data for banks, government agencies and ministries, embassies, consulates and intergovernmental organizations, and some general information pertinent to companies considering investment projects.

1427. **L'Enquête Démographique Intercensitaire.** Djibouti: Ministère de l'Intérieur des Postes et Télécommunications, 1991. 141 p.

A collection of government-collected demographic statistics, with some textual interpretation. The tables of data are fairly clearly presented. A helpful table of contents is provided.

1428. **Guide Pratique de la République de Djibouti.** Djibouti: L'Office National du Tourisme et de l'Artisanat, 1987. 111 p.

The traveler looking for practical information of any kind will be disappointed in this guide, which despite its title consists almost entirely of large, colorful, glossy photographs of fun things to do or see in Djibouti. There is a small amount of text and some maps.

1429. **Petit Guide de Djibouti.** Djibouti: Association Démocratique des Français de Djibouti, 1991. 118 p.

An informal local publication meant to assist the French-speaking expatriate becoming settled in Djibouti. There is simple descriptive material about the country, and quite a bit of practical information about baggage, vaccinations, visas, transport, local schools, etc.

1430. Aubry, Marie-Christine. **Djibouti: Bibliographie Fondamentale (Domaine Francophone).** Paris: Éditions l'Harmattan, 1990. v, 169 p.

A bibliography of sources in French, grouped into broad subject areas: physical geography and description, human activity (history, politics, culture, economics) and literature. The book includes two interesting sketch maps. Indexes of personal and corporate names are provided.

1431. Aubry, Marie-Christine. **Djibouti l'Ignoré: Récits de Voyage.** Paris: Éditions l'Harmattan, 1988. 248 p. ISBN 2-7384-0060-4.

This fascinating scholarly monograph includes a number of features valuable for reference work. There is an extensive and sophisticated bibliography, including some 59 firsthand accounts of travel and exploration in the area, among them works by Arthur Rimbaud, Pierre Loti, Pablo Neruda and Pierre Teilhard de Chardin. There is a glossary of unusual terms, five specialized historical maps, a names index, and eight pages of period illustrations.

1432. Carton-Dibeth, Véronique. **Manuel de Conversation Somali-Français: suivi d'un Guide de Djibouti.** Paris: Éditions l'Harmattan, 1988. 80 p. ISBN 2-7384-0090-6.

The Somali language is used by more than seven million people in the Horn of Africa generally, but this paperback guide is meant specifically for French-speaking visitors—both tourists and expatriates—to Djibouti. In addition to the vocabulary and grammatical summaries, there are phrases, expressions and conversational forms. Two maps and a simple orientation guide (practical information about the currency, hotels, transport, etc.) are included.

1433. Clarke, W. Sheldon. **A Developmental Bibliography for the Republic of Djibouti.** [Djibouti]: Private printing, 1979. Unpaginated.

A retrospective compilation of literature (articles and books) on the history of Djibouti, topically arranged. Many sources in French are included, and dates of publication reach well back into the 19th century. Related material on other states in the Horn of Africa is included. There is an author index. This reference represents a helpful source of hard-to-find information.

1434. Schraeder, Peter J. **Djibouti.** Santa Barbara, CA: ABC-Clio Press, 1991. xxxix, 239 p. *World Bibliographical Series;* v. 118. ISBN 1-85109-084-3.

The World Bibliographical Series being produced by Clio provides access for the English-speaking reader to a variety of materials: books and monographs, journals, bibliographies and reference works, theses and dissertations, conference proceedings, and sometimes more specialized information (e.g., manuscript catalogs). Fully-annotated entries (some volumes are annotated better than others) cover history, geography, economics and politics, culture, social customs and religion. Attention is paid to language, literature and the arts as well. An introductory essay and map are provided, and an index of authors, titles and subjects. Sometimes other helps (a glossary or chronology, for example) may be included. Each volume covers one individual country, but in some cases closely-related content overlaps: Somalia and Djibouti, Ethiopia and Eritrea, and so on.

Websites

1435. Djibouti. Société des Télécommunications Internationales de Djibouti (STID). **www.intnet.dj/**
Links to business/commercial, cultural and political information about Djibouti.

1436. Djibouti (Agora Djibouti). L'Actualité et la Culture de Djibouti en Ligne. **www.djibouti.org/**
Attractive, informative site in French and English.

Eritrea

Reference Sources

1437. **Bibliography on Eritrea.** Rome: Research and Information Centre on Eritrea, 1982. x, 235 p.
Introductory material in this volume is in English, but the works cited (books and articles) are written in a variety of European languages. Coverage of works in Italian is particularly good, which of course is important for historical research on the Horn of Africa. Entries are grouped under broad topical headings, and a little more location help is given by the index. Entries are not annotated.

1438. **Eritrea: a New Beginning.** London: United Nations Industrial Development Organization, 1996. ix, 76 p. *Industrial Development Review Series.*
A volume of hard-to-find information on the industrial and overall economic capacity of Africa's newest sovereign country. There are plenty of figures and tables of data, with a helpful introduction and explanatory text.
Sections cover macro-economic policies, basic manufacturing issues (productivity, ownership, environmental concerns, etc.) and specific industrial output in food, clothing, leather, wood, chemicals and petroleum, minerals, machinery, paper, glass, and so on. Import figures are also reported where relevant. There is no index, but the table of contents is adequate.

1439. **Eritrea at a Glance.** Revised edition. Edited by Mary Houdek and Leonardo Oriolo. Asmara: International Guidebook Committee, 1996. vi, 209 p.
A practical guide meant to orient English-speaking expatriates becoming settled in Eritrea. This volume provides background information, descriptions of local culture and customs, information on housing, utilities, driving, shopping, postal and communication services, health care, schools and recreation opportunities. There is pertinent directory data and several black-and-white photos, and a phrase list in Tigrigna and Arabic. Many helpful street maps and an index are included.

1440. **Eritrea: Demographic and Health Survey.** Asmara: National Statistics Office, 1997. xx, 324 p.

Technical assistance provided by Macro International, Inc., with funding from the US Agency for International Development, as part of the Demographic and Health Surveys (DHS) program.

This detailed, current, comprehensive and carefully-prepared statistical survey of the population and health conditions of Eritrea is an important information source in a distinctly underserved area. Maternal and child health, fertility, education, access to treatment and media information, infectious disease, employment and housing are all measured and reported in scores of tables and figures. In addition, an interpretive text clarifies the data-processing techniques and points out the implications of this raw data.

The contents of the volume are well organized, though not indexed. Appendices provide technical notes about the data-gathering and statistical methods and verbatim copies of the questionnaires used.

1441. **Eritrea Post Report.** Released July 1996. Washington: Department of State Publication 10362, Office of Information Services. 15 p.; photos. SuDocs S1.127:Er4/996.

Department of State "Post Reports" are pamphlets containing basic information thought to be useful for U.S. government employees and their families being sent to a new location. Each report includes: a brief description of the "host country"—its climate, population, transport, tourist attractions, health services, etc.; specific information on the American Embassy and any consulates, housing, food and clothing, recreation opportunities, education for dependents; basic travel data on customs duties, currency, import restrictions, local holidays. Some issues provide a handy, clear and detailed street map of the area of the capital city surrounding the American Embassy (often hard to find in any other source).

1442. Abbink, J. **Eritreo-Ethiopian Studies in Society and History, 1960-1995: a Supplementary Bibliography.** Leiden: African Studies Center, Political and Historical Studies Division, 1996. 203 p. ISBN 90-5448-032-7.

An update to Abbink's *Ethiopian Society and History* (1990), this volume covers only the five-year period 1990-1995; hence the "supplementary" term in the title. The two works together constitute a retrospective bibliography reaching back to 1957.

The work covers the traditional topics of history, agriculture, politics, law, art and religion, but the writer notes an increasing interest in the literature in environmental/ecological and "socio-cultural" studies (p. 1). The entries are carefully organized by topic and chronology, and there is a substantial section on ethnology/anthropology divided into 56 language or tribal groups. Scholarly monographs and articles are included here, and some reference works (e.g., catalogs of manuscripts). There is an index of authors, but no title index.

1443. Fegley, Randall. **Eritrea.** Santa Barbara, CA: ABC-Clio Press, 1995. lix, 125 p. *World Bibliographical Series;* v. 181. ISBN 1-85109-245-5.

The World Bibliographical Series being produced by Clio provides access for the English-speaking reader to a variety of materials: books and monographs, journals, bibliographies and reference works, theses and dissertations, conference proceedings, and sometimes more specialized information (e.g., manuscript catalogs). Fully-annotated entries (some volumes are annotated better than others) cover history, geography, economics and politics, culture, social customs and religion. Attention is paid to language, literature and the arts as well. An introductory essay and map are provided, and an index of authors, titles and subjects. Sometimes other helps (a glossary or chronology, for example) may be included. Each volume covers one individual country, but in some cases closely-related content overlaps: Somalia and Djibouti, Ethiopia and Eritrea, and so on.

1444. Iyob, Ruth. **The Eritrean Struggle for Independence: Domination, Resistance, Nationalism, 1941-1993.** Cambridge: Cambridge University Press, 1995. xiv, 198 p. *African Studies Series;* 82. ISBN 0-521-47327-6.

A scholarly monograph summarizing and analyzing the prolonged process of independence for the state of Eritrea. Two unusual maps, an effective index, meticulous source notes and a current bibliography of official publications, newspapers and periodicals, books and journal articles, interviews, speeches and videos increase the reference value of the work.

1445. Killion, Tom. **Historical Dictionary of Eritrea.** Lanham, MD: Scarecrow, 1998. xli, 535 p. *African Historical Dictionaries;* no. 75. ISBN 0-8108-3437-5.

A convenient reference based upon extensive firsthand knowledge of Eritrea's rocky road to independence. Important places, people and organizations in Eritrea's history are defined and described in unusually full, informative alphabetized entries. A chronology and subdivided bibliography are provided; there is no index, but entries contain cross-references. The four detailed sketch maps are not beautiful to behold but convey a great deal of hard-to-find information. A narrative introduction offers a concise summary of the nation's geography, history and population groups.

1446. Langknecht, Ludwig. **Eritrea: ein Reiseführer.** Heidelberg: Kasparek, 1995. 148 p. ISBN 3-925064-19-2.

A handsome introduction to Eritrea, emphasizing background and description of the geography, population, culture, religion, history and attractions. Appealing photos (both black-and-white and color), small drawings, maps and city plans and fact boxes enrich the text. A small section of basic, practical information for travelers is included; there is a simple glossary, bibliography and index.

1447. Paice, Edward. **Guide to Eritrea.** Second edition. Old Saybrook, CT and Chalfont St. Peter, Bucks, England: Globe Pequot; Bradt Publications, 1996. ix, 192 p. ISBN 1-56440-951-1.

Attractively printed and illustrated with clear maps, city plans and color photos, this guide is a useful introduction to Eritrea. About one-third of the book is description and background, while two-thirds is practical information for the visitor. The volume provides information about the smaller towns and country-side, not just the capital, assuming that the reader will make forays into less-traveled areas. A Tigrinya vocabulary and an index are included.

1448. Papstein, Robert. **Eritrea: a Tourist Guide.** Lawrenceville, NY: Red Sea Press, 1995. 117 p. ISBN 1-56902-011-6.

An informative travel guidebook, spoiled by poor print quality and binding. The maps and photos are not effectively reproduced; even some of the text is hard to read. The emphasis here is on practical ready-reference information, not description or background. There is a simple index.

Journals

1449. **Eritrean Studies Review.** Semiannual; 1996- . Lawrenceville, NJ: Red Sea Press. ISSN 1086-9174.

A new journal devoting its attention to the affairs of Africa's newest sover-eign nation. Education and literacy, business and the economy, agriculture and the peasantry, archaeology, constitutional law, voting and nation-building are all reflected in the first volume. The journal is a publication of the Eritrean Studies Association.

Websites

1450. Eritrea. Dehai Eritrea Online. **www.primenet.com/~ephrem/**
News and links.

1451. Eritrean Network Information Center (ENIC). **eritrea.org/EIB/control/main.html**
News, culture, tourism, education, business and other information.

Ethiopia

Reference Sources

1452. **Annotated Bibliography on the Population of Ethiopia.** Compiled by Abdulahi Hasen, Tesfayesus Mahary, and Jelaludin Ahmed. Addis Ababa: Population Information Network for Africa, 1990. xx, 205 p. *Country Bibliography Series;* no. 4.

Published under the auspices of the United Nations, this bibliography in-cludes very lengthy and detailed annotations—full summaries or abstracts of the contents of most of the works cited. These tend to be scholarly or technical studies of demographic phenomena. There is a rough index, marred by a publishing error (some pages are reversed).

1453. **Country Profile: Ethiopia.** Annual; 1997 . London: Economist Intelligence Unit.

This annual supplement to the quarterly EIU *Country Reports* aims to provide more extensive background reading and statistical tables. Each volume serves as a useful reference source. In 1997, Ethiopia was set off from the other countries of the Horn in its own profile.

1454. **Documents on Ethiopian Politics.** Edited by Borg G Steffanson and Ronald K. Starrett. Salisbury, NC: Documentary Publications, 1976. 3 v.

Limited edition (100 copies).

In three volumes, the compilers have assembled some 160 documents pertaining to Ethiopia's history between 1910 and 1929, during the emergence of Haile Selassie as the nation's leader. The collection is arranged chronologically and reproduced as is, in facsimile form, without caption, annotation or commentary—just a title in the table of contents. Documents in cursive handwriting or poor-quality typescript may be hard to read; on the whole, the later documents are more legible.

Previously unpublished, many of these materials were discovered in the National Archives of the United States; most of them are confidential political reports addressed by American consuls back to the State Department. Some diplomatic documents from European capitals, Ethiopian materials in translation, accounts by private observers and other contemporary correspondence and excerpts from press reports are included.

Vol. 1 covers the decline of King Menelik II and Selassie's early career, 1910-1919; Vol. 2 details his consolidation of power, 1920-1929; Vol. 3 deals with the activities of the foreign powers in Ethiopia (England, France, Italy, Germany and the United States) during the same period. There is one rough map in Vol. 2. The entire work is indexed by name and subject at the end of the third volume.

1455. **Ethiopia, a Country Study.** Fourth edition. Edited by Thomas P. Ofcansky and LaVerle Berry. Federal Research Division, Library of Congress. *Area Handbook Series.* Washington: Department of the Army, 1993. xxxvi, 412 p. ISBN 0-8444-0739-9; ISSN 1057-5294; SuDocs no. D101.22: 550-26/993

Also available online at **lcweb2.loc.gov/frd/cs/cshome.html**

Each book in this series deals with "a particular foreign country, describing and analyzing its ... systems and institutions, and examining the interrelationships of those systems and the ways they are shaped by cultural factors " (Foreword). The books use a similar five-part structure: historical setting, the society and its environment (sociology, anthropology, geography), the economy, government and politics, and national security. Areas studies specialists prepare each of these five parts, rather like signed encyclopedia articles. The volumes include a capsule "Country Profile," some black-and-white photos, maps and figures, several useful tables of population, trade and other data (in an appendix), a bibliography, glossary of terms and an extensive, well-organized index. The tables often provide data that would be difficult to obtain from any other source: e.g., a country's exact or estimated supply of major aircraft, air defense weapons, naval vessels, field artillery and armored vehicles.

1456. **Ethiopia Post Report.** Revised Aug 1996. Washington: Department of State Publication 10363, Office of Information Services. 16 p.; photos. SuDocs S1.127:Et3/996.

Department of State "Post Reports" are pamphlets containing basic information thought to be useful for U.S. government employees and their families being sent to a new location. Each report includes: a brief description of the "host country"—its climate, population, transport, tourist attractions, health services, etc.; specific information on the American Embassy and any consulates, housing, food and clothing, recreation opportunities, education for dependents; basic travel data on customs duties, currency, import restrictions, local holidays. Some issues provide a handy, clear and detailed street map of the area of the capital city surrounding the American Embassy (often hard to find in any other source).

1457. Abbink, J. **Eritreo-Ethiopian Studies in Society and History, 1960-1995: a Supplementary Bibliography.** Leiden: African Studies Center, Political and Historical Studies Division, 1996. 203 p. ISBN 90-5448-032-7.

An update to Abbink's *Ethiopian Society and History* (1990), this volume covers only the five-year period 1990-1995; hence the "supplementary" term in the title. The two works together constitute a retrospective bibliography reaching back to 1957.

The work covers the traditional topics of history, agriculture, politics, law, art and religion, but the writer notes an increasing interest in the literature in environmental/ecological and "socio-cultural" studies (p. 1). The entries are carefully organized by topic and chronology, and there is a substantial section on ethnology/anthropology divided into 56 language or tribal groups. Scholarly monographs and articles are included here, and some reference works (e.g., catalogs of manuscripts). There is an index of authors, but no title index.

1458. Abbink, J. **Ethiopian Society and History: a Bibliography of Ethiopian Studies, 1957-1990.** Leiden: African Studies Centre, 1990. 407 p. *Research Reports;* no. 45. ISBN 90-70110-86-5.

A compilation of over 5400 books and articles in a wide range of European languages, on all aspects of Ethiopia's past and present. Entries are organized by topic, including headings for 66 different ethnic groups. Material on cultural and creative activities is presented, as well as politics, sociology and economics. There is an index of authors. Entries are not annotated, but the titles are usually quite descriptive of content.

1459. Bonk, Jon. **An Annotated and Classified Bibliography of English Literature Pertaining to the Ethiopian Orthodox Church.** Metuchen, NJ: Scarecrow and the American Theological Library Association, 1984. xi, 116 p. *ATLA Bibliography Series;* no. 11. ISBN 0-8108-1710-1.

Prepared by an expert bibliographer and authority on the history of missions, this is a fully-annotated, tightly-focused compilation of books and articles covering the life, learning, worship and polity of one of the world's most venerable churches. Coverage extends from the ancient roots of the church to its activities today. Entries are divided into five main topical clusters, though these are not always self-explanatory: e.g., a sizable literature on the archaeology of early church sites is compiled under "Organization and Government." There is a basic keyword index.

1460. Geist, Gérard. **Les Européens en Éthiopie aux XVIème et XVIIème Siècles: Bio-Bibliographie d'après les Travaux de Camillo Beccari, Complétée par d'autres Éditions Anciennes ou Actuelles.** Nice: Université de Nice, 1983. ix, 189 p. *Travaux du Laboratoire d'Histoire Quantitative;* Séie Actes, Materiaux no. 1.

A record of the early activities of the Jesuit Fathers in Ethiopia and their contemporaries. Portugese missionaries began to arrive as early as 1555, and were expelled around 1640. Editor Camillo Beccari organized and catalogued their documents and correspondence in a huge multivolume work, 1905-1919; Geist has selected the relevant parts and built upon Beccari's work with additional information.

This edition presents a rather indistinct typescript (including some direct quotes from the documents), a chronology of "Les Pères de la Compagnie," an index, and an illegible map. Entries are arranged by early correspondent (including non-Jesuits, and some non-Portuguese), with biographical data as well as a record of the extant documents.

1461. Gräber, Gerd, Anjelika Gräber, and Berhanu Berhe. **Äthiopien: ein Reiseführer.** Heidelberg: Kasparek, 1997. 225 p. ISBN 3-925064-21-4.

This guidebook consists almost entirely of background information about Ethiopia's geography, history, population, religion, culture and political life, with lengthy descriptions of the "Städte und Sehenswürdigkeiten," including all of the places and tourist attractions one is likely to visit. Only one small section (pp. 201-216) is devoted to practical advice for the traveler. For this reason, the volume is actually a convenient, readable and attractively illustrated introduction to Ethiopia. Many photos (black-and-white and color), maps and city plans are provided, as well as simple fact boxes about cooking, various development projects, the Amharic alphabet, etc. There is some directory data, and a simple index.

1462. Hidaru, Alula and Dessalegn Rahmato. **A Short Guide to the History of Ethiopia: a General Bibliography.** Westport, CT: Greenwood Press, 1976. xi, 176 p. *African Bibliographic Center, Special Bibliographic Series;* New Series, no. 2. ISBN 0-8371-9284-6.

This interesting work is no longer current, but remains a valuable source for its period; it was prepared at a time when writing about Ethiopia was a highly-charged undertaking politically. The citations are for the most part organized by topic. Materials cited were published almost entirely in English, even Ethiopian government publications. When the title does not define a work's content, the entry is very briefly annotated.

The volume lacks a few important helps, such as a subject index and a list of periodicals represented, some of which are quite obscure. Unfortunately, the crowded typescript pages are hard to read. A little patience, however, will uncover some worthwhile materials.

1463. Kloos, Helmut and Zein Ahmad Zein. **Health, Disease, Medicine and Famine in Ethiopia: a Bibliography.** Westport, CT: Greenwood, 1991. xvi, 404 p. *African Special Bibliographic Series;* no. 13. ISBN 0-313-27488-6.

A compilation of over 4000 sources—mostly articles in medical and scientific journals—documenting Ethiopia's health concerns: infectious diseases, food and nutrition, chronic and non-infectious disorders, perinatal and maternal health. In addition, the work covers such topics as accidents or injury/trauma, health care services and delivery, mental health, traditional or herbal medicine, and the special problems of famine, displacement of populations and the needs of refugees. The work is organized by topic and provides author and subject indexes.

1464. Kropp, Manfred. **Die Äthiopischen Königschroniken in der Samm-lung des *Däggazmac* Haylu: Entstehung und Handschriftliche Über-lieferung des Werks.** Frankfurt am Main: Verlag Peter Lang, 1989. 327 p. *Heidelberger Orientalische Studien;* Band 13. ISBN 3-8204-9484-7; ISSN 0721-3069.

A volume for the specialist containing the text/facsimile, translation, commentary and detailed manuscript notes of classical Ethiopian royal chronicles dating from the 18th century. The volume includes a sophisticated bibliography, several genealogical tables and plates showing the calligraphy of the manuscripts themselves.

1465. Lockot, Hans Wilhelm. **Bibliographia Aethiopica; die Äthiopi-enkundliche Literatur des Deutschsprachigen Raums.** Wiesbaden: Franz Steiner Verlag, 1982. 441 p. *Äthiopistische Forschungen;* Band 9. ISBN 3-515-03347-5.

A very extensive and carefully-prepared compilation of materials on all aspects of Ethiopian studies published in German. Articles and scholarly studies from a vast variety of periodicals and collective works are cited here; it is doubtful that any electronic index could provide similar access to this literature, particularly materials published before 1980.

There are no annotations, and the citations are given in a condensed form, with many abbreviations, evidently in order to pack as many onto a given page as possible. Studies of geography and wildlife, all branches of culture (literature, religion, language, art, etc.), sociology, law, the economy, health and development, are included; history is especially well covered. Using the bibliography requires patience, however, as it is indexed by personal name only, and there are no topical subheadings.

1466. Milkias, Paulos. **Ethiopia: a Comprehensive Bibliography.** Boston: G. K. Hall & Co., 1989. 694 p. *Reference Publications in Area Studies.* ISBN 0-8161-9066-6.

A vast compilation of materials, including monographs, government documents and articles, arranged in broad topical categories alphabetically by article. The entries are not annotated. Materials published in English, Amharic, Tigrigna, Oromic (Oromo), German, Italian, French and—in some cases—Russian, Greek, Dutch and Swedish, are all, apparently, within the work's scope. The chronological range reaches from antiquity up to 1988. The work emphasizes "thousands of transliterated Amharic texts which have never appeared before" (Preface), most of them holdings of the National Library of Ethiopia and Addis Ababa University. Unfortunately, the too-broad topical headings (e.g., "literature," or "religion") are not helpful, and there is no subject or keyword index.

1467. Mueller, Q. **Äthiopien: Länderdossier für Hilfswerkvertreter (-innen) bei Befragung von Asylsuchenden.** Zürich: Schweizerische Zentralstelle für Flüchtlingshilfe, 1990. 84 p.

A manual for those interviewing refugees and evaluating their requests for asylum in Switzerland. This handbook serves as a record of the causes and effects of the surge of refugees fleeing persecution in Ethiopia in the 1970s and 1980s. It explains the events leading up to the revolution of 1974, the Derg regime and its political and social fallout. It presents a country profile, summaries of Ethiopia's history, descriptions of the religious and cultural characteristics of the people, all in a concise form written for the layperson and suitable for ready reference. There is a relevant bibliography, a detailed chronology of events, several maps and a table of abbreviations/acronyms.

1468. Munro-Hay, Stuart and Richard Pankhurst. **Ethiopia.** Santa Barbara, CA: ABC-Clio Press, 1995. xxxiii, 225 p. *World Bibliographical Series;* v. 179. ISBN 1-85109-111-4.

The World Bibliographical Series being produced by Clio provides access for the English-speaking reader to a variety of materials: books and monographs, journals, bibliographies and reference works, theses and dissertations, conference proceedings, and sometimes more specialized information (e.g., manuscript catalogs). Fully-annotated entries (some volumes are annotated better than others) cover history, geography, economics and politics, culture, social customs and religion. Attention is paid to language, literature and the arts as well. An introductory essay and map are provided, and an index of authors, titles and subjects. Sometimes other helps (a glossary or chronology, for example) may be included. Each volume covers one individual country, but in some cases closely-related content overlaps: Somalia and Djibouti, Ethiopia and Eritrea, and so on.

1469. Prouty, Chris and Eugene Rosenfeld. **Historical Dictionary of Ethiopia.** Metuchen, NJ: Scarecrow, 1981. xv, 436 p. *African Historical Dictionaries;* no. 32. ISBN 0-8108-1448-X.

The first half of this work provides ready-reference material identifying individuals and place names, and thumbnail sketches of important factors and events in Ethiopia's long history: for example, "The Welwel Incident." It also defines many uniquely Ethiopian vocabulary terms, like *nebura-ed* or *zemecha*. There are brief descriptive entries on more general topics, such as music and instruments, nationalization of resources, wildlife, and the status of women in the society. The second half of the work consists of an extensive bibliography (not annotated). An index offers access to additional topics not appearing as entries.

1470. Schwab, Peter. **Ethiopia: Politics, Economics and Society.** Boulder: Lynne Rienner, 1985. xx, 134 p. *Marxist Regimes Series.* ISBN 0-931477-00-X.

From a vantage point several years later, this book is like a time capsule of Ethiopia's Marxist/Derg period. It sets forth the policies and ideology of the movement, the structures it established, and its effects upon agriculture and the economy, education, health, religion and international relations. The volume provides two good maps, a basic country profile, several tables of figures and organizational charts, a bibliography and an index.

1471. Tareke, Gebru. **Ethiopia, Power and Protest: Peasant Revolts in the Twentieth Century.** Cambridge: Cambridge University Press, 1991. xxi, 272 p. *African Studies Series;* 71. ISBN 0-521-40011-2.

This specialized monograph contains unusual features worthy of note: clear, detailed, close-up maps of the rural provinces of Ethiopia that have experienced agrarian unrest, a concise glossary of uniquely Ethiopian terms, a meticulous index, a sophisticated bibliography and precise source notes that could be valuable for reference work. The study concentrates on three provinces—Tigrai, Bale and Gojjam—giving it a transparent structure that makes specific topics easy to find. Documentary material from primary sources is often included.

Websites

1472. Abyssinia Cyberspace Gateway. Community Resource on the Web. **www.cs.indiana.edu/hyplan/dmulholl/acg.html**

Links to attractive and informative pages on Djibouti, Ethiopia, Eritrea, Somalia and Somaliland.

1473. Addis Tribune. **AddisTribune.EthiopiaOnline.Net/**
Full-text online version. In English.

1474. Ethiopia Online. **etonline.netnation.com/**
News, business, tourism, culture and entertainment links.

Somalia

Reference Sources

1475. **Somalia, a Country Study.** Fourth edition. Edited by Helen Chapin Metz. Federal Research Division, Library of Congress. Washington: Department of the Army, 1993. xxxvii, 282 p. *Area Handbook Series.* ISBN 0-8444-0775-5; ISSN 1057-5294; SuDocs no. D101.22: 550-86/993

Also available online at **lcweb2.loc.gov/frd/cs/cshome.html**

Each book in this series deals with "a particular foreign country, describing and analyzing its ... systems and institutions, and examining the interrelationships of those systems and the ways they are shaped by cultural factors " (Foreword). The books use a similar five-part structure: historical setting, the society and its environment (sociology, anthropology, geography), the economy, government and politics, and national security. Areas studies specialists prepare each of these five parts, rather like signed encyclopedia articles. The volumes include a capsule "Country Profile," some black-and-white photos, maps and figures, several useful tables of population, trade and other data (in an appendix), a bibliography, glossary of terms and an extensive, well-organized index. The tables often provide data that would be difficult to obtain from any other source: e.g., a country's exact or estimated supply of major aircraft, air defense weapons, naval vessels, field artillery and armored vehicles.

1476. **The United Nations and Somalia, 1992-1996.** New York: United Nations Department of Public Information, 1996. 526 p. *United Nations Blue Book Series;* vol. VIII. ISBN 92-1-100566-3; UN Sales no. E.96.I.8.

This volume records the difficult history of UNOSOM, the famine of 1992 and the collapse of the Somalia mission in rather antiseptic terms. But the importance of this work for research and reference is the collection of the full text of 116 documents emerging from this affair: "resolutions of the General Assembly and of the Security Council, statements by the President of the Security Council, reports and letters of the Secretary-General, appeals for humanitarian assistance and communications from UN member states and regional organizations" (p. 101). A month-by-month, sometimes day-by-day chronology of the affair is provided. There is a subject index to the documents, and a general index to the volume itself.

1477. Castagno, Margaret. **Historical Dictionary of Somalia.** Metuchen, NJ: Scarecrow, 1975. xxviii, 213 p. *African Historical Dictionaries;* no. 6. ISBN 0-8108-0830-7.

Though dated now, this is of course an historical dictionary, so in a retrospective sense it is still useful. An interesting introduction, simple chronology, clear monochrome map and bibliography add to the reference value of the work. Entries are direct, concise and readable, and take care to define unique cultural terms (such as "gabay," "jamaha" and "midgan") , as they identify important historical persons, places and events. There is no index, but entries are cross-referenced. A new edition of this work would be most welcome.

1478. DeLancey, Mark W. et al. **Somalia.** Santa Barbara, CA: ABC-Clio Press, 1988. xxviii, 191 p. *World Bibliographical Series;* v. 92. ISBN 1-85109-038-X.

The World Bibliographical Series being produced by Clio provides access for the English-speaking reader to a variety of materials: books and monographs, journals, bibliographies and reference works, theses and dissertations, conference proceedings, and sometimes more specialized information (e.g., manuscript catalogs). Fully-annotated entries (some volumes are annotated better than others) cover history, geography, economics and politics, culture, social customs and religion. Attention is paid to language, literature and the arts as well. An introductory essay and map are provided, and an index of authors, titles and subjects. Sometimes other helps (a glossary or chronology, for example) may be included. Each volume covers one individual country, but in some cases closely-related content overlaps: Somalia and Djibouti, Ethiopia and Eritrea, and so on.

1479. Lewis, I. M. **A Modern History of Somalia: Nation and State in the Horn of Africa.** Revised, updated and expanded edition. Boulder and London: Westview Press, 1988. xiii, 297 p. ISBN 0-8133-7402-2.

This scholarly work provides an in-depth background for Lewis' more popular *Understanding Somalia.* Indeed, this volume may be the closest thing to a comprehensive reference history of the people and their territory. Bibliographical notes, three maps (the same three as in Lewis' other work, but better reproduced here) and a useful index are included.

1480. Lewis, I. M. **Understanding Somalia: a Guide to Culture, History and Social Institutions.** Second edition. London: HAAN Associates, 1993. 111 p. ISBN 1-874209-41-3.

Prepared by the author of the ethnographic study *Peoples of the Horn of Africa* and many related works, this guide offers an introduction to the anthropology, history, society and economy of "the Somali ethnic region." Brief, clearly-organized and enumerated sections make specific material fairly easy to find, though there is no index. A bibliography, chronology and glossary are provided; two appendices reproduce the text of important diplomatic documents from 1993. Tables and diagrams of demographic data and three quite detailed maps are included.

1481. Salad, Mohamed Khalief. **Somalia: a Bibliographical Survey.** Westport, CT: Greenwood Press, 1977. 468 p. *African Bibliographic Center, Special Bibliographic Series;* New Series, no. 4. ISBN 0-8371-9480-6.

The complier has attempted a "comprehensive bibliography of the Somali nation" (Introduction), and does list without annotation almost 4000 titles covering exploration, the colonial and independence eras, up to about 1975. The list incorporates works in English, Italian, French, German and Somali (but not Arabic). The entries are topically arranged, and there are no indexes.

Websites

1482. Abyssinia Cyberspace Gateway. Community Resource on the Web. **www.cs.indiana.edu/hyplan/dmulholl/acg.html**

Links to attractive and informative pages on Djibouti, Ethiopia, Eritrea, Somalia and Somaliland.

1483. Somali Press Online. **home.ica.net/~somalipress/**

In the Somali language.

NAMES INDEX

Reference is to entry number.

351

TITLES INDEX

Reference is to entry number.

365

Titles Index 385

SUBJECT INDEX

Reference is to entry number.
Terms in boldface type are those most frequently consulted for this region.